Learning to Read
with Literature

Learning to Read with Literature

DONNA L. WISEMAN
Associate Dean, College of Education
Professor of Reading and Language Arts
Texas A&M University

ALLYN AND BACON
Boston London Toronto Sydney Tokyo Singapore

Series Editor: Sean W. Wakely
Series Editorial Assistant: Carol L. Chernaik
Production Administrator: Annette Joseph
Production Coordinator: Holly Crawford
Editorial-Production Service: The Bookmakers, Incorporated
Cover Administrator: Linda K. Dickinson
Cover Designer: Suzanne Harbison
Manufacturing Buyer: Megan Cochran

Wiseman, Donna L. (Donna Louise)
    Learning to read with literature / Donna L. Wiseman.
      p.   cm
    Includes bibliographical references (p.) and index.
    ISBN 0-205-13241-3
    1. Reading (Elementary)—United States.   2. Literature—Study and
teaching (Elementary)—United States.   3. Children—United States—
Books and reading.   I. Title.
LB1573.W574   1992
372.4'1—dc20   91-44748
                                                                                          CIP

Printed in the United States of America

10 9 8 7 6 5 4 3 2 1   97 96 95 94 93 92

Photo Credits

Gabriel Carranza—p. 332; Nancy Howard—p. 72; Kathleen Hurley—pp. 14, 126, 198, and
201; John Norris—pp. 16, 23, and 340; John M. Norris—pp. 210, 233, 241, and 314.

Acknowledgments

p. 1 reprinted with permission of Bradbury Press, an affiliate of Macmillan, Inc. from *Freckle
Juice* by Judy Blume. Illustrated by Sonia O. Lisker. Copyright © 1971 by Judy Bloom.
Illustration copyright © 1971 by Sonia O. Lisker.
p. 22 from *Lincoln: A Photobiography* by Russell Freedman. Copyright © 1987 by Russell
Freedman. Reprinted by permission of Clarion Books, a Houghton Mifflin Co.
p. 24 adapted from Lynn K. Rhodes and Curt Dudley-Marling, *Readers and Writers With A
Difference* (Heinemann Educational Books, Inc., Portsmouth NH, 1988).

Acknowledgments continued on page 368, which constitutes an extension of the copyright page.

For
My husband John,
who constantly teaches me patience and belief in myself
My father Ephraim,
who has always taught me about lifelong learning
My daughter Angela,
who is reteaching me the joys of becoming a teacher
My son Christopher,
who has taught me a great deal about public education

CONTENTS IN BRIEF

CONTENTS

11   Families, Communities, and Children's Reading   328

PREFACE

This book was written to help future teachers begin to comprehend reading and the reading instruction process. I say "begin to comprehend" because learning about teaching and reading is a long-term endeavor. Just as answers and approaches are established, a new wrinkle emerges that must be evaluated and assimilated. This text, *Learning to Read with Literature,* reflects two wrinkles: using children's literature to teach reading, and viewing reading instruction as an integrated, meaningful classroom endeavor. All the traditional components of instruction are included in this text, but may be discussed in different ways or illustrated with distinctive activities. Some of the approaches included but not usually part of a reading methodology text include cooperative learning techniques, writing process, reader response, and metacognition. Other considerations that are significant to the text discussions are the importance of revaluing readers with difficulties, honoring diversity in the classroom, and involving parents in the reading development of their children.

The first chapter attempts to build a foundation for language-based reading. A description of the reading process and the assumptions that guide the entire text are presented in this chapter. In order to guide children to lifelong reading, a teacher must be a reader and a writer, so I spent some time discussing teachers' literacy. The second chapter enumerates and characterizes materials that can be used during literature-based reading instruction. Literary values, elements, and genres that serve as the basis for selecting excellent literature for classroom use are described. This chapter can be used flexibly because some readers of this text are well grounded in children's literature and will need only to refer to this chapter, and others will study the chapter in order to develop an awareness of children's literature. This is a text devoted to a literature-based approach, but the basal reader is a major component of many reading programs and descriptions of the approach are included in this chapter and throughout the text.

The third chapter describes the organization and management of reading. Usually placed at the end of such books, I placed it at the beginning to provide an overview of what a total reading program involves. It may be best to read this chapter two times: once at the beginning of the course and again at the end.

Except for the first two chapters, each chapter has a similar organization. Each discussion begins with some of the current beliefs and understandings about the major topics presented in the chapter. The general discussion leads to a list of several assumptions suggesting instructional processes and activities. I have referred to the wonderful world of children's literature throughout the discussions of activities and approaches. Each chapter includes a discussion of writing and reading. The effects of cultural and language differences on reading instruction are included in each chapter because diverse languages and cultures affect reading instruction.

Chapters 4 through 10 present traditional topics of reading instruction discussed in the context of literature-based instruction. The final chapter, on parental involvement, represents another trend evident in many of the current school reform movements.

I would like to thank and acknowledge the many people who have contributed to this text. A number of teachers provided ideas, feedback, favorite books, and activities. Some of the teachers I especially want to thank are Roberta Chapman (Caldwell ISD, Caldwell, Texas), Jennifer Dunham, Nancy Howard, Dianna Anderson, Ginger Cherbonnier (Bryan ISD, Bryan, Texas) and Donna Logan (Brenhem, Texas). You will see their ideas throughout this text. I would also like to thank Dr. Lea Ann Barton, East Texas State University, and my Summer 1990 graduate reading class who provided a great deal of feedback and useful suggestions after reading the text. I also want to thank the many undergraduates at Texas A&M University who inadvertently contributed to this text. The future teachers at my university constantly inspire and amaze me by using all their talents and energies to invigorate the profession of teaching. Their presence in teacher education programs provides inspiration and hope for the future of reading instruction and public education in general.

I offer a special type of gratitude to the reviewers: Patricia L. Anders, University of Arizona; Richard Chambers, Boston University; Karin L. Dahl, University of Cincinnati; Colleen P. Gilrane, University of Illinois; Mary Jett-Simpson, University of Wisconsin—Milwaukee; Jesse C. Moore, East Stroudsburg University; P. David Pearson, University of Illinois; Sam Sebesta, University of Washington; Lynn A. Smolen, University of Akron; and Kelly Thompson, Eastern Kentucky University. These colleagues sometimes were excruciatingly honest, but always took the time to help me to rethink what I was doing. They helped me modify this text—several times. I want to thank my editors, Carol Wada of Prentice-Hall and Sean Wakely of Allyn and Bacon, who were able to moderate and guide my enthusiasm so that I could produce this text.

1

UNDERSTANDING THE READING PROCESS

Andrew had plenty of time to look at Nicky's freckles. He sat right behind him in class. Once he even tried to count them. But when he got to eighty-six Miss Kelly called, "Andrew . . . are you paying attention?"

"Yes, Miss Kelly," Andrew said.

"Good Andrew. I'm glad to hear that. Now will you please pick up your chair and join your reading group? We're all waiting for you."

Andrew stood up in a hurry. His reading group giggled. Especially Sharon. He couldn't stand that Sharon. She thought she knew everything! He picked up his chair and carried it to the corner where his reading group sat.

"You may begin, Andrew," Miss Kelly said. "Page sixty-four."

Andrew turned the pages in his book. Sixty-four . . . sixty-four. He couldn't find it. The pages stuck together. Why did Miss Kelly have to pick him? Everyone else already had their books opened to the right page.

Sharon kept giggling. She covered her mouth to keep in the noise, but Andrew knew what was going on. He finally found page sixty-four. Right where it was supposed to be . . . between pages sixty-three and sixty-five. If he had his own freckles he wouldn't have to count Nicky Lane's. Then he'd hear Miss Kelly when she called reading groups. And nobody would laugh at him.

—Judy Blume, *Freckle juice*

READING is an extremely complex process that is affected by many factors, including language, intelligence, culture, and emotions. Reading instruction reflects the complexity. At times the instructional process appears to be an exact science and at other times, an incredible mystery. Experienced teachers may be amazed or baffled with the reading development of each student who enters their rooms. One of the most important factors in elementary teacher preparation is developing an understanding of the reading process and establishing a framework for reading instruction. This chapter will provide a background for understanding the process of reading and its relationship to language development. In addition, the chapter will begin explaining reading instruction and the role of teachers in classroom instruction. Some of the questions this chapter will answer are:

1. What is literacy?
2. How is reading related to the language processes?
3. What are some specific ways a reader relies on the language system?
4. What are the behaviors associated with efficient reading?
5. What are the basic principles of learning language that guide reading instruction?
6. What is literature-based reading instruction?
7. What is the role of the teacher in literature-based reading instruction?

Foundations of Literacy

The goal of reading instruction should be to produce literate members of society who have the abilities to communicate with and about written language. Literate people use their reading ability to help them understand the written language as found in such materials as a daily newspaper, directions for a video cassette recorder or microwave oven, writing by Stephen King, Larry McMurtry, or William Shakespeare, and texts related to their work or study. Our society requires a large and diverse range of reading abilities if an individual is to succeed.

Literacy is not obtained simply by producing individuals with the ability to read and understand texts. Literate people should be able to use written language to create new ideas, solve problems in work and recreation, and generally to think on a high level. Daily life constantly requires us to make decisions or solve problems as a result of encountering written materials. We may need to interpret a manual to unlock the ignition in our new car, survey a cereal box to determine if the contents will complement our diet, or understand written directions that guide us to our airport gate. Interpretation of written material is becoming more necessary to ensure success in work and play. It wasn't so many years ago that individuals in our society could succeed without control of written language. But, one has only to read a United States tax form to realize the demands of reading ability have increased during the last few decades.

Literacy results from both the needs of a particular society and the demands of the learner's community and family situation. Different societies have different reading and writing requirements. Even within a society the reading and writing requirements may differ. Look, for example, at the different literacy requirements of a teacher and an engineer. Both occupations require a high level of literacy, but a teacher must have a set of literacy skills different from a person who builds bridges and highways. A comparison of the materials that both the teacher and the engineer read each day will demonstrate the differences. To understand what the engineer must read, one must have an understanding of math, statistics, building design, and other technology. The engineer may read graphs, tables, and a technical style of writing. The vocabulary is very content-specific and may define such words as *plane, thrust,* or *formula* differently than do other members of our society. The teacher's reading material requires an understanding of child development, psychology, reading development, instructional methods, motivation, and so on. A teacher may need to know how to read curriculum guides, children's literature, test results, and research studies. A teacher's reading vocabulary also may reflect the profession in much the same way as the engineer's use of specific terminology. Such words and phrases as *instructional objectives, literature-based instruction,* and *process* must be understood within the context of the profession. In addition, literate teachers must possess an understanding of literacy skills so that they are able to explain terms and concepts on many different levels.

This does not mean that people in different occupations do not share some aspects of literacy. Both the teacher and the engineer must understand their insurance policies, tax laws, bank statements, and (most probably) must be able to read a manual that accompanies a computer program. Literate people have skills that allow them to use written language in all aspects of their lives.

Children are not born literate. Literacy develops naturally as children interact with the environment, long before they enter school (Harste, Woodward, & Burke, 1984; Holdaway, 1982; Teale, 1986; Wiseman, 1984). As soon as children are born they begin interacting with their surroundings, learning about communication, and building the foundations for literacy. Children learn about language as they are read to, engage in conversation, and hear others use language. Literacy development continues as children use language to accomplish tasks and to take care of their needs.

Oral language forms the basis of literacy development during the preschool years. But the focus changes as children begin their schooling. When school becomes a part of literacy development, the emphasis on acquiring written language increases. Literacy instruction in early elementary school years traditionally has emphasized reading. In fact, reading has become a symbol of success or failure in the education of children. Evaluation of our nation's entire educational system often is based on reading acquisition rates. Concerned residents, describing the literacy of our nation, often will use the reading ability of public school children to illustrate the success (or failure) of our schools. The general public's concern about literacy and therefore reading is reflected throughout the educational system. Needless to say, parents are concerned deeply with the reading success of their children, and elementary teachers view literacy and reading instruction as among the most important responsibilities of teaching.

Principles of the Reading Process

Descriptions, explanations, and definitions of the reading process abound. Those who attempt to understand and define reading must consider the physical aspects of the eyes, memory mechanisms and attention, anxiety, risk-taking, the nature and uses of language, speech, interpersonal interactions, sociocultural differences, learning theory, and child development (Smith, 1985). Considering all of these factors impact reading to make it a complex process, it is no wonder that there are so many ways to explain how reading happens. Everyone, including preschool children, has beliefs and assumptions about reading and reading instruction. (For example, a common belief of first grade children is that they will begin reading the first day of school.) Teachers almost always hold identifiable beliefs about reading. Even when teachers are unable to express their views explicitly, their instructional approaches to reading reflect specific views (Harste & Burke, 1977; Lee, 1987). This textbook establishes a particular view of the reading process, too. There are several principles that serve as a foundation for understanding reading as it is presented in the following pages.

Reading Is Language

Reading, along with speaking, listening, and writing, is considered to be a language process. Common elements of oral and written language emphasize the relationship between the processes. Language processes have common sounds, sentence arrangements, vocabularies, and meanings. Another element of language processes is the experience of the user. Personal experiences affect the way one understands what is read or heard, as well as what is discussed when talking and writing.

Children's proficiency in oral language affects their reading and writing development. The more experiences children have with oral language, the more background they have to apply to their written language acquisition. For example, children who have parents who talk with them about a wide range of subjects and ideas and read orally will be better prepared to read. Children's reading abilities directly affect their writing development. Reading helps build vocabulary and contributes to understanding decoding skills that are used when writing.

The interrelatedness of the language processes suggests that reading, writing, listening, and speaking are mutually supportive. Growth in one language process supports total language development. Reading instruction can be enhanced by taking into account the mutual reinforcement of language processes. The most effective reading instruction will be effective language instruction.

Reading Is Developmental

Accepting reading as a developmental process implies that individuals may develop reading abilities at different rates and with different patterns. It is easy to see this during the preschool years. Some children begin to read and write, with seemingly little effort, before they start school. They have a natural interest in letters and words, ask questions, and participate in activities that allow them to gain meaning with unfamiliar texts. Other children may have access to books but never read without assistance. While it is natural to accept differences in children's physical, emotional, and social growth, the developmental nature of reading is not always recognized when children begin formal schooling. There are reasonable patterns of reading development, but one child's reading development can vary greatly from another's (Sulzby, 1981). A kindergarten child may, for example, read a book by turning pages, following the words with a finger, and reciting a story that is different from what written in the book. Although this is not what an efficient reader would do, it is demonstrating the child's knowledge of the reading process. Very few teachers would be concerned about a kindergarten child who displays this behavior, but if a first or second grade reader exhibits this behavior a teacher is less accepting. The first grader who demonstrates behavior expected from a preschool child may be displaying developmentally appropriate behavior depending on access and prior experiences with books. The behavior of each child should be evaluated on the basis of individual development.

Reading Is Learned by Reading

One condition necessary for learning oral language is an environment filled with spoken language and opportunities to use spoken language. This same assumption should be made for learning how to read and write (Newman, 1985). To learn to read, one must have plenty of opportunities to use books and other written materials. Readers must understand what written language does and that the text does convey meaning (Smith, 1985). Only contact with books and print will develop this concept. When children are very young, they need adults to read to them, write with them, and talk with them about what they are doing until they can read for themselves. After they begin to develop reading strategies, they must continue practicing in order to become more efficient and flexible. There is no way to become a good reader other than to read.

Reading Is Meaningful

The learning of oral language in preschool years occurs in an environment in which language is used purposefully. Children learn oral language by having reasons to use it and working to make themselves understood. The same must be true of learning how to read. Meaningful reading develops from and uses authentic texts for real life purposes. Teale (1986) identifies real life purposes as those occurring naturally in daily routines, entertainment, learning situations, work, religion, interpersonal communication, and literature. Real life purposes should be reflected in meaningful instruction.

Language and reading instruction are meaningful when learners have a certain amount of control over the process. Readers who have some choice in selecting materials and determining how to respond to written language will feel they are engaged in a meaningful activity. If readers to not understand why they are reading certain material and if they are not allowed a wide range of responses, then it is difficult for them to understand the purpose of reading. When there is no recognized purpose, reading becomes meaningless.

Reading Is Social

The desire to read is based on the social need to understand others and the world around us (Goodman, 1986). If there were no need to understand our world, which is full of language and print, there would be no reason to learn how to read. Even the value a reader places on reading is based on social and familial contexts. If family and friends believe that reading is important, that belief easily will become an important aspect of the reader's system.

The social influences go beyond establishing the need and the value of reading. A reader's understanding is affected by personal, social, and cultural values. Past experiences that reflect readers' social and cultural lives affect how readers understand what they read. Reading cannot be isolated from social and cultural education.

Reading also is affected by social interaction. As a reader shares and interacts with others, comprehension and understanding develop or are modified. Social interaction provides feedback to support and increase understandings gained from written language. Think of the times you have read a text and didn't understand the concepts. After attending a class lecture and discussing the material with others, you may have been able to understand the content better or you may have modified your ideas about the material. By discussing and reacting to reading, readers receive feedback. Feedback can be the natural interaction of reader and peers, older and younger acquaintances, and respected adults.

Language Systems

Learning to read is affected by the principles of learning language, as discussed above. Reading also is tied to language learning by common rules and information. Readers possess information about the rules of spoken and written language. Even at a very early age children begin establishing rules about how language is used and while reading use the language rules as they understand them. They expect the language rules they have established to apply to the texts they are reading. Much of what allows children to communicate with others is intuitive and they cannot explicitly explain a great deal of their knowledge and understandings (Goodman, Watson, & Burke, 1987).

You expect the words of this text to be written according to the rules you have acquired about language. A great deal of prior knowledge of language and the world comes into play as you begin to read this chapter (Goodman, Watson, & Burke, 1987). Language rules can give you clues to the material or can cue or suggest what the text is about. The structure of language offers three distinct cue systems that help you understand text. Graphophonics, syntax, and semantics provide systematic cues that enable readers to be successful and efficient in their search for meaning.

Graphophonics

Graphophonics is the relationship of the sounds of language and their graphic display. Graphophonics includes spelling, letter–sound representations, and the relationship between spelling and sound (Goodman, Watson, & Burke, 1987). Graphophonic knowledge allows readers to expect certain letter combinations and suggests which combinations of letters and sounds are most acceptable in English. Graphophonics is one of the basic differences between the written language processes of reading/writing and the oral language processes of listening/speaking. Oral and written language systems differ in that reading and writing use graphic symbols to convey messages, and listening and speaking use sound symbols to convey messages.

Children must learn that the squiggles they see on the paper represent meaning. Although they have been successful at learning the meanings of many oral language symbols, children may find graphophonics difficult because the English language does not have a strict one-to-one relationship between its symbols and its sounds. For example, the letter *c* can sound like the *c* in *cat* or the *c* in *city,* and any vowel can represent any number of sounds. Efficient readers have developed an understanding of graphophonics and use that knowledge to suggest the meanings of written words.

Syntax

Syntax is the morphological relationship and interrelationship of words. Grammar is a term commonly used to refer to this language system. Children learn a great deal about syntax while developing their oral language skills. By the time children come to school they can comprehend and produce sentences that include verbs, nouns, and modifiers in appropriate order. They usually use morphological rules to know when to use *s, ed,* and *ly.* Their sentences are more or less complete, and they use articles such as *the, an,* and *a,* in their sentences. As they are exposed to written language they begin developing an understanding of punctuation. All this developing knowledge of language is used in reading.

Effective readers will draw on their knowledge and experience of patterns in oral and written language to predict and confirm text. To illustrate, a reader will be relatively assured that the rules of syntax suggest that after the article *the,* a noun or noun clause will follow, or a reader may assume that after a noun appears in a sentence, there will be a verb. The assumption the reader makes is that reading is arranged like familiar language and will follow the rules and cues associated with what is known about syntax. The question an effective reader asks when relying on syntax is, ''Does this sound like language to me?''

Semantics

Semantics refers to how readers understand the world, meanings and concepts that have been acquired through experiences. Everything readers have in their backgrounds or experiences is available to help establish an understanding of text. The more experiences a reader possesses about what is being read, the easier it is to understand. For example, if one reads in the newspaper about some event, such as a recent San Francisco earthquake, after hearing about it on several television newscasts, it is much easier to understand the material. If the reader has experienced an earthquake or lived in San Francisco, it is even easier to understand the phenomenon by reading about it. However, if a reader is attempting to understand an event or occurrence for the first time, it is not as easy to gain meaning from the text. It is more difficult to comprehend unfamiliar information.

Efficient readers use their knowledge of the world to predict and understand text. They are given cues or hints about the reading material based on what they have experienced. As readers confront written symbols, they expect them to make sense based on what they know and understand. The semantic cue system they have established will allow them to predict and make sense of the text. The question an effective reader asks when relying on the semantic system during reading is, ''Does this make sense to me?''

Efficient readers use graphophonics, syntax, and semantics to give them cues to the meaning of the text they are reading. Knowledge of the reading process, language, and the world is used to construct a meaning suggested by written language.

The Reading Process

Reading is not always thought of as being active, but when readers gain meaning from a text it is, in fact, an active and constructive procedure (King & Watson, 1983). Reading is active because the reader constantly is solving a series of problems or questions while attempting to find out what the author is trying to say (Goodman, 1986; Smith, 1988). Reading is constructive because readers are building meaning based on what they already understand and what the author intends for them to understand. This active process is continued by using relevant, available information and making decisions about the meaning of the text.

Discussing your own reading behavior may provide insights about the activities taking place as you approach this text on reading instruction. During the efficient reading process, you are involved actively in several behaviors or strategies: sampling the print, predicting the meaning, confirming or rejecting the prediction, and finally integrating the author's information (Goodman, Watson, & Burke, 1987).

Sampling

Reading involves sampling the text. An efficient reader may not read every single word or identify each individual graphophonic symbol of the text. In fact, if a reader tries to read each word or "sound out" each individual sound, the reading process is slowed and meaning may be lost. The reader samples instead of trying to absorb all the information available. The amount of text sampled during reading depends upon how much the reader knows about the material presented. The more the reader understands about the topic, the less graphic information is required during the reading process. Smith (1985) describes this as a trade-off between printed and known information.

> *The more nonvisual information you have when you read, the less visual information you need.*
>
> *The less nonvisual information you have when you read, the more visual information you need.*
>
> *. . . The more you know in advance about a book, the easier it is to read. You can read an easy book faster, you can read it in smaller print, and you can read it in a relatively poor light . . . The eyes have more work to do if the book is difficult. This is not an uncommon phenomena; the better you are acquainted with a person, or a kind of car or tree, the easier it is to recognize them at a distance. (p. 15)*

It will be easier to understand the text of this book if you have a background in education and education-related courses because you can predict the meaning of some of the text. You can make a trade-off between what you already know and understand about reading and reading instruction and use that information so that you will not need to process every textual element. An engineering major, however, would not have as much experience with the topic and to understand the concepts would need to process a great deal more of the text.

Efficient readers are able to balance the trade-off between written and unwritten information and only sample the printed material in order to construct meaning from the text. Sampling is not the only active process occurring during reading. As text is sampled, the reader begins to predict. You probably did not read every word in this book or this chapter as soon as you had it in your possession. Perhaps as you began this chapter, you sampled the information. You may have glanced at the index, flipped through the pages, read the captions of some of the pictures. You even may have sampled some of the first lines of paragraphs and read the end of chapter questions. All this sampling provides information and better prepares you to predict the meaning of the text.

Prediction

Along with sampling the material, readers predict much of what is expected in the text. The knowledge of all three language systems, graphophonics, syntax, and semantics, is used to predict its meaning. The prediction strategies of efficient readers are not random guessing, but the elimination of what is unlikely (Smith, 1985). Thus, sampling results in readers using their knowledge to make educated guesses about what comes next or what the author is trying to convey. Or, said another way, sampling leads to eliminating what the written material is not about.

Good readers begin predicting as soon as text is placed before them. For example, as soon as you picked this textbook up at the bookstore, you probably began using your past experiences to predict what you would read when you opened it. Your experiences in other education courses and the information you may have gleaned from those who have taken the course supplied you with information that allowed you to begin predicting the nature of reading methodology. The title of the textbook allowed you to make additional predictions. You may have predicted that this book would discuss methods of teaching reading, and you expect that you will know more about reading instruction after reading this book. You would be very surprised after sampling and predicting if, when you opened the book, it was full of recipes or presented aerobic dance exercises. If the information were totally different from what you expected, you could not confirm your predictions.

Confirming

As the reading process continues, readers confirm or eliminate their predictions by continuing to sample. As you began reading this first chapter, you may have sampled and predicted, and you were able to determine whether your predictions were on target. Once you opened the book you found the topics presented were about reading instruction, just as you predicted. You confirmed your predictions. As you read further into the text you continued to sample, predict, and confirm.

If you have never read about sampling and prediction in relationship to reading, you probably were not able to predict as easily. Your predictions may not have come as rapidly, and you may have not been able to confirm whether your predictions were on the right track. You occasionally may have stopped your reading and said, "Now, what did that mean?" or, "That just doesn't make sense." You may have had to reread the information with new predictions that could be confirmed. Once your predictions were confirmed, you may have said under your breath, "O.K., now I get it." When you "get it," you have integrated the information. As the information begins to make sense you are able to integrate what you predict and confirm it with information you already have about teaching reading.

Integration

When readers confirm their predictions, they are able to integrate the information with what they already know. When reading information is integrated, a level of comprehension has occurred. If the reader is unable to sample, predict, or confirm effectively, no integration occurs and the reader comes away from the experience thinking, "I didn't understand any of the material."

It is hoped that this text makes sense so far and you are able to integrate the information. If by chance you possessed absolutely no prior knowledge of the topics in this chapter and had to process all the printed material instead of sampling it, reading this far into the text would have taken you a very long time. In addition, if the information did not match the predictions you originally made, it would have become difficult for you to confirm your predictions and integrate the information with what you already knew—you would probably have given up before getting this far.

Reading is more difficult when you do not possess information about the topic. For example, many of you may have been introduced to economics for the first time when you entered a university. As you picked up your economics text, you may not have been able to make many predictions about what you could expect. You may have had to sample more material before making predictions, and you may have read very slowly. Perhaps as you continued sampling and predicting, some of your predictions were not confirmed and the information was not integrated until you spent some late night hours before an exam going over and over the text. It is just more difficult to sample, predict, confirm, and finally integrate the information when you don't have previous knowledge of the topic.

These behaviors begin when readers approach print, but do not occur in a linear fashion (King & Watson, 1983). Readers do not first sample and predict, then confirm, and finally integrate. Rather, the processes of sampling, predicting, confirming, and integrating occur in concert almost without the readers' conscious knowledge. If a reader uses one strategy in isolation or fails to use each strategy, the reading process is disrupted and fluent reading ceases. Effective readers balance their use of reading strategies and cuing systems successfully (Goodman & Burke, 1980).

Reading Instruction

Effective reading instruction must include consideration of how children learn language, use language systems, and understand written language. If the reading process seems complicated, it is, and there have been many approaches and structures over the years to help children succeed with written language.

The basal reader has been by far one of the most influential and widely used methods of teaching reading and for several decades has served as the foundation for reading instruction. Basal readers are collections of reading material produced especially for reading instruction. Basals include such materials as specially prepared texts for reading, specific teacher directions, workbooks, suggestions for individual activities, and other related materials. There is emphasis on learning letters of the alphabet, sight words, vowel sounds, vocabulary, and comprehension skills, such as identifying the main idea, reading for facts, and many other identified objectives. (See Chap. 2 for a complete discussion of the basal reader.) The basal emphasis has resulted in 50 to 75 percent of today's teachers using basals for reading instruction.

In 1985, *The Report of the Commission on Reading, Becoming a Nation of Readers* (Anderson, R., Hiebert, E., Scott, J. & Wilkinson, I.) suggested that perhaps the reliance on basal readers is not a positive approach to reading instruction. In a discussion of formal reading instruction, the report stated, ''. . . some authorities wonder whether school reading programs . . . adequately prepare children for genuine literature . . .'' (p. 67). This comment indicated that those knowledgeable in reading instruction were beginning to question the wisdom of the dependence on the basal.

We have only to look at the methods of teaching reading for the past forty years to see that we have focused on basal readers and ignored one of the greatest resources for reading development. Children's literature can be exciting and motivating, encouraging literacy and thinking. In addition, the wide variety of topics available in children's literature can meet the needs of the diverse classrooms of the United States today.

The conjectures of the mid-eighties have given way to a strong trend in the nineties. One of the most recent inclinations in reading instruction suggests that classroom programs should provide children with many opportunities to read high quality literature (Boehnlein, 1987; Hiebert & Colt, 1989; Holdaway, 1982; Larrick, 1987; Newman, 1985). The state of California has gone so far as to set up a statewide instructional approach that integrates literature into reading programs (Alexander, 1986; McGee & Richgels, 1990). Many other states are supporting the use of literature by providing instructional suggestions and guidelines that encourage the use of a wide range of reading materials. The term used to describe the instructional reading approach that uses children's literature and a wide range of reading material to teach reading is *literature-based reading instruction.*

Many programs and practices claim to be literature-based, but there are several elements that must be present when literature is effectively used to encourage children to be readers. Obviously, literature-based reading instruction focuses on allowing children to read meaningful and motivating literature and texts. During reading instruction, children deal with a wide variety of reading and writing materials. The stories and texts are those written to be read for enjoyment, as opposed to texts that are written for instruction. Literature-based instruction uses complete texts.

Literature-based reading instruction supports all the basic principles associated with language and reading development outlined in the beginning of this chapter. Children are encouraged to experiment and become familiar with books and other varieties of print. Much time is allowed for actual reading and exposure to readers as role models. Literature-based instruction allows the child to select reading materials and for planning activities geared to individual interests and abilities. Literature is a natural basis for children to collaborate, receive responses to their questions about books, and be encouraged to read and write (Martinez & Teale, 1987). Table 1.1 compares and contrasts factors associated with literature-based and basal instruction.

It is apparent that quality reading instruction must include more than the basal readers for elementary students, and the basic premise of literature-based instruction is that children will read good literature. However, literature-based instruction is more than including literature in a basal series or a reading lesson. Literature-based instruction also involves making conscious decisions to allow children to act like real readers during classroom activities. The attitudes and philosophies of teachers are as important as the materials selected for instruction. Teachers and programs that use the literature-based approach consistently invite all children to read high quality literature in their earliest school experiences and to explore language through children's literature.

The values of literature-based reading programs are many and will be reiterated and substantiated throughout this text, but there are some benefits that should be recognized at

TABLE 1-1   Comparison of literature and basal programs

	Literature-based	*Basal Approach*
Materials	Uses children's literature and children's writing to encourage reading comprehension	Uses materials written and selected to focus on identified reading skills
Selection of materials	Teacher and child select materials	Textbook publishers design materials
Literature's role	Main focus	If literature is used, it usually is in a supportive role or through excerpts included in the basal collections
Teacher's role	Facilitator, guide, model	Responsible for reading activities and manages the basal plan
Student's role	Actively involved, responding, making decisions	Receives formal, direct instruction based on basal plan
Instructional focus	Actual reading and responding to text with oral and written language	Guided reading and completion of suggested activities and exercises
Amount of reading	Large quantities of materials selected by child and directed by teacher	Short selections are read and reread together with teacher's guidance
Response to reading	Children produce varied responses to their reading	Children complete worksheets and exercises suggested by basal plan, discuss questions presented in teacher's guide

the outset. One of the most recognizable values is the absorption and exposure to content, vocabulary, and linguistic complexity that children's literature can provide (Cullinan, 1987; Jalongo, 1988). Children tend to take over the language they hear and read, delighting and amazing teachers when vocabulary and literary concepts appear in the children's day-to-day speech. Children's literature provides them with a strong model for building their language capabilities.

A second value of children's literature is that reading can contribute to children's understanding of the world around them. Books broaden perspectives about others, help develop understandings and concepts not ordinarily experienced, and build imaginative worlds that encourage the development of thinking. These values are broad and generic, but even if they were the only products of using literature to assist children's language and reading development, the inclusion of children's literature could be justified.

The Role of the Reading Teacher

Over the years the teacher has been recognized constantly as the factor that really makes a difference in instruction. The teacher who takes on the responsibility of implementing literature-based instruction will direct literature selections, encourage reading of a wide variety of materials, and provide opportunities for sharing reactions and learning in all areas of instruction. Reading instruction involves planning for children's writing and discussion, but the nature and direction of learning are guided by children's responses. To accomplish this, the role of the teacher must reflect several functions.

A major responsibility of the teacher of a literature-based curriculum is to be familiar with children's literature since children will reflect what teachers know. However, it is not enough for teachers to know and use literature in classroom activities; they also must appreciate and demonstrate excitement about the literature they use (Jalongo, 1988). This is not difficult since good literature generates a great deal of enthusiasm. Teachers who use a literature-based curriculum profess that teaching is exciting and dynamic when the great wealth of available reading material is used for instruction.

Actions of important adults are as important to children's learning as the instructional activities in a classroom. A teacher who demonstrates a love of literature and reading is a valuable lesson for children. When children see teachers and others reading, they begin to understand the importance and necessity of becoming literate. Teachers in a literature-based classroom should never hesitate to show that they love books and written language. Donald Graves (1990) quotes a teacher who loves books by sharing some of her writing:

> *I love books. I don't just love to read them. I like to hold them, run my fingers lightly over the covers, the pages, the pictures. I like to dream the stories waiting between the covers. I even like to smell books . . . especially old books, books from my childhood, those given to me by people all but forgotten but for the book they left . . . I am delighted when some tiny trace of a previous reader is evident in the pages: a turned page, the petal of a rose, a cookie crumb, a slip of a bookmark, or best of all a name inside the cover. (p. 31)*

Jennifer understands the importance of reading to her first grade children.

The teachers of literature-based curricula have a responsibility to discover and use the interests and needs of their students to guide written language explorations. One of the basic tenets is that children select books and influence instruction. When children make decisions about their reading, the curriculum becomes more meaningful, and purposeful engagement in texts is assured.

Teachers of literature-based curricula should view themselves as collaborators in learning. This may mean that they are willing to take the child's perspective. They become coaches and cheerleaders as their students construct meaning from the texts they encounter. This does not mean that teachers do not plan, structure, and meet instructional goals. It simply means that teachers are aware and consider the children's developmental responses and needs for learning.

The literature-based teacher establishes the risk-free and comfortable environment so necessary for learning. Making books available and using the literature in classroom instruction is important, but allowing children to discuss a book and encouraging children to see, feel, think, and associate as they read becomes an important component of the teacher's role (Petrosky, 1980). Children must feel comfortable before they begin the experimentation and hypothesizing necessary for learning to read and write.

Teachers must view themselves as professionals who understand reading, learning, children, curriculum, and methodology. Understanding the instructional process means that teachers view themselves as learners. They will learn from their children as they read and write together, with their children as they focus on content, and about their children as they observe the learning process.

Writing and Reading Instruction

One of the assumptions discussed in this chapter is that reading instruction should focus on all four facets of language. Instruction in reading and other language skills is integrated so that children perceive reading, writing, listening, and talking as a series of communication options available to them for many purposes. The language processes become mutually supportive. Growth in one language process supports the growth of all aspects of language.

Writing is the language process most often recognized as explicitly supportive of reading instruction. Today, educators tend to view reading and writing as parts of the whole communication process (Hennings, 1990). Effective language instruction will accept reading and writing as two components of one entity: literacy. Instruction during the 1980s encouraged teachers to focus on reading/writing relationships during reading instruction and that trend most likely will continue. Instructional principles identified by Shanahan (1988) explain how reading and writing best can enhance a child's literacy development.

1. Teach both reading and writing. This is a fundamental tenet of literacy instruction. A reading program that does not include writing is not complete. Reading and writing (and speaking and listening) fit together, and it is difficult to imagine how they could occur in isolation.

2. Introduce reading and writing in the earliest grades. It's never too early to encourage children to read and write. Research in the 1980s revealed that children are curious about print from an early age and this curiosity can be used during early literacy instruction. Most children are beginning to write before entering kindergarten (Tompkins, 1990), and teachers help children by having them read and write about interesting topics.

3. Reflect the developmental nature of written language. Teachers should use what they know about literacy development during reading instruction. They should accept their students' attempts at writing and allow them the opportunity to experiment.

4. Emphasize the relationship of reading and writing. Teachers should trust that allowing opportunities to learn about writing will help children understand the reading process. The relationships of reading and writing should be the basis for many instructional activities, which will help children become aware of these relationships.

5. Make the connections between reading and writing explicit to children. Teachers should discuss reading and writing with children and let them learn how to talk about the processes. Children should be encouraged to understand what it takes to become readers and writers and should be able to describe their own behaviors when engaged in either process.

6. Teach reading and writing in a meaningful context. Children should be able to see why they are reading and writing. They should accomplish goals as they read and write.

Writing is an important part of reading instruction. It can be used to help children understand both the text and the reading process. Writing can contribute to children's ability to read by encouraging them to explore print and discover how to produce their own ideas. Writing is a form of learning and understanding; sometimes ideas are clarified or expanded as children write.

The end result of writing is an audience for the material. Writing by children can become an important part of classroom reading material. Some of the most popular materials available for classroom reading are the ideas and insights provided by children learning to write.

Learning Differences

Cultural and language differences sometimes are considered roadblocks to reading instruction. It is important to understand the impact that speaking a different language

Writing provides opportunities for children to understand the reading-writing connections, respond to what they read, and write texts for other readers.

or being a member of a specific culture can have on literacy development. Every aspect of language instruction is affected by the cultural background and language experiences of the children learning to read.

Cultural Differences

Cultural differences, once observed only in special instances, are now the rule for most classrooms. Classrooms are full of a rich diversity of backgrounds—children from a wide range of countries with differing religious and ethnic practices. Educators long have worried about the disproportionate number of minority group children who do not learn to read (Ogbu, 1985), and there was a time when educators believed that reading difficulties could be inherent to some cultures. That explanation no longer is acceptable. Cultural differences do not mean that children are deficient in experience, but they may mean that they have experiences different from those of others in the classroom. Culturally different children come to school with styles of learning and patterns of interaction and communication that are different from their peers and the adults at school (Ogbu, 1985). Teachers responsible for teaching children from many cultures should understand the differences and use their awareness to enhance instruction for all children.

Some of the learning difficulties attributed to culture arise from the teachers' expectations. For many years teachers accepted that a culturally different child would learn differently. One of the first steps a teacher can take to eliminate learning difficulties is to accept the child and honor the differences. It is the very wise teacher who uses the differences to enrich reading and writing instruction.

Teachers must consider how cultural, economic, and other factors affect the way children respond to schooling. Schools also should recognize that cultural backgrounds develop and influence children's learning. Each chapter will provide a section that discusses how a teacher can include approaches and methods that encourage all children to become literate.

Language Differences

In the 1990s, teachers will have more chances to hear many different languages in their classrooms than ever before. Often, children in classrooms are learning English for school while maintaining their native language at home and in their communities. Learning to read and write English as a second language can be a difficult and frustrating experience or a natural challenge, depending on the instructional approach. An effective reading teacher can affect a child who speaks a different language in many ways.

All children who come to school speaking a language other than English are not the same. Often, the nonnative speakers are lumped together just because they speak different languages. But teachers need to recognize that different children possess different levels of fluency and literacy. Just as in the case of native English speakers, there are great differences among nonnative speaking children in how fast and well they learn to speak, read, and write English.

Most nonnative speaking children will be able to speak the language of the home, but there will be differences in oral fluency. Some of the children may have had schooling in another country, and others may not have attended school. Some students may be extremely efficient in their oral and written native language. Experience shows that children who have learned to read in another language will make the transition to reading in English more easily than children who have no reading experience in any language. Teachers should view each child as an individual and to attempt to find the most effective learning situation for each child.

Most schools offer specific programs for students who are learning English as a second language. As a result, a regular classroom teacher will have various levels of responsibility for these students. There are schools that completely isolate non-English speakers in classrooms where subjects are taught as the children learn to speak English. However, other schools have programs that allow these children to mingle with English speakers. Still other schools may not have any organized programs for learning English as a second language and the classroom teacher provides all instruction.

Bilingual learners need not be totally proficient at understanding and producing English to begin to read and to derive considerable meaning from their reading (Goodman, Goodman, & Flores, 1979). They will learn English by using and hearing it. Listening to stories read aloud or participating in discussions of appropriate reading material in English are examples of effective activities for students with limited English abilities.

Students who come to school with a different language can benefit from the same considerations we give those students who are native English speakers. Much instruction appropriate for beginning readers is effective with students who are learning to communicate in English.

The teacher can establish an environment that encourages success at learning to read and write English by establishing certain provisions. Students should be supported and accepted in a rich language environment. Children who do not speak English as their first language should have many opportunities to hear English, to speak English, and to read and write English. They will need to see others read and write English and will need to take part in discussions. Children's literature can serve as the foundation for all activities designed to expose non-English speakers to English (Hough, Nurss, & Enright, 1986).

Providing opportunities for non-English speakers and children who are fluent in English to talk and work together can benefit all children in a classroom. Peers can be the best teachers of children who are learning to speak English. They encourage the risk-taking necessary to learn language. Opportunities for talking during the work and play of a school day can contribute to second language learners' vocabulary and language. In the same way, exposure to children who speak a language other than English can enrich the cultural awareness and understandings of English speakers. Language differences should be recognized as a strength of the American culture, and classroom instruction should encourage children to understand and appreciate one another no matter what language is spoken.

Students' successes should be recognized explicitly. As with any children, the nonnative speaking child needs to have opportunities to succeed at school. Once a child succeeds, the teacher should let the child know that progress has occurred.

Teachers should recognize behavior differences of children who speak a different language. Children may not always respond in the expected way when they are learning English as their second language. They may mix languages or respond in ways not usually produced by a child who speaks English as a native. It is important for teachers to expect and accept this behavior as part of the learning process.

DISCUSSION AND ACTIVITIES

1. Use a reading interview as a basis for discussing the reading process with at least three people. Use the interviews to discuss the following questions.

    a. How do each of the people you interview define reading?
    b. What do they feel is important about reading instruction?
    c. Do they relate reading and language?
    d. Do their views differ from the ideas presented in this first chapter? Try to compare differences you might observe in the way people talk about reading.

2. Write an autobiography about your past as a reader both in and out of school (Bixby, 1988). Remember a time or a person in your life, a school year, a class, an event, a teacher that contributed to your reading habits. Describe a situation or person that had a good or bad impact on your reading. Focus on how this event affected you and how you feel about it now.

Share your draft with a partner from class to get reaction to your writing. Try to identify events that contribute to your personal definition and theory of reading. The class may want to analyze the positive and negative aspects that students write about in their autobiographies. [See the Anthony L. Manna and Sue Misheff article in the *Journal of Reading* of November 1987 entitled, ''What Teachers Say About Their Own Reading Development,'' (pp. 160–168) for an example.]

3. Why do you believe that children's literature has been ignored as an instructional approach during the last two or three decades? Interview a teacher with at least twenty years of experience to see how she or he explains the nearly exclusive use of the basals. Discuss this question with your classmates, and keep track of how your ideas change during the semester.

4. Try to be aware of how you go about the reading process. What do you do when you don't understand a passage? Identify a text that you read rapidly. Why do you read it so fast and still understand the material? Compare what you do when you read a text that is difficult and a text that is very easy.

5. List the literacy demands of your daily life. Compare the demands with a college-age peer in another major. Compare your reading with that of older members of your family who may not be in school. What does a comparison suggest to you about literacy requirements in our society?

RELATED READING

Harste, J., Woodward, V., & Burke, C. (1984). *Language stories and literacy lessons.* Exeter, NH: Heinemann.

> *This book does a good job of demonstrating explicitly how language and reading develop-ment are interrelated. It also describes how children begin to learn how to read and write and how they view what they are doing.*

Smith, F. (1985). *Reading without nonsense* (2nd ed.). New York: Teacher's College Press.

> *This book describes the reading process in-depth by elaborating on the importance of prediction during the reading process.*

———. (1989). Overselling literacy. *Phi Delta Kappan, 70* (5). 352–360.

> *Smith has been a pioneer in supporting language-based literacy instruction. He has written many important articles and books that discuss the importance of viewing reading and writing instruction as a natural outgrowth of using language. In this particular article, Smith argues that the ways in which we teach reading and writing may destroy the literacy we are trying to create.*

Tunnell, M.O., & Jacobs, J. (1989). Using "real" books: Research findings on literature based reading instruction. *The Reading Teacher.* 470–477.

> *Tunnell and Jacobs present some convincing arguments regarding the use of literature to teach reading. This is one of the first of many articles in the* Reader Teacher *to advocate the use of children's literature as the foundation of reading instruction.*

REFERENCES

Alexander, F. (1986). California reading initiative. In B. Cullinan (Ed.), *Children's literature in the reading program.* Newark, DE: International Reading Association.

Anderson, R., Hiebert, E., Scott, J., & Wilkinson, I. (1985). *The report of the commission on reading: Becoming a nation of readers.* Urbana, IL: Center for the Study of Reading.

Bixby, M. (1988). Autobiographies of language users. In C. Gilles, M. Bixby, P. Crowley, S.R. Crenshaw, M. Henrichs, F.E. Reynolds, & D. Pyle (Eds.), *Whole language strategies for secondary students.* New York: Richard C. Owen.

Boehnlein, M. (1987). Reading intervention for high risk first-graders. *Educational Leadership. 44,* (6) 32–37.

Buchanan, E. (Ed.). (1980). *For the love of reading.* Winnipeg, Manitoba, Canada: The C.E.L. Group, Inc.

Chambers, A. (1983). *Introducing books to children.* Boston: Horn.

Cullinan, B.E. (1987). Inviting readers to literature. In B.E. Cullinan (Ed.), *Children's litera-ture in the reading program.* Newark, DE: International Reading Association.

Fisher, C., & Terry, C.A. (1990). *Children's language and the language arts: A literature based approach.* Boston: Allyn & Bacon.

Graves, D.H. (1990). *Discover your own literacy.* Portsmouth, NH: Heinemann.

Goodman, K. (1986). *What's whole in whole language?* Portsmouth, NH: Heinemann.

Goodman, K., Goodman, Y., & Flores, B. (1979). Reading in the bilingual classroom: Literacy and biliteracy. Rosslyn, VA: National Clearinghouse for Bilingual Education.

Goodman, Y.M., & Burke, C. (1980). *Reading strategies: Focus on comprehension.* NY: Holt, Rinehart and Winston.

Goodman, Y.M., Watson, D.J., and Burke, C.L. (1987). *Reading miscue inventory: Alternative procedures.* NY: Richard C. Owens.

Harste, J.C., & Burke, C.L. (1977). A new hypothesis for reading teacher research: Both teaching and learning of reading are theoretically based. In P.D. Pearson (Ed.), *Reading: Theory, research, and practice.* Twenty-sixth Yearbook of the National Reading Conference. Rochester, NY: NRC, 32–40.

Harste, J., Woodward, V., & Burke, C. (1984). *Language stories and literacy lessons.* Exeter, NH: Heinemann.

Hennings, D.G. (1990). *Communication in action: Teaching the language arts.* Boston: Houghton Mifflin.

Hiebert, E., & Colt, J. (1989). Patterns of literature-based reading instruction. *The Reading Teacher, 43* (1), 14–20.

Holdaway, D. (1982). Shared book experience: Teaching reading using favorite books. *Theory into Practice, 21* (4), 293–300.

Hough, R.A., Nurss, J.R., & Enright, D.S. (1986). Story reading with limited English speaking children in the regular classroom. *The Reading Teacher, 39,* 510–514.

Jalongo, M.R. (1988). *Young children and picture books: Literature from infancy to six.* Washington, DC: National Association for the Education of Young Children.

King, D., & Watson, D. (1983). Reading as meaning construction. In B. Bushing & J. Schwartz (Eds.). *Integrating the language arts in the elementary school* (pp. 70–77). Urbana, IL: National Council of Teachers of English.

Larrick, N. (1987). Illiteracy starts too soon. *Phi Delta Kappan, 69* (3), 184–189.

Lee, S.C. (1987). *Teachers' perceptions of the process and function of theories of language learning.* Unpublished doctoral dissertation, Texas A&M University: College Station, TX.

Manna, A. L., & Misheff, S. (1987). What teachers say about their own reading development. *Journal of Reading, 31* (2), 160–168.

Martinez, M., & Teale, W. (1987). The ins and outs of a kindergarten writing program. *The Reading Teacher, 40,* 444–451.

McGee, L.M., & Richgels, D.J. (1990). *Literacy's beginnings: Supporting young readers and writers.* Needham Heights, MA: Allyn and Bacon.

Newman, J.M. (1985). Insights from recent reading and writing research and their implications for developing whole language curriculum. In J.M. Newman (Ed.), *Whole Language: Theory in Use.* Portsmouth, NH: Heinemann.

Ogbu, J.U. (1985). Cultural-ecological influences on minority school learning. *Language Arts. 62,* 860–869.

Petrosky, A.R. (1980). The inferences we make: Children and literature. *Language Arts. 57,* 149–156.

Shanahan, T. (1988, March). The reading-writing relationship: Seven instructional principles. *Reading Teacher. 41* (7), 636–647.

Smith, F. (1985). *Reading without nonsense* (2nd ed.). New York: Teachers' College Press.

———. (1988). *Understanding reading* (4th ed.). Hillsdale, NJ: Lawrence Erlbaum Associates.

Sulzby, E. (1981). Crossing the bridge from pre-reading to reading. *Early Years,* 38–39, 46.

Teale, W.H. (1986). The beginnings of reading and writing: Written language development during the preschool and kindergarten years. In M. R. Sampson (Ed.), *The pursuit of literacy: Early reading and writing.* Dubuque, IA: Kendall/Hunt.

Tompkins, G.E. (1990). *Teaching writing: Balancing process and product.* Columbus, OH: Merrill.

Trealease, J. (1985). *The read aloud handbook.* New York: Viking/Penguin.

Tunnell, M.O., & Jacobs, J. (1989). Using "real" books: Research findings on literature based reading instruction. *The Reading Teacher. 42,* (7), 470–477.

Wiseman, D. (1984). Helping young children make steps toward reading and writing. *The Reading Teacher, 37* (4), 340–346.

Zarrillo, J. (1989). Teachers' interpretations of literature-based reading. *The Reading Teacher, 43* (1), 22–28.

_2_

PROVIDING READING MATERIAL

Mostly, he [Lincoln] educated himself by borrowing books and newspapers. There are many stories about Lincoln's efforts to find enough books to satisfy him in that backwoods country. Those he liked he read again and again, losing himself in the adventures of Robinson Crusoe *or the magical tales of* The Arabian Nights. *He was thrilled by a biography of George Washington, with its stirring account of the Revolutionary War. And he came to love rhyme and rhythm of poetry, reciting passages from Shakespeare or the Scottish poet Robert Burns at the drop of a hat. He would carry a book out to the field with him, so he could read at the end of each plow furrow, while the horse was getting its breath. When noon came, he would sit under a tree and read while he ate. "I never saw Abe after he was twelve that he didn't have a book in his hand or in his pocket," Dennis Hanks remembered. "It didn't seem natural to see a feller read like that."*

. . . Folks liked young Lincoln. They regarded him as a good humored, easy going boy—a bookworm maybe, but smart and willing to oblige . . .

—Russell Freedman, *Lincoln: A Photobiography* (1988 Newbery Medal winner)

Oₙₑ of the teacher's tasks when establishing literature-based reading instruction is to provide students access to a wide range of reading material. The provision of reading material is an enormous job that contributes to the success of literature-based instruction and activities. Availability of reading material affects how often students read, their attitudes toward reading, their achievement in reading (Rhodes, 1979), and even the quality of their writing. This chapter will discuss the various materials available for reading and instruction and will answer the following questions:

1. What material is appropriate for literature-based reading instruction?
2. How does a teacher become acquainted with the materials?
3. What criteria are used to determine high quality literature?
4. What material other than children's literature should be accessible to students?

A most important factor in guiding students to select and read literature and for planning literature-based instruction is knowing which authors are writing for children and what children are reading. Teachers who are planning literature-based curricula

Children's literature offers a wide variety of reading opportunities.

read children's literature and listen to how children talk about it. A knowledge of children's literature is necessary to discuss with children what they read, to guide them in their explorations of literature, and to facilitate children's learning through literature. Together, teachers and children will become acquainted with authors, illustrators, literature series, characters, and events.

Students' developmental levels, interests, motivations, and abilities provide guidelines for determining what reading materials should be available. In addition, teachers must consider state and local curriculum requirements, availability, funding, and the purposes of various texts as well as instructional goals and their own personal preferences.

Rhodes and Dudley-Marling (1988) considered all factors to make suggestions that guide a teacher in selecting materials for classroom reading. Box 2.1 presents an outline of the questions the teacher will want to consider when choosing reading material for the classroom.

Literature-based reading instruction is supported by a wide variety of materials, and reading teachers should familiarize themselves with any that would motivate their students to read for many purposes. Materials include children's literature (picture

BOX 2-1

Guidelines for Selecting Material

1. Were the materials written for authentic communication? Were the materials written to communicate a feeling, idea, information, or story, or were they written to teach or reinforce reading skills?

2. Do the materials use natural language? Can children use their knowledge of syntax and semantics while they read?

3. Are the materials relevant to the background and experience of students? The information in the text should match the children's experiences.

4. Do the materials invite lengthy engagement in reading? Children can be encouraged to spend a longer time with books when the texts are longer or the material is motivating.

5. Do the materials encourage divergent responses? Children should be able to share many ideas, reactions, and experiences after they read.

6. What can the student learn about the world as a result of using the materials? Students should be able to find value in the materials they are reading.

7. Are the materials representative of out-of-school materials? Children should read the same types of books that they will read without classroom incentives.

Source: Adapted from L. Rhodes, and C. Dudley-Marling, *Readers and Writers with a Difference* (Portsmouth, NH: Heinemann, 1987).

books and trade books), "pop" literature (lyrics, comics, and joke books), basals, newspapers, magazines, and student-written publications. In addition, there are several instructional aides that encourage students to participate and engage in reading. Computers, audio tapes, videos, films, and filmstrips can be an important part of reading instruction. These commercially produced materials, combined with student writing, provide a wide range reading material for the classroom.

Literature-based Instruction

A recent review of research on literature-based reading instruction (Tunnell & Jacobs, 1989) documents the success of programs that use a great deal of children's literature and reflects the recent and common theme that supports the inclusion of children's literature in reading instruction and materials (Hiebert & Colt, 1989; Zarrillo, 1989). One obvious characteristic of literature-based reading instruction is its use of literature written for children's enjoyment instead of material written and organized for teaching children. The authors of high quality children's literature write and illustrate books to create a mood, convey a theme, or share an exciting plot without considering the reading skills that might be required or encouraged by reading the material. Rhodes and Dudley-Marling (1988) and others refer to the materials written specifically to share, teach, or entertain as "authentic" materials. Authentic material is used to motivate children to read and to help them understand behaviors associated with efficient reading. When the teacher wishes to emphasize specific reading strategies, the focus is accomplished within the context of children's reading and writing.

A second characteristic of literature-based instruction is the many opportunities for children to select their reading material. Although some books are suggested by the teacher as a result of specific instructional objectives and others are read by the entire class or small groups, there is always a large classroom library so that children may have opportunities to select reading material that is personally interesting and motivating. This is a great contrast from traditional instructional approaches that are completely teacher directed and planned.

Literature-based reading instruction is a viable approach to reading instruction for several reasons. One benefit is that allowing children to choose reading material motivates them to read and improves their attitudes toward reading (Tunnell & Jacobs, 1989). It also allows children to take a personal interest in reading (Fuhler, 1990), so children view reading as something done for a purpose. In addition, using a wide variety of reading materials in the classroom offers opportunities to represent many lifestyles and cultures.

The basic characteristics and activities associated with literature-based instruction are supported by the principles of learning language. For example, reading literature encourages and supports the development and understanding of all forms of written language. Well-written books provide an impressive model of language and exemplary vocabulary that children can use in their own written and oral language (Fuhler, 1990). Children's responses to literature also can provide a time for using many of the language processes. Reading, writing, listening, and speaking are ways of responding to a variety of literature.

Reading is the basic activity of literature-based instruction, and the skills associated with reading are learned through use rather than skill drills and activities that focus on isolated reading skills. The more often children read, the more successful they will be at reading. Another basic activity associated with literature-based instruction is social interaction. Children are encouraged to discuss, write, share, debate, compare, and enjoy literature together. Since most of what is known about language is learned in the presence of others (Harste, 1990), interaction associated with literature enhances and supports language development.

The list of benefits is lengthy, but there are also concerns commonly associated with the implementation of literature-based instruction. One of the greatest concerns has to do with the evaluation and monitoring of development in a curriculum that is extremely individual. Because the literature-based instruction trend follows on the heels of widespread development of testing and evaluation, many are concerned by what they view as inadequate evaluation. Since skills measured on standardized tests are not the focus of instruction, other methods of monitoring growth and development are more appropriate. Checklists, retellings, discussions, self-evaluations and student's collected writings (described in Chap. 9) are examples of ways to monitor and evaluate children's progress. If these methods are developed and organized in a workable manner, they can explain a great deal more about children's reading than a standardized test score.

One of the first things to confront a teacher who wishes to implement literature-based instruction is the lack of classroom libraries. When establishing a literature-based program, there is a great deal of pressure to provide a large number and variety of books. It may take time to provide easy access to books for individual reading and unit planning. But support for literature-based instruction will encourage schools to continue to build classroom libraries and make classroom sets of literature available.

Literature-based instruction requires much planning and organization. Some teachers may feel that preparing for literature-based instruction is only one more thing to accomplish in a busy and hectic career. Those teachers who do embark on it feel well rewarded and find that implementation becomes easier over time. Working in small planning groups and forming teams of teachers make the job of planning, organizing, and teaching reading a collegial and enjoyable affair.

Children's Literature

There are a number of different ways to use literature as part of reading instruction (Cullinan, 1987), but the first step for any teacher who wishes to prepare for literature-based reading instruction is to become familiar with the diverse and ever expanding world of children's literature. Children's literature can represent many styles, media, genres, and creative presentations. But most of the books can be categorized as either picture books or novel-length books. Often picture books are identified as most appropriate for primary grade children and novel-length books as most appropriate for upper grade children. While this is not entirely true, it is at least a beginning for a discussion of the two main formats of children's literature.

Picture Books

It is difficult to find a definition of picture books that will be universal to all people familiar with the format. Different people will recognize different books as picture books. Picture books are usually identified as books that use both pictures and text to convey the meaning of the story. The pictures can't tell the story alone nor can the text tell the story as completely without the pictures. Words and pictures contribute to the meaning of the text. But even the acknowledgement that words and pictures work together will fail to fully delineate picture books. A special case would be the wordless books that tell their stories with pictures.

Picture books were developed to motivate young children to read and traditionally we think of *Mother Goose,* ABC books, counting books, concept books, wordless books, fantasy, traditional books, and books that tell about common experiences as picture books. These books are easily recognized as more suitable for preschool, kindergarten, first, and second grades. However, there are many picture books that are relevant in content and theme for middle school children. Even adults are intrigued by the beautiful artwork and multiple levels of meaning and interest presented in picture book format.

Novels

The books that are longer and do not have pictures to match each line of text generally are directed at children who are at least in the third grade. Novel-length books can be fiction or nonfiction and may include high quality artwork, but there is no doubt that the book would not be identified as a picture book. *Swan Lake* (Helprin, 1989) is a good example—it includes the high quality artwork of Chris Van Allsburg, but would not be classified as a picture book because of its extended text. Other examples of novel-length books would include most of the winners of the Newbery Medal discussed later in this chapter. Novel-length books are generally more appropriate for older children to read, although, as might be expected, they are not always that easy to categorize. For example, *Charlotte's Web* (White, 1952) includes a fairly long and involved text, but is appropriate for very young elementary students.

The term *trade book* is used to refer to books not written for instruction that are of a size and cost easy for children to purchase, share, and trade. They include picture books and novel-length books. Trade books' subjects can cover almost any topic and can represent any genre or type. (See the latter part of the chapter for a complete discussion of genre.) Trade books can be funny or sad, offering a look at everyday happenings or a single worldwide event.

Nearly forty thousand children's trade books are in print (Huck, Hepler, & Hickman, 1987) and four thousand more are published each year (Lukens, 1989). There are just too many books to know each one, and the list of children's literature keeps growing. Teachers need to develop the skill of selecting books appropriate for classroom use. One way to begin acquiring the knowledge necessary for selecting books for classroom reading is to become familiar with children's literature award winners.

Award Winners

Although the award winners are not the only books valuable for children to read, they present a standard for judging the others. Certainly, there are high quality and motivating books that have not won awards, and many of them are excellent for classroom use. Those who begin with familiarizing themselves with award winners quickly branch out to find their personal favorites that may or may not include award winning books.

The two most prestigious awards for children's literature in the United States are the Caldecott and Newbery medals. The Caldecott is named for Randolph Caldecott, a nineteenth century English illustrator of children's books, and is awarded to the outstanding picture book of any given year. A cursory review of the Caldecott Medal winners reveals a wide and diverse range of lovely picture books that could be used at many different grade levels. The classic Caldecott Medal winner, *Where the Wild Things Are* (Sendak, 1963), demonstrates the longevity and high quality artwork that is typical of Caldecott winners. *Where the Wild Things Are* (Sendak, 1963) has provided pleasure to children for more than twenty-five years and is still a delight to read to young children. The Sendak classic, which presents the main character Max meeting "wild things" in his dreams, can be compared with a more recent winner, *Shadow* (Brown,

1982), a sophisticated rendition of a French poem, to illustrate the range of topics and artwork found among the award winning picture books.

The John Newbery Medal is presented each year to the author of a book that makes the most significant contribution to children's literature. The books recognized by the Newbery Medal are more appropriate for children in upper grades and provide a wide range of topics, styles, genres, and appeal. The Newbery winners include such well-known favorites as *Bridge to Terabithia* (Paterson, 1977), with a strong theme of friendship and tragedy, *Jacob, Have I Loved* (Paterson, 1981), which discusses the issues of sibling rivalry, and *Lincoln: A Photobiography* (Freedman, 1987), which is an in-depth study of the president.

The Newbery Medal has been awarded by the American Library Association every year since 1922, and the Caldecott Medal has honored illustrators since 1938. Each year there are several books in each category that are named ''honor books'' and should not be overlooked in a survey of the award winners. The medal winners are stamped with round gold seals and the honor books with silver seals that quickly become recognizable to teachers and children who read a great deal of children's literature. A complete list of the winners is presented in an appendix to this text.

There are several other awards given to children's books. Some are international, such as the Hans Christian Andersen Prize, which recognizes a children's author or illustrator every two years. Americans who have won this award include the illustrator Maurice Sendak and the author Paula Fox. The Laura Ingalls Wilder Medal is given to honor an American author or illustrator who has made a lasting contribution to literature in our country. Two of the most recent recipients of this award were Jean Fritz and Maurice Sendak.

Two examples of states that allow children to vote for favorite books are Texas and Michigan. Texas has the Bluebonnet Award, the winner of which is selected by a statewide poll of fifth graders. Michigan's Young Readers' Award provides an opportunity for teachers and children to collaborate on selecting favorite books. Many more states have award winners that are worthwhile for teachers to become familiar with. A list of many of the state awards is included in the appendix.

Evaluating Picture Books

Because of the great number of picture books available to a teacher who wishes to use them in the classroom, it is important to understand the criteria for selecting those representative of good literature.

1. The first criterion to consider is the appropriateness of the book for the children who will be using it. The children in the classroom should be able to understand and enjoy the concepts presented. The vocabulary and use of language are among the factors that determine appropriateness. For example, *Shadow* (Brown, 1982) may not be appropriate for most first graders because of its use of complicated concepts and language:

The eye has no shadow.
All the children of the Moon
And of the Sun,
The Earth, the Water,
The Air, the Fire.
Own no shadow.
Shadow itself has no shadow.

The images and language of this text can be contrasted with the simpler *Brown Bear, Brown Bear, What Do You See?* (Martin, 1983), which is more appropriate for young children:

"Redbird,
Redbird,
What do you see?"
"I see a yellow duck
looking at me."

These two samples of picture book texts demonstrate the enormous range of language in picture books and underscore the importance of age and developmental appropriateness in providing picture books for the classroom.

The language of well-written picture books is much like poetry and usually flows easily. In well-written texts, the language produces images, encourages imagination, and presents children with examples of language they might not hear in their every day world. The recent Caldecott Medal winner *Owl Moon* (Yolen, 1987) is an excellent example of the wonderful use of language in a picture book.

It was late one winter night,
Long past my bedtime,
When Pa and I went owling.
There was no wind.
The trees stood still
As giant statues.
And the moon was so bright
The sky seemed to shine.
Somewhere behind us
A train whistle blew,
Long and low,
Like a sad, sad song.

2. The quality of the picture book's content and illustrations must be considered when selecting for classroom use. Picture books for even very young children should have themes and something worth saying. For example, the classic *The Tale of Peter*

Rabbit (Potter, 1902) has a strong theme of obedience that has been enjoyed by children for years. Peter is the naughty rabbit who disobeys his mother and visits Mr. McGregors's garden. He avoids being caught by McGregor, but loses his hat and shoes and becomes ill as a result of running through the wet garden without a hat or shoes.

Picture books' stories need fast action and a well-developed storyline. Children like story action that is immediately evident and a storyline that is easy to follow. The classic picture book, *Where the Wild Things Are* (Sendak, 1963), carries its main character Max off on a great adventure within the first two sentences. As soon as Max dresses in his wolf suit ". . . and produces mischief of one kind or another," the action begins, and children are caught up with the story.

The enjoyment of a picture book depends a great deal on the quality of the pictures. The pictures should be well done and support the story. For years, artists have been experimenting with appropriate and effective art for picture books. As a result, there are books with line drawings, such as *Madeline's Rescue* (Bemelmans, 1953), books with woodcuts, such as *Once a Mouse* (Brown, 1961), books in brilliant hues of primary colors, such as *Drummer Hoff* (Emberly, 1967), and a wonderful example of collage in *A Snowy Day* (Keats, 1962). With so many talented and creative people working to produce wonderful and inviting books for children of all ages, it is no wonder that a wealth of artistic talents and techniques is evident in the artwork of children's literature.

Recent technology reproduces magnificent artwork to support the texts of picture books. One has only to review the picture books of the 1980s to see beautiful and creative presentations accompanying children's literature. No matter what artwork is used to present the information in picture books, the media should match the mood and themes of the story. A good example of match between mood and story is represented by the classic presentation of big bold monsters painted in tempera in *Where the Wild Things Are* (Sendak, 1963) and the character of bold, brave Max.

3. The shape, size, and general attractiveness of the books must be evaluated. Some children love to look at very small books while others will want to hold larger books. If a teacher is going to share the book with the entire class, the size must be taken into consideration. When teachers learn what their students enjoy and use that knowledge to select books, they will be able to increase the enjoyment of the literature.

When the content of the story, the language used to tell the story, and the pictures work together, the magic of a picture book is obvious. There is nothing quite as rewarding as finding a wonderful picture book to share with children. It is not unusual for picture book characters and events to become intertwined in the daily routine of the classroom. The characters become an integral part of the classroom, and the teacher may hear children refer to a character or events long after the book has been returned to the shelf.

Literary Elements

Teachers need to understand the literary elements of children's literature to select books for the classroom and guide children in their reading. Children should be exposed to the terminology of literature from an early age so that they can more intelligently discuss what they are reading.

Character Development

An author employs many methods to help us understand the characters in a story. A reader gets to know characters by actions, feelings, description, and speech. Children want the character of a story to be involved in action and to make decisions (Lukens, 1989). Children need to understand the decisions and actions of a character, and they enjoy a story in which the main character is involved in an accident or something unexpected.

Plot

Plot is the order of how things happen in a story. Picture books with the simplest story line should contain a well-defined plot. Good plot development does not occur by mere coincidence, nor should the sequence of events depend on emotion and tearjerker passages. A good plot must have conflict. Without some need for decision-making or action, a story is boring (Lukens, 1989).

Just as young children enjoy fast plots in picture books, older children prefer stories that are action-packed, start fast, and contain some conflict. Many times a good book will involve two or more conflicts. In the recent Newbery honor book *Hatchet* (Paulsen, 1987), the reader is quickly inaugurated into two levels of conflict. The conflict caused by the pain of the main character's reaction to his parents' divorce develops within the first pages. The main conflict is established after a plane crash that leaves the main character stranded in the Canadian frontier. Both conflicts contribute to the plot or sequence of events.

Theme

The theme is the reason the author wrote the story and includes the central idea or moral the author wishes to convey. The classic *Charlotte's Web* (White, 1952) sets forth the theme of the importance of friendship. No child can read this popular classic without realizing that good friends are valuable assets in their lives. Themes in good children's literature are not didactic or preachy and provide children with insights into their own lives.

Setting

The setting includes the time and location of the story. Children's literature may involve an integral setting that contributes to the plot. An example is *Julie of the Wolves* (George, 1972), which tells of a young girl's ordeal as she travels through the tundra. The setting is established as the antagonist, and much of the conflict is based on Julie's survival in the harsh, cold, wild environment. The setting is necessary to the story line. The setting in stories like *Tales of a Fourth Grade Nothing* (Blume, 1972), which takes place in an apartment complex, does not affect the events and is considered a backdrop.

If the setting is essential to the understanding of the story, the author should make the reader experience it. Children usually do not enjoy long, involved descriptions of settings, so the most effective description is woven through the action and plot (Lukens, 1989).

Point of View

The point of view considers who tells the story. The story may be told by the main character or another character in the story (first person); the author or an all-knowing character (third person or omniscient); an objective or dramatic point of view that explains all the events and feelings and lets the reader come to conclusions (Lukens, 1989). An understanding of point of view will contribute to the students' overall comprehension of the story.

The maturity of the reader must be considered when evaluating the point of view. Children have not experienced many of the events and emotions that they read, so it is difficult for them to draw on their experiences. Children's literature needs to clarify events through objective descriptions of actions and speech (Lukens, 1989). One reason picture books are so valuable to use with younger children is that the pictures provide a strong reinforcement of point of view.

Style and Tone

The teacher who helps students focus on the style and tone of the story is encouraging very high-level comprehension skills. The discussion of style can include a consideration of the author's arrangement of words; the tone of the story is the feeling that the author wants to convey. The style and tone of a story should be evaluated for freshness of words and language and the attitude of the author toward the story. An example is *Hey, Al* by Arthur Yorinks with pictures by Richard Egielski (1986) which has a definite, unique style:

> *Al, a nice man, a quiet man, a janitor, lived in one room on the West Side with his faithful dog, Eddie. They ate together. They worked together. They watched TV together. What could be wrong?*
> —Excerpt from *Hey, Al* by Arthur Yorinks. Copyright ©
> 1986 by Arthur Yorinks. Reprinted by permission of Far-
> rar, Straus and Giroux, Inc.

The distinctive style of Yorinks is recognizable in a funny, offbeat passage from *Louis the Fish* (1980):

> *One day last spring, Louis, a butcher, turned into a fish. Silvery scales. Big lips. A tail. A salmon.*

Louis did not lead, before this, an unusual life. His grandfather was a butcher. His father was a butcher. So, Louis was a butcher. He had a small shop on Flatbush.

> *Steady customers. Good meat. He was always friendly, always helpful, a wonderful guy.*

—Excerpt from *Louis the Fish* by Arthur Yorinks. Copyright © 1980 by Arthur Yorinks. Reprinted by permission of Farrar, Straus and Giroux, Inc.

The short sentences and clipped speech of Yorinks suggests the accent of New York or Boston. Egielski's illustrations of apartment living and large city shops support the writing style evident in the text. In contrast, the writing style of McKissack's *Mirandy and Brother Wind* (1988), is more indicative of the smooth, slow dialect of the south and is reflected in Jerry Pickneys's illustrations of the rural community of Ridgetop where the main character of the story, Mirandy, tries to outsmart Brother Wind.

> *"Sure wish Brother Wind could be my partner at the junior cakewalk tomorrow night,"* say Mirandy, her face pressed against the cool cabin window. *"Then I'd be sure to win."*
>
> *Ma Dear smiles. "There's an old saying that whoever catch the Wind can make him do their bidding."*
>
> *"I'm gin' to,"* say Mirandy. And she danced around the room, dipping, swinging, turning, wheeling. *"This is my first cakewalk. And I'm gon' dance with the Wind!"*

—From *Mirandy and Brother Wind* by Patricia C. McKissack, illustrated by Jerry Pinkney. Text copyright © 1988 by Patricia C. McKissack. Illustrations copyright © 1988 by Jerry Pinkney. Reprinted by permission of Alfred A. Knopf, Inc.

As soon as children are exposed to literature they should begin to use the terms associated with its elements and language. Children who grow up with this terminology will be able to look for the elements in everything they read as well in as their own writing. They also can also use the terminology to discuss any genre or type of book.

Genres of Children's Literature

The term used to refer to the different types and categories of literature is *genre*. Almost all stories and texts written for children can be classified as a certain genre: traditional, fantasy, historical fiction, contemporary, or informational. Genres of children's literature may be found in either picture or novel formats. There are several different genres or categories of children's literature appropriate for classroom use and each has identifiable characteristics.

FIGURE 2-1   The text and pictures of *Mirandy and Brother Wind* illustrate a distinctive style and mood.

Source: McKissack, P.C. (1988). *Mirandy and Brother Wind.*

Traditional Literature

Traditional literature has its origin in storytelling. Eventually the stories told by the common working folk of long ago were collected and recorded for others to read. These stories include epics and ancient stories, ballads and legends, fantasy, folk songs, fables, and myths. The values of using folklore in the classroom are many:

1. Traditional literature selections are basically good stories that move quickly, usually are humorous, and almost always end happily. They are great fun to share in the classroom (Huck, Hepler, & Hickman, 1987).

2. Traditional literature fosters imagination and encourages children's fantasies (Huck, Hepler, & Hickman, 1987). Those of us who grew up wanting to be Cinderella or the handsome prince can understand the impact of imagination. Many children imagine they are the characters of traditional literature or invite the characters to become part of their fantasy play.

3. Traditional literature provides a foundation for appreciating and understanding literature, art, and dance (Norton, 1991). There are many references to traditional literature in modern literature and art.

4. Traditional literature provides a vehicle for understanding different groups and cultures. The customs, speech, and dress of characters in traditional literature reflect differing cultures and periods.

5. Traditional literature represents universal qualities of mankind. It is easy to understand the basic values represented in traditional literature. Reading traditional literature helps develop an understanding of others in the world.

Traditional literature usually has a plot presented in a series of episodes and maintains quick action. Repetition is a basic element, making the stories easily adaptable for beginning or troubled readers. The time and place are established quickly: the introduction presents the conflict, characters, and settings in a few sentences. The conclusion incorporates only a few details.

Characters are not well-developed and represent some specific quality. The beautiful girl is virtuous, humble, patient, and loving. Stepmothers are mean and cruel. Very little is known about the feelings and motives behind actions. For example, Cinderella is beautiful, kind, hardworking, and mistreated, but the reader knows nothing about her or why she responds and acts as she does.

One of the unusual features of traditional literature is the motifs. Motifs are the smallest part of a story that exist independently. There are several common motifs in traditional literature. For example, the motif of three is presented in the *Three Billy Goats Gruff, Goldilocks and The Three Bears,* and numerous stories that have three wishes, guesses, or gifts. Other motifs include long sleeps or enchantments, magical powers, magical transformations, magic objects, wishes, and trickery.

There are many versions of traditional literature. Most experts believe that since traditional literature derives from basic human needs and understandings, all cultures have similar stories. As a result, there are five hundred versions or variants of Cinderella from different parts of the world. These variants will have the same plot, but different characters, settings, and motifs. A popular version of *The Three Little Pigs* is a tongue-in-cheek rendition of the wolf's point of view. The wolf introduces his version of the well-known tale in *The True Story of the Three Little Pigs!* (Scieszka, 1989) by writing:

I'm the wolf. Alexander T. Wolf. You can call me Al. I don't know how this whole Big Bad Wolf thing got started but it's all wrong.

Criteria for identifying quality literature should be considered when selecting traditional literature for classroom reading. Traditional literature should retain the flavor of oral storytelling, maintain the presence of early retellings, and represent culture in a dignified manner. In particular, there should be no stereotyping of women or minorities in the stories. One way to select high quality literature from the many stories available is to look for versions by talented artists that maintain traditional characters and the flavor of the folk heroes.

Fantasy and Science Fiction

When a story includes some element that cannot happen in the natural world, the story is defined as fantasy (Norton, 1991). Fantasy can have its roots in folk tales, legends, and myths. Much of the fantasy seems very familiar to those who know and love traditional literature (Huck, Hepler, & Hickman, 1987). The most important reason to use fantasy in the classroom is its contribution to the development of imagination. Fantasy worlds can take the reader to outer space, worlds where animals talk or people never grow old. There is no place where the mind cannot visit when reading fantasy.

There are several types of fantasy that can be used with children during reading instruction. Very young children love animal fantasy in which animals dress up and talk like humans. Stories that feature the fantasy of animal worlds provide children with opportunities to learn the difference between fact and fiction. Even after children realize the differences in real and make-believe, memorable animal characters like Wilbur and Charlotte from *Charlotte's Web* (White, 1952), Peter Rabbit, and Winnie the Pooh are staples in young children's lives.

Another type of fantasy presents small worlds by acquainting the reader with miniatures or toys involved in action on a minuscule scale. *The Borrowers* (Norton, 1953) establishes a fantasy world under a country kitchen in which a miniature family has an exciting world built around those items that huge adults constantly seem to be loosing.

Other stories present time as the element that produces the fantasy. These stories may leap into the past or the future and transport children to a different age. The classic *Wrinkle in Time* (l'Engle, 1962) shares the adventures of children who travel long distances in time and space and overcome evil to find their scientist-father who disappeared.

Some types of fantasy are produced when aspects of other genres of literature and imagination are combined. Quest and adventure stories are produced when the author invents ancient hero and adventure themes based on folklore. Quest stories often include characters who slay dragons and hunt for magic swords in King Arthur's time. This fantasy classification is a curious mix of traditional and science fiction.

Science fiction and fantasy are really the same type of literature with one difference. Science fiction generally makes the comment that technology will affect humans. Much science fiction is intense and concerned with high level social issues, but some science fiction is filled with excitement and humor. Flexibility of ideas and thoughts and a well-developed imagination are encouraged by reading science fiction.

When evaluating science fiction, the technological and scientific information must be presented accurately, and the story should help the reader consider values and science thoughtfully. For example, children experience the horrors of nuclear warfare by reading the powerful *Z for Zachariah* (O'Brien, 1975), which describes a young girl's struggle after being one of only two people to survive a nuclear attack. Imagine the irony of this fast-moving science fiction when the main character discovers that the other person left in her part of the world wants to harm her.

When selecting fantasy for reading instruction, the teacher evaluates the books according to the criteria for high quality children's literature. High quality fantasy must meet all the basic requirements of a good story; in addition, the fantasy world must be plausible, and the characters and events should stay within the framework of the world that has been created. All the stories should create an aura that allows the reader to suspend belief in the real world.

Historical Fiction

Historical fiction is usually a story that could have happened but in a particular period of time past. It presents accurate events with a fictional character and plot. Factual history and real characters may be intertwined with fictional characters, conflicts, and plots.

Johnny Tremain (Forbes, 1946) is an example of an authentic historical novel. As Esther Forbes was researching a biography of Paul Revere, she read many books about apprentices in the revolutionary period. After completing extensive research and writing her book about Paul Revere, she wrote a fictional children's novel based on historical facts. The considerable research that supports *Johnny Tremain* (Forbes, 1946) provides opportunities to learn factual information in an extremely entertaining account of the revolutionary war period. The historical events are accurate and authentic, but the research is thoroughly assimilated in the plot and theme, making the facts seem like a part of the story.

There are other representations of historical fiction that reconstruct a period in which the author did live. For example, Laura Ingalls Wilder retells a personal family experience in fictional form in her "Little House" books. The 1990 Newbery Medal winner, *Number the Stars* (Lowry, 1989), is the author's account of what actually happened to a Danish friend who saved the lives of Jewish neighbors during World War II. The genre of historical fiction in these two examples is based on real experiences in the authors' lives. While neither Wilder nor Lowry completed the extensive research associated with Forbes' work for her *Johnny Tremain,* they compiled accurate and historical information from the people who lived in the time they were writing about. (Lowry does indicate in the afterword of her book that she completed some research, but the basic story line was developed from her friend's experience.)

Occasionally a story will endure until it acquires historical significance. The *Snow Treasure* (McSwigan, 1942) was published as a contemporary story, but has endured and remains an exciting presentation of a World War II event. It is only the highest quality of book that will survive many years and still be enjoyed by children.

Historical fiction allows a child to experience the past and enter the conflicts, the suffering, and the joys of other times. As children read about problems of the past that reflect contemporary issues, a feeling for the continuity of life is established. The reading of historical fiction helps children develop a sense of history and judge the mistakes of the past and produces an awareness that the past influences the events of the future.

Good historical fiction must meet the requirements of a good story and some additional goals. Stories of the past must be authentic and accurate when presenting the facts, setting, language, and characters of another time. Not only must the characters reflect the language and live in an accurate setting, but they must represent the thinking and values of the time period without being stereotypical (Cullinan, 1989). Historical fiction is based on true events, blending factual information with fictional plots.

Biographies bridge historical fiction and nonfiction books (Huck, Hepler, & Hickman, 1987). The biography of a person may be presented as a narrative account and focus on documented facts. The recent Newbery Medal winner *Lincoln: A Photobiography* (Freedman, 1987) is a good example of the high quality biographies available for children to read. Biographies should meet criteria for good informational books and be written in a way that motivates reading and encourages discussion.

Nonfiction

The number of topics presented in nonfiction books for children is almost endless. It is not possible for a teacher to know all nonfiction books available for teaching reading and other subjects. A more reasonable way to approach this large and varied genre of literature is to understand the general types of informational books available. Some of the general types of nonfiction books include:

1. Concept books. These books begin with a familiar concept and move toward something unfamiliar. The books can never be substituted for actual experiences, but should be used to enrich those experiences. Such basic concepts as "up" and "down," "open" and "shut" can be demonstrated in concept books.

2. Picture books. Information sometimes is combined with pictures to present information to children. Tommie dePaola has a series of books, including *The Quicksand Book* (1977) and *The Cloud Book* (1975), that explain topics while telling a story. However, all books with pictures do not tell stories. Many informational picture books, despite format and illustrations, are not directed at early elementary age children and contain difficult concepts and involved explanations not suitable for very young children.

3. Photographic essays. The essay relies upon the camera to document information and emotion journalistically. These books may use actual newspaper pictures and articles to present stories.

4. Identification book. These are generally naming books and are particularly common for scientific categories of animals, plants, body parts, and so on. In the simplest form an identification book may have the picture of an object, label, and a small

description written below. When developed for older children, the descriptions and explanations become more detailed, precise, and complex.

5. Life cycle books. The life cycle books cover all or some part of the development of a human, animal, or plant. Usually the books are presented very objectively, although sometimes animal subjects will have names, but not the power of speech.

Informational books are a good way to integrate children's literature in the curriculum and provide children with opportunities to read about special interests. When selecting informational books for children, the teacher should make sure they are written by reputable experts, present accurate factual material, and include formats and vocabulary appropriate for the children to read.

Poetry

Poetry uses condensed language to explore feelings and events. It relies on the use of imagery to reproduce perceptions in the mind. Poetry can be contemporary and fresh or it can be a part of our oral heritage. We sing and chant naturally many times during our lives. Rituals at church, songs on the radio, and commercials on television all capitalize on the joy that organized language arrangements contribute to our lives. Poetry comes naturally to young children.

Poetry for children differs from adult poetry only in that the theme and subject focus on children's interests. Children's poetry will encompass all the feelings and experiences of childhood. When children have a choice they will select humorous poems with clear-cut rhyme and rhythm. The narrative is a popular poetic form, and favorite topics are familiar experiences and animals.

Poetry is available in several different forms. It often accompanies texts about common topics in basal readers or other anthologies. There also are many good children's poetry collections available. *Sing a Song of Popcorn* (de Regniers, 1988) is an anthology that features many favorite children's illustrators and many delightful verses arranged together in such themes as ''Fun with Rhymes,'' ''Mostly Weather,'' ''Spooky Poems.'' *Poems of A. Nonny Mouse* (Prelutsky, 1990) is a collection of the rhymes we often hear and suggests that the poets who were once anonymous have been identified. A. Nonny Mouse presents many of her best works with the help of Jack Prelutsky, who collected and illustrated many of her most famous poems. Occasionally one poem will be the subject of a single picture book. *Stopping by the Woods on a Snowy Evening* (Frost, 1978) is a wonderful presentation of a favorite in which the artwork contributes to the mood and feeling of the poem.

Contemporary Realistic Fiction

Imaginative fiction that accurately reflects life is realistic fiction. Realistic fiction includes everything that could conceivably have happened to real people. Children consistently select contemporary realism as their favorite because it reflects their own lives. It is important for children to read contemporary realistic fiction for several reasons. This genre can assist children in gaining a greater understanding of themselves, deepen their compassion for others, reassure them that they are not different from others, help them to gain insights about experiences they have not had, and provide models for ways to approach life (Huck, Hepler, & Hickman, 1987).

The many examples of contemporary realism indicate the wide variety of reading material available for children. There are mysteries, animal stories, and adventure tales as well as literature that present everyday events in funny, serious, and thoughtful ways. Children can view situations common to their own and have other experiences vicariously.

Two of the more popular authors of contemporary realism who have been writing for several generations are Judy Blume and Beverly Cleary. Beverly Cleary introduces us to an entire neighborhood of friends like Ramona, her dog Ribsy, and her friend Beezus, who deal with the problems of growing up in a humorous and thoughtful way. Almost everyone can relate to Ramona's worrying about her father's smoking habit and the fact that he can't find a job in *Ramona and Her Father* (Cleary, 1977). The Christmas scene that concludes the story is one that provides insights into the spirit of Christmas and family. Cleary's Newbery Medal winning *Dear Mr. Henshaw* (1983) introduces the reader to Leigh Botts, who becomes a friend to all through his journal entries about adjusting after his parents' divorce.

Perennial favorite Judy Blume writes about a multitude of subjects and concerns of preteenagers. *Tales of a Fourth Grade Nothing* (Blume, 1972) is an uproariously funny account of how a younger sibling can be a nuisance, and it introduces young ''Fudge'' as a character for later books. *Are You There God? It's Me, Margaret* (Blume, 1970) and *And Then Again, Maybe I Won't* (Blume, 1971) are read widely by upper grade children, but cover sensitive topics that a teacher might want to avoid for whole class discussions or instructional focus.

Two contemporary authors have written about popular topics and produced series that children find appealing. Ann Martin is the author of the enormously popular *Baby Sitter's Club* series and other books about contemporary problems, including *Missing Since Monday* (1986), which discusses child abduction, and *Just a Summer Romance* (1987), about the first love of a fourteen-year-old girl. Both are topics sure to capture the attention of fourth, fifth, and sixth grade readers. Judy Delton is another series writer, whose work includes the ''Angel'' series, which discusses the courtship and marriage of a single mother and the daughter's reactions and feelings about her new father.

There are several contemporary fiction titles about boys. Gary Paulsen won a Newbery honor award by describing a young boy's survival after an airplane crash and a divorce in *Hatchet* (1987). He describes a young Native American's quest to discover himself and his culture in *Dogsong* (Paulsen, 1985). *The Winter Room* (Paulsen, 1989) is the story of a young boy growing up in Minnesota, and it describes his family and friends. Louis Sachar focuses on the funny-sad antisocial behavior exhibited by an elementary age boy in *There's a Boy in the Girl's Bathroom* (1987).

Contemporary realistic fiction has a particularly wide range of appeal due to the many topics, plots, and characters. All children can find topics of interest in this genre. Use of contemporary literature in the classroom can encourage and motivate children to read about characters like themselves.

Controversial Subjects

The content of contemporary realism for children has changed dramatically in the past fifteen years. Topics that may not have been appropriate in the past are presented in recent contemporary realism. Teachers must be aware that some topics in children's literature are controversial and reflect the social problems of the world we live in. Parents might not always approve of their children discussing and reading about sensitive issues in school. Sex, violence, religion, and extreme value systems are always subject to objections when used as a basis for instruction. Teachers should consider the community, parents, and children before presenting questionable topics during reading instruction.

Major complaints from parents have focused on books used in school that are about realism, sexism, and racism. Some parents prefer children not be disturbed by what they read nor to entertain ideas different from their families' views. Generally when parents object to books used in the schools it is because they are afraid that their child will be corrupted.

Teachers occasionally decide to use books that include topics that might be considered objectionable. If the book has sufficient import in literary quality or learning material, the teacher may decide to use the book for classroom instruction. Often teachers need to be familiar with books with controversial subjects, not because they will be used during instruction, but in order to respond to their students' discussions and questions about the books. Many of these books can be the foundations for discussions of such tough societal issues as divorce, drugs, sex, abuse, and diseases. If a teacher decides to use or suggest books that present special issues or deal with mature topics, there are some general criteria to consider (Rudman, 1984):

1. The book should include realistic solutions to problems that children might face. Realistic perspectives are particularly important if the book is being used to help children find answers or solve a specific problem.

2. The characters should behave plausibly, humanely, and responsively. The characters need to reflect the values and goals demonstrated by the community in which the children live.

3. The language should be acceptable and free of bias reflecting religious views and ethnic prejudice.

4. The book should include accurate and current information on subjects of a sensitive nature. The nature of many controversial subjects changes almost daily, and books need to reflect the most current information and attitudes.

5. The books should meet high literary standards, include good writing, and avoid sensational conflict.

6. As with all selections for children, any book that includes sensitive topics should be appropriate for a student's developmental level. There are some books and topics appropriate for junior high that could not be used in early primary years.

Teachers can protect themselves from complaints by knowing books that are recommended to their students as well as the books their students are reading. Every

TABLE 2-1   Censorship Distinguished from Professional Guidelines: Examples

EXAMPLES OF CENSORSHIP	EXAMPLES OF PROFESSIONAL GUIDELINES
1. EXCLUDE SPECIFIC MATERIALS OR METHODS *Example:* Eliminate books with unhappy endings.	**1. INCLUDE SPECIFIC MATERIALS OR METHODS** *Example:* Include some books with unhappy endings to give a varied view of life.
2. ARE ESSENTIALLY NEGATIVE *Example:* Review your classroom library and eliminate books that include stereotypes.	**2. ARE ESSENTIALLY AFFIRMATIVE** *Example:* Review your classrooms library. If necessary, add books that portray groups in nonstereotypical ways.
3. INTEND TO CONTROL *Example:* Do not accept *policeman*. Insist that students say and write *police officer*.	**3. INTEND TO ADVISE** *Example:* Encourage such nonlimiting alternatives for *policeman* as *police officer, officer of the law,* or *law enforcer*.
4. SEEK TO INDOCTRINATE, TO LIMIT ACCESS TO IDEAS AND INFORMATION *Example:* Drug abuse is a menace to students. Eliminate all books that portray drug abuse.	**4. SEEK TO EDUCATE, TO INCREASE ACCESS TO IDEAS AND INFORMATION** *Example:* Include at appropriate grade levels books that will help students understand the personal and social consequences of drug abuse.
5. LOOK AT PARTS OF A WORK IN ISOLATION *Example:* Remove this book. The language includes profanity.	**5. SEE THE RELATIONSHIP OF PARTS TO EACH OTHER AND TO A WORK AS A WHOLE** *Example:* Determine whether the profanity is integral to portrayal of character and development of theme in the book.

Source: Board of Directors of the National Council of Teachers of English, *Statement of Censorship and Professional Guidelines,* 1982. Reproduced with permission.

school should have a clearly defined system for dealing with complaints. Generally, if parents feel they have been heard and their concerns have been considered, they will accept the school policies. However, if parents or other groups insist on pressuring a school to remove a book from the classroom or school, they are assuming the role of a censor.

There is a fine line between censorship and selection of books for children. Teachers select books because they have something of value to offer to children. A book is censored when the beliefs of individuals or groups are imposed on everyone. Censorship involves banning, removing, or restricting books from any situation. The National Council of Teachers of English contrasted censorship and professional guidelines in the 1982 statement that appears in Table 2.1.

Newspapers, Magazines, and Periodicals

Options for classroom reading include materials that are regularly read in the home and workplace. Children should become familiar with newspapers, magazines, periodicals, and the many materials written for children. The children's publications *Weekly Reader* and *Scholastic Magazine* are two periodicals found most commonly in classrooms. Many other magazines and periodicals are available and reflect a wide range of interests and concerns. Outdoor life, science, and black culture are examples of themes represented in the periodicals listed at the end of the chapter.

Some adult materials are appropriate for use in the classroom. Newspapers are the most widely read material published and should be in the classroom (Cheyney, 1984). *Time* and *Newsweek* can become part of classroom reading material, too.

Student Writing

Texts that children write can become a valuable addition to classroom reading material. A collection of student-written texts will evolve from many of the activities conducted in literature-based reading instruction. These materials should be approached just as any of the other credible reading material. Activities and methods that encourage student writing are mentioned in later chapter discussions of this textbook.

Basal Readers

Certainly the choice materials for reading instruction are children's literature and other authentic selections, but since many schools use the basal readers, a discussion of the materials and practices associated with them is warranted. Basal textbooks have been a part of reading instruction for many years and are the mainstay of many programs. As a result, the basal reader is the most frequently read material in elementary school. Current trends suggest exclusive use of the basal should be discouraged and basal readers never should be the total reading program. Modern teachers regard the basal as one of many reading materials that can support children's reading development.

There is a difference in the quality of literature used in various basal series and even within a series or a single basal reader. A few basal series meet Rhodes and Dudley-Marling's selection criteria for literature in the classroom (see Table 2.1), and there are individual texts in all basal series that meet the criteria. The basals that include high quality reading material are a resource for teachers. Teachers should use their knowledge of children's literature and information from university courses and librarians to make decisions about the use of the basal during reading instruction.

Basal readers are collections of graded texts appropriate for readers in kindergarten through eighth grade. The selections are used by a class or by groups within the class specifically for reading instruction. Basals form the core of a reading lesson and typically are organized and grouped in units by themes. In addition to reading selections for the children, each basal reading unit provides the teacher with study and discussion questions, poetry, and other material related to the theme.

Basal selections represent a wide variety of genres (e.g., science fiction, historical fiction, contemporary realism, biography, fantasy, and contemporary realism). Sixty-five to seventy-five percent of basal selections are narrative and presented in story form, as opposed to being informational or factual (Flood & Lapp, 1986). There are two types of reading material in the basal series (Baskwell & Whitman, 1988). Some current basals incorporate literature that has been written by well-recognized children's authors. Often the texts and illustrations appear exactly as they did in the original publication. However, there are times that basal companies change the illustrations or language of the texts to meet requirements for material for a certain reading level. The second type of material found in basals is text written to teach specific skills. If the planners of the basals believe that children need to practice a certain skill, they will produce material that encourages use of that skill.

In addition to the graded texts, the basals include several resources that assist in planning, instructing, and evaluating reading instruction. Basal series' supplements include teachers' manuals, workbooks and worksheets, tests, and other aides.

Teachers' Manual

The teachers' manual is a complete plan for presenting reading lessons. Suggested plans are designed to provide teachers with guidance through each page of reading, suggest vocabulary lessons, delineate strategies and skills to emphasize with each lesson, guide follow-up questions, suggest enrichment, and present methods of assessing children's achievement.

Student Workbooks

Student workbooks are usable strategy and skill pages that offer opportunities for children to complete individual work independently. Workbook pages provide independent practice with the skills and strategies emphasized during lessons taught when the teacher and students are reading the story together. Some basals also provide teachers with ready-made worksheets that can be reproduced for the children and serve the same role as the workbook.

Keeping Records

Many basal publishers provide tests that measure students' progress and also provide ways for the teacher to keep records of children's progress. Test masters are provided so that teachers can duplicate the tests that accompany the suggested instruction. Many basals also provide placement tests that assess children and match their level of skills with a particular basal. Almost all basals suggest methods of keeping track of children's progress through the basal series.

Computer Software

Two trends are apparent with regard to basals and computers (Balajthy, 1987). The first is that basal publishers are providing computer-based management systems to help the teacher keep records and provide subskill and placement tests. In addition, publishers are producing software that can be used to encourage basal skill development.

Records and Tapes

Publishers of basal readers provide numerous and varied supplements that complement their companies' reading programs. Supplements may include taped dramatic readings of the stories, filmstrips to accompany the texts, video cassettes to motivate the reader, and other multimedia materials. If these supplements are done well and support well-written basal texts, they have the potential to offer motivational benefits.

Classroom Libraries

The focus on literature-based reading instruction has encouraged basal publishers to include additional reading material as a supplement to the standard basal. Usually, supplemental readers reflect the themes in the basal reader and represent high quality literature. Class sets of the same story or collections of a variety of materials to supplement theme units are among optional basal materials.

.There are many basal reader programs available, but individual teachers do not usually select the basal series for their classrooms. Typically, every five or six years a committee of teachers is appointed by an educational agency at the state level to select 5 to 10 basals to be used in the state. The basal readers selected become known as *state-adopted basal readers.* After the selection process is completed at the state level, each school district repeats the selection process and one or two of the state-adopted basal readers are approved for use. The local selection committee may make decisions about which workbooks, supplemental readers, tests, and other materials will be purchased for schools. In other cases, school district policy allows individual teachers to select the support materials to accompany the basal reader. Some school districts allow teachers to include children's literature as a choice of materials.

Proponents list several advantages to the basal reader approach. Basal readers are easy and accessible. Basals may be the only way to provide multiple copies of one story and can be a resource for children for reading and sharing common material. Teachers can select stories that are interesting to children, well-written, and meet the criteria for acceptable reading material.

Basals also reduce the pressure to generate reading lessons. A new teacher may feel overwhelmed if there are no suggestions for reading lessons. What do you do first? What must be taught during a specified amount of time? It makes sense to use basals as one resource as teachers learn to cope with the everyday duties of the classroom.

Supporters of basals suggest the techniques and instructional procedures promote an organized approach to reading instruction and provide a structure and support for many teachers. They argue that teachers welcome the suggestions and guidance for the order of activities and lessons. Basals provide a framework not available for other approaches.

There are many criticisms of the basal readers. One of the most disturbing results of basal use is the absence of actual reading time. Students spend up to 70 percent of the time allocated for reading instruction in independent practice or working on worksheets and other related skills and drills (Fisher et al., 1978). This distracts from the time that can be reserved for reading in the classroom.

A second criticism of the basal approach is that too much time is spent practicing phonics and learning specific rules of pronunciation and other language generalizations, some of which have a low rate of utility in real reading. Any time an instructional approach focuses on drills and skills to the exclusion of reading and discussion of good literature, it can be criticized for its detrimental effects on reading and literacy development.

Basal instructional patterns also are associated with an overemphasis on correctness to the detriment of thinking and comprehension when answering questions (Durkin, 1981). The questions and guides provided for teachers often suggest that only one answer is acceptable and discourage the thinking and problem-solving that should be an important feature of reading instruction.

The stories in basal readers long have been criticized as boring because of their limited vocabulary and rigid adherence to skill sequences. Most basal series contain stories with controlled vocabulary, not allowing in early readers words that are long or sentences that are complex. It was once thought that the words and sentences that children read must be governed closely to control the reading difficulty for children. The result of controlled vocabulary and language is stilted language and an unnatural style. Many basals are working to overcome this criticism by including high quality stories in the reading material.

Finally, the basal approach may be criticized for including too many activities, stories, and skills, without adequate guidance for selecting and excluding some activities. Teachers should be encouraged to make educated decisions about the basal, including use of stories and activities. When teachers feel that children do not need the activities listed in the guides, they should be encouraged to skip them and spend the time engaged in more meaningful activities. Teachers should be flexible when approaching basal use and be ready to supplement and revise instruction-based on the feedback from the children.

It is important to remember that it is not simply use but the total reliance on the basal that is questionable. To completely eradicate the basal with disregard for the structures and resources provided to teachers would be as inadvisable as the abandonment of children's literature has been. The key to using the basal is making choices in regard to the stories, activities, and suggestions and selecting activities according to the overall goals of a strong reading program.

Basals are a fact of life in most elementary schools; future teachers need to consider how they will use them to their best advantage. Teachers can be provoked into heated discussions of the advantages and disadvantages of the basal. Probably, the bottom line to this controversy is that basals have been overused in recent years. At the least, current reading instruction should integrate other types of literature with the basal reading series. A good way to supplement or supplant the basal is to consider the wealth of reading material available in high quality children's literature.

Other Media

Many stories can be told in print or film. Prints, slides, filmstrips, films, and videocassettes provide adaptations of children's books or versions of traditional stories. The content of print or film should be evaluated with some of the same considerations used when selecting literature (England & Fasick, 1987).

The most common nonprint media used in the classroom are audio recordings. Stories can be presented on long-playing records, cassette tapes, and compact discs. Recordings generally fall into the categories of music, stories, and poetry. Stories that are read dramatically, with music and other accompanying sound effects, can encourage future reading and discussion.

The popularity of the video cassette recorder (VCR) offers yet another way to introduce well-loved stories to children. The most effective way to include VCRs in the classroom is to read the story and watch it as a follow-up. Films and filmstrips also can be used to motivate and interest the young reader. Children know the visual well and respond immediately and it can serve to interest readers and nonreaders in printed materials.

Interactive video technology will offer many options as soon as cost allows its introduction in classrooms. One exciting aspect of video discs is the presentation of information through combinations of still shots and action sequences with stereo sounds. The visual quality of the videodisc is much superior to video tapes (Rickelman, 1988).

In addition to evaluating the subject matter of nonprint material, teachers should assess the way in which the medium itself is used. Images should be clear and precise to present the story in a lively, creative way. The overall cost should be considered. Reviews of new media can be found in professional journals and in periodicals devoted to new technology and audio-visual presentations.

Computers and Reading

Teachers are beginning to use computers to support many aspects of reading instruction. There are many reasons for using computers: novelty, flexible descriptions, innovative formats, interesting graphics, amazing speed, and easy text manipulation (Geoffrion & Geoffrion, 1983).

Because computers and software change so rapidly, very few specific programs are mentioned here. The goal of the discussion about computers is to explore the special capabilities of computers. Computer technology will only continue to improve and provide new materials and methods for reading instruction; the following descriptions suggest three ways to use computers that seem especially adaptable to literature-based instruction (Anderson, 1988; England & Fasick, 1987).

1. Problem-solving programs are particularly valuable for developing comprehension skills. Not many programs are designed to promote problem-solving skills and many of the programs are relatively new (Whitaker, Schwartz, & Vockell, 1989). One of the classic problem-solving programs is *Oregon Trail,* which focuses on social studies while guiding students through a series of decisions necessary for completion of a journey across the United States.

2. Word processing programs encourage children to write their own stories. Word processing can encourage children simultaneously to learn to enjoy reading and writing and provides instant text when very young children dictate stories to the teacher. Desktop publishing software provides an inexpensive method for creating illustrated classroom newspapers or magazines. The popular *Print Shop* by Springboard is one of the most flexible desktop programs. Desktop publishing has the potential to offer a great deal of student-written material for reading instruction.

3. Access to different computer bulletin boards and message systems can provide additional reading material and requires different strategies as children communicate with people in many parts of the country. Reading skills can be strengthened because children need to read rapidly to follow the print appearing on the screen.

Computers will not offer a complete reading program. As with all materials, the teacher's planning and decisions are the key to successful use of computers in reading. Computers are a tool and offer a different way to present instruction and reading material to children. A modern education system must provide children with opportunities to learn about computers and other technology; reading will be the major vehicle for teaching the effective use of technology (Rickelman & Henk, 1989).

Many software programs will be available for teachers to use during reading instruction. Teachers should make sure that the software programs encourage and support the reading curriculum presented in the classroom. In other words, if a teacher believes that reading should not be fragmented, computer programs that are extremely skills-based should not be used. The software should be based on sound learning and teaching assumptions. The best software will not imitate common instructional methods, such as worksheets and workbooks, but uses technology to add motivation, flexibility, graphics, and speed to help children learn how to read.

Selecting Culturally Diverse Material

Reading instruction should use materials that recognize many races, religions, languages, and social backgrounds are represented in the United States. The literature used for reading instruction should include content that is relevant to both culturally and linguistically different children. There should be an extra effort to ensure that children are exposed to a wide range of cultures and languages in the literature they read.

Literature selected to represent the differences in our country should be evaluated for general literary value and the image of the culture presented in the text and illustrations. There are several considerations in selecting books that represent cultural and language differences:

1. Reading material should include the diversity and range of cultural and language groups in our country. Children in the classroom must relate to the reading material. They should recognize that their cultures and language are represented in some of the material they read at school. When children never read about their cultures at school, a subtle statement is made about the acceptability of their backgrounds. Children may decide that their race or culture is not as important as those of the children in their instructional material.

2. Reading material should avoid stereotyping any group. All depictions of characters should encourage the reader to recognize differences among groups of people. Children should realize that there are good people and people who make mistakes in every group. The literature should reflect the differences of people of the same language and culture.

3. Reading material should present a realistic perspective of different groups. During the last ten years there have been many fine books published that reflect the social and cultural traditions of black children in America. Culturally conscious fiction has certain recurring features that offer all children, but especially black children, a perspective in fiction that is uniquely African-American (Sims, 1982).

Unfortunately, there are not as many good books for members of other minority groups represented in our classrooms. Many of the books about Hispanics, for example, are stereotypical (Huck, Hepler, & Hickman, 1987) or represent traditional genre. It may be even more difficult to find good literature about Asian-Americans, Moslems, or Buddhists. Basals are beginning to include a wider representation of children from our pluralistic society, and it is probably only a matter of time before there is high quality literature available about many of the groups in our diverse society.

DISCUSSION AND ACTIVITIES

1. Read one Newbery Medal or honor book. Use the criteria presented for high quality books to figure out why the book was honored. Share your book and observations in small discussion groups.

2. After the class is divided into small groups, complete one or more of the following activities to familiarize yourself with picture books:

  a. Select five early Caldecott Medal winners and five recent Caldecott winners. Compare the content, artwork, media, and subject matter to see what changes have occurred in children's literature over the years. Report your findings to the class.

  b. Select several picture books that have not received awards and decide within your group which book is the most enjoyable. Use the evaluation criteria to justify why you selected the book. Report your findings to the class.

  c. Decide whether your group will investigate *Mother Goose,* counting books, alphabet books, or concept books. Collect several books from one group. Decide which of the books you would prefer to use in the classroom. Use the evaluation criteria to justify your choice. Report your findings to the class.

  d. Identify an award-winning illustrator and writer. Maurice Sendak, Chris Van Allsburg, Arnold Lobel, and Marcia Brown are a few of the very special children's illustrators and writers. Collect all the books that you can find by one author. Review the books and decide what is consistent in the author's style, content, artistic presentation, or any other interesting feature that you can identify.

3. Find several books with some representations of different cultural groups. Evaluate the books on the basis of what should be considered when selecting books for the classroom. Decide whether the book you selected is of high literary quality and if it represents the cultural group in a fair and unbiased way.

4. Watch a video cassette presentation of a book that the class has read. Or, have half the class read a book and the other half watch the film presentation. Make a list of advantages and disadvantages of each method used to get to know the book.

5. Divide into small groups of four or five and collect samples of all types of written material suggested in the chapter. Review the materials according to the criteria discussed in the chapter.

RELATED READING

Professional

Much is written about children's literature that could not be presented in one chapter of a reading methods textbook. Many books and articles can explain most of the topics presented in this chapter in much more depth. The following resources provide additional information.

The journals *Language Arts* and *The Reading Teacher* include reviews of newly published children's books and many ideas about technology and computer usage. There are many excellent children's literature texts. The texts listed below are classics that many teachers have used during their college and professional careers.

Cullinan, B.E. (1989). *Literature and the child.* New York: Harcourt Brace Jovanovich.

> *Cullinan has created a beautiful source book for children's literature that includes many suggestions for classroom use. The cover illustration by Trina Schart Hyman is striking and reflects the excitement and beauty of the children's books Cullinan describes in the text.*

Huck, C. S. , Hepler, S., & Hickman, J. (1987). *Children's literature in the elementary school* (4th ed.). New York: Holt, Rinehart & Winston.

> *Huck has been helping teachers become familiar with children's literature for many years. She and her colleagues share their knowledge and enthusiasm for literature in this valuable resource.*

Norton, D. (1991). *Through the eyes of a child.* Columbus, OH: Merrill.

> *This is a good introduction to children's literature. It provides many excerpts as well as color plates from children's literature. It suggests individual books within certain genres of literature.*

Three other books are excellent resources for learning more about children's literature and using it in the classroom:

Cullinan, B.E. (1987). *Children's literature in the reading program.* Newark, DE: International Reading Association.

> *International Reading Association published this text and acknowledges it is one of their top selling books. It contains helpful practical suggestions for teachers who want to use literature throughout the curriculum.*

Lukens, R. J. (1989). *A critical handbook of children's literature* (4th ed.). New York: Scott Foresman.

> *This book discusses how to evaluate and judge high quality children's literature. It contains numerous excerpts from a wide array of children's literature.*

Rudman, M.K. (1984). *Children's literature: An issues approach.* New York: Longman.

> *This book is mainly a reference that suggests books pertaining to specific issues of interest to children.*

There are several books that serve as bibliographic sources and can help teachers find lists of books on a specific subject. One of the most recent is Lima, C. (1989) *A to Zoo: Subject access to children's picture books* (3rd ed.). New York: Bowker.

Children's Literature

Bemelmans, L. (1953). *Madeline's rescue.* New York: Viking.
Brady, I. (1976). *Wild mouse.* New York: Scribner's.
Brown, M. (1961). *Once a mouse . . .* New York: Scribner's.
———. (1982). *Shadow.* New York: Scribner's.
dePaola, T. (1975). *The cloud book.* New York: Holiday House.
———. (1977). *The quicksand book.* New York: Putman.
de Regniers. (1988). *Sing a song of popcorn.* New York: Scholastic.
Emberly, B. (1967). *Drummer Hoff.* Illustrated by E. Emberly. New York: Prentice Hall.
Frost, R. (1978). *Stopping by the woods on a snowy evening.* Illustrated by S. Jeffers. New York: Dutton.
Keats, E.J. (1962). *The snowy day.* New York: Viking.
Martin, B. (1983). *Brown bear, brown bear, what do you see?* Illustrated by E. Carle. New York: Holt, Rinehart & Winston.
McKissick, J. (1988). *Mirandy and Brother Wind.* Illustrated by J. Pinkney. New York: Knopf.
Potter, B. (1902). *The tale of Peter Rabbit.* New York: Warne.
Prelutsky, J. (1989). *A. Nonny Mouse.* Illustrated by H. Drescher. New York: Knopf.
Sachar, L. (1987). *There's a boy in the girls' bathroom.* New York: Knopf.
Scieszka, J. (1989). *The true story of the 3 little pigs!* Illustrated by L. Smith. New York: Penguin.
Sendak, M. (1963). *Where the wild things are.* New York: Harper & Row.
Van Allsburg, C. (1981). *Jumanji.* New York: Houghton Mifflin.
Viorst, J. (1972). *Alexander and the terrible, horrible, no good very bad day.* Illustrated by R. Cruz. New York: Atheneum.
White, E.B. (1952). *Charlotte's web.* New York: Harper & Row.
Yolen, J. (1987). *Owl moon.* Illustrated by J. Schoenherr. New York: Philomel.
Yorinks, A. (1980). *Louis the fish.* Illustrated by R. Egielski. New York: Farrar, Straus, Giroux.
———. (1986). *Hey, Al.* Illustrated by R. Egielski. New York: Farrar, Straus, Giroux.
Zelinsky, P. O. (1986). *Rumpelstiltskin.* New York: Dutton.
Zemach, H, (1983). *Duffy and the devil.* Illustrated by M. Zemach. New York: Farrar, Straus & Giroux.

Other Genres

Blume, J. (1970). *Are you there God? It's me, Margaret*. New York: Bradbury.
———. (1971). *Then again maybe I won't*. New York: Bradbury.
———. (1972). *Tales of a fourth grade nothing*. Illustrated by R. Doty. New York: Dutton.
Cleary, B. (1977). *Ramona and her father*. New York: Morrow.
———. (1983). *Dear Mr. Henshaw*. New York: Morrow.
Delton, J.(1986). *Angel's mother's boyfriend*. Boston: Houghton Mifflin.
———. (1987). *Angel's mother's wedding*. Boston: Houghton Mifflin.
Forbes, E. (1946). *Johnny Tremain*. Illustrated by L. Ward. Boston: Houghton Mifflin.
Freedman, R. (1987). *Lincoln: A photobiography*. New York: Clarion.
George, J. C. (1972). *Julie of the wolves*. Illustrated by J. Schoenherr. New York: Harper & Row.
Helprin, M. (1989). *Swan Lake*. Illustrated by C. Van Allsburg. Boston: Houghton Mifflin.
l'Engle, M. (1962). *A wrinkle in time*. New York: Farrar, Straus & Giroux.
Lowry, L. (1989). *Number the stars*. New York: Houghton Miffin.
McSwigan, M. (1942). *Snow treasure*. Illustrated by M. Reardon, New York: Dutton.
Martin, A.M. (1986). *Missing since Monday*. New York: Holiday.
———. (1987). *Just a summer romance*. New York: Holiday.
Norton, M. (1953). *The borrowers*. New York: Harcourt, Brace.
O'Brien, R. (1975). *Z for Zachariah*. New York: Atheneum.
Paterson, K. (1977) *Bridge to Terabithia*. New York: Cromwell.
———. (1981) *Jacob have I loved*. New York: Cromwell.
Paulsen, G. (1985). *Dogsong*. New York: Viking.
———. (1987). *Hatchet*. New York: Bradbury.
———. (1989). *The winter room*. New York: Orchard.
White, E.B. (1952). *Charlotte's web*. Illustrated by G. Williams. New York: Harper & Row.
Wilder, L. I. (1953). *Little house in the big woods*. Illustrated by G. Williams. New York: Harper & Row.

Publishers of Children's Periodicals

Child Life
1100 Waterway Blvd., Box 567B
Indianapolis, IN 46206

National Geographic World
National Geographic Society
Washington, DC 10036

Ebony Junior
Johnson Publishing Co.
820 S. Michigan Ave.
Chicago, IL 60605

Highlights
Box 269
Columbus, OH 43272

Boy's Life
Boy Scouts of America
1325 Walnut Hill La.
Irving, TX 75038–3096

Humpty Dumpty
Box 567
Indianapolis, IN 46206

Jack and Jill Magazine
1100 Waterway Blvd.
Box 567B
Indianapolis, IN 46206

Your Big Backyard (for younger readers)
1100 Waterway Blvd.
Box 567B
Indianapolis, IN 46206

Ranger Rick
National Wildlife Federation
1412 16th St., NW
Washington, DC 20036

Stone Soup: A Magazine by Children
Box 83
Santa Cruz, CA 95063

These weekly children's periodicals are often found in the classroom:

Scholastic Action or *Scholastic Sprint*
Scholastic Magazines
902 Sylvan Ave.
Englewood Cliffs, NJ 07632

Weekly Readers
Xerox Educational Publications
1250 Fairwood Ave.
P.O. Box 444
Columbus, OH 43216

REFERENCES

Anderson, J. (1988). Computers and the reading teacher: An Australian perspective. *The Reading Teacher, 41*(7), 698–700.

Balajthy, E. (1987). What are basal publishers doing with computer-based instruction? *The Reading Teacher, 41*(3), 344–345.

Baskwill, J., & Whitman, P. (1988). *Moving on: Whole language sourcebook*. Ontario, Canada: Scholastic TAB.

Cheyney, A.B. (1984). *Teaching reading skills through the newspaper* (2nd ed.). Newark, DE: International Reading Association.

Cullinan, B. (Ed.). (1987). *Children's literature in the reading program*. Newark, DE: International Reading Association.

———. (1989). *Literature and the child* (2nd ed.). New York: Harcourt Brace Jovanovich.

Durkin, D. (1981). Reading comprehension instruction in five basal reader series. *Reading Research Quarterly, 16* (4), 515–544.

England, C., & Fasick, A.M. (1987). *Child view: Evaluating and reviewing materials for children*. Littleton, CO: Libraries Unlimited.

Fisher, C.W., Berliner, D., Filby, N., Marliave, R., Cohen, L., Dishaw, M., & Moore, J. (1978). *Teaching and learning in elementary schools: A summary of the beginning teacher evaluation study*. San Francisco: Far West Regional Laboratory for Educational Research and Development.

Flood, J., & Lapp, D. (1986). Forms of discourse in basal readers. *Elementary School Journal, 87,* 299–326.

Fuhler, C. J. (1990). Let's move toward literature-based reading instruction. *The Reading Teacher, 43* (4), 312–315.

Geoffrion, L., & Geoffrion, O. (1983) *Computers and reading instruction*. Menlo Park, CA: Addison-Wesley.

Harste, J. (1990). Jerry Harste speaks on reading and writing. *The Reading Teacher, 43* (4), 316–318.

Hiebert, E., & Colt, J. (1989). Patterns of literature-based reading instruction. *The Reading Teacher, 43* (1), 14–20.

Huck, C., Hepler, S., & Hickman, J. (1987). *Children's literature in the elementary school*. New York: Holt, Rinehart & Winston.

Lukens, R. J. (1989). *A critical handbook of children's literature* (4th ed.). Glenview, IL: Scott, Foresman.

Norton, D. (1991). *Through the eyes of a child*. Columbus, OH: Merrill.

Rhodes, L.K. (1979). *The interaction of beginning readers' strategies and texts displaying alternate models of predictability*. Unpublished doctoral dissertation, Indiana University: Bloomington, IN.

Rhodes, L.K., & Dudley-Marling, C. (1988). *Readers and writers with a difference: A holistic approach to teaching learning disabled and remedial students*. Portsmouth, NH: Heinemann.

Rickelman, R. J. (1988) Interactive video technology in reading. *The Reading Teacher, 41* (8), 824–826.

Rickelman, R. J., & Henk, W. A. (1989). Meeting tomorrow's challenge. *The Reading Teacher, 43* (1), 78–79.

Rudman, M. K. (1984). *Children's literature: An issues approach*. New York: Longman.

Sims, R. (1982). *Shadow and substance: Afro American experiences in contemporary children's fiction*. Urbana, IL: National Council of Teachers of English.

Tunnell, M. O., & Jacobs, J.S. (1989). Using "real" books: Research findings on literature-based reading instruction. *The Reading Teacher, 42* (7), 470–477.

Whitaker, B.T., Schwartz, E., & Vockell, E. (1989) *The computer in the reading curriculum*. Watsonville, CA: Mitchell; New York: McGraw-Hill.

Zarrillo, J. (1989). Teacher's interpretations of literature-based reading. *The Reading Teacher, 43* (1), 22–28.

3

ORGANIZING AND PLANNING READING INSTRUCTION

The kids in Room 207 were misbehaving again.
Spitballs stuck to the ceiling.
Paper planes whizzed through the air.
They were the worst-behaved class in the whole school.
"Now settle down," said Miss Nelson in a sweet voice.
But the class would not settle down.
They whispered and giggled.
They squirmed and made faces.
They were even rude during story hour.
And they always refused to do their lessons.
"Something will have to be done," said Miss Nelson.
The next morning Miss Nelson did not come to school. "Wow!" yelled the
*   kids. "Now we can really act up!"*
They began to make more spitballs and paper planes.
"Today let's be just terrible!" they said.
"Not so fast!" hissed an unpleasant voice.
A woman in an ugly black dress stood before them.
"I am your new teacher, Miss Viola Swamp."
And she rapped the desk with her ruler.
"Where is Miss Nelson?" asked the kids.
"Never mind that!" snapped Miss Swamp. "Open those arithmetic books!"
Miss Nelson's kids did as they were told.
They could see that Miss Swamp was a real witch.
She meant business.
Right away she put them to work.
And she loaded them down with homework.
                                —Harry Allard & James Marshall, *Miss Nelson Is Missing*

EVERY teacher's secret nightmare is that their class will behave like Miss Nelson's. One way to prevent the mayhem is to plan and organize classroom reading and writing activities effectively. Effective reading instruction is the competent orchestration of many factors. In addition to twenty to thirty children and one teacher, reading instruction involves a large assortment of reading materials, record-keeping, transitions from activity to activity, and behavior management. Organizing and planning well may be the key to successful teaching and learning in literature-based instruction.

This chapter will discuss several aspects of classroom organization and instructional planning and specifically answers the following questions:

1. What planning must occur before instruction?
2. How are decisions made about the strategies, skills, and texts used when teaching reading?
3. Is there a physical room arrangement that encourages the best reading achievement as well as a love of reading?
4. How is reading instruction scheduled?
5. How are children grouped for literature-based instruction?
6. What does a day or week of reading instruction look like?

Foundations of Planning and Organization

Careful planning encourages and motivates children and helps avoid behavior and discipline problems (Robinson & Good, 1987). Teachers who plan and organize daily routines and schedules based on the needs of their students, the nature of the reading process, and high quality reading material will have a greater opportunity to encourage reading and writing development. Planning and organization should contribute to predictable classroom procedures, establishing a comfortable environment, and reflect realistic expectations of the teacher.

It is important that children find reading instruction fairly predictable. Once procedures are established the structure should be consistently and comfortably maintained. School may provide some children with a structure not present elsewhere in their lives. Other children will find that the regular routines of home life are supplemented by school schedules. This does not mean that teachers who are effective organizers do not respond to children's desires, interests, and concerns. On the contrary, effective teachers are willing to accept children's ideas and incorporate their interests, feelings, and needs into the daily routines (Robinson & Good, 1987). Teachers should be willing to change daily planned instruction to better meet the needs of their students. Children's interest and attention may be affected by personal events, such as the acquisition of a new puppy or discussion of a favorite television show watched the night before, and effective teachers will value what is happening to the child over the organizational objectives. There are times when classroom events such as a special visitor, worldwide events such as the dismantling of Russian communism, or national events such as a presidential inauguration suggest that the regular routine be abandoned and reading activities be refocused. Generally, however, students should know what to expect from the reading instruction routines.

Basic procedures and routines should be established in a comfortable, nonthreatening atmosphere, and children should be assured that they will succeed if they participate. To illustrate: If a teacher plans independent reading activities for children who have had a great deal of experience with independent reading, it is right to plan for a reading period of twenty to thirty minutes. However, if a class has never spent time reading independently, five minutes might be more realistic. Five minutes is short enough to ensure success, and the teacher will not have to make rules that threaten the shared atmosphere of the activity.

Teachers' expectations of children's achievement are also an important aspect of classroom organization. Teachers' expectations of their students will affect what is presented, how it is presented, and the attitudes of both the teacher and the children. If the teacher realistically establishes a five-minute independent reading time and fully expects the students to participate successfully, the chances of a positive experience are much higher than if the teacher believes that the children will not be able to sit for five minutes and read. Expectations affect all aspects of management and organization.

Good plans must include logical implementation. The best plans can be ineffective when a teacher does not take the time to inform and prepare students before instruction. Literature-based teachers spend a great deal of time establishing classroom procedures early in the year. Effective implementation of reading routines is more probable when children understand and can predict what is taking place. Activities associated with reading instruction should be clearly identified, described, and demonstrated before children are asked to participate. For example, teachers who are using reading conferences in their instructional plans may not have good results if they announce to children that they will participate in a conference, bring small groups of children to the front of the room, and begin asking questions about a book. A more successful approach might involve several weeks of preparation during which children learn how to select books, read selections on their own, keep records, and participate in discussions about literature. Teachers illustrate procedures associated with conferences through activities and discussions for the whole class, role playing, and demonstrations before expecting all children to participate successfully.

Instructional organization and planning requires the teacher to make many decisions. State-mandated curricula, commercial programs, and other requirements may influence some of what the teacher does. State and local mandates may require that certain instructional elements be presented, specific materials be used, or certain topics taught. In the end, teachers maintain a great deal of control of the physical environment of the classroom, curriculum (what is taught), time allotments and scheduling, grouping procedures, and instructional strategies (how material is presented and goals met) (Dreher & Singer, 1989).

Assumptions of Effective Organization

All teachers develop their own style of organization, but all effective organization and planning is based on basic assumptions.

Planning Is a Most Important Factor in Organizing Reading Instruction

One way to assure effective reading instruction is to approach it with a well-devised plan. Although some of the most wonderful moments in a classroom occur on the spur of the moment, most instruction is the result of thorough planning.

Organization of Reading Instruction Is Affected by Many Factors

Some of the factors affecting plans for classroom reading instruction can be controlled by teachers and some cannot. State and local mandates may require that teachers include certain instructional objectives, teach certain topics, and sometimes include specific materials. Teachers must understand the role of state and district guidelines when planning instruction.

Predictable Routines Are Important Elements of Literature-based Instruction

Children should know what to expect. Routines contribute to how comfortable children feel during instructional activities and how successful they will be in learning how to read.

Teachers' Expectations of Children's Behavior Affect Organization for Reading

Most organizational plans are based on what a teacher expects. Expectations should be realistic, yet move the children along.

The basic assumptions of planning and organization should be considered when making decisions about all aspects of reading instruction. The teacher will learn to use many strategies to support an organizational plan. Some of the more obvious and concrete concerns are arranging the physical aspects of classroom organization, responding to a reading curriculum, scheduling activities, grouping children for instruction, and establishing instructional routines.

Physical Arrangements

A logical place to begin planning is the physical arrangement of the classroom. Literature-based teachers plan a classroom that will support routines and instruction. Arrangements will vary according to the amount of space, equipment, and furniture available. The room's size, space, and shape are relatively constant, but teachers can arrange the furniture and equipment to suggest an emphasis on reading and reading-related activities. Classrooms should invite movement from small groups to individual work to whole class sharing. Reading and writing material should be easily accessible for little people. If possible, quiet spaces should be provided as well as space for group work. The classroom becomes a space that reflects a teacher's philosophy and children's work, and facilitates learning. Figure 3.1 suggests one way to arrange a classroom and consider all the activities and needs of teachers and students.

Classrooms that support literature-based instruction are flexible, and desks, chairs, and tables should be movable so that the room can be rearranged for certain activities. In general, a room should provide a large space for whole class instruction and sharing, a smaller area off to one side for small group work, a display and book

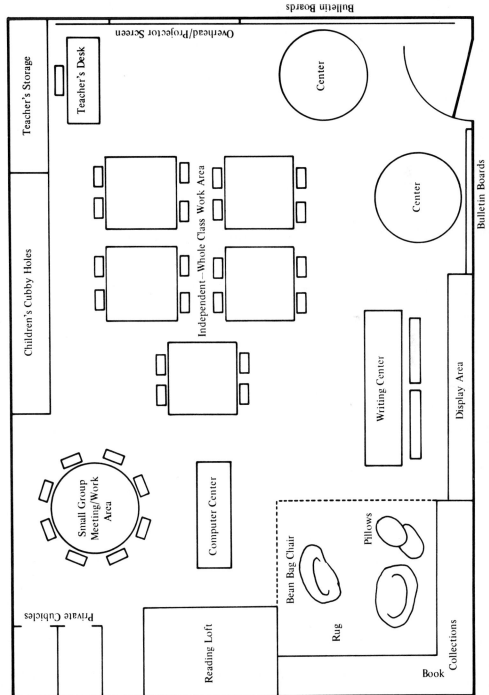

FIGURE 3-1 This classroom is arranged so that children are encouraged to read and write. The arrangements encourage social interaction and provide space for varied classroom activities.

shelves for library materials, individual work spaces, and room for several types of centers. (see Figure 3.1) Centers can be tables, rugs, or carts that contain materials for a specific activity such as listening, math, or reading, or a special interest center for a week-long study, a current event, or other short-term classroom exhibits.

The physical arrangement of the classroom, materials, and equipment can make a statement about the philosophy of instruction. Classrooms can be arranged to say, "Let's read, talk and write about what interests us." Classrooms also may suggest a child-centered focus and a challenge to try things. Circular arrangements or round tables stimulate interaction. A circular arrangement of individual desks or round tables could be used for discussion sessions. Group conferences, small group work, and whole class discussions also could take place in a circular arrangement.

Display Areas

Space for displaying children's work is an important feature of a literature-based classroom. Usually, classrooms have bulletin boards or other areas for children's work exhibits. Writing and artwork can be hung from the ceilings to make up for lack of bulletin boards. Writing can be hung with clothespins on strings draped across a section of the room.

Books and other literature should be displayed and easily accessible. Book cases, shelves, and other display areas are available in most classrooms. If there is a lack of shelves and bookcases, wooden or plastic shelves or cartons can help a teacher display reading material.

Whole Group Instruction Area

A large area of the room should be devoted to whole group instruction. The desks should be in view of the board and/or projection screen. Some teachers allow children to sit on the floor during group discussions and specific arrangements should be made if that is allowed. The atmosphere the teacher wishes to convey can determine how the whole group instruction area is established.

Individual Work Areas

Some areas of the classroom should allow children to pull away from the group when they need quiet time to read and write. Space protected by file cabinets, book cases, or other classroom furniture can be used for individual activity. When space is not abundant, special lofts, or quiet corners can be designed to provide individual reading niches. Children enjoy crawling into corners, cubby holes, and special places to read favorite books. Some teachers have room for a comfortable chair or sofa that is to be used only for reading. Even cardboard boxes can provide special hideouts where children can read during their independent reading time.

Permanent Centers

Some centers in the classroom will be established permanently. Library and reading centers should be familiar and established areas in the room. Rugs, beanbag chairs, sofas, and rocking chairs add character to the permanent arrangement of the classroom and invite children to read. Writing and publishing centers can be an important part of class routines.

Print and Media Center

A classroom involved in reading and writing may need several focal points or centers that allow students to accomplish their work. For example, there may be a corner or a desk devoted to tape recorders and head sets where children listen to recorded versions of popular reading material or their own writing. Another table in the classroom might be equipped with all types of paper and writing implements. Reference material should be placed in another part of the room so that children can complete their research. Computer centers that support reading and writing should be easily accessible. Listening centers and art centers may come and go as units are developed and used.

Theme Centers

Occasionally, teachers may need to devote space in the room to a particular emphasis, such as a current event or a story related to other activities in the classroom. Furniture can be arranged, and books, equipment, and other props can be gathered to support a theme or unit. Motivational devices at this center could be accompanied by teacher-suggested activities that children can accomplish independently. When a theme unit is exhausted, the room is put back in order and new centers are established.

Reading Curriculum

A second factor that must be considered when organizing reading instruction is the curriculum or what and how reading is presented. Most school districts have a curriculum document that explains and delineates reading instruction for each grade level. The curriculum document will have a section devoted to the strategies and skills to be introduced, retaught, and emphasized for each grade level. The district curriculum may reflect statewide curriculum or a basal reading series. These documents include lists of skills or strategies to be mastered, objectives to be met, and even suggest activities for the children. The district curriculum may go so far as to mandate the time in the school year that the strategies are introduced. An example of a typical school-wide curriculum is demonstrated in Box 3.1.

Many state education agencies offer suggestions and guidelines for reading instruction. State guidelines may suggest not only the curriculum, but other organizational constraints. For example:

Teachers in Texas are required to teach essential elements. These are goals that strongly influence the curricular framework whereby school districts develop the objectives for each grade level . . . district requires grades on report cards to be stated in percentages ranging from fifty to one hundred. Texas requires that school districts throughout the state issue report cards once every six weeks using either letter grades or numerical forms. (Woodley & Woodley, 1989, p. 74)

Well-designed curricula can be a great help for teachers and provide guidance for organizing reading instruction. A positive way to use the curriculum guides is to

---

BOX 3-1

Reading Objectives from a School-wide Third Grade Integrated Language Curriculum

Grade 3: First Six Weeks

Comprehension

- In fictional and nonfictional selections, the student will identify the *main idea/topic and supporting details.*
- After reading a nonfictional selection, the student will identify the *details* to support the topic and/or main idea.
- The student will verbalize reading strategies (i.e., using picture cues and context clues, skipping a word) to gain meaning from a given selection.
- The student will use study strategies (i.e., skimming, surveying) to gain meaning from a given selection.

Language/Vocabulary

- Given a passage, the student will identify the meaning of an unfamiliar word by using *context clues.*
- Given any word with a prefix or suffix or both, the student will orally identify the *base word.*

Study Skills

- The student will select a book for individual need/interest.
- The student will identify and use the parts of a book (i.e., cover, spine, pages, title page, contents, dedication, table of contents, index, and glossary).

Source: Spring Branch Independent School District, *District Language Arts Curriculum Guide.* (Spring, TX, 1989).

---

consider the stated objectives as a framework for instruction and an outline from which classroom activities can be designed. The negative aspect of curriculum guides is that teachers often interpret curricular plans literally and translate guidelines directly to instruction without regard for the unique characteristics of their students. If a curriculum guide states that all first graders will know beginning consonant sounds, and teachers interpret this to mean that individual lessons on beginning consonant sound will be taught specially to each first grader, the curriculum guide may have a negative effect on instruction. Literal interpretation may result in reading instruction that does not meet the needs of the students or tends to fragment instruction into unmeaningful activities that children do not need. Instruction based on curriculum guides can become stilted and unresponsive to individual classrooms.

Teachers should use the curriculum to guide their decisions, but a good curriculum is a tool and does not provide a complete reading plan. One of the first tasks for a teacher is to find out how flexible the school district is about the existing curriculum. In reality, most districts allow flexibility in using the curriculum document; an understanding of the role of a school's curriculum is important for teachers making decisions about reading instruction. Successful teachers will be familiar with the suggested curriculum so that they may use it as a guide to plan literature-based instruction that meets the needs of their children.

Some school districts ask that a teacher use the curriculum document and basal series to prepare for reading instruction. Principals and experienced teachers are good resources in guiding beginning teachers in the flexibility of the documents. A realistic way for beginning teachers to establish their reading procedures is to start with the structure suggested by curriculum guides and include routines that use children's literature.

Literature-based Instruction

Literature-based instruction can be organized in many different ways. Three patterns that describe how literature-based instruction can be implemented in a classroom (Hiebert & Colt, 1989) illustrate different interpretations of curricula.

1. The teacher leads instruction and selects the literature. This pattern is teacher-oriented. The teacher who establishes this pattern of instruction may use the curriculum guide to define the objectives and goals of instruction and to select activities and literature that meet that goals of the curriculum. Activities are guided and evaluated by the teacher.

2. The teacher leads but students contribute to discussions and the selection of literature. Teachers may provide a great deal of guidance, but allow children to say what they feel about the reading materials and activities and which books they want to read. Children may select some of the reading material and activities for reading instruction.

3. The teacher encourages students to select literature and reading activities. This approach is entirely student-oriented. Children select materials, pace their reading, and choose activities related to their reading. This pattern of instruction is the individualized reading instructional approach described in chapter 4.

Some teachers use elements of all three patterns at the same time or use the patterns sequentially. In fact, there may be times when one pattern is preferable. Some classrooms are so independent that they can be entirely self-paced and regulated, and other classrooms require more teacher guidance. Children who have had experience with literature-based curriculum will learn independence and tend to be self-directed. Children who have had little involvement with literature will require more guidance. Teachers will vary in how comfortable they feel about independent work. They, too, will be more comfortable giving responsibility to children when they have had experience with literature and literature-based programs.

Basals

Basically, the traditional organization of instruction is teacher-oriented and relies upon the completion of skills and strategies as suggested by the basal series. The basal organization controls what is taught, how it is taught, and in what order instruction is presented to students. The concerns associated with the misuse of the basal are enough to show that basals alone simply are not adequate for teaching reading. Considering what is known about motivation for reading, the negative and positive effects of basal instruction, and the excitement offered by children's literature, a reading program that does not include children's literature simply is not adequate. Basals can be viewed as one source of material for children to use, but not necessarily as a curriculum plan. The suggested plans that accompany the basals can be used as a framework or plan for reading instruction and do give teachers ideas about where to start their instruction. However, under no circumstances should the basal be the only source of material and the sole plan for reading instruction.

Themes and Units

A most effective strategy is to plan reading instruction around a particular theme. Theme units are complete plans for reading instruction based on a topic that can be integrated into many of the subjects discussed during the day (Pappas, Kiefer, & Levstick, 1990). Unit or theme plans may be made for any length of time, but usually last one or two weeks. Upper grade units may take longer since students may be with a teacher one period a day or because the reading may involve longer texts than in the lower grades.

Unit themes may be developed in several ways. Teachers get ideas from children's interests, an interesting artifact, a specific book, drama, or other material (Pappas, Kiefer, & Levstik, 1990). To select a child-oriented, interesting theme, the teacher must take several steps.

1. Select the focus of the integrated or theme unit in order to organize planning. Holidays suggest natural themes, but favorite books, authors, or current events can become the focus of the unit. A unit might have a science or social studies theme or can begin in the basal (Baskwill & Whitman, 1988).

The basal or subject area texts (such as science and social studies) can be used with thematic units in two ways. Basal stories or textbooks can be one resource, just as any other reading material. They also can be used to provide the teacher with activities and reading material that contribute to the development of a unit.

A second method is to use a children's literature selection as the focus for activities. This method is particularly effective when class sets of books are available so that all children can read the material. All children read the book that is the foundation of the unit and then read related books individually.

Another way to plan theme units is to select the theme from among interests of the children, identify several books with the theme, and use the books as the foundation. When a teacher is willing to explore themes not presented in textbooks, the number of topics for classroom exploration is infinite, and the teacher's and childrens' individual interests can be reflected. One important facet of theme selection is to make sure that the focus is interesting and a wide variety of materials is available.

2. After the theme is identified, establish instructional goals and objectives. The theme often will suggest certain activities, or a teacher may design a unit to meet specific objectives. For example, if the district curriculum requires that a teacher provide opportunities for children to compare and contrast, a unit that compares and contrasts traditional literature can be planned.

Themes can embrace many subjects for reading and writing. Once a topic is identified, numerous activities and books can become part of instruction. See Box 3.2 for an example of how a theme can be used when *The Polar Express* (Van Allsburg, 1984) is the focus.

Themes can be developed in similar ways around a book-length text. The units would last longer and perhaps be more complex than those developed with picture books, but there would be opportunities for meeting everyone's interests and needs when using a story with multiple themes and ideas.

3. Select an exciting way to introduce the theme. This may be done with drama, video cassette recordings, guest speakers, poetry reading, field trips, or brainstorming. Often a single book or story may introduce an involved unit of study. Only a teacher's creativity limits the type of introduction.

4. Develop a plan to guide learning during a unit. Teachers need to identify specific goals, activities, schedules, and materials to guide the class through the unit. Even though there is a specific plan, flexibility and responsiveness to the children's goals and interests might necessitate rearrangement. But initial planning should never be left to chance. The teacher should have a definite and well-considered plan for guiding children through the reading and which activities will take place.

BOX 3-2

Teaching Ideas for *The Polar Express* as a Theme

Social Studies

Map Skills:

- Locate the North Pole on a map
- Make an imaginary trip to the North Pole

History:

- Research discovery of North Pole

Christmas customs and traditions:

- Study gift-giving traditions
- Study eight days of Hanukkah
- Research the origin of Santa Claus

Art

- Study the art work of Van Allsburg
- Make Christmas ornaments
- Cut out snowflakes

Language Arts

Writing:

- Describe favorite holiday gifts
- Tell the story of a lost item
- Describe the first holiday gift of your choice
- Relate events in the story to things that really happen

Drama:

- Produce a Reader's Theater based on *Polar Express*
- Read favorite sections aloud

Reading:

- Read other books by Chris Van Allsburg
- Read and compare other holiday stories
- Share holiday poetry

Music

- Sing holiday songs
- Sing the song "Silver Bells"
- Play holiday music with bells

Science

Weather:

- Study how snow is formed

Biology and Wildlife:

- Talk about reindeer

Ideas That Can Lead to Activities in other Subject Areas:

- Take a field trip on a train
- Invite a train conductor to be a guest speaker
- Eat chocolate bars and hot chocolate for a snack

5. Evaluate and monitor as part of the plan. Evaluation is necessary to monitor the needs of the children as well as to provide feedback on the effectiveness of instruction. The chapter on monitoring and feedback presents many different methods for monitoring reading and writing activities.

6. Never hesitate to collaborate with others. Interacting with colleagues, librarians, and other professionals will provide teachers with ideas that will expand the unit presentation. For example, a music teacher might be able to extend the unit into related music or the librarian may help focus children's library time to support the unit.

Unit planning is easier if teachers work together and share ideas. Units can be used more than once, and variations can be made for each year or for a particular group of children. Roberta Chapman and several third grade teachers worked together to plan two weeks of reading around one book. As a result, the book *Two Bad Ants* (Van Allsburg, 1988) became a way to integrate teaching of science and reading in a highly motivating and exciting way (see Box 3.3).

Grouping Children

Children can be arranged and grouped in many different ways for reading instruction. Different activities and goals, of course, will require different groupings. Distinctive classroom mixtures will require different arrangements since the way individuals work together commands various organization patterns. The key to arranging and managing the classroom is to be flexible and experiment with different groupings to find the best one for the children, the activities, and the materials for a particular activity. Children often are placed in small groups to ensure that each child has an opportunity to participate. Not all children will volunteer in large group settings, and small groups can encourage a great deal of interaction. Small groups also are more manageable than the whole class and can be assigned special projects.

There are many ways to arrange children in small groups. Any organization should avoid labeling children, and efforts and responses from group work should be positive and successful. Beneficial group work is accomplished when the organization is based on student and instructional needs.

Flexible Grouping

One way to arrange children in small, manageable groups is to establish flexible grouping practices. Membership in flexible grouping terminates when the specific goal for which the group was established is reached. Small groups can be established for long periods of time or may be set up for short-term projects. Group membership also is flexible, based on the objectives and goals of the group.

The goals and objectives of the small, flexible groups should be well-known to the teacher and the students. The type of follow-up activities should be carefully delineated

──── **BOX 3-3** ────────────────────────────────

Description of Unit Schedule and Activities

First, the ants go to the wall, climb up, and go inside the bowl of crystals. The two bad ants decide to stay and eat all the crystals. In the morning, a spoon scoops up the ants and plunges them into a cup of coffee. Just before they are swallowed, the cup is set back down. The ants climb out, rest in a piece of bread, but then get toasted. The ants are then rocketed out onto the water faucet. Water forces them into the garbage disposal. They are battered when they get out and go to rest in a light plug. But they are shot out of the plug like a bullet! When they see the crew of ants, they decide to get some crystals and just go home. The ants were joyful and grateful to be home!*

Day 1 Activities:

Teaching Objectives:

1. The children make predictions about the story.
2. The children observe ants and write notes.
3. The children share observations.
4. The children understand the vocabulary words.

Introductory Activities:

■ The teachers show the cover of the books and encourage the children to predict what insect the book might be about. The teacher elicits, from the cover picture, what the book might be about. All predictions are recorded for later reference.
■ After predictions are established, the students and teachers go outside with their journals and pencils and find ants on the playground. They record their observations of the ants in nature. The students and the teacher experiment with the ants by providing bread crumbs for them to move to their holes, and the children record their observations as the ants climb trees, move bread crumbs, disappear in their holes, etc. The children then return to the classroom and share their observations. The teacher records the observations on the board.
■ The teacher introduces vocabulary words by writing them on the board and allowing the children to predict what the words mean. Words such as *deemed, hovered, rocketed,* and *battered* are discussed at length.

Day 2 Activities:

Teaching Objectives:

1. The children identify vocabulary in context and check predictions.
2. The children identify setting.
3. The children identify *ed* verbs.
4. The children identify synonyms.

BOX 3-3 *Continued*

- The children review the observations about the ants and the teacher reads the story asking the students to listen for the vocabulary as she reads.
- The teachers ask the children to identify the three settings of the book and associate vocabulary with the settings in the story.
- Children use the text to identify *ed* suffixes.

Day 3 Activities:

Teaching Objectives:

1. The children identify words in text that use suffixes.
2. The children summarize the plot (events) of the story.
3. The children improve their comprehension by asking questions about the text.

- The teacher has the students retell the story to partners in their own words. Then the pairs write the summary together checking for the correct sequence. A class summary is compiled from the pairs and an overhead is used to write the class summary (see summary at the beginning of this explanation).
- The teacher and the students then participate in a Request activity (Chapter 6) in which the students and teacher ask each other questions.

Day 4 Activities:

Teaching Objectives:

1. The children sequence the story using the story summary.
2. The children summarize the story by drawing a cartoon.

- The teacher passes out a typed sequential summary developed by the students the day before. The students cut up the summary, scramble the order, and then reorganize the order by numbering each statement.
- They also are asked to underline the words with *ed* suffixes.
- The children summarize the story in one sentence and draw a picture to illustrate the summary statement.

Day 5 Activities:

Teaching Objectives:

1. The children learn specific facts about ants.
2. The children categorize information about ants.

Continued

BOX 3-3 *Continued*

3. The children follow directions and make an ant out of supplies provided.

■ The teacher shares another story about ants, and the students and teacher write facts about ants on the board. They answer such questions as ''How do they look?'' ''Where do they live?'' and ''What do they do?'' The class develops a fact sheet about ants. The teacher passes out the body parts of an ant and materials for each child to make an ant.

Day 6 Activities:

Teaching Objectives:

1. The children develop questions for interviews.
2. The children record answers from interviews.
3. The children organize their ideas into a paragraph.
4. The children focus on descriptive words used to discuss ants.

■ The teacher repeats the factual story about ants and with the children writes questions that the children will ask each other about ants. The children in pairs ask each other about ants, answering the questions in writing. They then cut sentence strips from the interview pages and organize the information given by their partners into three basic categories: what ants look like, where they live, and what they do. These sheets become the basis for developing their own description of an ant. The answer to each question becomes the framework for developing a paragraph in a descriptive writing activity. The children are encouraged to illustrate their descriptions.

*This summary of *Two Bad Ants* by Chris Van Allsburg was written by Roberta Chapman's third grade class.

---

and monitored. Buchanan (1980) and Harp (1989) suggest several types of small, flexible groups that can contribute to classroom organization:

1. Special project groups can work on activities that accompany the reading. Special projects can be expanded reading, drama, art, or writing after reading a common text. For example, after reading the Chinese variant of *Little Red Riding Hood, Lon Po Po* (Young, 1989), groups can be formed to become experts on other versions of *Little Red Riding Hood*. They can read the variants and compare them to the version that the entire class read.

2. Interest groups can be established to allow small groups of children to read, discuss, and complete activities based on common interests. Children who are interested

in a particular sport, hobby, or subject can be grouped together to complete common reading or discuss what they have read.

3. Research groups are established to locate, organize, and report information. Research groups are particularly appropriate for instruction in social studies, science, and art. Before research groups are required to work on their own, they should be taught research skills needed in the small group. Many of the skills can be demonstrated in whole class settings before children are placed in small groups.

4. Brainstorming and categorizing groups usually are short-lived and are established to begin reading, discussing, or writing. Children can be placed in small groups to list everything they know about a concept or a topic or to design questions they would like to answer during a study.

5. Instructional groups are formed when more than one child could benefit from teacher-led instruction. These groups are disbanded when all group members understand the strategy, skill, or concept.

6. Expert groups may be formed and assigned a topic on which they are supposed to become "experts." They become resources for the rest of the class. Expert groups may be required to do some research, be familiar with a particular portion of the text, or perfect some skill.

Cooperative Grouping

Cooperative learning describes grouping arrangements that establish a common goal and assign shared responsibilities for learning. Cooperative learning activities can be applied to any area in the curricula, but are particularly effective in reading instruction. Usually, four or five children form the cooperative group that works together to solve some problem or complete a task. Individual work is down-played, and the work of the entire group is recognized for evaluation. The idea is that the team members are responsible for motivating all in the group to learn.

When teachers use cooperative learning to accomplish a goal, there are guidelines for introducing the organizational strategy (Harp, 1989; Uttero, 1988):

1. Make the rules and procedures of cooperative learning very clear. After a teacher decides what is to be accomplished cooperatively, then demonstration and instruction should accompany procedural instruction. Children should be explicitly aware of what should happen in the cooperative groups. One third grade has established the following rules for cooperative learning group work.

> You are responsible for your own work and behavior.
> You must help anyone in your group who needs your help.
> You must do your part in the group.
> If you disagree, you must explain why.
> Ask the teacher for help only when everyone in the group has the same question.

Cooperative learning provides opportunities for children to read and write together in small groups as shown in the above photos.

─── **BOX 3-4** ──────────────────────────────────

Cooperative Learning Lesson

Task: Each group will produce a comparison of versions of a fairy tale. The teacher will have discussed variants and methods of comparison in advance.

Group responsibilities:

1. Choose two books that represent variants of a fairy tale.
2. Involve each group member in the activities.
3. Assign roles and responsibilities.
4. Use format for comparison of fairy tales.
5. Add findings to class format.
6. Evaluate group performance after completion.

Individual responsibilities:

1. Read the two stories to be compared.
2. Contribute to summary of the two fairy tales.
3. Contribute at least two ways the stories are alike.
4. Help the entire group complete the format for comparing fairy tales.
5. Help the group decide who will add information to the class compilation.

Evaluation:

1. Produce group summaries of two fairy tales.
2. Evaluate group skills in making decisions, achieving goals, and helping each other.
3. Evaluate the contribution to class compilation.

──

2. Organize the groups. The groups of three to six students are mixed in abilities. Each of the group members will be assigned a specific task. The third grade teacher, who uses cooperative learning groups on a daily basis, suggests the following assignments:

> Secretary—Monitors the group assignments and turns in the work to the teacher.
> Materials monitor—Passes out materials to the group.
> Recorder—Writes responses from group members during group activities.
> Reporter—Reports responses from group members during large group discussions.

3. Describe the purpose of and rationale for the activity and the tasks required of the children. Many of the routines discussed in this book can be assigned as cooperative

learning activities. Cooperative learning groups can accomplish supportive reading activities, vocabulary building activities, or any other work that is logical for more than one person to do. Work in the small cooperative groups should be meaningful and motivating.

4. Explain and demonstrate. Do not expect the children to be able to do what you ask until you have taken time to introduce the activity. The activity can be introduced gradually through whole class instruction, role playing, or demonstration.

5. Observe how the students work in groups. Cooperative learning teaches children to be independent, but requires careful guidance from the teacher. During activities the teacher notes problems, helps solve problems, and guides activities. Even though the children are responsible for accomplishing their goals, the teacher still is involved actively.

Research shows favorable results from cooperative learning. Children who participate in group work seem to develop better social abilities, interdependence on peers, personal independence, and more accountability for their accomplishments (Harp, 1989). Cooperative learning (see Box 3.4) is a strategy that works well with reading and language arts activities and the study of many other subjects.

Instructing the Whole Class

Whole class grouping is not used for reading instruction as often as one might imagine. While it is not the best arrangement for all types of instruction, there are some specific activities that can be very successful if the whole class is involved. Discussions, enrichment activities, genre introductions, reading aloud, and instruction can be accomplished with a whole class. It is a useful arrangement for presenting information for several reasons:

1. Whole class instruction is efficient. Presenting the information to the entire class at one time can free the teacher to provide more attention to individuals and small groups.

2. Whole class instruction provides students with time to interact with those of differing abilities and opinions.

3. Whole class activities contribute to establishing a classroom community.

Surely one of the most important activities that can occur during whole class instruction is that of sharing new and exciting books. The teacher or students can be called upon to read selections to the class or to share why they are enjoying a particular book. There is no better way to demonstrate the importance of reading to children than to devote time to sharing reading material.

Learning and presenting some strategies can be more economical during whole class instruction. This is an excellent way to present routines for discussing literature, ways to monitor reading, and responses to literature. In addition, author and genre studies may be introduced to an entire group at one time. Small groups and individual work can follow whole class instruction and focus on different aspects of the main theme of instruction.

Whole class approaches avoid labeling or focusing on special abilities and offer an opportunity for a wide range of interests and abilities to be recognized. Children at all levels can participate easily in whole class sharing and instruction. Even if all children do not participate in discussions, they can learn a great deal by listening. The information gained in large group discussions can be a basis for small group activities.

Almost any type of activity that can be accomplished in small groups can be done in whole classes and vice versa. The activities for the entire class should offer something for everyone. In-depth discussion or strategy instruction that applies only to a few students should be saved for smaller groups.

Conferences

Conferences, discussed in chapter 4, are a small group strategy that can be used to encourage, monitor, evaluate, and guide students during reading instruction. Conferences can be arranged with individuals, small groups, or whole classes. The teacher is responsible for planning and organizing the structure normally used in each situation.

The role of the teacher changes in a conference. While the teacher may provide the structure for what happens during the conference, the activities are directed by students who are responsible for selecting the discussion topic, identifying strategies to focus on, or selecting literature to use. The thing for the teacher to remember during a conference is that the student should do most of the talking. Conferences are a time to listen and support students in their reading and writing. Questions to guide a conference and other organizational considerations are suggested in other parts of this text.

Student Pairs

Tutoring or pairing is an effective arrangement. Children can be paired in numerous ways to support the instructional organization. Pairs can be used to accomplish a goal, clarify an instructional objective, or tutor each other in a particular strategy.

Students can be paired to accomplish some goal, such as those suggested for cooperative learning arrangements. There are some specific activities, such as assisted readings or paired readings (see chapters 5 and 9), that require pairing. Written conversations also are based on pairing children. Teachers can pair students to provide each with practice in a particular strategy. Sometimes children can explain an idea more clearly to their peers than a teacher. In a reciprocal situation, one child might share her or his understanding of a topic and the second child will discuss the same topic.

Peer tutoring allows a more able child to help a less able child (Topping, 1989). The value of peer tutoring is not only help for the one being tutored: research demonstrates that the tutor also gains in reading skills. One of the benefits of peer tutoring is extra practice in a one-to-one setting. Students of all abilities can benefit, and students can be grouped with the same or different sexes and still produce results. There are other benefits: improved self-concept, better social relationships, and more positive attitudes toward reading (Topping, 1988).

Cross-age tutoring also has potential for many benefits. Arranging for situations in which older children tutor younger children is particularly effective for upper grade children who have reading problems. A fifth grader may be available simply to listen to a first grader read, take dictation, or provide extra read-aloud time for a younger child. Tutoring across grade levels can provide teachers with a great deal of help in the classroom and allow younger children to receive some individual attention.

Individual Activity

There may be times when children work independently. Daily plans must include projects for children to complete on their own without direct teacher supervision. While children are working independently, the teacher is free to meet with small groups and individuals. Individual activity must be planned carefully because of the potential for discipline problems.

The most obvious opportunity for independent, individual activity is silent reading. Silent reading requires quiet, uninterrupted periods when children can concentrate. During some regularly scheduled reading times, it is imperative that the teacher read with the students, but there will be other times when children read independently. Children will need to read additional material after group work, class discussions, conferences, or to meet instructional objectives. Children should have a book available for recreational reading at all times. In addition, they may explore subjects on their own or research their own interests.

Writing also will be done independently. Journal entries, responding to literature, or writing narratives should be completed independently without guidance from the teacher. Summarizing discussions, research efforts, and writing in different genres should occupy a great amount of children's class time. Independent work also can include artwork, listening to tapes with headsets, or completing records.

The classroom described in this chapter is one that hums with busy children talking about what they are reading and writing. There do need to be times for children to pull away to study or read on their own. Quiet corners of the room provide areas where children can work without being disturbed by classroom activity. When planning independent work in the classroom, it is important to be sure that children understand the routines and logistics. If children know explicitly what is expected of them during independent work time, there will be a better chance that the classroom will run smoothly and productively.

Ability Grouping

For many years teachers have placed children into reading groups according to their abilities. Usually, ability levels in reading are measured by some form of standardized testing, and children are placed into groups according to common performance. For example, all children who have test results that reflect a particular grade level will be placed together. Ability grouping is designed to reduce the wide range of differences among students so that more effective instruction can be provided. Grouping during reading instruction has been a widely accepted procedure in the United States.

Recently, however, ability grouping has come under intense scrutiny and is no longer viewed as the optimum method of arranging children for reading instruction. There are several reasons for this happening. Particularly disturbing is the research that questions the effectiveness of grouping children with similar abilities, suggesting that there are dismal results. "Almost without exception, reviews from the 1920s to the present have come to the same general conclusion; that between-class ability grouping has few if any benefits from student achievement," according to Slavin (1987). Teachers should consider carefully ability grouping practices and the effects it could have on children.

Several detrimental practices are associated with ability grouping:

1. Ability grouping labels children. Children easily discover that they are in the "high" or "low" groups. Often, the label will affect the child's self-concept and opinion of reading for years to come. There is an example of a doctoral student who still believed he was not a good reader because he had never been in the top reading group during his elementary schooling. The results of grouping are long lasting; most adults can remember which group they were in during reading instruction.

2. The groups remain constant through several years of schooling. It is seldom that children move from one group to another. Once placed in a reading group in first grade, the same children most probably will be together in successive years. This suggests that early ability grouping predicts future achievement and expectations.

3. The instruction varies between groups. Those in the lower groups usually receive a different quality of instruction. Children in low groups tend to do less reading than other groups of children. Teachers interrupt children in the low group more often, come to their aid sooner, and focus their attention on small parts of language to the exclusion of discussions of comprehension and understanding. Many of these differences in instruction only continue the reading behaviors that put the children in low groups in the first place.

4. For years members of minority groups have been overrepresented in low groups. Although there has been a great deal of discussion as to why this happens, the fact remains that it does. Children whose language and culture are different seem at a disadvantage on achievement tests, so ability groups reflect this discrepancy.

Basal reading programs may encourage ability grouping since they generally are based on the acquisition of a set of skills. If children do not acquire the skills, they may be identified as needing special attention or requiring reteaching because of their "deficit." Children often are grouped together because they need to acquire those skills and strategies they are "missing" according to lessons and objectives in the basals. This may perpetuate the ability groups.

It would be more realistic to encourage teachers to use ability grouping only under special conditions and for short periods. Perhaps grouping children together to learn a particular skill or strategy might be useful. But, once the strategy has been learned, the group should be eliminated. If a teacher recognizes that five or six children do not know how to identify proper nouns in historical fiction, a group can be formed to work on the strategy. When children are competent, the group is abandoned.

Time and Scheduling

Another important thing to remember when planning reading instruction is that children need a predictable schedule (Baskwill & Whitman, 1988). Children want to know what to expect in their lives, and while they can be flexible, predictability helps them feel in control. Most writers (Atwell, 1987; Cambourne, 1988; Baskwill & Whitman, 1988; Buchanan, 1980) dealing with classroom organization for literature-based instruction suggest that class time should be arranged to include the following daily activities:

1. *Whole class instruction or focus time.* Atwell (1987) calls this time "mini-lessons," Cambourne (1988) refers to the time as "whole class focus," and Baskwill and Whitman (1988) label it "shared language time." Whatever label is used, each day the teacher should plan for time and activities when the entire class works together. This is the time when the teacher focuses the activities and takes care of the organizational part of instruction. Whole class instruction may be a time to teach new strategies, discuss a new genre, or to talk about what is expected of each student in the classroom. The teacher might use this time to read aloud or to provide time to write responses to class activities. This time is very flexible, depending on teaching objectives and the age of the group.

2. *Independent reading time.* Everyone in the class must read independently each day. During some of this time the students should be allowed to make independent selections of reading material and have control of their reading. Even children in kindergarten can be expected to have daily independent reading time when they are looking at pictures or pretending they can read. Some independent reading time should be assigned in response to assignments or discussions introduced during the whole class time. Independent reading time may occur with the entire class reading at the same time or with part of the class reading while the teacher works with small groups. The rules for independent reading should be established early, and everyone should be aware explicitly of how this time is conducted. Atwell's suggested rules for reading workshop are examples of explicitly stated directions for independent reading time (see chap. 4, Box 4.2). These rules should be used as a guide for developing an individual classroom's routine for independent reading since teachers and students will develop rules that work best for them.

3. *Reading and writing activities.* Independent reading can form the basis for all other planned reading and writing activities. Instructional time should be an expansion of the independent reading. Cambourne (1988) feels that reading instruction should involve children in two types of activities: elective and compulsory. Elective activities are chosen by children from a variety of options. As the classroom procedures evolve from the first of the year, children can be introduced to their options and how to select the activities. These activities might be a specific format, such as writing in journals about what they have read, participating in small discussion groups, or completing

additional reading on the topic. The compulsory activities are those the teacher requires individuals, small groups, or the entire class to complete. Compulsory activities will meet some instructional goal and be more teacher-directed. These activities can include strategy lessons, genre introductions, or comprehension activities. As children work individually, the teacher will have time to demonstrate, discuss, and provide guidance to individuals and small groups of readers.

4. *Sharing time.* Sharing sessions culminate the time allotted for planned instruction. Discussion provides opportunities to verbalize and talk about what children have read and written in their independent work. Sharing time provides opportunities to discuss books, share personal writing, teach, evaluate, and learn, and gives the teacher opportunities to evaluate the effectiveness of instruction. Sharing time is different from class focus time, when the teacher may have specific plans and objectives. Sharing time is guided by what the children are accomplishing and what they wish to share.

Table 3.1 illustrates activities and time allotments that might be logical for several grade levels (Robbins, 1990).

TABLE 3-1   Time Guidelines and Sample Activities for Literature-based instruction

Activities	Grades 1–2	Grades 3–4	Grades 5–6
Read to children	daily 10–20 min.	daily 15–30 min.	daily 15–30 min.
Children and teacher read aloud together (repeat favorites)	3–5 wk. 10–30 min.	only occasionally	
Independent reading, material chosen by student	daily 10–20 min.	daily 15–30 min.	daily 15–30 min.
Guided reading activities	daily 20–45 min.	daily 30–45 min.	daily 30–45 min.
Children and teacher write	3–5 wk. 10–20 min.	only occasionally	
Writing	daily 15–30 min.	daily 30–40 min.	daily 30–40 min.
Teacher-directed mini-lessons	daily 5–10 min.	daily 5–10 min.	daily 5–10 min.
Sharing	daily 10–20 min.	daily 10–20 min.	daily 10–20 min.
Subject reading	daily	daily	daily

Instructional Plans

When future teachers take undergraduate courses, they may be required to develop several instructional plans and units. These plans are usually very detailed and require complete descriptions of activities. After several years of teaching, their plans are usually not quite as detailed unless a unit or activity is being presented for the first time. The plan in Box 3.3 was completed by Roberta, an experienced teacher presenting the ideas and activities to her third grade class for the first time. How much a teacher writes in plans will be guided by personal preference and administrative requirements. Some schools require a certain level of planning be completed and available to the principal or supervisor in case the teacher is absent and someone else must take care of classroom instruction.

Lesson plans are an outline of what usually takes place in the classroom and suggest goals and objectives as well as the logistics for managing twenty children. When implementing a unit or activity for the first time, the plans often are specific and descriptive. After a teacher has acquired several years of experience, the plans may only refer to activities without explaining the progression.

Writing

The management and organization of writing-related activities are part of the organization of reading instruction. Plans for reading always should include opportunities to write, and writing usually is a result of what happened during reading activities. Writing becomes a natural progression for sharing ideas from reading, extending concepts and thinking, and clarifying ideas. Instructional organization for writing usually has two aspects: keeping track of the writing and responding to each writing assignment.

Journals are one way to organize writing activities. By requiring children to write regularly in journals, as suggested in the reading workshop, teachers and children both know when, what, and how to write. The writing is kept in one place, and everyone should understand the procedures. Routine procedures such as journal writing will relieve the teacher of planning each writing assignment in detail.

Teachers can use folders to keep track of the writing, too. Manila folders can be the home for writing that is in progress, completed lists of writing assignments, and suggestions for further writing. Folders provide a place to collect samples, records of conferences, and publications, and generally organize all writing materials. It is easy to incorporate the idea of folders into the management of the classroom if the teacher is using the concept of portfolios, discussed in the chapter on evaluation, and monitoring reading behaviors.

Another important consideration that accompanies writing activities is the individual and small group discussions centering on students' writing activities. These small group meetings may be composed of teachers and one or more students and are usually called writing conferences. Conferences can impact scheduling and room and grouping arrangements. A routine and setting for the conferences must be established in the classroom so that they will be efficient and well managed. A teacher should establish where the conferences will occur, a structure for the conferences, and what the student should bring to each meeting. Considerations regarding writing conferences will be similar to those discussed about reading earlier in this chapter.

Learning Differences

Instructional organization must consider learning differences within the classroom. Some specific factors should be remembered when planning for a class that has language and cultural differences. However, much of what should be considered is simply good instructional technique. It is not difficult to manage and organize a classroom that recognizes different cultures and languages when using a wide range of literature for instruction. The following suggestions should come as no surprise and are easy to implement.

Culture

The classroom should be a place where children from many social and cultural backgrounds meet and learn together. Classroom organization can provide many opportunities for students to learn about each other as individuals. Some prejudices and misunderstandings can be overcome in classrooms where activities are carefully planned and organized. One way to challenge cultural prejudices is to allow children of all cultures many opportunities to interact and discuss (Cohen, 1986) what they have in common and how they are unique.

In addition, there are some basic principles that teachers should remember when organizing a class representing several cultures. Effective organization recognizes that children have different interests, learning styles, and abilities. Understanding the potential differences and using that knowledge to organize instruction can improve the learning environment for everyone.

Cultural awareness may require that a teacher consider the way children are arranged for classroom activities. Some cultures encourage children to work cooperatively with others when completing projects or solving problems. Other cultures stress the importance of individual, task-oriented work. Most children are social, however, and all children will respond to a collaborative learning arrangement such as group work or cooperative learning. The issue of competition must be considered, too. Competition can be detrimental to children who have been raised to cooperate to complete a task.

Cultural considerations should take into account the content presented during instruction. For example, some children will learn better if the content involves people. Black and Mexican-American children are among those who will be more interested in content if people are involved in the descriptions and explanations (Sleeter & Grant, 1988). They would much rather read and discuss how people react to certain situations than about concepts not tied in to real life. Content may need to be presented in different ways to meet the interests of all students. Suppose a teacher recognizes that some of the children in the classroom will be more interested in learning if human reactions are a part of the content? When the teacher presents a lesson on comparison and contrast, the lesson might focus on comparing and contrasting the behavior of the characters, instead of comparing and contrasting the elements of a story.

Another aspect to consider when planning instruction is to make sure that materials account for cultural differences. Materials should be meaningful to children or no learning will occur, no matter how much planning takes place. Children certainly will respond differently when reading material including characters that are not unlike themselves. In addition, the room can be decorated to reflect social themes, cultural diversity, and students' interests (Sleeter & Grant, 1988).

Teachers can meet the needs of culturally different children by providing a wide range of opportunities to interact with others. Cultural differences also can be recognized when a variety of flexible and cooperative grouping arrangements are used. Finally, teachers will need to make sure that materials that represent children's cultural and individual backgrounds are used in instruction.

Language

No one organizational and instructional approach takes care of all the languages spoken by children in the classroom. The activities, materials, and responses effective for all children should benefit those children who are learning how to speak English. However, there are some things that a teacher must remember when planning instruction for the child who is learning English.

Group work offers the best opportunity to expose the child to peers who speak English (Cohen, 1986). Group work should include a great deal of nonverbal cues so that the child who is learning English can understand what is going on. Children's learning can be enhanced by accompanying reading and writing activities with real objects. For example, before reading about farm life, a visit to a farm where animals can be observed will increase a child's understanding of text. If a visit to the farm is not possible, stuffed or wooden animals can provide concrete examples for the abstract ideas presented in text. Another was to increase understanding is to provide opportunities for physical activity and creative expression (Rosenbusch, 1988). Acting out stories in pantomime is a good example of how to include speakers of different languages in reading instruction.

Thematic approaches to reading and writing are particularly valuable for speakers of different languages. Themes can be based on a story or text accompanied by illustrations that support meaning. Hands-on activities should accompany instruction. McGee and Richgels (1990) suggest that books such as *Strega Nona* (dePaola, 1975) and *The Magic Porridge Pot* (Galdone, 1976) can become the basis for activities that lead to discussions about magic and pasta. Children could make spaghetti and invite guests to the room for a luncheon. Activities could include children dictating to the teacher about the events that occurred in the classroom. This provides the children with opportunities to learn and use English in a meaningful way.

DISCUSSION AND ACTIVITIES

1. Meet in a small group with others from your class and try to identify the most important element of classroom planning and organization. Can you identify and agree on just one element? What does that suggest to you about the organization of reading instruction?

2. If you had to develop a lesson to present to children, what would be the first thing you would do? Outline what you would do to plan a lesson and a unit. Describe the plan you would use for reading instruction.

3. What might interfere with the instructional plan for a classroom? How could you mold an unexpected event into a reading lesson?

4. Pretend you had all the space you needed and resources you wanted. What would your idea classroom look like? (You may have to identify an ideal grade level.) Remember, this is just a dream.

5. Work in small groups and outline a weekly routine for reading instruction. What daily and weekly activities do you feel are necessary in effective reading instruction?

RELATED READING

Professional Reading

Pappas, C.C., Kiefer, B., & Levstik, L.S. (1990). *An integrated language perspective in the elementary school.* New York: Longman.

> *This text presents a detailed account of how to set up an integrated language unit. It is particularly helpful since it presents examples at many levels and in great depth. It will take a teacher from step one, deciding how to select a unit topic, to the evaluation phase of the planning.*

Robinson, R., & Good, T. (1987). *Becoming an effective reading teacher.* New York: Harper & Row.

> *Robinson and Good have developed a methodology text that reflects their vast knowledge of classroom management and teacher expectations. Chapter 8 presents an involved discussion of teacher expectations and its relationship to reading instruction.*

Children's Literature

There are several resources to help a teacher develop theme units. Two of the most accessible are listed:

Children's Books in Print is an annual comprehensive index of children's books in print. The books are listed by author, title, and illustrator. This reference is available at most libraries and book stores.

Subjects Guide to Children's Books in Print is an annual publication of children's literature grouped by subject. This book is an invaluable reference for planning and developing units. It is available at most libraries and some book stores.

Theme: Music and Dance

Akerman, K. (1988). *Song and dance man*. Illustrated by S. Gammell. New York: Knopf.

> *This recent Caldecott Medal winner could serve as the basis for studying vaudeville and tap dancing. It also offers a picture of a wonderfully warm grandfather–grandchildren relationship.*

Arrogon, J. (1989) *Lullaby*. Illustrated by T. Radzinskier. San Francisco: Chronicle.

> *The text of this book sounds like music. It is a lilting story, soothing as a lullaby.*

dePaola, Tomie. (1983). *Sing, Pierrot, sing*. New York: Harcourt Brace Jovanovich.

> *dePaola says that this book is done in mime, which means it is classified as a wordless picture book. This is the story of a mime who tries to win a beautiful lady in love with another man. Pierrot is heartbroken when he finds that she does not love him, and children offer him friendship for comfort.*

Griffith, H.V. (1986). *Georgia music*. Illustrated by J. Stevenson. New York: Greenwillow.

> *Georgia sounds and a harmonica reproduce the sounds and music of the South in this story of grandfather and granddaughter. The grandfather introduces a young girl to the sounds and music and then she must use the same to help him laugh again after he must leave his Georgia cabin.*

Isadora, R. (1979). *Ben's trumpet*. New York: Greenwillow.

> *The beautifully done black-and-white artwork presents a story of inner city musicians in a study of shapes and visions of jazz.*

———. (1981). *Jesse and Abe*. New York: Greenwillow.

> *Another Isadora book done in black and white, it tells a story that complements* Song and Dance Man. *Jesse's grandfather Abe is a doorman at a 1920s theater where vaudeville is performed. Although the vaudeville stage is the background, the main theme involves the relationship of the old man and the boy.*

Simon, C. (1989). *Amy the dancing bear*. Illustrated by M. Datz. New York: Doubleday.

> *An irrepressible bear dances even though it is time to attend to life's routines. Although young children are delighted with a bear who dances past bedtime, older children might be able to understand how creativity in art and music cannot be stopped.*

Yorinks, A. (1988). *Bravo Minsky*. Illustrated by S. Egielski. New York: Farrar, Straus & Giroux.

> *This zany text introduces us to a genius who could do anything, but only wants to sing. Believe it or not, there is a tie-in between the message in this book and* Amy the Dancing Bear. *Both describe the unrelenting drive of truly talented people.*

Novels

Paterson, K. (1985). *Come sing Jimmy Jo*. New York: Dutton.

> *For some reason* Come Sing Jimmy Jo *is a Paterson book that has not received much attention. This story illustrates that being extremely gifted is not always all that it's cracked up to be. Sometimes the extremely talented Jimmy Jo wishes he could be like all the other people his age instead of touring the country and singing on radio and television.*

Paulsen, G. (1985). *Dogsong*. New York: Viking.

This book may be an unlikely tie-in to a discussion of books on music and dance, but is included since the main character keeps hearing a tribal song as he faces the harsh, cold Alaskan environment. This book could encourage discussion of the songs that all of us carry in our heads or hear when we go about our daily work.

Voight, C. (1983). *Dicey's song.* New York: Atheneum.

Dicey's sister is a talented musician who has a difficult time learning how to read and do other school work. While the sister's plight is not the main conflict in the story, there is enough description of it to start a discussion of how individuals display different talents.

Other Books Mentioned in This Chapter

Ahlberg, J., & Ahlberg, A. (1986). *The jolly postman or other people's letters.* Boston: Little, Brown.
dePaola, T. (1975). *Strega Nona.* Englewood, NJ: Prentice Hall.
Galdone, P. (1976). *The magic porridge pot.* New York: Clarion.
Van Allsburg, C. (1985). *The polar express.* Boston: Houghton Mifflin.
————. (1988). *Two bad ants.* Boston: Houghton Mifflin.
Young, Ed. (1989). *Lon Po Po.* New York: Philomel.

REFERENCES

Atwell, N. (1987). *In the middle: Writing, reading, and learning with adolescents.* Portsmouth NH: Boynton/Cook-Heinemann.
Baskwill, J., & Whitman, P. (1988). *Moving on: Whole language sourcebook.* Ontario, Canada: Scholastic.
Buchanan, E. (Ed.). (1980). *For the love of reading.* Winnipeg, Manitoba, Canada: C.E.L. Group.
Cambourne, B. (1988). *The whole story: Natural learning and the acquisition of literacy in the classroom.* Auckland, New Zealand: Ashton Scholastic.
Cohen, E.G. (1986). *Designing groupwork: Strategies for the heterogeneous classroom.* New York: Teachers College Press.
Dreher, M.J., and Singer, H. (1989). The teacher's role in students' success. *The Reading Teacher, 42* (8), 612–617.
Harp, B. (1989). When the principal asks "What do we put in the place of ability grouping?" *The Reading Teacher, 42* (7), 534–535.
McGee, L.M., and Richgels, D.J. (1990). *Literacy's beginnings: supporting young readers and writers.* Boston, MA: Allyn & Bacon.
Pappas, C.C., Kiefer, B.K., and Levstik, L.S. (1990). *An integrated language perspective in the elementary school.* New York: Longman.
Robbins, P.A. (1990). Implementing whole language: Bridging children and books. *Educational Leadership, 47* (6), 50–55.
Robinson, R., & Good, T.L. (1987). *Becoming an effective reading teacher.* New York: Harper & Row.
Rosenbusch, M.H. (1988). Teaching methodology: A child centered approach. In R. Benya and K.E. Muller (Eds.), *Children and languages: Research, practice, and rationale for the early grades.* New York: National Council on Foreign Language and International Studies.
Slavin, R. E. (1987). Ability grouping and student achievement in elementary schools: A best-evidence synthesis. *Review of Educational Research, 57* (3), 293–336.
Sleeter, C.E., & Grant, C.A. (1988). *Making choices for multicultural education: Five approaches to race, class, and gender.* Columbus, OH: Merrill.

Topping, K. (1988). *The peer tutoring handbook: Promoting cooperative learning*. Cambridge, MA: Brookline.

———. (1989). Peer tutoring and paired reading: Combining two powerful techniques. *The Reading Teacher, 42* (7), 488–494,

Uttero, D.A. (1988). Activating comprehension through cooperative learning. *The Reading Teacher, 41* (4), 390–395.

Woodley, J.W., & Woodley, C. E. (1989). Whole language, Texas style. In K. S. Goodman, Y. M. Goodman, & W. J. Hood (Eds.), *The whole language evaluation book*. Portsmouth, NH: Heinemann.

_4_

INDEPENDENT READING

He started reading Amanda Beal's book his second day in town and fin-ished it that afternoon. Ordinarily he would have returned it immediately, but he was so fascinated by the story of the Children's Crusade that he kept it and read it the next day. And the next.

When he wasn't reading, he was wandering. When most people wander, they walk. Maniac Magee ran. Around town, around the nearby townships, al-ways carrying the book, keeping it in perfect condition.

★★★★★

And he loved the quiet times after Hester and Lester went to bed. That's when he read Amanda's books. When he had gone through about half of them, he figured it was time to tackle the encyclopedia A.

Problem was, Amanda was always reading it. And she vowed she wasn't giving it up not even to Maniac, till she read everything from Aardvark to Aztec. To make matters worse, the supermarket offer had expired, so there were no other volumes.

The more Amanda would not let go of the A, the more Maniac wanted it. It reached the point where she had to hide it whenever she wasn't reading it. Unbe-knownst to her, Maniac always found it. He would get up even earlier in the morn-ing, read it by flashlight for a while, sneak it back, and go trotting with Bow Wow.

—Jerry Spinelli, *Maniac Magee* (1991 Newbery Medal winner)

INDEPENDENT reading is the basis of literature-based reading instruction. The overall goal of reading instruction in the schools is that children learn to read and continue reading outside of school without a teacher's direction. Successful reading instruction encourages children to read at home, away from school, in their spare time, and during free time at school. This chapter addresses the issues of independent and recreational reading and answers the following questions:

1. Why should teachers be concerned about children's independent reading behavior?
2. Is there a relationship between independent reading and reading achievement?
3. Can classroom activities encourage independent reading?
4. How is independent reading different from instructional reading?
5. How can instruction incorporate independent reading?

Books and reading can provide children with many rich experiences and expose them to many aspects of life. Teachers who inspire independent reading better the lives of their students. "The poorest man in the world is the man limited to his own experience, the man who does not read," write Fader and McNeil (1967, p. 4). Every child should learn how to read, and every child should emerge from organized reading instruction able and willing to read independently.

Independent reading behaviors do not develop by chance or without guidance (Herber & Nelson-Herber, 1987), and teachers can help students develop independent and recreational reading habits by designing school activities that encourage such behavior. Teachers can encourage independent reading by turning children on to reading and convincing them that they can rely on books for information and entertainment throughout their lives. When teachers make books accessible, read aloud in the classroom, encourage independent reading at school, and allow time to discuss literature, children view reading as a highly valued activity (Buchanan, 1980) that can be incorporated into all aspects of their lives.

Foundations of Independent Reading

Statistics demonstrate that people in our society are not reading as much as they once did. Cullinan (1987) reports that a book industry study reveals that 80 percent of all books are read by 10 percent of the population. Trelease (1989) substantiates Cullinan's concerns and reports an alarming decline in the number of books read in the classroom. In surveys of children's book reading habits since the late 1960s, he has found that children are reading less and less. When he asked children what they were reading, they could name only their textbooks.

People who read on their own must learn how to do so, and as they continue to read, they will add to their knowledge of the process. As readers interact with print, they use their skills and abilities in new and expanded ways. Even efficient readers develop new reading interests, acquire new vocabulary, perfect reading skills, and rely on others to "explain, demonstrate, clarify, embellish, evaluate" (Herber & Nelson-Herber, 1987, p. 586). The development of independent reading strategies is an important, but often overlooked objective of most reading programs.

Independent reading is any reading that children do without the teacher selecting the material, preparing instruction, or guiding them. Independent reading may support classroom instruction, as when a teacher plans for children to read independently in response to a social studies assignment or requires independent reading during reading instruction. Independent reading also arises from children's desire to read.

When children read simply because they feel it's a good way to spend free time, independent reading becomes recreational. It may or may not be related to their school work. Children who read for recreation are demonstrating their potential for lifelong reading habits. Recreational reading is a highly desired outcome of all reading instruction.

Recreational reading has a positive effect on reading achievement in school (Anderson, Wilson, & Fielding, 1988; Greaney, 1980; Walberg & Tsai, 1984). That children can improve reading achievement by reading outside of school should be enough reason for teachers to plan to develop students' independent and recreational reading habits. It makes sense that the more children read, the better they are at reading, and some of the practice must occur out of school and during children's free time. A teacher may encourage independent reading by requiring it during instruction, but the desire to read recreationally must be nurtured because books compete with television, video games, computers, and other forms of entertainment. Parents can do much to encourage reading outside of school, but teachers can affect children's reading habits, too.

Teachers often see themselves as influencing what children do in the classroom and may not realize that they can affect reading behaviors outside of school. There is evidence that teachers influence how much time children spend reading outside of school (Anderson, Wilson, & Fielding, 1988). Children may read books discussed in class, mimic reading behavior of peers and teachers, and respond to their teacher's prodding by reading on their own time. Smart teachers capitalize on their influence.

Independence is gained by learning and practicing how to be an independent reader (Herber & Nelson-Herber, 1987). Students will not become lifetime readers unless they frequently read for recreation (Sanacore, 1990). When teachers include independent reading in their instruction, children learn how to apply reading techniques and habits to their daily lives. Children can benefit from knowing where to find books, how to select books and, most important, what books are available for reading.

Some think teachers' influence on children's attitudes toward recreational reading is highly significant. Instilling a love for reading and demonstrating the benefits of spending time with books can, indeed, make a difference in a child's life. The important message for children is that lifetime reading is valuable. If teachers do have such a great influence, it is because they are aware of their impact and plan and carefully select classroom activities to encourage independent and recreational reading.

Independent Reading

The assumptions about independent and recreational reading that teachers can make are simple and brief. These assumptions justify classroom activities that promote independent reading.

Independent Reading Does Have a Positive Effect on Reading Achievement
When children read on their own, reading scores and comprehension increase. Children become better readers by reading, and independent reading is one way to practice. In addition, when independent reading is the focus of some classroom activities, a love of reading and books can be instilled.

School Activities Can Encourage Independent, Outside Reading
The teacher's inclusion of independent reading in classroom activities makes a difference in the amount of reading children do outside the classroom. Teachers who provide opportunities for independent reading in the classroom and discuss and share books with children encourage them to read on their own.

Encouraging Independent Reading

The opportunities teachers provide for independent reading are among the most enjoyable activities of the school day. Independent reading should be free of grading, testing procedures, and other academic restraints. Independent reading can be a pleasurable and relaxing time for both teacher and students.

Access to Books

The first step in encouraging independent and recreational reading is to provide an inviting atmosphere and a large number of books and other reading material. Inviting atmospheres can be created with beanbag chairs, rugs, or partitions to isolate the reading corner. Some classrooms have reading lofts, reading tents, and reading couches as incentives for children to take time for reading. In as many ways as possible, the classroom should say, "Come on in, let's read."

Another aspect of inviting children to read is to not associate failure or unpleasant activities with independent, pleasure reading (Sanacore, 1990). Some reading should be allowed that does not require follow-up, evaluation, or even discussion. If any follow-up is required for independent reading, the activities should be creative and enjoyable. Independent reading should be part of a risk-free environment in which children can experiment with topics, titles, and reading strategies.

Books of all kinds should be available for children to read, but they may not always be available in each classroom. The resourceful teacher finds ways to provide books and other reading material with a limited or nonexistent budget. Books from home libraries, city and school libraries, and personal collections can broaden the classroom library. Secondhand book sales sponsored by libraries and service clubs are an inexpensive way to stock classroom libraries. High quality literary selections from outdated basals can be made into skinny books. (Skinny books usually present one story or one concept and are made easily by putting a cover on individual stories from old basals, selections from trade books, short story collections, magazines, or other sources.)

Another valuable source of classroom reading material should be children's original writing. Children who are reading and writing will produce a great many manuscripts that can become reading material for the classroom. The student-written pieces can be collected, bound, and displayed as regular reading material. These manuscripts should have a respected position in the classroom library and will be some of the most popular reading material available.

One of the rewarding institutions for avid readers is the library. Children who are not familiar with the library at first may be overwhelmed by the size and enormity of a large book collection. This is an important reason for children to have access to a small classroom library where they can learn about selection, variety, and range of reading material on a small scale. Classroom library experiences can prepare them for learning about a library in an unthreatening situation (Robinson & Good, 1987).

It is also important that children learn to feel comfortable among larger library collections. Children who are not familiar with the library may be taught to use the card catalog and identify appropriate books. Most school librarians will provide opportunities for children to learn about the school library, but children also know that city libraries are resources for independent and recreational reading. A field trip to the library or a visit from the city librarian can provide incentive to learn what is in the library. Modern city libraries offer much more than books and may lend pictures, video cassette recordings, audio tapes, records, and other materials.

Teachers can support library usage by assigning research that requires library work or requiring children to have books available for independent reading. The best way to learn about a library is to use it to accomplish some task. Children who begin using the library to find answers, interesting information, and books to read during early school years will continue to rely on the institution when they grow up.

Children may not always choose to read high quality literature. Some children will go for long periods of time reading only "Nancy Drew" books or books about a single subject such as baseball. Teachers must resist the temptation to pass judgment on the books children select. If children are reading, it is enough. On the other hand, teachers can recommend to those who may need to expand their reading range books about a particular topic or another author the student might enjoy.

Introducing New Books

Children must know what is available before they will read books in their spare time. Introducing books encourages all readers, including the narrowly focused reader, to read a wider range of books. There are numerous and flexible methods for introducing books that some in the classroom might enjoy. One of the most common ways to spark an interest in new books is for the teacher or another student to read exciting excerpts. Reading aloud can be a "teaser" to share a portion of an exciting book or it can be a time to introduce an entire book or author.

Interesting books can be advertised by children who have read them. Readers can produce advertisements on bulletin boards, make covers indicating the plots of the books, or try to sell classmates with short talks about the books. Books also can be introduced through video cassettes, popular movies, or computer programs. By far the simplest method of introducing a book to a classroom is to have it available and provide opportunities for discussion.

Reading Aloud

Reading aloud to children, especially young children, is one of the most important things that teachers do to promote reading outside of classrooms (Anderson, Wilson, & Fielding, 1988; Cosgrove, 1987). Almost all primary classrooms allow time for children to read together each day. Once children begin reading independently, the amount of time devoted to reading to them usually declines. By the time children are in upper grades, it may be difficult to carve out time to read. But the value of reading aloud is measurable no matter the age of the students. Reading aloud builds class spirit and provides a time for children to share adventures. In addition, when children are read to, positive attitudes toward reading increase, independent reading behaviors develop, and comprehension levels improve (Cosgrove, 1987). Butler (1988) provides a list of several advantages of reading aloud to children; those that relate specifically to encouraging independent reading include:

1. Children can hear stories that may be too difficult for them to read themselves. Young children or children with reading problems can benefit greatly.

2. Reading aloud provides a good model. The teacher demonstrates the reading process by reading aloud. It also suggests the importance of reading and encourages children to take time to read independently.

3. Reading aloud generates interest in reading all types of literature. Reading a wide variety of material introduces children to literature they might not know. Children can learn about books they have yet to read, authors they want to know, or books they want to reread. They may find titles and genres to read independently.

4. Reading aloud can introduce children to characters and events that may motivate them to read more. There are many memorable characters that become part of children's lives and will motivate them to read sequels or other books. Often, characters become friends and part of classroom activities. One second grade class read about Paddington Bear (Bond, 1958) at the beginning of the year, and a small stuffed Paddington accompanied the students through many adventures during the year. The three Paddington books became very popular, and the second graders wrote about Paddington, talked about him, and allowed him to comfort them when needed. He became a member of the classroom. At the end of the year, the parents knew how much Paddington meant to the children and collected money to replace the small, worn Paddington with a new 3 1/2-foot-tall Paddington. That Paddington still oversees the classroom.

It is particularly important to read aloud to children who have not been read to at home. Children who are not exposed to books in the home should be read to in the classroom, no matter their ages or reading abilities. Younger children who have not been read to may need extra doses. They can meet with the teacher for an extra session, have opportunities to listen to recorded texts while following the print, or be paired with a buddy who might assist in reading favorite books aloud. Upper grade children can benefit from reading aloud, too. There is no more valuable way to spend time than presenting children with experiences that introduce them to literature.

Reading to older children is important, too. Taking time to share books sends the message about the importance of reading. Reading aloud should be so important that the class finds time each day to read. Reading aloud also provides an opportunity for introducing new texts, characters, and genres to older children. Reading exciting portions of stories to children can induce them to read more. Reading aloud exposes children to ideas and concepts they may not have found on their own. Sharing difficult concepts and vocabulary is not nearly as overwhelming, particularly for less experienced readers, as reading something challenging alone. Reading aloud is an activity that is valuable for all ages and should not be abandoned after primary grades.

Discussion

Interactions of students and teachers contribute to positive attitudes about reading and increased reading achievement (Anderson, Wilson, & Fielding, 1988). All of us enjoy discussing a book that we have really enjoyed and children are no exception. Reading opportunities can be enhanced by planning for formal and informal discussions of books that children are reading independently. Discussions can be based on almost any premise, but informal discussions in small groups or as an entire class about what individuals are reading can give the students time to share and inform others about books.

Studying authors is one way to introduce new books through discussion or reading aloud. Focusing on an author during discussions and reading activities can familiarize children with different styles, ideas, and subjects as well as provide a common forum for discussion. Author/illustrator Chris Van Allsburg's texts and illustrations are easy for children to recognize. He has become a favorite of children during the ten years he has devoted his considerable talents to writing and illustrating children's books. Judy Blume and Beverly Cleary are perennial favorites who focus on contemporary problems and issues that many children must confront. Teachers can establish a format for focusing on authors or allow children to determine which authors are discussed.

Genre studies are another way to introduce a variety of new books. Children can focus on traditional literature, historical fiction, contemporary literature, poetry, or fantasy during their independent reading time. Discussions can compare, contrast, or present different aspects of the genres. Discussions that focus on a variety of types of literature expose children to genres they might not have read before.

Children can be encouraged to discuss books each night with parents or siblings (Lamme, 1987). Young children can take books home to share and discuss. The school day can begin with a discussion of what was read or what they discussed with their parents the night before. Older children can share ideas with parents and siblings from books they are reading and discussing at school. The exchanges can enrich the understandings of an entire classroom.

Sharing Favorite Books

Providing time to share and discuss favorite books is a simple and effective method to encourage independent reading. Teachers can do much to encourage reading by sharing their personal favorites. Books enjoyed as a child, books discovered as an adult, or books found through professional reading can be shared with the classroom. When the books are made available afterward, the odds that children will select them to read independently are increased.

Children can share their favorite books with each other. Many children find out about books from their peers and friends. A classroom that provides opportunities for sharing capitalizes on the natural influence children have on each other and contributes greatly to the development of independent reading habits.

Another way to hook children on reading is to invite adults who are important to children to share literacy events. Adults other than teachers can serve as role models for reading during independent classroom reading, read their favorite books aloud, or read books along with the class and take part in discussions. This is a good time to encourage parental involvement in classroom activities or invite other community role models to join the class. Favorite football or baseball players or TV personalities probably would enjoy spending time reading with students.

One school devoted an entire day to having community leaders share their favorite books. The mayor, police officers, nurses, doctors, and TV and sports personalities brought their favorite books to the school to share with students. Every child in the school had the opportunity to listen to two or three adults discussing their favorite books and their ideas about reading. The experience became a powerful message about the importance of reading and the enjoyment others derive from books.

Reading Real Material

One way to instill the importance of reading outside the classroom is to include materials used regularly outside school. Teachers should take every opportunity to demonstrate to students the importance of reading in adults' lives. Magazines and newspapers, very real opportunities for reading, can be a part of the classroom environment. Children see adults reading these materials and realize that they are an important part of reading.

If real material is used in the classroom, real reading behavior is the focus. Much popular reading material is opinionated and requires critical reading skills for comprehension. When children are reading opinionated material, they should compare and contrast opinions and viewpoints. Sports, current events, and television reviews can be read critically, allowing students to evaluate what is important, what is presented realistically, or what is biased. Descriptions of the same events from different sources will help children understand the importance of recognizing bias in daily reading.

Children can learn job-related reading. Students can interview adults with different jobs to learn about the reading demands of their particular situations (Robinson & Good, 1987). Adults sharing their daily reading material and habits give children reasons for continuing their reading development. This can prove to be a real eye-opener about the need for reading in our world. Teachers and colleagues could be interviewed about what they read daily. But, interviews with nurses, auto mechanics, television repairers, and other working adults help children understand the wide variety of needs that reading meets. This also will help children understand why reading is so important to their futures.

Independent Reading in Subject Areas

Sanacore (1990) suggests that independent reading in certain subjects such as science, social studies, humanities, and even math can encourage lifetime reading habits. He supports the inclusion of children's literature in instruction in all subjects and implies that using children's literature throughout the curriculum has the potential to help children enjoy reading. There are several aspects of children's literature that support Sanacore's thesis. The wide variety of texts available allows children with many different interests to identify material that is important to them. The different formats and lengths of children's literature can add to the pleasure of learning. Children who might not enjoy reading a social studies textbook, for example, can't avoid learning about the Civil War in *Across Five Aprils* (Hunt, 1964) or the Revolutionary War in *Johnny Tremain* (Forbes, 1946).

Sanacore also believes that independent reading and material read aloud by the teacher can support learning and encourage children to read for enjoyment. Learning about different subjects provides a reason for reading and listening to the material. Children learn about a topic, experience pleasurable reading, and are reinforced in the joy of reading while they are reading independently about certain subjects. The types of books appropriate for different topics are discussed in chapters 2 and 8.

Specific Strategies

Some specific types of classroom instruction encourage free choice of reading material. The strategies presented in this section encourage much independent reading in the classroom and often require teachers to provide opportunities for discussion and other follow-up. The strategies suggested in this section use independent reading as the basis for instruction.

Sustained Silent Reading (SSR)

One of the basic strategies for providing independent reading time in the classroom is sustained silent reading (SSR). Sustained silent reading also is called DEAR (Drop Everything and Read), WEIRD (We're Engaged in Independent Reading Daily), SQUIRT (Super Quiet Undisturbed Individual Reading Time), or DIRT (Daily Independent Reading Time). These are just some of the names for classroom reading based on the premise that children simply need time to read what they want. SSR is one way that teachers can use scheduled classroom time to promote independent reading (Anderson, Wilson & Fielding, 1988). Children participating regularly in SSR understand that this time is set aside to read books of their choice for a specific length of time. Sustained reading opportunities encourage independent reading and have a positive effect on attitudes toward reading (Moore, Jones, & Miller, 1980).

The rules for SSR are simple. The entire class, including the teacher, selects material to read. Children and teacher read silently for a preset amount of time, with no interruptions. Parents, principals, school nurses, and gym teachers can be guests of the class during this time and read their own books. This allows children to see that many people in their lives believe that reading is important.

SSR should become a ritual. Children can make signs for the door that state "PLEASE DO NOT DISTURB, WE ARE READING." The beginning of SSR can be signaled by someone placing the sign on the door and end at the sound of a common kitchen timer. The rules for SSR should be clear and explicit. The teacher indicates the amount of time to be spent reading and sets the timer to keep the time. Children should have a clear understanding of such logistics as how they obtain reading material for the time allowed for reading, where they may sit, or if they may move around after the timer starts.

Everyone reads during SSR time. No one disturbs the readers, and formal follow-up is not required. Even when the teacher does not require follow-up, children may want to discuss and show the books they read. Many teachers respond to the children's desire to share by closing SSR time with discussion or journal writing. After children have spent time with good books, there is much to share and time for it should be provided.

One way to assure success is to make sure that children have books to read during SSR time. Very young children should be encouraged to have two or three books in their possession when the SSR time begins. A basket of books provided by the teacher can help them make selections for SSR. Beginning readers will need to select some books that have been read in class or shared at home (Rothlein & Meinbach, 1990). Beginners and those who have some difficulty reading texts should be encouraged to use wordless picture books during SSR. Newspapers, children's periodicals, reference books, and student-authored texts also can be read during SSR.

Older children should be given responsibility for identifying books to read, but the teacher can help them plan for SSR. The teacher has opportunities to suggest titles during conferences, when responding to journals, or during class discussions. Books that both students and teachers identify as suitable for independent reading are usually favorites. When a child has an extremely difficult time finding enough to read during SSR, the teacher can offer books directly or suggest three or four titles the child might enjoy.

Children have to learn how to spend time reading. When SSR is first implemented in the classroom, a very short time may be devoted to reading. After some experience with SSR, older children may read for thirty minutes at a time. Younger children's ability to sit quietly and look at books will develop over time. But even immature kindergarten children can be expected to sit and look at books for five or ten minutes.

One of the values of SSR is that children see the teacher reading, and it is imperative that the teacher do so. It is not the time to grade papers or plan for the next activity. Reading during SSR is one way the teacher can demonstrate that reading is an important activity. The example set by the teacher can make a strong impact on a child's view of reading. Children may not have many opportunities to see adults read because adults may read late at night when children are in bed, or when children are not around. When children witness adults in their lives engaging in recreational reading, it sends the message that grown-ups believe reading is important. Children need models who read actively and regularly, both in and out of school, so that they will view reading as an activity done places other than school.

Literature Groups

Although sharing time is not usually a specific result of SSR, many teachers find that children need to talk about the books they are reading independently. The easiest way to share is in a whole class setting, but some children may not feel comfortable talking about what they've read in a large group. One way to provide an opportunity for talking about books is to establish regular times when small groups of children discuss a book they all have read. Other small group discussions might focus on a theme common to different books, books from series or the same genre, or books by the same author. Literature groups allow children to share independent reading informally.

Conferences

When students read independently, teachers must find a way to respond, question, and monitor individual student progress and activities. Conferences are individual or small group meetings that provide teachers and children with opportunities to discuss independent reading. The discussions provide teachers with information that can help monitor and guide students' future reading activities. Conferences may be regularly scheduled with students or can be initiated by the teacher or student if there is a need. As a result of a conference, children can determine future reading selections, share what they have read independently, discuss their reactions to reading, and develop strategies that encourage independent reading. Reading conferences are different than small groups formed for teacher planned instruction, since the students determine the topics and direction of discussion. The main objective of a reading conference is to provide students with an opportunity to interact with an individual or small group about the books they are reading. Another result of the conference can be that teachers have the opportunity to encourage students to read a wide range of literature. Atwell (1987) talks about using conferences to nudge students toward certain books and ideas. Discussing books and ideas with a teacher and other peers can encourage readers to rethink, reread, and find other interesting reading materials.

Conferences have four parts (Pappas, Kiefer, & Levstik, 1990): sharing, questioning, oral reading, and encouraging and guiding.

1. Conferences can begin by allowing children to share what they have been reading. If they are keeping written logs of their reading material, they can be invited to read some of their entries to the teacher.

2. The teacher listens to what the child has to share and asks questions about the reading material. If it is a small group conference the teacher invites children to question each other about their independent reading.

3. The conference includes opportunities to read orally as children provide examples, prove points, or share favorite parts. During the conference the teacher notes and records oral reading behavior for later reference.

4. The children and teacher discuss reading plans. Children can identify what they would like to read next, and teachers can guide them to the stories and books that meet their goals. At the conclusion of a conference, children should have a plan for the next few days of reading activities.

The four components of a conference can be used at any grade level to encourage and respond to independent reading. Once children learn the logistics of a conference, they can conduct conferences with each other.

Peer conferences give children opportunities to discuss their reading. Conferences may be arranged and structured by the teacher or may occur spontaneously when a collegial atmosphere is established in the classroom. In a classroom that is continuously sharing what is being read, it is not unusual to have student-initiated conferences. Often, informal conferences between students are reflections of teacher-led conferences (Calkins, 1983). Teachers report that children will conduct a conference with questions, procedures, and even mannerisms identical to those of the teacher. This is another example of the impact of role models on young children.

Sample questions, such as those in Box 4.1, can be used to begin discussions during conferences.

BOX 4-1

Questions for a Reading Conference

General Questions About the Book

- What did you learn from this book?
- What is your reaction to this book?
- Were there events that made you think of something that has happened in your own life?
- What was your favorite part of the story?
- If you could change part of the book, what would you do?
- Have you read other stories that remind you of this story?

Questions About the Characters

- Would you like this character if you knew him or her in real life?
- How did the author make you like or dislike this character?
- How did the character change?
- What would you have done if you were the character?
- How was the character like or unlike you?
- Compare this character with another character you have read about.

Questions About Literary Elements

- Would this book make a good movie? Was it exciting? Adventurous?
- How did the author help you understand the setting? Have you ever visited a place like the setting of this story?
- What part of the story was hardest for you to understand?
- Is there any part of the story that you find uninteresting?
- Were there parts of the story that use language especially well?
- How did the author use language differently?

Individualized Reading Instruction

One instructional approach that encourages independence in reading is the individualized reading approach. Individualized reading emphasizes students' self-pacing and selection of reading material. Individualized reading instruction is monitored by a teacher who organizes and oversees activities. When an individualized instructional approach is used, children take responsibility for their progress and feel more in charge of their learning (Butler, 1988), but the teacher is aware of what activities they are attempting.

There are several characteristics identified with individualized reading instruction:

1. There is a great deal of print available for children to read. For children to select their own reading material, the teacher must use well-stocked classroom collections as well as public and school libraries.

2. Children choose what they read with the teacher's guidance. Usually, children read material that reflects their interests and abilities, but there are times the teacher may select a theme or assign certain work related to the reading, and the children are free to select material that will meet the objectives. For example, the assignment might be to read a novel about the Civil War. The teacher is responsible for choosing the theme, but the students select the reading material.

3. Individual and small group conferences provide time for the teacher to discuss the books with the children and present lessons that may be needed. Reading conferences are critical to individualized reading instruction because they are a time for children to interact with the teacher about what they are reading. During conferences teachers may check on comprehension, identify difficulties in reading, encourage ideas for writing, and provide guidance for further reading.

4. Activities and projects are planned to follow up the reading. There should be a variety of activities for sharing what has been read. Sometimes, however, children feel the book they read was not very special, so they should be allowed to simply record their reading without completing a long, involved activity.

5. Record-keeping is done by children and teachers. One way to keep records is reading logs (see Figure 4.1). Children can keep track of their reading in a journal or use short, structured forms. The records are used to monitor progress, plan for instruction, and identify reading problems that children might need help with. The records and observations serve as a basis for individual, small, and large group conferences.

Teachers should include observations and anecdotes in records of children's behaviors and work during individualized reading instruction. They may take notes during conferences or watch how children respond during independent reading times. They note children's choices of reading materials and any problems they may have during oral or silent reading.

Individualized reading instruction can be the entire reading program or a way to include literature in a basal approach. There are many ways to implement the procedures, and teachers almost always will modify the basic format to fit their needs. One structure designed for individualized reading is the readers' workshop.

FIGURE 4-1   Reading logs provide a structure for children to help with the record keeping associated with literature-based instruction.

Title	Author	# of Pages	Start Date	Finish Date

Readers' Workshop

Atwell (1987) has adapted some of the features of the individualized reading approach for an independent instructional approach called readers' workshop, which includes four aspects: mini-lessons, independent reading, dialogue journals, and sharing opportunities.

1. *Mini-lessons.*
        Short, planned, teacher-directed sessions begin the reading period each day. When teaching children how to participate in readers' workshop, the mini-lessons are used to present procedures and routines. For example, the mini-lesson format can be used to teach the logistics and expectations of the dialogue journal or to explain the routine of independently selecting reading material. As students learn the routines of readers' workshop, mini-lessons begin to focus on such activities as studying authors, reading and discussing a poem, short story, or opening book chapter, or introducing a certain genre. The teacher can use mini-lessons to present comprehension strategies, vocabulary development, or word studies. The short lessons provide opportunities for the teacher to demonstrate a skilled reader's behavior and oral reading to the students.

—— **BOX 4-2** ——————————————————————————————————

Rules for Reading Workshop

1. Students must read for the entire period.

2. They cannot do homework or read any material for another course. Reading workshop is not a study hall.

3. They must read a book (no magazines or newspapers where text competes with pictures), preferably one that tells a story (e.g., novels, histories, and biographies rather than books of lists or facts where readers can't sustain attention, build up speed and fluency, or grow to love good stories.)

4. They must have a book in their possession when the bell rings; this is the main responsibility in coming prepared to class. (Students who need help finding a book or who finish a book during the workshop are obvious exceptions.)

5. They may not talk to or disturb others.

6. They may sit or recline wherever they'd like as long as feet don't go up on furniture and rule # 5 is maintained. (A piece of paper taped over the window in the classroom door helps cut down on the number of passersby who require explanations about students lying around with their noses in books.)

7. There are no lavatory or water fountain sign-outs to disturb me or other readers. In an emergency, they may simply slip out and slip back in again as quietly as possible.

8. A student who's absent can make up time and receive points by reading at home, during study hall (with a note from a parent or study hall teacher), or after school.

Source: From Atwell, N. (1987). *In the middle: Writing, reading, and learning with adolescents.* Portsmouth, NH: Heinemann. p. 154.

——

2. *Independent reading.*

Much of the instructional time is devoted to independent reading, with students following established guidelines. Guidelines best-suited for individual classrooms evolve, but Atwell (1987) presents classroom rules as an example of how to establish the routine of independent reading (see Box 4.2).

3. *Dialogue journals.*

Students respond to independent reading time with dialogue journals in which they write to the teacher in a spiral notebook using a friendly letter format (Oberlin & Shugarman, 1989) to describe what they are reading. The children share the thinking process that results from what they read. The teacher reads each journal entry and responds, which is an important feature. Atwell (1987) suggests that teachers respond "specifically and personally" (p. 178) to what the children have written. The journals are not a place for working on mechanics of writing, but a forum for sharing and responding to the readers' ideas. The journals, Atwell says, are considered a "a first draft chat, not polished pieces of writing" (p.178). There are no corrections made in the journals; interesting questions from teachers and children stimulate the dialogue (see Figure 4.2).

Atwell (1987) also suggests that the teacher use student-to-student dialogue journals to provide more audiences for reactions to independent reading. Occasionally, classmates can respond instead of the teacher. Not only does this give the teacher some help in responding to an entire classroom, but provides the writer with different perspectives.

    4. *Sharing.*

    Sharing is an important part of reader's workshop. Some sharing can occur in conferences, which provide time for individualized instruction, focusing on students' concerns, and gaining insights into their feelings and reading behavior. Most important, the conferences, small group interactions, and whole class discussions provide opportunities to share what is read.

Reading Centers

Learning and reading centers have evolved from an emphasis on individualized instruction (Tierney, Readence, & Dishner, 1990) and can be used to motivate, encourage, and provide opportunities for following up on independent reading. Reading centers are formed when there is an area in the classroom where students have access to reading material, suggestions for follow-up, and space for responding to books read independently. The object of establishing space, books, and materials devoted to student-chosen reading and activities is encouraging independent reading.

    The center might support a display of books on a certain topic or by a particular author, from which students select books to read during independent reading opportunities. After reading the students return to the center to work independently or in small groups, discussing, and writing about the material they have read. The center includes a multitude of suggestions for record-keeping and responding to texts. Children select the type of follow-up they wish to pursue. For example, a center might be established to make a large number of Chris Van Allsburg books available for independent reading. Children could select any Van Allsburg title from the display. After reading the book, students select from a wide range of follow-up activities, from simply recording the title, date, and name of the reader to elaborate artwork based on the book. Several different activities, such as comparing his bizarre plots, looking for common themes in the artwork in his books, or preparing the story to read aloud to younger children, could be suggested as follow-ups. The students are free to select an activity or read another book.

    The reading center might focus on generic follow-up activities for children to select. However the reading center is established, the teacher will want to make sure that logistics and rules are explicit so that children will understand what is expected when they are working there.

Readers' Clubs and Book Fairs

Some elementary schools have established a time during the day when all interested students can contribute to discussions of books. Teachers devote a lunch time to meeting with children who like to discuss books, or children spend a recess time discussing their favorite books. Readers' clubs may be restricted to a certain grade level or combine readers of several ages and abilities. Usually, readers' clubs incorporate more than one

FIGURE 4-2 Children's journal responses provide the teacher opportunities to interact about the literature.

Adam   Nov. 9, 1990
Dear Mrs. Bertin   I just
got finish reading <u>Something good</u>
It is a very good book Tyya and
her father, brother and sister. Her
brother and sister get to have
sweets and she dose'nt. The worst part
in the book is when Tyya puts al'
but 100 boxes of ice cream in her
cart and it makes amess. The part I
wish that would happen to me
is I wish I could yell in
a grocery store. The thing I
wouldnt want to happen to me
is nock down 500 apples.

Continued

FIGURE 4-2   *Continued*

Dear Adam,

    I'm glad you told me about Something Good. I just read it tonight. I really laughed when the lady thought Tyra was a doll and put a price tag on her head. When I read it I thought that Tyya's dad wouldn't let her get sweets. It doesn't say that her brother and sister got sweets. Go back and reread to see if you agree.

                 Love,
                 Mrs. Bertin

FIGURE 4-2 *Continued*

The part I didint like was oh there was no part I did not like. Some of the caters are all the kids in the train, johnation and his mom and Dad. I relly relly would recommend this book to you Because It is a great book and it has alot of betles in it and that was the end of my story.

Sincerely, Dawn

Reading √+++
Grammar √+

Dear Dawn,   Oct.31, 1990
    Your work is incredible! I think you are really growing as a reader & writer. I can tell reading and writing are important to you! Love, Miss D.

classroom. No follow-up assignments or requirements are made. It can be as simple as establishing a weekly or monthly time when children know they can meet in the library or a classroom to discuss books.

Book clubs often are sponsored by publishing companies that cater to elementary-age children. The clubs offer inexpensive monthly selections. Some book club orders (such as *Weekly Reader* and *Scholastic*) are placed by the teacher, who can receive free books based on the number of books paid for by students. Some of the common book clubs include:

Scholastic, 730 Broadway, New York, NY 10003.

- See-Saw Book Club (kindergarten and grade one)
- Lucky Book Club (grades two and three)
- Arrow Book Club (grades four and five)

Another school-wide event to promote interest in independent reading is a book fair. Book fairs invite each grade level to display creative reactions to certain children's books. Children can design displays to highlight their favorite books and promote reading. Classes decide on specific authors or genres their displays will emphasize and design charts, mobiles, book covers, and dioramas to represent the books. On a given day or week, the book fair is conducted in the library or in the hallways.

Another type of book fair often is used by parent–teacher organizations to raise money. The groups display books for sale at reasonable prices. The books are supplied by children's book publishing companies and can be purchased for less than $2.00. Many children add to their libraries during the book fairs.

Writing

Children who read and write at school usually read and write outside of school. If children are writing in response to their school reading, they also begin to write about independent reading. It is a positive step for children to share some writing that is an outgrowth of their recreational reading or that was completed outside of school.

Some writing is a natural extension of independent reading. Journals can be used to accumulate reactions, records, and evaluations of books read by children. Teachers can require a certain format or allow the students to establish the method of responding in journals. Journal writing is more successful if someone responds to the entries. The responses can be in writing or oral. Journals can be adapted to almost any goal a teacher may have for independent reading.

Writing offers a way for a teacher or peers to respond to an individual's independent reading. It is a way to share and get reactions from the teacher or other classmates. Burke (1988) suggests written conversations as a method of responding to books. After children have read books, they can break into pairs and discuss their books through writing. There is no talking allowed, and the entire discussion is written on a single sheet. This allows ''quiet discussion,'' while encouraging writing development.

Writing that is required in reaction to independent reading should be avoided so that it does not cause a negative reaction to the reading. In many cases children will want to share their reactions to a book. Never let it be said that children avoid reading independently so they will not have to write about what they read. Although writing (and discussion) are excellent ways to structure responses and provide feedback to children's independent reading, there may be times when independent and recreational reading is completed without any follow-up.

Other Media

Headsets, tape recorders, video cassette recorders, and other audio-visual equipment contribute to increased book use and enthusiasm for books (Morrow, 1987). Sets of prints and slides can serve as a basis for group presentations and discussions of reading (England & Fasick, 1987). Filmstrips and traditional films seem antiquated with the easy access of video cassettes. But many classics are available on film, and some schools may not yet have developed their collections of video cassettes. No matter what type of video support a teacher uses, each has the potential to increase interest and motivation in independent and recreational reading.

There are several ways to use film and cassettes in the classroom. Books can be introduced with audio-video methods, or stories already read can be enjoyed once again through dramatization on film. Comparison and contrasts can be made after viewing a favorite story. Children can spend a great deal of time discussing the casting of the main character or if the mood of the book is supported by the artwork and music of the film. Each of these discussions leads to greater understanding of literary elements as well as contributing to the understanding of individual stories.

The Effect of Television on Reading

Television has been recognized as a culprit in the decline of reading by children. Lately, the consensus about television viewing is that in moderation there is no effect on reading achievement (Anderson, Wilson, & Fielding, 1988; Williams, Haertel, Haertel, & Walber, 1982). A subtle effect of television viewing may be that children must have high quality literature to tear them away from television. Television is exciting and action-packed, and children need books and literature that offer exciting stories, imaginative illustrations, and much thought-provoking material to pull them away from the TV.

One way to encourage reading is to use the television to stimulate reading. Students could read books about favorite stars or characters, or television filmmaking. Television also can encourage children to enjoy remakes of favorite classroom stories. Public television often shows filmed versions of high quality literature.

If teachers are aware that a high quality story will be featured on television, they can encourage independent reading of the book or read parts of the book that might entice children to watch the program. "Reading Rainbow" is a Public Broadcasting Service television show that presents the reading of a high quality book and relates the book to other interesting social studies, art, music, and science facts. The show often ends by suggesting additional reading. The "After School Specials" on a commercial network occasionally dramatize favorite children's stories. Teachers can tape favorite stories and use the taped versions as extensions of classroom reading material. Independent reading is encouraged when the TV is used as a motivator.

Movies can be used in the same manner. Such characters as E.T., Batman, and Darth Vader can become classroom companions through children's reading and writing. Even calmer characters, like Winnie the Pooh and Peanuts, can be seen in different ways with classroom movies and films. Children can become involved in the real characters of movies through reading, too. They can read biographies of favorite film stars or read magazine and newspaper articles critiquing and discussing favorite movies.

Selecting television programming and determining which shows are of high quality can become a lesson in real reading. Children can be encouraged to make wise choices in television watching by reading and reviewing television schedules. This is meaningful reading that can motivate any child with its usefulness. Children can be encouraged to read before watching TV and to keep written logs of their television experiences. Written summaries and critiques of television programming can be regular classroom activities. Reading critiques from newspapers can encourage children to make wise choices before seeing movies. Children also can be encouraged to write their own critiques of movies and television shows for others to read.

Learning Differences

No matter the background or language abilities of the students in a classroom, they can benefit from independent reading activities. Because students choose their independent reading material, children with differences in abilities and backgrounds can interact with text important to them. The teacher has two major concerns when adjusting independent reading activities for all the children in the classroom: motivating children to read and making interesting literature accessible to all students.

It is important that book collections include a wide range of subjects to appeal to various cultures and languages. The reading needs of all children in the classroom should be met. Librarians and teachers should search for books that treat ethnic characters fairly and realistically. To select books representing differing cultures for independent reading, the following criteria should be considered (Nauman, 1987):

1. There should be a realistic and authentic perspective of all cultures represented in the books, with an absence of stereotyping and inclusion of different lifestyles, socioeconomic status, interests, and abilities.
2. Some books should reflect the language of the culture.
3. Historical and political issues relating to the cultural group should be presented with accuracy and dignity.
4. Illustrations should be accurate.

These criteria assure that children can relate to the books available for independent reading. A major concern is that books and materials be available for children with limited ability in English. This can be a problem since it may involve providing material in Spanish, French, Italian, Hungarian, Vietnamese, Japanese, Thai, Chinese, Farsi, or Laotian. (Students from large metropolitan areas like Houston may speak 85 to 110 different languages.) A teacher with limited resources can make sure that wordless picture books, predictable English books, or student-written texts are available for independent reading.

Independent reading allows children of different backgrounds to incorporate their interests and knowledge into instruction. During independent reading, all students must meet the same requirements, but they do so with reading materials they choose. This is one way to provide an individualized approach in a classroom that includes children with many different backgrounds. Furthermore, the wide variety of reading materials and topics will be reflected in discussion and writing so that all children can be aware of the multi-ethnic and cultural differences in the classroom. Independent reading offers a time when reading can be adapted for children of all backgrounds.

Providing plenty of opportunities for children from different cultural backgrounds to see role models reading may be particularly important. Community members representing different cultures can be called upon to discuss how they view reading and to share favorite books. It is particularly effective if community members can share books that reflect language and cultural differences. Inviting adults from different backgrounds to take part in SSR is a good way to promote reading habits among all children.

Teachers also should be aware of how different cultures and backgrounds affect how their students view the importance of independent reading. Children may be coming from homes that do not value written language as the most important form of communication. This does not mean that these children cannot learn to appreciate independent reading, and teachers should never assume that children from different cultures will not be independent readers. Recognition of differences allows teachers to plan for various responses in the classroom.

Sometimes parents who have not had much reading and writing experience do not know how to encourage recreational and independent reading and writing. They may not have books or other reading material in the home. It is difficult for children to see the importance in reading if their home life does not reflect the need. Households that focus on television, radio, and stereos will not use written language as much as households that value written language. When reading is not viewed as important, there may not be material available or quiet times provided for reading. Parents need to be educated about the importance of independent reading. Methods of encouraging parental involvement in the literacy process are discussed in chapter 11.

DISCUSSION AND ACTIVITIES

1. Establish small groups to experiment with readers' workshop activities. During the mini-lesson, one student can prepare a discussion of picture book illustrations (see chap. 2). Each member of a small group should bring a picture book to read after the short lesson. After a few minutes of independent reading, each member writes an informal letter to a partner about his or her book and its illustrations. The letters are exchanged and the partner supplies responses and guidance to what was written.

2. After reading several selections of children's literature, divide into pairs and practice conducting a reading conference. Try discussing a specific book using some of the questions suggested in this chapter. Don't be restrained by the suggestions and let the conference be free-flowing if it seems appropriate. See if you can guide your partner to a decision about what the next children's reading selection might be.

3. Role play a teacher discussion that might occur about independent reading time in the classroom. Have one of your classmates take the role of a teacher who is supportive of independent reading time and encourages SSR activities in the classroom. Instruct a second student to take the role of a teacher who feels too pressed for time to allow daily SSR time. Encourage each one to justify his or her position.

RELATED READING

Professional

Atwell, N. (1987) *In the middle: Writing, reading, and learning with adolescents.* Portsmouth, NH: Heinemann.

This book provides the complete concept of readers' workshop. Atwell discusses the conceptual framework, specific activities, and provides examples of dialogue letters. If you are serious about implementing readers' workshop in the classroom, this book is a must.

Fader, D. N., & McNeil, E.B. (1967). *Hooked on books: Program & proof.* New York: Berkley.

Hooked on Books *is a classic that describes how to motivate reluctant high school readers. The original version (cited) is no longer in print. But there is a more recent edition that may be easier to obtain, perhaps from a library. Fader and McNeil write about secondary students, but have something to say to all teachers who wish to encourage their students to read.*

Gilles, C., Bixby, M., Crowley, P. Crenshaw, S., Henrichs, M., Reynolds, F., & Pyle, D. (Eds.). (1988). *Whole language strategies for secondary students.* New York: Richard C. Owens.

This book includes many suggestions to support independent and recreational reading. It also includes methods of motivation and responding to literature.

Watson, Dorothy. (Ed.). (1987). *Ideas and insights: Language arts in the elementary school.* Urbana, IL: National Council of Teachers of English.

No doubt about it, this text has a great many ideas about language arts in the elementary classroom, many of which encourage independent reading.

Children's Literature

Bond, M. (1958). *A bear called Paddington.* Illustrated by Peggy Fortnum. Boston: Houghton Mifflin.

Forbes, E. (1946). *Johnny Tremain.* Illustrated by L. Ward. Boston: Houghton Mifflin.

Hunt, I. (1964). *Across five Aprils.* Chicago, IL: Follett.

REFERENCES

Anderson, R.C., Wilson, P.T., & Fielding, L.G. (1988). Growth in reading and how children spend their time outside of school. *Reading Research Quarterly, 23* (3), 285–303.

Atwell, N. (1987). *In the middle: Writing, reading, and learning with adolescents.* Portsmouth, NH: Heinemann.

Buchanan, E. (Ed.). (1980). *For the love of reading.* Winnipeg, Manitoba, Canada: C. E. L. Group.

Burke, C. (1988). Book-sharing through written conversation. In C. Gilles, M. Bixby, P. Crowley, S. Crenshaw, M. Henrichs, F. Reynolds, and D. Pyle (Eds.). *Whole Language Strategies for Secondary Students.* New York: Richard C. Owens.

Butler, A. (1988). *The elements of a whole language program.* Crystal lake, IL: Rigby Education.

Calkins, L. (1983). *Lessons from a child.* Portsmouth, NH: Heinemann.

Coody, B. (1973). *Using literature with young children.* Dubuque, IA: William C. Brown.

Cosgrove, M.S. (1987). *Reading aloud to children: The effects of listening on the reading comprehension and attitudes of fourth and sixth graders in six communities in Connecticut.* Unpublished doctoral dissertation. Storrs, CT: University of Connecticut.

Cullinan, B.C. (1987). Inviting readers to literature. In Bernice Cullinan. (Ed.), *Children's literature in the reading program.* Newark, DE: International Reading Association.

England, C., & Fasick, A.M. (1987). *Child view: Evaluating and reviewing materials for children.* Littleton, CO: Libraries Unlimited.

Fader, D.N., & McNeil, E.B. (1967). *Hooked on books: Program & proof.* New York: Berkley.

Greaney, V. (1980). Factors related to amount and type of leisure time reading. *Reading Research Quarterly, 15* (3), 337–357.

Herber, H.L., & Nelson-Herber, J. (1987). Developing independent learners. *Journal of Reading, 30* (7), 584–588.

Lamme, L.L. (1987). Children's literature: The natural way to read. In Bernice Cullinan (Ed.), *Children's literature in the reading program.* Newark, DE: International Reading Association.

Moore, J.C., Jones, C.J., & Miller, D. C. (1980). What we know after a decade of sustained silent reading. *The Reading Teacher, 33* (3), 445–450.

Morrow, L. M. (1987). Promoting intercity children's recreational reading. *The Reading Teacher, 41* (3), 266–274.

Nauman, A. K. (1987). School librarians and cultural pluralism. *The Reading Teacher, 41* (3), 201–205.

Oberlin, K. J., & Shugarman, S.L. (1989). Implementing the Reading Workshop with middle school LD readers. *The Journal of Reading, 32* (8), 682–687.

Pappas, C.C., Kiefer, B.K., & Levstik, L.S. (1990). *An integrated language perspective in the elementary school: Theory into action.* New York: Longman.

Robinson, R., & Good, T. (1987). *Becoming an effective reading teacher.* New York: Harper & Row.

Rothlein, L., & Meinbach, A. M. (1990). *The literature connection: Using children's books in the classroom.* Glenview, IL: Scott, Foresman.

Sanacore, J. (1990). Creating the lifetime reading habit in social studies. *The Journal of Reading, 33* (6), 414–418.

Tierney, R.J., Readence, J. E., & Dishner, E.K. (1990). *Reading strategies and practices: A compendium.* New York: Allyn & Bacon.

Trelease, J. (1989). *The new read aloud handbook.* New York: Penguin.

Walberg, H.J., & Tsai, S. (1984). Reading achievement and diminishing returns to time. *Journal of Educational Psychology, 76* (3), 442–451.

Williams, P. A., Haertel, E. H., Haertel, G. D., & Walber, H.J. (1982). The impact of leisure time television on school learning. *American Educational Research Journal, 19* (1), 19–50.

5

EMERGING LITERACY

WORLDS I KNOW
I can read the pictures
by myself
in the books that lie
on the lowest shelf.
I know the place
where the stories start
and some I can even say
by heart,
and I make up adventures
and dreams and words
for some of the pages
I've never heard.

But I like it best
when mother sits
and reads to me
my favorites;
when Rapunzel pines
and the prince comes forth,
or the Snow Queen sighs
in the bitter north;
when Rose Red snuggles
against the bear
and I lean against Mother
and feel her hair.

We look at stars
in Hungary—
back of the North Wind
over the sea—
the Nutcracker laughs;
the Earl King calls;
a wish comes true;
the beanstalk falls;
the Wester wind
blows sweet and low,
and Mother gives words
to worlds I know.

—Myra Cohn Livingston, *Worlds I Know and Other Poems*

Rᴇᴀᴅɪɴɢ is probably one of the most exciting and rewarding learning experiences for parents, teachers, and children. Helping children become literate is particularly delightful since children are natural language learners. By the time most children begin school, they have demonstrated great potential for learning language. Their oral language development is easily observed as they acquire and use vocabulary, develop complex sentence structures, and use language for many reasons. Generally, adults take children's oral language development for granted and expect that children will be able to communicate their needs and wants at a very early age. Amazingly, most children become effective oral communicators by the time they are four or five years old. When one considers the monumental task that children accomplish within a few years, it seems amazing that so many are successful communicators before they start to school.

Adults expect children to learn to speak at young ages, but they do not always anticipate that children may learn to read and write before they start school. Writing and reading during the preschool years is not as obvious or as recognizable (Henderson, 1986) as children's speaking abilities, usually because adults are not familiar with behaviors associated with the emergence of literacy. Once adults know what to observe, they will see a great deal of evidence that suggests children are learning about written language at a very early age. Behaviors such as recognizing familiar logos, reading or writing names, becoming interested in letters, and understanding how to handle books indicate that literacy is beginning to emerge.

Literacy behaviors are learned in environments that provide many opportunities to interact with print and experiment with reading and writing. Environments and adult reactions to early attempts at reading and writing encourage literacy. But teachers and other adults must understand the process of acquiring written language in order to support children's learning. This chapter will attempt to answer some of the questions related to beginning reading and writing development. Some of the questions that will be answered include:

1. What early experiences encourage literacy development?
2. What type of behaviors do successful beginning readers and writers exhibit?
3. How are beginning reading and writing related?
4. What experiences must children have when learning to read and write?
5. How is beginning reading instruction different from reading instruction for efficient readers?

Historically, children were not expected to learn reading and writing until the age of six, and for many years educators viewed the development of early literacy as the responsibility of educational programs in kindergarten and first grade. In the 1970s and 1980s research and education began to reflect a greater understanding of how children learn to read and write. In fact, children begin to learn to read and write long before they start school and encounter formal instruction. That early school instruction should continue to encourage an already developing knowledge of language and print is a common assumption of beginning literacy instruction.

Written Language Development

Knowledge of how children learn to read and write has grown greatly in the last few years because of contributions from many different areas. Psychologists, linguists, and educators, just to mention a few, have investigated written language development from their unique perspectives. The result of all the scrutiny has been a shift in the way adults view children's early attempts to read and write. These new views are based on the contributions of several well-known theorists.

Although Jean Piaget wrote about child development as early as 1930 and some of his ideas have been questioned recently, his theories of early childhood education have implications for beginning reading instruction (Piaget, 1970). One contribution is the belief that children must learn through concrete actions and exploration. Piaget was one of the first theorists to suggest that children cannot be told how to do something, but should learn by doing. Accordingly, the best way to teach reading and writing is to involve children in reading and writing.

Piaget (1970) also suggested that children know a lot about what is required for learning to take place. He felt that in the right environment, children would learn what they need to succeed in their world. This theoretical view is widely supported by more current researchers and theorists who believe that children who find themselves in supportive, literate environments go about the business of becoming readers and writers.

A third Piagetian contribution to beginning reading instruction was the concept that children's learning experiences are developmental. His theory is the foundation for accepting that children's knowledge can be very different from adults' and changes as experience is gained. Children's early attempts at reading and writing may not be what adults expect from efficient readers. Think of the very young child who sits with a book, pointing a finger at the words and reciting in a sing-song voice. The child may or may not approximate the text in the book. While this is certainly not adult behavior, it is developmentally appropriate for the young child. It is particularly easy to demonstrate the innovative behavior and developmental nature of children's early writing attempts (writing is discussed later in this chapter).

Those who have studied development of children's literacy more recently than Piaget have continued to build on his ideas. Ferreiro and Teberosky (1982) add to the Piagetian view that children must be involved actively in reading and writing. They believe that children's concepts of reading and writing are shaped by related activities and tasks that parallel their understandings of other things in their world (Ferreiro, 1985). This theory is reflected in the common event of a child watching her mother write a letter. The child begins to question her mother about what she is doing or maybe even crawls up on her lap to watch. The mother provides the child with a paper and pencil to write a letter. The child pretends she is writing, folds the paper, and it is put into an envelope and mailed. The child learns about communication, the mail carrier and mailbox, letter writing, how to hold a pen, that letters are written on special paper, and so on. Written language was only one part of what the child learned. Thus, as children learn more about their world through experimentation and exploration, their understanding of written language expands. The belief that children's reading and writing are shaped by their play and experiences underscores the importance of involving children with print at an early age.

Many researchers (Harste, Woodward, & Burke, 1984; Teale, 1984) emphasize the social aspect of early literacy. Since children almost always live in an environment that involves more than one person, they learn language as they interact with others. From a very early age, children want and need to communicate and their attempts to use language are based on the need and desire to make their thoughts and wishes known to others. Children learn language to get things done—by explaining, imagining, requesting, protesting, or asserting. Children find it necessary to express meanings for a variety of reasons and purposes (Watson, 1983). Learning language takes at least two individuals.

Written language development depends on interacting with others in another way, too. The responses to children's attempts at language indicate that adults expect and intend for children to communicate (Snow, 1983). Intention becomes an important motivator in children's early attempts at language. Motivated by the desire for children to communicate, parents of very young children respond to babbling as if it were talk. They may say, ''Is that want you want?'' or ''You don't say!'' to nonsense sounds made by the child. The expectation that children will learn language provides feedback from adults and motivates children's early attempts.

The association of meaning with print is evident as children begin to read and write. Children who sit and go through the motions of reading a text intend for the book to reflect what they know about print. They use pictures or memory to pretend to read aloud and mimic adults who have shared books with them. Children who write fully intend to convey meaning (Watson, 1983). Children will scribble long, involved messages and hand them to adults to read. If the adult asks the child what it says, the child will respond with the message intended.

Another consideration is the recognition of the impact of the home environment on learning. The experiences that children have with print at home affect their views of reading and writing during instruction. Children's homes offer a great diversity of experiences. Teachers of beginning readers should be prepared to provide a variety of experiences for children from different backgrounds. The value of reading, the accessibility of material for reading and writing, and the opportunity to experiment with print before school must be considered when planning instruction for beginning readers.

Finally, there is the relationship between reading and writing. The interrelatedness of the language process is by far one of the most important ideas affecting early literacy instruction in the last decade. Numerous researchers '' . . . have moved away from defining reading and writing separately and toward defining them more broadly as literacy,'' according to Sulzby (1986, p. 219). The recognition of the reading–writing relationship implies that beginning reading instruction cannot exist without writing. The two processes are mutually supportive, and teaching reading and writing should not be isolated.

There are many ideas about how children learn to read and write. Children learn to read and write when the environment provides them with opportunities to experiment with print actively and interact with others about their efforts. Even when they have opportunities for experimentation, children develop differently, according to their own needs. As children begin learning about print, they begin displaying certain behaviors.

Emerging Literacy Behaviors

There are several behaviors children display that should be recognized, identified, encouraged, and expected. They often are overlooked because teachers and other adults do not know what to anticipate. Even the children themselves don't realize that certain behaviors suggest that they are well on their way to reading and writing. An awareness of what children do as they learn about reading helps teachers encourage young readers and writers.

Reading

Holdaway (1979) identifies reading-like behavior as an important feature of early literacy. He suggests that children produce ''spontaneous approximations'' of adult reading behaviors. They may sit with a book, cross their legs, turn pages in order, and repeat words in a sing-song manner, mimicking adults. Much of what very young children do when learning how to read and write is spontaneous and joyful (Strickland & Morrow, 1988) and has been described as ''literacy play.''

Children demonstrate a knowledge of books and reading in several different ways (Robeck & Wiseman, 1982). They may recognize that books are to read, know that words are in books, understand certain labels associated with books (such as titles, authors, and pages), recognize other reading material, separate print from pictures, and indicate some understanding of proper sequence in print. Some children may be able to isolate a single word from all the words on a page, match spoken and written words, and even read. Observation of children who have not begun their formal schooling indicates how much can be learned by young children naturally.

Most book use and reading can be clustered (Lass, 1982): 1) interest in and skill with print, 2) interest in and ability with written words, 3) interest in books as playthings, 4) enjoyment of the content of books, 5) oral language play, and 6) interest in writing. The six categories of early reading behavior indicate that children have a lot to learn. Most of these behaviors can appear quite early in a child's life under the right conditions.

Researchers have provided quite a long list of what young children do that indicates they are beginning to understand the reading process. *Memory reading* is one example.

Many parents describe how their young children will not allow them to miss words or skip pages during bedtime reading. After hearing a book read several times, young children will be able to recite or "read" the book as well as an efficient reader. Doake (1980) describes the word-by-word recitation of a text as *memory reading* and gives it as evidence that young children are becoming aware of what is involved in the reading process. Doake points out that early experiences with print encourage young children to begin developing an understanding of what must occur during reading. As a result, many children demonstrate the very close approximation of reading a text by memory and mimicking the actions of an efficient reader. He feels that memory reading is a necessary behavior that many children will attempt before becoming efficient readers. In any case, children who are demonstrating memory reading are very aware of the reading process and it usually is only a matter of time before memory readers can read unfamiliar print.

Everyday print plays an important part in children's early reading attempts (McGee & Richgels, 1990). Since children's daily routines place them in contact with street signs, food labels, and commercial advertisements they may learn a great deal about the print in their environment. Much of their initial understanding of literacy comes from what they learn from cereal boxes, candy wrappers, and television advertisements. Most children recognize the STOP in signs, the EXIT above doors, and the McDonald's symbol and name. Print and its familiar uses may form the basis for early reading.

Everyday print can become a part of the classroom. Familiar printed items such as a McDonald's bag, cereal boxes, and milk cartons can be used to encourage reading and writing. Children can transfer their knowledge about everyday print to classroom activities as they write about grocery story adventures, list favorite toys, read and write about favorite restaurants, and so on. Some teachers allow their beginning readers to include words from everyday print in lists of "Words I Can Read." Teachers can use everyday print to introduce numerous reading and writing activities.

Writing

Children learn about reading and writing in concert. There is a basic connection in the two processes at the beginning phases of learning (Henderson, 1986). As children begin demonstrating reading-like behaviors, they also are capable of producing many writing-like behaviors.

Drawing and scribbling play an important role in writing development. Children begin learning about writing tools and the basics of making marks on the paper with their first drawings and scribbles. They may find that using a writing tool is fun while they are learning to control their movements (McGee & Richgels, 1990). Often, early drawing represents a message or some other meaning the child wishes to convey. It is not long before children attempt to tell stories or explain concepts associated with their drawings. The drawings become symbols for objects or ideas. When children begin to view their drawings as ways to convey ideas or make rudimentary attempts to label their work, their drawings can be said to be representative. Representative drawings are often a child's first attempt to convey meaning through written symbols.

Drawing and scribbling precede use of letter-like forms and real letters. As children are exposed to print and continue to experiment with producing written forms, they may begin to produce letter-like figures as Figure 5.1 illustrates. It is not long until they

FIGURE 5-1 Producing letter-like figures demonstrates that children are beginning to realize that writing has certain forms.

begin to write some recognizable letters, usually those that are in their names. Activities should encourage experimentation with written language and recognize the importance these early attempts have on learning.

Read (1975) has shown that while children's first attempts to write may not appear too meaningful because of the random arrangement of letters and unconventional spelling, children often are using printed language meaningfully. Using several features of letters, children create their own spellings, which Read has termed *invented spellings*. Read (1975) and Chomsky (1976) believe that inventing spelling is a concrete way for children to acquire written language.

Read (1975) identifies several features of invented spelling. In early attempts, one letter may represent an entire word. For 5-year-old Ericka, IHRADIKDALSNO meant "I hate rain and I kinda like snow."

Michael used letter names to represent certain phonemes as he wrote the query, "HOWOLDIS YOURHILD" ("How old is your child?"). Here his spelling of *child* begins with an *H*, probably because the letter name for *h* articulates the *sh* or *ch* sound (āch). Michael did this again when he wrote, "I WOULD LIKE TO GO A PISHOR" ("I would like to draw a picture"). The soft *g* sound forms the same mouth position as the *dr* in draw, and to this 5-year-old, *go* appeared to be the logical choice of letters to represent the sounds articulated in *draw*.

As children continue to learn about written language, they begin using vowels in their invented spellings. Beers (1980) calls this strategy *vowel substitution*. Children spell long vowels by matching the sound that is heard, as Ericka did when she spelled *snow* "Sno." Other vowel sounds may be represented by close approximations of sounds and letter names. Children's first attempts at vowel usage often involve substitution of one vowel for another. Chris substituted vowels as he wrote "I'M rollre skateing vare her so mI Foot is herteen" ("I'm roller skating very hard, so my foot is hurting").

Close scrutiny of children's writing reveals much experimentation (Holdaway, 1979). One young writer produced a book with the contraction *I'm* spelled "II'm," "i'm," and "Iemm." This writer did not produce the correct spelling but showed he had learned enough to start writing close approximations of the word he wanted.

Young children's writing offers a great deal of information about their control of and capabilities in written language. They may produce unconventional writing, but children intend for their writing to have meaning. Adults who are translating their writing may need to ask children to interpret messages and explain their intentions. When children begin talking about their own language, knowledgeable adults note another demonstration of emerging literacy.

Knowledge and Control of Reading

One of the more recently identified factors affecting children's beginning literacy skills is their ability to explain how written language is used and how it works. A child's explicit consciousness of the language process may result in his or her ability to discuss, direct, and control attempts at reading and writing (Morrow, 1989). The knowledge and ability to discuss and control reading and writing are known as *metalinguistic aware-*

ness. Young children's metalinguistic awareness may be one of the best measures of their later abilities in reading and writing.

Conversations that reveal metalinguistic knowledge may reflect some of the delightful experimentation evident in children's beginning reading development. The following conversation between a five-year-old and his mother demonstrates one child's emerging metalinguistic knowledge:

> *The mother was driving and the child was in the passenger seat studying the name of the car, which was written on the glove compartment.*

Child: Mom, (pointing to the name *Pacer* written on the glove compartment) the "cee" in Pacer should really be an "ess."

Mother: Why do you say that, Chris?

Child: Because that "cee" makes exactly the same sound as the "ess" in *stop sign.*

Chris was using his own experiences and knowledge to make sense of the messages in his world and to explain how he thought language should work. Although the explanation is not accurate, Chris is displaying a developing metalinguistic knowledge by attempting to talk about language and its uses.

Young children demonstrate their metalinguistic knowledge in very specific ways (Rowe & Harste, 1986). When they correct themselves or realize that they have produced or read print that is not standard, they are indicating that they have knowledge of their language. Children also demonstrate metalinguistic knowledge when they attempt to make sense of how language works, as the conversation between Chris and his mother demonstrated. Finally, when children attempt to transfer their knowledge of language from one situation to another, they are indicating that they have developed metalinguistic knowledge. If Chris had used his understanding of the *s* sound from *stop* to explain why he spelled a word in a certain way, he would have been transferring his knowledge from one situation to another.

Children often are able to demonstrate their metalinguistic abilities when discussing their writing attempts. They may identify the purpose of writing, explain why they are spelling words in a particular way, or what their inventions mean. Sometimes it is easiest to observe metalinguistic abilities during writing because a product evolves and children have something to discuss.

Changing Views of Literacy Development

For years it was accepted that reading readiness was measured with standardized tests. The assumption behind reading readiness was that children must learn specific skills before they can read and write. Children were tested on such things as letter name knowledge, visual discrimination, and auditory discrimination. Often, writing was not encouraged until children exhibited certain reading-related skills.

The reading readiness view is not as widely accepted as it once was. While there are still reading programs that treat emerging literacy as a uniform process, recent research discourages this view and suggests that there is no magic number of words children need to recognize, letters they need to be able to form, or words they have to be able to spell before they can be encouraged to read and write by themselves (Newman, 1985). Although they may not produce conventional responses to written language, even very young children demonstrate strategies that allow them to explore the world of print through their reading and writing.

Beginning reading and writing instruction should include recognition of children's print-related knowledge. Most children arrive at school with a great deal of information about literacy, and teachers need to discover what young children understand and how they can use their knowledge about reading and writing. This can be done best by observing experimentation and sharing during reading and writing activities (Hall, 1987).

Assumptions of Emerging Literacy

What we know about how young children learn to read and write suggests several important ideas and assumptions that can be applied to early instruction. The major goal of formalized instruction should be to extend the literacy development of the preschool years and help children build reading skills as they learn to enjoy reading. There are several ways to promote literacy, and they are surprisingly easy to incorporate in early school experiences.

Young Children Need a Print Rich Environment in Order to Become Literate

From the moment children are born they are surrounded by oral language. The noises and sounds of their world are difficult to avoid, and it isn't long before a young child begins experimenting and playing with talking. The same circumstances apply to establishing a learning environment for reading and writing. Children should be surrounded by print and reasons to learn and use print. Where there are reasons for learning to read and write and children cannot avoid exposure to written language, learning to read and write can occur as naturally as learning to speak (Cambourne, 1988). Written language must be an important part of children's daily lives.

The Most Important Activities for Children Who Are Learning to Read and Write Are Reading and Writing

Early instruction should provide numerous opportunities for developing literacy skills and practicing reading and writing. There should be many opportunities to handle and read books. Writing has not always been considered an important aspect of beginning reading instruction, but recent research and instructional trends emphasize the impact of writing on reading development. Even very young children can be exposed to books, paper, and pencils and be encouraged to learn their uses in concrete ways.

Children Should Be Allowed to Produce Responses That Are Not Conventional

Young learners will not demonstrate standard, conventional behaviors during their first reading and writing attempts. This is particularly apparent in their writing. Children need opportunities to experiment with language and should be encouraged to continue their attempts at both reading and writing. Teachers need to recognize that certain unconventional behaviors such as memory reading and invented spellings are acceptable. An environment that encourages the risk-taking associated with beginning reading and writing rewards approximations (Cambourne, 1988).

Children Should Learn to Read and Write in an Environment That Includes Social Interaction

Social interaction provides motivation and enjoyment for children as they read and write. It also furnishes occasions for children to receive feedback about their reading and writing endeavors to guide their literacy development. The feedback they get will determine much of how they feel about reading and themselves as language users. Feedback must be nonthreatening and should encourage children to continue to take the risks necessary for learning to read (Buchanan, 1980).

Beginning Reading Instruction

Children arrive for their first day of school with a variety of print-related knowledge. The knowledge young children possess is neither generic nor consistent. Their abilities and experiences with print already differ in kindergarten. Children may need different kinds of practice with print, depending on what they have experienced before coming to school.

Once teachers understand beginning literacy behavior and how children go about acquiring the behaviors, an effective instructional program can be developed. Literature-based reading instruction offers many opportunities to support children. Literature contributes to positive self-concepts, offers many opportunities for developing fluency in reading and writing, and focuses on meaningful experience (Weaver, 1990).

Children's Literature

Children's literature is a necessity in beginning reading instruction. Literature does more than teach beginning readers how to read; it also contributes to language development, amuses the senses, allows response and emotion, and exposes children to thoughts and ideas (Jalongo, 1988). All kinds of literature can be used during children's initial encounters with print, but when teachers begin introducing children to reading strategies and children first attempt to read on their own, there are certain types of literature that can encourage and support their efforts.

Predictable Books

Books particularly good for beginning reading are those with text that is predictable in some way. Since prediction is such a necessary reading strategy, it is important to include books that allow children to use their knowledge of language and the world around them. Several favorite children's books illustrate the features of a predictable

book. Repeated phrases in a book like *Brown Bear, Brown Bear* (Martin, 1983) allow
children to anticipate the text easily.

> Brown Bear,
> Brown Bear,
> What do you see?
> I see a redbird
> looking at me.
> Redbird,
> redbird,
> What do you see?
> I see a yellow duck
> looking at me.
> Yellow duck,
> yellow duck,
> What do you see?

Bill Martin provides a lively text that is easy to remember and predict as early as
the first reading.

Most predictable books provide a very close match between text and pictures. *The
Bus Ride* (1971) has a simple picture of a girl getting on a bus; the words below the
picture read, "The girl got on the bus." By expressing exactly what is depicted in the
picture, children "read" the text that appears on the page. *The Very Hungry Caterpillar*
(Carle, 1970) provides two familiar sequences (e.g., Monday, Tuesday, Wednesday, and
one, two, three) that allow children to use familiar information to predict what will come
next in a story. Text that reads, "On Monday, I ate one apple,/ On Tuesday, I ate two
pears . . ." allows children to predict that by Wednesday the caterpillar will eat three
items. All three of these classic examples of predictable books provide text with familiar
vocabulary and language. Children love these books, and their predictable texts encourage
reading-like behavior after introduction.

Cumulative style is a special case of predictable books. *Drummer Hoff* (Emberly,
1967), with its building of characters and action, provides many opportunities for
children to predict the text. On the first page the text reads, "Drummer Hoff fired it
off," followed by the second page, which reads, ". . . Sargeant Crowder brought the
powder, but Drummer Hoff fired it off . . ." Each page adds another character who
contributes to the action, and another line is added to the text. Rhyme and rhythm also
produce predictable stories. Poetry and song can be learned easily and read as children
identify the rhyme and rhythm.

Predictable books are extremely valuable because children quickly learn the repetitive patterns and use the predictability to understand what efficient readers must do.
Predictable books introduce them to methods of prediction (Tompkins & Webeler, 1983)
and that strategy helps them with comprehension. Sharing predictable books with children helps them develop a love for reading, feel successful about reading, learn about
the reading process, and develop concepts about print and story. A list of predictable
books is included at the end of the chapter.

Big Books

Big books are oversize versions of children's books. Most big books are predictable and are used in beginning reading programs, although they can be used effectively with older efficient readers in special instances. (Using a big book as a model for older children who are producing books for young children would be an example.) The text and illustrations of a big book are large enough to enable a group of children to read the print and see the details of the pictures. With a book of traditional size, only one or two children who are close to the teacher can read the print as the story is read aloud. Big books are designed for the home reading or the *lap method* at bedtime when parent and child sit closely together and read. The proximity of the two allow the child to follow the text as the mother reads and rereads the story.

Many children's literature and basal publishing companies are producing oversize editions of favorite children's books, and it may be difficult to select which books are good for use in the classroom. Criteria for picture books can provide a guide for selecting commercial big books. These books should meet the criteria for high quality children's literature (see chap. 2). They also should be made of durable materials, be illustrated with pictures that are easy to see, and use type that is easy to read from a distance.

The instructional procedures for big books and predictable books are similar. Basically, children are exposed to repeated readings and encouraged to predict and read along. As children follow along as the words are read, they begin to recognize individual words and letters and associate meaning and the printed symbols. The big books offer the advantage of being able to share the text and allow children the chance to develop concepts about words, letters, and punctuation as the teacher reads aloud (Holdaway, 1979). Reading along with predictable books allows children to mimic successful reading behavior (Lynch 1986).

Big books and predictable books enable teachers to extend joyful reading experiences to groups of children. Positive reading activities in early school years can affect attitudes and achievement in later reading. Handy and Holdaway (1980) consider the enjoyment of early reading experiences to be the single most important condition for reading achievement.

Children benefit from teachers reading predictable and big books aloud, but additional activities should be part of classroom use. There are some specific procedures for instructional uses of both types of books.

Introduction

The reading aloud of a predictable or big book can begin with the entire class discussing book covers and illustrations on the front cover. Children can discuss the term *title* and predict a title for the book, based on the cover illustrations. After children have made several predictions, the teacher can read the title while pointing to the words on the front cover. The teacher next solicits predictions about what will happen in the story. As children make suggestions, the teacher should record them on the board or a chart for further reference.

The front cover of the story can be opened, and the children can investigate the inside pages. This is the time to discuss the publication information, title page, and dedications. The teacher can point to and read the author's name and explain that the author is the person who wrote the book. The illustrator can be introduced in the same way. This is an excellent time to focus on parts of the books and to introduce terminology such as author, illustrator, copyright, and dedication.

Reading

Before the teacher reads the text the predictions can be reviewed. During the initial reading, the entire story is read aloud from beginning to end. The story is read enthusiastically to make the reading experience enjoyable. At the end of the reading, the predictions are reread and compared with what really happened in the story. Children can be asked to share their reactions to the story.

Repeated Reading

The stories can be reread as often as children want to hear them. Children may respond to the rereadings in several different ways. They may repeat phrases immediately after the teacher has read (*echo reading* is described later in this chapter). During repeated readings children can be encouraged to read the predictable phrase each time it appears. As soon as children have the confidence, they should read along in parts they know. After several readings children will read the story in unison.

Many of the big-book publishers provide small individual books to accompany the large books. Small reproductions of the books increase the value of oral reading experiences immensely. As the teacher reads the large version, the children can handle the smaller books, turn the pages, and follow along as the story is read.

Discussions of the stories provide opportunities for literary terms to be introduced and discussed. Pointing out the characters and the setting in picture books is the first step to identifying and developing an understanding of literature.

Extending the Stories

There are many ways to use the stories of predictable and big books. Predictable texts can easily be made into oral cloze (Holdaway, 1979) activities in which children provide words omitted by the reader. *Cloze* is a strategy in which a reader inserts a word that has been omitted from a text. While reading *The Very Hungry Caterpillar* (Carle, 1970) aloud, the adult reader can omit the days of the week or the numbers for the children to insert. *Brown Bear, Brown Bear* (Martin, 1983) invites participation by filling in omitted phrases and words during the oral reading. The oral cloze procedure helps a child confirm the predictability of written language. Nursery rhymes and highly predictable poetry also would be effective oral cloze material.

Another activity that uses predictable and big books also provides reading and writing experience. A book with a repeated phrase is read to children. The teacher and class discuss the repeated phrase and reread parts of the story that include the phrase. Finally, individual children are asked to produce an original phrase modeled on the phrase in the book. The phrase is written on paper and the child illustrates it. This procedure was used with *Rain Makes Applesauce* (Scheer, 1964), which "talks silly talk" with such phrases as "Monkeys live in gumdrop trees and Rain Makes Applesauce/Stars are made of soap, soap, soap and Rain Makes Applesauce." After reading

Predictable books, such as Rain Makes Applesauce, *involve beginning readers in reading, writing, oral language, and artwork.*

and discussing the story, 5-year-old Hillary dictated: "I wear my bathing suit without no top and Rain Makes Applesauce." Her friend Dustin wrote, "Clouds hid in a tree and Rain Makes Applesauce."

Both children illustrated their phrases, which became a part of a book produced by their kindergarten class. In addition to verbally recalling their personal contributions to the book, many children were able to "read" their classmates' contributions (see Figure 5.2).

Wordless Picture Books

Wordless picture books can be enjoyed and understood by children of different backgrounds, cultures, languages, and reading levels. Because the stories are conveyed through pictures, the books appeal to many different reading situations. "Wordless books are ideal for encouraging language growth, stimulating intellectual development, motivating creative writing, and evaluating a child's language skills," Norton writes (1990, p. 180). These books are particularly valuable for classrooms in which children speak languages other than English as their primary languages.

In wordless picture books, a sequence of detailed illustrations tells the story. Even with pictures, the story is often repetitive, so the predictable nature of the implied text helps the reader read the story presented in the illustrations.

FIGURE 5-2 A teacher read *Rain Makes Applesauce* and the children talked "silly talk" before writing captions and drawing pictures to illustrate their dictations.

Wordless picture books provide a wonderful opportunity for children to become authors. Children can discuss the pictures and write the story from their perspective. Although technically the children are only writing (or dictating) their personal interpretations of the illustrations, they are authors of the text as they interpreted it. Children's interpretations can be dictated and recorded by the teacher, by an older student from a different grade, or can be recorded by the children themselves. Final productions can be bound and should be read, reread, used, and valued as significant contributions to the classroom library (See Figure 5.3).

FIGURE 5-3 After studying and discussing the wordless picture book, *A Boy, a Dog, and a Frog,* Hamon, a second grader, dictated this text to his teacher. After the story was typed, he and his mother illustrated the story.

The boy woke up the next morning, and the frog was gone.

The boy looked into his boot and into the jar.

He opened the window and called the frog and said, "Where are you, my frog?"

The boy said, "Where are you, my frog?" Down fell the dog.

Easy to Read Books

Easy to read books are designed specifically for children with beginning reading skills (Norton, 1990). Usually, easy to read books contain pictures and text that match, just as in a picture book. However, the stories usually are written with a controlled vocabulary so that young readers can read the text independently. Controlled vocabularies may place such restrictions on language used in the text as using a certain number of words to tell the entire story, allowing only words that contain a limited number of letters, or using sentences that do not exceed a certain number of words.

Controlling the vocabulary sometimes results in very contrived and stilted language and often the books do not meet high literary standards. But some authors have managed to produce delightful books even with the language constraints. Arnold Lobel has produced several examples of high quality, easy-to-read books with his award-winning Frog and Toad stories.

The Basal Approach

The basal approach to reading instruction embraces the assumption that beginning readers must possess certain skills before learning to read. Kindergarten and first grade basals have as their goal the mastery of a list of skills very similar to this:

- Recognizing shapes and colors
- Matching parts of objects to the complete object
- Matching words
- Learning about capital and lowercase letters
- Identifying initial consonants
- Recalling details
- Forming categories
- Summarizing
- Sequencing
- Predicting
- Building background
- Rhyming words
- Context clues

The instructional sequence for beginning readers provides opportunities for them to practice the skills associated with prereading levels. Workbook activities, discussion questions, and other classroom activities focus on developing an understanding of skills. Often the basal readers focus on oral language as an essential part of beginning to read. Many activities will be suggested to encourage children to discuss, describe, answer questions, and share ideas. Eventually the focus on oral language guides teachers to write down children's language to use as reading material (see the section on language experience). The basals developed for beginning reading instruction have pictures to initiate discussions, pages with single letters representing the illustrations, and one word texts that give children practice recognizing words on sight. Decoding, vocabulary development, and oral reading are skills that become the focus of instruction. Many of the more recently published basals include children's literature selections and writing activities to complement the instruction. Workbooks, stories written on large charts, and cards with single words to be learned are designed to coordinate with skills, literature selections, basal texts, and oral language activities during instruction.

The basal activities for beginning readers should be evaluated and used with the same considerations mentioned in the discussion of basal readers. It is particularly important to evaluate basal readers by comparing the strategies with what we know about emerging literacy. The instructional approach should encourage the behaviors associated with early reading and writing, foster risk-taking and experimentation, focus on meaning, and invite social interaction. Basal approaches and activities that use children's literature to support language learning opportunities can be a valuable resource for the teacher of beginning readers. However, basal series and activities used to the exclusion of children's literature and that fail to encourage some of the activities that are known to encourage literacy development should be avoided.

Specific Strategies

There are many different activities and strategies particularly appropriate for beginning reading instruction. Whether they use the basal reader, children's literature, or a combination of the two approaches, teachers will identify several instructional techniques that they feel are effective with children who are learning to read. Some activities should always be part of children's first experiences in school, no matter what instructional approach is used or what the teacher prefers.

Reading Aloud

The single activity most important for ensuring success in reading is reading aloud to children (Chomsky, 1972). Frequently reading a variety of material aloud encourages children to expand their listening, speaking, and writing vocabularies and increases their knowledge of books.

Reading aloud is fun, simple, and cheap (Trelease, 1989). There is not an easier activity to plan, implement, and enjoy.

Although each teacher establishes a routine for reading aloud, the following sequence illustrates the range of possibilities (Butler, 1988):

Plan
Select and read a book before presenting it to the children. Teachers who share a book without reading it themselves are inviting trouble over content. Many modern books contain themes and language that might be offensive to parents. Even picture books can include topics, pictures, and certain ideas that can cause controversy. *Sylvester and the Magic Pebble* (Steig, 1969), an award winner, has caused concern because of its stereotypical portrayal of a mother who waits on the father, does all the cooking and cleaning, and knits in her spare time. Sendak's intriguing fantasy, *In the Night Kitchen* (1970), once was kept off library shelves because a nude child became part of a dream. A recent version of *Little Red Riding Hood* was banned in one California school district

because Little Red Riding Hood carried a bottle of wine to her grandmother. Picture books that include questionable material may be unavoidable, but teachers should be prepared for children's questions or responses.

Reading aloud can simply be for pure enjoyment or can result in assignments. If the intent is other than simple enjoyment, the purpose should be identified and some planning should be done. Reading aloud might introduce a topic or theme for study, a story, author or illustrator, a new genre, literary devices, or material for discussion and activities. When a specific instructional objective is intended, the teacher should plan fully to ensure a solid and productive lesson.

Set the Scene with Children

Prediction is a good introduction to reading aloud. Read the title, show the cover, and discuss what the children think the story will be about. Children can predict what type of story they expect as well as its story line. If information about the author is available, a discussion may be appropriate before reading aloud.

An important part of setting the scene for reading aloud is to help the children link the story with their own experiences. This can be accomplished by reminding them of other, similar stories they may have read or by discussing activities that relate to the story. Such background should be provided especially when the story contains new or unfamiliar concepts.

Read the Text

The story should be read with expression, and the teacher should demonstrate that reading aloud is an enjoyable experience. Children will use the teacher as a model for their own oral reading performances.

Discuss the Story

Even if the reading aloud is for pure enjoyment, the children probably will want to discuss the story or even hear parts of it read again. There is nothing wrong with taking time to discuss parts of a wonderful book the class has discovered.

Reading aloud often is the first step to additional reading, writing, drama, artwork, or other types of play. The number of appropriate activities is almost infinite.

Two warnings about organizing the reading aloud time are in order. Teachers should not overlook the value of spontaneity. If another teacher or child wishes to share a new-found book, that is certainly enough to warrant taking time to read the story. (The only caution with spontaneous reading is to be relatively certain that there is no objectional material in the book.) Teachers also should feel comfortable about voicing opinions or putting a book aside. If children's interests are waning or there is a sense that they are not enjoying the book being read aloud, there is nothing wrong with acknowledging it. This tells children that they may exercise taste.

Language Experience

Language experience is an instructional approach to beginning reading that involves the learners' experiences, thoughts, and language to produce class-written material for the children to read. The teacher acts as a scribe and writes what the children have to say. The result becomes reading material used in instruction.

Language experience is very flexible and can be used with different size groups, readers of different abilities, in many situations, and to satisfy several instructional objectives. Burke and Jurenka (undated) suggest the following sequence for instruction:

1. Provide or focus in on an experience. An experience that easily adapts to whole class or small group instruction is sharing a piece of literature. Other activities that provide material for language experience might include any event that happens in the classroom, the community, world, or school.

2. Establish a reason for recording the experience. A reason for recording what children say makes the experience more meaningful and exciting. The reason may be as simple as providing text for children to illustrate or adding their version of a particular story to the classroom collection. Identifying the purpose allows children to consider their audience and format.

3. Discuss ideas before recording them. Discussion is one of the most critical aspects of language experience. Talking about the story invites young learners to explore all aspects of the experience. The teacher can use questions to clarify and expand ideas. The discussion should be used to elevate language experience from a list of events to a narrative or exposition.

4. Record what the children dictate. As children begin telling the story or describing events, the role of the teacher changes from leader to scribe. As teachers write what children dictate, they can help their students expand, clarify, and illustrate the text. Teachers will want to follow certain conventions as they record the children's ideas:

a. Use standard English spellings, regardless of dialect. Record *eds* and *s* endings whether they are enunciated or not.
b. Use standard punctuation. Language experience is a demonstration of punctuation and other conventions.
c. Use children's grammar and vocabulary. This is sometimes difficult for teachers who want to correct children so they will learn proper usage. It is important for children to see their ideas reproduced as they expressed them.

5. Reread and edit the story. The session should not end without the children hearing the completed text read aloud. The children should get an overall feel for what they dictated, and they should be allowed to change or add information to the text. This is a wonderful way to demonstrate and teach editing skills. Editing is particularly easy if the teacher has access to a word processor. One first grade teacher made changes on a large chart with carets, mark-overs, arrows, and writing in the margins. The first graders recopied the text to publish the book. It was no surprise that the children who had been exposed to all this scribbling and editing demonstrated editing skills when they wrote.

6. Reread the children's narrative at a later date. Too often, language experience activities end after the first reading and children never see the dictated texts again. There are many ways to preserve and reread their texts. Stories and texts may be preserved in a wall chart, duplicated and copied for each child, produced in a class book, typed and bound in limited edition library books, published as a shape books, produced as collections on file cards, filed in folders, or displayed on bulletin boards.

When the texts are preserved, they can be read by many people, including the author, the subject of the story, parents, other children in the room or school, classroom visitors and helpers, or other adults in the school. One first grade teacher regularly sends collections of class narratives home for children and parents to share.

Almost anything can become a subject for dictation. Donna Logan had her kindergarten class dictate its experiences in making a jack-o-lantern. Later, she typed the narrative in large type and sent the story home with each child (see Box 5.1).

Captions

Caption writing is an experience for very young children. After children draw pictures, cut them out of magazines, or take photographs, they dictate captions for the pictures.

BOX 5-1 ━━

How To Make a Jack-o-lantern
written by K–11 kids

Brett and his mother brought us a pumpkin Friday afternoon. The pumpkin came from Milano.

Monday, we cut the pumpkin. We laid out the newspaper on the round table. Mrs. Logan got the spoon, the blue bowl, the little knife and the big knife and the black pen.

Mrs. Logan drew the eyes, the nose, the mouth, the ears and the top. She cut the "loop loop" top. The top wouldn't pull off. We thought a monster was holding the lid on. We thought Peter's wife was in the pumpkin. We thought a mouse was holding the lid on. Finally, Mrs. Logan got it off.

Mrs. Logan got the gunk out. The gunk looked like orange spider webs. The pumpkin had a whole lot of gunk in it.

Next, Mrs. Logan cut the triangle eyes out. Mrs. Logan cut the circle nose out. Mrs. Logan cut a big smile with three teeth. Mrs. Logan cut two square ears out, so the jack-o-lantern could hear and learn.

Next, we had to clean the mess up.

Then, Mrs. Logan put a candle on a pan and put it inside the jack-o-lantern. Mrs. Logan lit the candle and turned the lights out. The room looked:

like a sunshine
like the jack-o-lantern glowing in the dark,
spooky and
like Halloween.

K–11 is how Logan's school identifies her classroom. She often refers to her children as "K–11 kids." Dictated Oct. 28, 1990.

The teacher writes a caption down exactly as the child states it. This material is reread to the children, and they are encouraged to repeat what they have written. Captioned pictures can be displayed on bulletin boards, hung on clotheslines with clothespins and strung across a wall, or bound in a class publication.

Writing captions is a good way to begin each kindergarten or first grade day. As children arrive in the morning, they meet with the teacher or an aide who takes a sentence or two of dictation. After they have their dictated sentences, the children can be invited to draw pictures to illustrate their sentences. The finished products can be displayed on a bulletin board or some other manner and become the publication for the day.

Supportive Reading

Strategies for beginning readers should include activities that deliberately provide support and help in reading in one of four ways (Buchanan, 1980):

- using material that is meaningful and purposeful,
- using predictable material,
- practicing the material, or
- reading aloud with another person or group.

Supportive strategies allow children to enjoy good literature and to internalize the rhythm and flow of language as they gain confidence in their reading abilities. Repeated readings, choral readings, paired readings, and assisted readings are examples of supportive reading techniques.

Repeated Readings

Repeated, shared reading provides enjoyment and a meaningful context for beginning reading instruction. Each rereading should have a definite purpose. Repeated reading allows children and teachers to enjoy the story, discuss what happened, identify familiar words, and focus on parts of the books, vocabulary, prediction skills, or other aspects of reading. When children are beginning to read, repeated readings increase fluency (Rhodes & Dudley-Marling, 1988) and help them maintain the natural flow of language as they read.

Repeated readings of a text or part of the text aloud provide safe situations for young readers to experiment with print. As the teacher leads a group in repeated readings, correct handling of books and the actual mechanics of reading, such as following print, turning pages, and left to right progression, become internalized (Baskwill & Whitman, 1986).

One behavior that evolves from reading and rereading a story is memory reading. Young children who are not yet efficient at reading often ask to hear favorite books read repeatedly until they are able to recite the text from memory. Memory reading or reciting the text verbatim is a valuable contribution to efficient reading behavior (Doake, 1980). Repeated readings in the classroom allow children to gain experience with fluent reading. When the teacher does not have the time to participate in numerous repeated readings, tape recordings (either commercial or prepared by individuals working with children) provide a way for children to hear the story over and over. However, the importance of adult–child contact during reading should not be overlooked. Tapes and records only supplement children's experiences with books and should never take the place of an adult reading to a child. As children become more and more familiar with the text, they should be encouraged to read the parts they know aloud.

Choral Reading

While group oral reading may occur spontaneously, choral reading occurs when more than one voice recites in unison to entertain another group. Choral reading is dramatic and provides an opportunity for children to read with expression and meaning. Many types of material can be presented effectively with choral reading. It is best to use short, simple, imaginative selections that can be interpreted by voices. Choral reading is a good time to use the wonderful poetry written for children.

One key to choral reading is allowing children to make decisions about interpretation. The rereading to prepare for choral reading provides a built-in purpose for repeated reading. They can tape their efforts and listen to their verbalizations to make decisions about rearranging voices.

Voices can be arranged in many different ways. The simplest arrangement is to direct the entire class to read in unison. But choral reading is more fun and interesting when different arrangements are established. One child could read a line with the entire class or groups of students responding. Voices can accumulate as a poem continues to develop a crescendo, or voices can gradually drop off for diminuendo. During repeated readings, children can make decisions about volume, intensity, and speed. In addition, they can add movement and action or sound effects to their dramatic interpretations. The children can present their production to other classes, parents, or a group of their classmates.

Paired Reading

Paired readings are recommended for emerging readers or for older students who focus on individual words and sounds at the expense of fluency. Paired reading teams two individuals for the purpose of reading aloud. Usually, one of the readers is able to better read the text than the other. Support for the less effective reader is provided by the more confident reader. Reading in unison allows less efficient readers to read chunks of meaning and increases their comprehension (Buchanan, 1980).

The instructional material for paired readings can be a text, whole story, or book. When one or both of the readers is not efficient at reading, the text should be one that students already have heard and enjoyed or one that is very predictable. If the students have not heard the text previously, the teacher can read the story aloud so the students can begin to develop an understanding of the story.

After the students have heard the story at least once, the couples attempt to read aloud with proper intonation and emphasis of meaningful words while maintaining a normal speed. One of the readers should be able to read without interruption since the goal of paired reading is to allow beginning readers to read an entire text with assistance. After the reading is completed, discussion of the plot, vocabulary, and the main idea can follow.

Paired reading provides support and demonstrates fluent reading. Children are not afraid to try reading when another voice supports their efforts. The reading can occur with pairs of children, small groups, teachers' aides, parents, or with a tape-recorded version of the story.

Vocabulary and Word Recognition

One traditional focus for beginning reading instruction is vocabulary and word recognition. The procedure for vocabulary and word recognition often consists of drills and practice with beginning word sounds with work sheets or flash cards to train children to recognize words on sight. While there may be some justification for occasional use of these routine activities, other activities encourage vocabulary and word recognition and use instructional time more effectively. Many of the strategies appropriate for beginning readers are discussed in the chapter on vocabulary and word identification, but there are some that benefit young children.

Reading

The most effective strategy for developing vocabulary and word recognition in very young readers is reading. Reading predictable books and participating in accompanying assignments provides opportunities for children to become familiar with words and to practice vocabulary in a meaningful way. As children read, they constantly are exposed to and become familiar with letters and words in context. When children learn to read a predictable book from beginning to end, they begin to recognize words that contribute to specific stories. As the list of known words lengthens, the sight words can be keys for decoding new words in new contexts.

Oral and Written Cloze

Using text from predictable books to develop oral and written cloze enhances vocabulary and word recognition. To complete an oral cloze, children are invited to supply words omitted when the teacher pauses.

Written cloze exercises can be prepared by recording sentences from a favorite story on the chalkboard or elsewhere, substituting a blank for a particular word. The children can be instructed to say ''blank'' when reading the sentence. After reading whole passages, children suggest words to complete the meaning of a sentence. The suggested words can be recorded and discussed to determine the effects of those words on the meaning of the sentence. Adaptations of cloze include supplying a consonant at the beginning of the blank, soliciting a list of words to fit the blank, and checking the list to find a word that begins with the same letter. Or, to illustrate correct grammar, the root word could be inserted in the blank and students could provide the correct ending.

Sentence Strips and Word Cards

Sentence strips give children opportunities to manipulate text. Sentences from texts, including all punctuation, can be written on strips of paper, then cut into smaller segments to divide words and parts of sentences. Children can arrange the strips to recreate sentences or create new ideas. Children may need to refer to the original sentences to help them build new ones.

Another method is to write familiar text on note cards, one word per card. Children can match word cards and sentences to the text of familiar stories. Big books are especially good for this activity. Word cards and sentences that match the text of big books can be distributed to the children to match their sentence strips with the text as the teacher reads aloud. This focuses children's attention on words and allows children to become aware of how words are used in reading.

Language Experience

Dictated stories can be used to focus on certain letters and words. When children dictate stories and watch teachers write the letters and words, they become aware of the sounds and representations of letters and words. As teachers write, they can discuss basic ideas about sound symbols, spellings, and language use. Children understand much more about letters, sounds, and words when they produce meaningful texts.

Alphabet Books

Alphabet books, such as *Animalia* (Base, 1986) and *The Z Was Zapped* (Van Allsburg, 1987), provide occasions for children to play with letters and words within the context of literature. The text calls attention to individual letters and their sounds. When interesting words such as those in *Animalia* (Base, 1986) are used, teachers and children alike will focus on the vocabulary.

Zoophabets (Tallon, 1979) is told with nonsense words that allow children to practice decoding without the help of context. The important benefit of using alphabet books is skill practice within the context of real reading. In addition, not many children can resist the combination of complex vocabulary and intriguing illustrations in many of the good alphabet books.

Some books focus on certain rhymes, letter groups, or letter families. A small book called *Andy: That's My Name* (dePaola, 1973) introduces the reader to Andy and some older boys who steal his name, which he was pulling in a wagon. The big kids make all the words they can from Andy's name while he repeatedly asks if he can have his name back. One first grade teacher uses this book to study the word family *and* and then gives each of the first graders wagons made of tag board that holds their own names spelled in movable letters. This activity begins a week-long study of the letters and sounds in each of the children's names.

Independent Reading

Very young children should have plenty of time to spend with books. All reading should not be scheduled, planned, or directed by the teacher. Some time should be allowed for children to pick out books, monitor their behavior, and engage in quiet reading time. A primary classroom must have a display of accessible books to encourage children to read in their free time.

Time with books can be scheduled or encouraged during free time or independent activity times. Sustained silent reading (SSR) is time during the school day for uninterrupted reading of books selected by the children. The unique aspect of SSR is that the teacher also reads. The presence of a teacher involved in reading demonstrates that reading is important. SSR for young children might be somewhat noisier and more active than for older readers and may last a shorter time. But young children can spend independent time with books and learn about reading by doing it and by observing the teacher reading.

Writing

School should provide young children with many opportunities to experiment with writing. Writing is learned most easily when it is directly related to reading activities. Reading and literature serve important roles in developing children's perception of themselves as writers. Conversely, writing provides children with a foundation for continuing to develop their reading. Exposure to print familiarizes them with print and the way it works. Also, writing allows children a concrete way to experiment with print and language.

Children learning in a print-rich environment will develop natural interest in writing. As they work to communicate their ideas, they will begin producing letters, spellings, and ideas. Through experimentation and the feedback available in the classroom, children begin establishing an understanding of written symbols.

One of the most effective learning situations for young writers is to simply allow them to experiment with writing. They should have a great deal of time to try writing on many types of paper with different implements. In kindergarten and first grade this can be as simple as providing a table, with paper, pens, pencils, and crayons, where children can experiment with writing. One kindergarten teacher covers a table with butcher paper and encourages her young writers to write on it with magic markers. After all the children have had a chance to write on the table (they call it their journal), the entire class assembles to read the messages. The large paper is hung on the wall for all to enjoy for the remainder of the day.

Language experience is a first step in encouraging writing behavior. Teachers who recognize the importance of allowing children to write their words on paper make sure that there is time each day to produce captioned pictures or other language experience activities. One kindergarten teacher begins each day by meeting with her students individually to write a caption that is illustrated and displayed on the bulletin board as the ''news of the day.'' At the end of the week each child has a packet to take home to show what has happened during the school week.

Learning Differences

Children come to school with very different experiences with books and print. Many of the differences owe to families' different approaches to written language. Certainly some differences can be attributed to culture and language, and the teacher of beginning readers should be aware of the effect of the variants.

Culture

Cultural differences do not mean that children should have difficulty learning to read. However, cultural differences may affect the *way* children learn to read. Teachers should carefully select materials and approaches so that children can use their backgrounds and experiences when learning to read. There are basically four factors that teachers who work with beginning readers of different cultures should consider: consideration of a cultural frame of reference, inclusion of familiar cultural patterns, use of appropriate materials, and acceptance of the child as an individual.

One way to recognize different backgrounds and experiences in the classroom is to employ examples that focus on a cultural frame of reference. This means that teachers should become acquainted with the cultural groups represented in the classrooms. Teachers can help beginning readers by using customs, holidays, food, dress, and family and community games during instruction. Often, the children can help by sharing their backgrounds. Culturally aware teachers can use the differences positively in reading instruction by allowing all children to see and understand different ways of celebrating, dressing, and viewing the world.

Beginning readers will be more successful if they can use familiar cultural structures and patterns to begin their school and reading experiences. For example, most classes are oriented to written language and quiet, independent completion of tasks. The children's community may value verbalization, extensive oral development, and group completion of tasks. There are some American ethnic groups that highly respect the verbalization and display of oral language and those who are capable of talking are valued in their communities. This is in direct contrast to the classroom that respects and honors those who are experienced with written language and can complete tasks nonverbally and without a great deal of explanation. The teacher who understands these differences will accept differences in verbalization and provide opportunities for oral response as well as for quiet, independent work.

The materials for beginning reading instruction easily can reflect the cultural diversity of our country. A special effort should be made to use books and materials that include characters of different cultural backgrounds. The basals and children's literature publishers are beginning to provide such books. Traditional literature offers many options for cultural representation in the primary classroom. There is no excuse for not representing many cultures with high quality literature that everyone will enjoy. When this is done, all children in the classroom learn more.

The teacher's acceptance of the individual child is important. Children should be aware that it is possible to be a successful learner in class and maintain their cultural identities and security. Teachers can recognize and use cultural differences in instruction and also accept each child as an individual who possesses valuable attributes and talents. When children are accepted as individuals, they are able to respect school routine and benefit from the learning opportunities that are available.

Language

There is a much debate over the language of instruction for beginning readers who do not speak English. One view is that non-English-speaking children should be provided with beginning reading instruction in their native languages as well as in English until they can read in both languages. Some educators and politicians fear that instruction in two languages interferes with socialization as well as the achievement of the child. However, there is considerable evidence that quality bilingual instruction does promote academic achievement. In addition, global interdependence suggests that bilingualism is necessary for economic and social success in the future.

Some of the goals and instructional objectives of beginning reading instruction are not easy to meet when many different languages are represented in one classroom. The problem is compounded when teachers and children do not speak the same language. There are techniques designed to help children who are speaking English as a second language that do not require the teacher to speak the language of the child.

The teacher who is not bilingual or has not received training in teaching English as a second language can modify the activities and principles suggested for English-speaking children. These modifications include using a great deal of oral language (speaking and listening) and concrete and nonprint experiences to build initial vocabulary for the children. In addition, children who do not speak English will benefit from repeated activities, topics, and materials.

Specific instructional activities that help children who are limited in their English proficiency are language experience, predictable reading, supportive reading, repeated readings, and narrow reading (Krashan, 1986). *Narrow reading* allows a child to read many stories on one topic or stories by the same author. The stories and reading material can discuss the topic in many different ways. Each exposure to the same topic provides another opportunity to familiarize students with the vocabulary and concepts associated with the idea. It is apparent that narrow reading builds confidence and background experience.

DISCUSSION AND ACTIVITIES

1. Share a predictable book with a young child. Experiment with oral cloze and see how children fill in omitted phrases during reading. Report to the class and explain what you think the child's responses told you about reading ability and knowledge.

2. Identify a predictable book that can be used to emphasize beginning consonant sounds, and design a discussion and lesson to focus a child's attention on letters in the context of the story.

3. Hand a young child a book and observe what he or she does with it. See how many beginning reading behaviors the child demonstrates. Do the same after providing a young child with paper and a pencil.

4. In a small group, review several alphabet books that might be useful for presenting letter and sound recognition to young children. Discuss with the group why a book would be especially appropriate for young children.

5. List some activities that you might expect preschool children to participate in at home. What are some similar instructional activities that would provide the same types of experience?

6. List some of the experiences and activities you feel are necessary for children to begin to develop literacy skills successfully.

RELATED READING

Professional Reading

Baskwill, J., & Whitman, P. (1986). *Whole language source book.* Ontario, Canada: Scholastic.

A particularly helpful book for a beginning teacher. It includes specific instructions for daily routines, units, and evaluation.

Bissex, G. (1980). *GNYS AT WRK: A child learns to write and read.* Cambridge, MA: Harvard University Press.

Glenda Bissex chronicles the development of her son's reading and writing during the first few years of his life. This is an excellent book for those who love to watch very young children figure out their world. In addition, the reader will have a much better understanding of literacy development after reading this book.

Harste, J., Woodward, V., & Burke, C. (1984). *Language stories and literacy lessons.* Portsmouth, NH: Heinemann.

The three educators have collaborated on beginning literacy and what should happen in the classroom. Their text is illustrated with many writing samples and anecdotes from young children.

Jalongo, M.R. (1988). *Young children and picture books: Literacy from infancy to six.* Washington, DC: National Association for the Education of Young Children.

Jalongo believes that children learn much from picture books and that the process must begin with enjoyment. This book explains how teachers and parents can establish an environment that allows a child to become excited about literature.

Krashan, R. (1986). *Inquiries and insights,* Haywood, CA: Alemany.

Krashan provides a great deal of information about children who speak other languages. Usually his books provide theory and classroom examples.

McGee, L.M., & Richgels, D. J. (1990). *Literacy's beginnings: Supporting young readers and writers.* Needham Heights, MA: Allyn and Bacon.

These two authors discuss beginning literacy in ways that reflect the latest research and ways to talk about young children. Their care about and for children is evident in this book full of practical suggestions and current research.

Morrow, L.M. (1989). *Literacy development in the early years: Helping children read and write.* New York: Prentice-Hall.

This is one of many books to present a complete literature-based program for early literacy development. It is important to read current and updated ideas about beginning reading instruction.

Children's Literature

Base, G. (1986) *Animalia.* New York: Harry N. Abrams
The bus ride. (1971). Glenview IL: Scott Foresman.
Carle, E. (1970). *The very hungry caterpillar.* Lakewood, OH: World.
dePaola, T. (1973). *Andy: That's my name.* Englewood Cliffs, N.J. Prentice-Hall.
Emberly, B. (1967). *Drummer Hoff.* Illustrated by E. Emberly. Englewood Cliffs: NJ: Prentice-Hall.
Lobel, A. (1979). *Days with frog and toad.* New York: Harper & Row.
Martin, B. (1983). *Brown bear, brown bear, what do you see?* Illustrated by E. Carle. New York: Holt.
Scheer, J. (1964). *Rain makes applesauce.* Illustrated by M. Bileck. New York: Holiday.
Sendak, M. (1970). *In the night kitchen.* New York: Harper & Row.
Steig, W. (1969). *Sylvester and the magic pebble.* Old Tappan, NJ: Windmill.
Tallon, R. (1979). *Zoophabets.* New York: Scholastic.
Van Allsburg, C. (1987). *The z was zapped.* Boston: Houghton Mifflin.

Wordless Books

dePaola, T. (1978). *Pancakes for breakfast.* New York: Harcourt Brace Jovanovich.
Hutchins, P. (1971). *Changes, changes.* New York: Macmillan.
Mayer, M. (1974a). *A boy, a dog, and a frog.* New York: Dial.
———. (1974b). *Frogs goes to dinner.* New York: Dial.
McCully, E. (1984). *Picnic.* New York: Harper & Row.
———. (1985). *First snow.* New York: Harper & Row.
———. (1987). *School.* New York: Harper & Row.
Spier, P. (1977). *Rain.* New York: Doubleday.
Turkle, B. (1976). *Deep in the forest.* New York: Dutton.

Alphabet Books

Hoban, T. (1982). *A, b, see!* New York: Greenwillow.
Kitchen, B. (1984). *Animal alphabet.* New York: Dial.
Lobel, A. (1981). *On market street.* New York: Greenwillow.
Martin, B., and Archambault, J. (1989). *Chicka chicka boom boom.* Illustrated by L. Ehlert. New York: Simon & Schuster.
Sendak, M. (1962). *Alligators all around.* New York: Harper & Row.
Van Allsburg, C. (1987). *The z was zapped.* Boston: Houghton Mifflin.

Counting Books

Anno, M. (1982). *Anno's counting house.* New York: Philomel.
Bang, M. (1983). *Ten, nine, eight.* New York: Greenwillow.
Carle, E. (1971). *The very hungry caterpillar.* New York: Crowell.
Hoban, T. (1987). *26 letters and 99 cents.* New York: William & Morrow.
Hutchins, P. (1986). *The doorbell rang.* New York: Greenwillow.

Keats, E. J. (1972). *Over in the meadow*. New York: Scholastic.
Sendak, M. (1962). *One was Johnny*. New York: Harper & Row.

Concept Books

Carle, E. (1971). *The grouchy ladybug*. New York: Crowell.
———. (1975). *The mixed-up chameleon*. New York: Crowell.
Crews, D. (1978). *Freight train*. New York: Greenwillow.
dePaola, T. (1977). *The quicksand book*. New York: Holiday.
Dubanevich, A. (1983). *Pigs in hiding*. New York: Four Winds.
Hoban, T. (1974). *Circles, triangles and squares*. New York: Macmillan.
———. (1976). *Big ones, little ones*. New York: Greenwillow.
———. (1981). *Take another look*. New York: Greenwillow.
Martin, B. (1967). *Brown bear, brown bear, what do you see?* New York: Henry Holt.

Easy to Read Books

Hoff, S. (1959). *Sammy the seal*. New York: Harper & Row.
———. (1961). *Chester*. New York: Harper & Row.
Lobel, A. (1970). *Frog and toad are friends*. New York: Harper & Row.
———. (1976). *Frog and toad all year*. New York: Harper & Row.
Wiseman, B. (1970). *Morris goes to school*. New York: Harper & Row.
———. (1978). *Morris has a cold*. New York: Dodd, Mead.

Picture Storybooks

Burton, V. (1942). *The little house*. Boston: Houghton Mifflin.
Freeman, D. (1968). *Corduroy*. New York: Viking.
Galdone, P. (1972). *The three bears*. New York: Clarion.
Keats, E. J. (1962). *The snowy day*. New York: Scholastic.
Kraus, R. (1945). *The carrot seed*. Illustrated by C. Johnson. New York: Harper & Row.
McCloskey, R. (1941). *Make way for ducklings*. New York: Viking.

Predictable Pattern Books

Cowley, J., & Melser, J. (1980). *Mrs. Wishy-Washy*. San Diego: Wright Group.
Degen, B. (1983). *Jamberry*. New York: Harper & Row.
Mayer, M. (1980). *What do you do with a kangaroo?* New York: Scholastic.
Scheer, J. (1964). *Rain makes applesauce*. New York: Holiday.
Seidler, A. & Slepian, J. (1967). *The hungry thing*. New York: Scholastic.
Sendak, M. (1962a). *Chicken soup with rice*. New York: Harper & Row.
———. (1962b). *Pierre*. New York: Harper & Row.

REFERENCES

Baskwill, J., & Whitman, P. (1986). *Whole language sourcebook*. Ontario Canada: Scholastic–TAB.
Beers. J.W. (1980). Developmental spelling strategies of spelling competence in primary school children. In E.H. Henderson & J.W. Beers (Eds.). *Developmental and cognitive aspects*

of learning to spell: A reflection of word knowledge. Newark, DE: International Reading Association.

Buchanan, E. (Ed.). (1980). For the love of reading. Winnipeg, Manitoba, Canada: C.E.L. Group.

Burke, C., & Jurenka, N. (Undated). *Whole language approaches to initial reading–language experience.* Unpublished manuscript.

Butler, A. (1988). *The elements of the whole language program.* Crystal Lake, IL: Rigby.

Butler, A., & Turbill, J. (1987). *Towards a reading writing classroom.* Portsmouth, NH: Heinemann.

Cambourne, B. (1988). *Language, learning and literacy.* Crystal Lake, IL: Rigby.

Chomsky, C. (1972). Stages in language development and reading exposure. *Harvard Educational Review, 42,* 1–33.

Chomsky, C. (1976). After decoding: What? *Language Arts.* 53 (3), 288–296, 314.

Cox, C. (1988). *Teaching language arts.* Boston: Allyn & Bacon.

Doake, D. (1980, May). *Book experience and emergent reading behavior.* Paper presented at the annual convention of the International Reading Association, St. Louis, MO.

Ferreiro, E. (1985). Literacy development: A psychogenetic perspective. In D. R. Olson, N. Torrance, & A. Hildyard (Eds.), *Literacy, Language, and Learning.* Cambridge, MA: Cambridge University Press.

Ferreiro, E., & Teberosky, A. (1982). *Literacy before schooling.* Exeter, NH: Heinemann.

Hall, N. (1987). *The emergence of literacy.* Portsmouth, NH: Heinemann.

Handy, L., & Holdaway, D. (1980). *What do you do with a kangaroo? Teacher's manual.* London: Aston Scholastic.

Harste, J., Woodward, V.A., & Burke, C. L. (1984). *Language stories and literacy lessons.* Portsmouth, NH: Heinemann.

Henderson, E. (1986). Understanding children's knowledge of written language. In D.B. Yaden & S. Templeton (Eds.), *Metalinguistic awareness and beginning literacy: Conceptualizing what it means to read and write.* Portsmouth, NH: Heinemann.

Holdaway, D. (1979). *The foundations of literacy.* Aukland, New Zealand: Heinemann.

———. (1986). *Stability and change in literacy learning.* Portsmouth, NH: Heinemann.

Jalongo, M.R. (1988). *Young children and picture books: Literature from infancy to six.* Washington, DC: National Association for the Education of Young Children.

Krashen, R. (1986). *Inquiries and insights.* Haywood, CA: Allemany.

Lass, B. (1982). Portrait of my son as an early reader. *Reading Teacher, 36* (1), 10–18.

Lynch, P. (1986). *Using big books and predictable books.* New York: Scholastic.

McGee, L.M., & Richgels, D. J. (1990). *Literacy's beginnings: Supporting young readers and writers.* Needham Heights, MA: Allyn & Bacon.

Morrow, L. M. (1989). *Literacy development in the early years.* New York: Prentice-Hall.

Newman, J. (Ed.). (1985). *Whole language theory in use.* Portsmouth, NH: Heinemann.

Norton, D. E. (1990). *Through the eyes of a child: An introduction to children's literature* (3rd ed.). Columbus, OH: Merrill.

Piaget, J. (1970). *The science of education and the psychology of the child.* New York: Orion.

Read, C. (1975). *Children's categorization of speech sounds.* Technical Report No. 197. Urbana, IL: National Council of Teachers Committee on Research.

Rhodes, L.K., & Dudley-Marling, C. (1988). *Readers and writers with a difference.* Portsmouth, NH: Heinemann.

Robeck, C., & Wiseman, D. (1982). The development of literacy in middle class preschool children. *Reading Psychology 3* (2), 105–116.

Rowe, D.W., & Harste, J.C. (1986). Metalinguistic awareness in writing and reading: The young child as curricular informant. In D.B. Yaden & S. Templeton (Eds.), *Metalinguistic awareness and beginning literacy: Conceptualizing what it means to read and write.* Portsmouth, NH: Heinemann.

Snow, C.E. (1983). Literacy and language: Relationships during the preschool years. *Harvard Educational Review, 53* (2), 165–189.

Strickland, D. S., & Morrow, L. M. (1988). New perspectives on young children learning to read and write. *The Reading Teacher, 42* (1), 70–71.

Sulzby, E. (1986). Children's elicitation and use of metalinguistic knowledge about *word* during literacy interactions. In D.B. Yaden and S. Templeton (Eds.), *Metalinguistic awareness and beginning literacy: Conceptualizing what it means to read and write*. Portsmouth, NH: Heinemann.

Teale, W. (1984). Reading to young children: Its significance for literacy development. In H. Goelman, A. Oberg, & F. Smith (Eds.), *Awakening to literacy*. Exeter, NH: Heinemann.

Tompkins, G., & Webeler, M. (1983). What will happen next? Using predictable books with young children. *The Reading Teacher, 36* (5), 498–502.

Trelease, J. (1989). Jim Trelease speaks on read aloud to children. *The Reading Teacher, 43* (3), 200–206.

Watson, D. (1983). Bringing together reading and writing. In U.H. Hardt (Ed.), *Teaching Reading With the Other Language Arts*. Newark, DE: International Reading Association.

_6_

DEVELOPING COMPREHENSION STRATEGIES

*James was on his third sandwich and Maybeth was still nibbling at her
first. "How did it go?" Gram asked. "How many pages did you read?"*

*"Four," Maybeth answered softly, without looking up. "That's not
enough," she added.*

*Gram looked at Dicey, and Dicey sighed. "Is the book too hard?" Dicey
asked her sister's bent head . . .*

. . . "Was the book too hard?" she asked again.

*Maybeth shook her head. "I have to keep working, Mrs. Jackson said," she
told Dicey. "Only I can't remember what the words are, so I have to go back and
memorize the lists again. If I work, Mrs. Jackson says, everything will be all
right."*

*****

*Dicey went to stand behind James, who sat at the big wooden desk reading
a thick book. He looked up over his shoulder at her and marked his place on the
small print with a finger. "How long do you think it'll take to get the boat fixed
up?" Dicey asked him.*

"Not now, Dicey, I'm reading."

"What're you reading?"

"The Bible."

"Why?"

*James sighed. "Mr. Thomas said every educated man should. He said it's
one of the underpinnings of western civilization." His face lit up. "Isn't that an
idea? Underpinnings of civilization? As if—civilization were a big building, you
know? Besides there are some good stories in the Bible."*

*"And besides," Gram added in, "it was the fattest book on the shelves and
James always likes to read the fattest ones."*

"That's not true," James said.

"Isn't it," Gram answered.

*"And besides," James said, "if you have a big idea, you have to write it
down in a big book, otherwise you won't be able to explain all the complicated
parts."*

—Cynthia Voigt, *Dicey's Song* (1983 Newbery Medal
winner)

THE ability to comprehend and solve problems is an extremely valuable skill that contributes to the social, economic, and personal well-being of each individual. Reading comprehension is basic to all education and many recreations. Reading comprehension contributes to the quality of life of individuals and ultimately the quality of life in our society.

Developing effective comprehension strategies should be the major focus of reading instruction. Various approaches view comprehension somewhat differently but all views acknowledge the complexity of the process. Comprehension is an intricate cognitive process that is difficult to identify, assess, or teach explicitly. Teachers must develop an understanding of the process to guide their students in developing comprehension strategies effective for many types of texts. The questions that will be answered in this chapter include:

1. What factors contribute to understanding how to teach reading comprehension?
2. Do different purposes and materials require different comprehension strategies and responses?
3. What comprehension strategies do effective readers use?
4. Why must comprehension strategies be flexible and adaptable?
5. What is the role of instruction in guiding reading comprehension?
6. Why are listening, writing, and speaking necessary for developing comprehension?

Comprehension exists beyond the reading process and can be accomplished without using print. In fact, children acquire a great deal of understanding and comprehension of their world without reading. Before they enter school most of their understandings and interpretations of the world have been acquired without printed material. Reading offers another way to learn and understand events that children experience as well as a way to learn about things indirectly.

Foundations of Comprehension

Reading comprehension is the ability to gain understanding from written language and depends on an individual's ability to predict and ask questions (Smith, 1985). The knowledge and experiences of readers determine how questions are asked and understood. In order to guide children as they attempt to understand texts, several factors should be considered:

1. the importance of readers' prior knowledge,
2. how experiences, events, and information are organized in the readers' mind,
3. and the ability to control the personal reading process.

Prior Knowledge

The knowledge a reader brings to a text is a great influence on what is comprehended, learned, and remembered. Readers who possess and use prior knowledge about a topic are more likely to understand the material. Prior knowledge reduces uncertainty about a subject or topic, and answers to questions are more easily obtained (Smith, 1985). If the reader does not know something about the content, misinterpretation or failure to comprehend is likely.

When readers know much about a topic it is easy to make predictions about what will be found in the text. Conversely, if readers do not know much about the topic, it is difficult, if not impossible, to make predictions about text. For example, if you attempt to read a book written for a basic engineering class and you are not familiar with engineering, you may find it difficult to make predictions about the material. If you attempt to read the material, your rate may be slow, you will reread portions of the text often, and may give up before you finish it. Even if you are capable of reading the book aloud and discussing some vocabulary and isolated meanings, you have difficulty comprehending passages. Your inability to comprehend a text about engineering does not reflect your overall ability to comprehend. You still are capable of predicting, summarizing, inferencing, and relating what you remember about other topics, but you are unable to predict and answer questions about engineering. However, if engineering students attempt to read a text about reading instruction, they may understand most of the material, since everyone has experienced the reading process and instruction and will be able to predict something about the material. A reader who has acquired very little prior knowledge about a topic will find it more difficult to make accurate predictions and therefore construct meaning (Uttero, 1988).

Schemata Development

There is more to reading comprehension than the use of prior experiences. The schema or mental organization of prior experiences contributes much of how readers interpret and comprehend and what they expect from the text (Garner, 1987; Smith, 1988). Personal experiences can be organized in many categories or schemata. As you prepare for a career in teaching, you begin mentally to arrange information about children. Most of what you think and remember about children depends on organization. As you learn more and more, you develop categories for organizing the information. Within your schema for children you may have categories of children in your family, children for whom you have babysat, children on television, children in school, child psychology information, and so on. "Children" can be related to other schemata about school, babies, playtime, and families. There is also a link between "children" and books, writing, and reading. The schemata each person develops are highly personal and intricately related to form a organizational structure for personal experiences and understandings.

Schemata can change and grow to accommodate new information. As learning occurs, the categories within a schema are modified and new categories are built to form additional schemata. Reading is one way to add new information to an existing schema. Readers learn by adding new information to old schemata, modifying existing schemata, interrelating schemata, or building new schemata (Garner, 1987; Smith, 1988). As you complete this course you will build on your schema for teaching reading. You will modify some existing information, add new information, and form relationships among the categories of children, language, and learning.

Awareness of story schema greatly affects reading comprehension. Children who have been exposed to books will remember stories and expect new text to reflect anticipated components and arrangements. For example, children expect that stories have definite beginnings, middles, and ends. There is much evidence that children develop their ideas of what a story or text should be at a very early age, and their understandings of text organization become more complex as they grow older and are exposed to greater amounts of print (Mandler & Johnson, 1977). Adults who are experienced readers possess a story schema that includes a wide variety and complexity of text organization. Continued exposure to a wide variety of materials prepares a reader for the organizational differences between a romance novel and a textbook.

The most efficient reading occurs when the categories or schemata established in a reader's mind match the organization of the reading material. When stored knowledge fits with new information on the page, comprehension and learning occur with greater ease (Garner, 1987). (One of the purposes of the table of contents of a textbook is to help readers recognize its organization. If you haven't noticed the chapter organization for this text, it might make it easier for you to understand the information presented if you go back and reread the table of contents.) Readers expect new information to be presented in a way that fits their schemata. If new information does not fit into the schemata, the reader may fail to comprehend the information. There are several factors that may affect positively a reader's comprehension. Comprehension is easier when (Fitzgerald, 1989):

1. the information is organized,
2. the reader understands the organization of a particular text,
3. the reader possesses knowledge of the topic,
4. the reader understands relationships among categories presented in the reading material.

Differences in Responding to Texts

Different readers interpret texts in different ways, and there are times when prior knowledge and experience lead readers to very different conclusions and understandings. Paterson's *Park's Quest* (1988) tells the story of a twelve-year-old boy's efforts to learn about his father, who was killed in Vietnam. Park, the main character, finds that his mother is reluctant to discuss his father. He travels to his uncle's farm to meet his father's side of the family. An elementary school child whose father or uncle fought in Vietnam may understand the emotions and discussions of the war by responding in a personal manner or by relating to discussions and descriptions discussed at home. A child who grew up on a farm might have unique responses to the descriptions of farm life and might think of the uncle in the story as being like his own relatives who live on a farm. Both readers comprehend the story, but in very different ways.

Awareness of the impact of prior knowledge and schemata development on reading leads to a broader definition of the comprehension process. A discussion of differences in responses to literature and an understanding of the effects of various texts provide insights to their impact.

Response Approach to Reading

A reader's responses to a text are unique. Because of the varied experiences readers bring to material, they may come away with different understandings, images, feelings, and ideas (Gentile & Kane, 1989) as was illustrated by the *Park's Quest* (1988) example. Readers create an understanding based upon an interaction between their own background knowledge and the text. The reader-response approach to understanding text emphasizes the role of the readers' experiences, values independent interpretations, and consequently accepts innovative purposes for reading literature (Many & Wiseman, 1992). Instead of trying to identify the ''one right meaning,'' the reader-response approach does not judge a response as correct or incorrect but as appropriate or more appropriate based on what is presented in the text (Rosenblatt, 1978). From a reader-response perspective, it is valid to accept various reactions and interpretations of texts.

A response approach to literature values equally the diversity and uniqueness of what each child has to say about a book (Cullinan, 1989). This view encourages a teacher to accept the reader as active and important. This acceptance presents a much broader definition of comprehension than the traditional lists of skills. Reader-response theory puts the reader more in control of the outcome of reading, recognizes that each reader's response is worthwhile, and suggests the function of the text is to inform the reader. This idea discourages the teacher from controlling outcomes, thoughts, and emotions. Students with different backgrounds are encouraged to respond naturally and allow their ideas to be modified after reading new material (Probst, 1988). This may lead to lively discussions when children share their unique responses to a piece of literature.

A teacher's role in helping students establish meaning may involve some negotiation between response and text. If a reader establishes an understanding that is inappropriate to what the text says, the teacher guides or negotiates with the reader to reach a more appropriate understanding. For example, let us propose that you read this section on reader's response and came away with the understanding that this approach is applicable only to romance novels. That response is partly the intent of this section and you certainly have understood the concept to some degree, but it was hoped that the text would produce a somewhat different idea of reader-response than that limited interpretation. Your professor allows you to share that understanding in class and the ensuing discussion of what the professor and classmates understand about the text will help you negotiate the meaning or call attention to aspects of the text that you might not have noticed (Probst, 1988). You use the discussion and rereading of this and other texts to contribute to your understanding of the concept. Your comprehension of reader response may change after considering your ideas, those of your peers and instructors, and a closer reading of the text.

Reader-response theory suggests that each reader is capable of a legitimate response based on experience. This assumption complicates the reading process since the reader is required to take a personal perspective. The results of taking a personal perspective during reading compel the reader to participate in the reading process and ultimately to grow and change. This reinforces the belief that the reader is very active and responsible during the comprehension process. Comprehension requires an environment that allows free expression of thoughts, a group that trusts one another, and literature that provokes response (Probst, 1988).

Exposition and Narrative

There are differences in the organizations and purposes of texts, and readers' comprehension is affected by the nature of the texts they read. Texts may be defined as *narrative,* giving an account or telling a story, or *expository,* explaining a concept or event (Murth, 1990). Many of the materials used in schools—traditional, contemporary, fictional, fantastic, and historical literature—are considered narratives. However, nonfiction books, periodicals, school subject area texts, and basal readers often include a great deal of exposition. Children's abilities to understand various texts may be developmental, and there are indications that children from fourth grade on develop increasing abilities to read exposition (Mandler & Johnson, 1977).

There are similarities in reading both types of texts. Reading any text requires prediction and hypothesis. Background information must be gathered before one reads narrative or exposition, although there may be a greater need to develop a specific background when approaching exposition. For example, if you persisted in reading the engineering text used as an example earlier in this chapter, you would benefit from a discussion of why you want to read the material and the experiences you've had with the topic, just as you might before reading any narrative. It is also important, however, to build an understanding of engineering and the related concepts to be presented in the text. Knowledge of the subject is especially important when a reader must understand an explanation or description of a certain concept.

One of the most important aspects of understanding information is knowledge of text structure (Slater & Graves, 1989). An understanding of text suggests that readers expect a certain organization. Children who are familiar with story books come to school with developing schemata for stories. But when children confront exposition for the first time, they confront a structure that is unfamiliar. Understanding what is conveyed in an unfamiliar structure can be very difficult. Comprehension can be increased by familiarizing the reader with the text structures for exposition. Information about the purposes and methods of various text organizations helps children to know what to expect and how to go about understanding the information (Probst, 1988). (Expository reading will be more fully explored in chapter 8.)

Knowledge and Control of Reading

The understanding and monitoring of thinking, language, and reading skills is known as *metacognition.* Metacognition includes understanding the reader, the reading process, and the strategies used in reading (Garner, 1987). Implementing metacognitive strategies to improve comprehension is likely to occur before, during, and after reading a text. Babbs and Moe (1983) suggest the following activities are involved in metacognition:

Readers Consciously Control Their Reading

Readers who use metacognition have the self-confidence to control the reading process. They know they can read the material and decide if it is too complex, decide whether they need to read the material, and produce a situation that allows comprehension to occur. Effective readers also recognize when comprehension is not occurring and will know what to do to so that they can understand the material.

An example of effective reading may help you understand how you use metacognition as you read. You began reading this chapter to understand the material and establish how you would use it later. Your instructor may have asked you to prepare for a class discussion, write a response to the chapter, or study for some type of evaluation. Or, you may have wondered about reading comprehension and read the material to learn more. You read an amount of text that allowed you to get what you wanted from it. Your reading process may have depended upon the outcome you desired. If you realized that you were not comprehending the text, you may have reread the material, read another book about the same topic, or waited until after class discussion to read the material. As an efficient reader you were able to use your knowledge of the reading process to control and regulate your activities.

The Reader Establishes the Goal

An important part of controlling the reading process is knowing why the material is being read. Efficient readers can make a statement like ''I will read this material to find out . . .'' The ability to establish a purpose for reading allows readers to do what they want to do. A reader who is metacognitively aware can establish the reasons for reading and read to accomplish that goal.

If you are reading this material to take part in a class discussion or to clarify class lecture notes, you will read very differently than if you are reading to respond to answers on a quiz. When preparing for a quiz, you may read more slowly and repeat your reading, even verbalize to gain deeper understanding. When reading to contribute to a class discussion, you may develop a thorough understanding of one portion of the text since you have the freedom to contribute to any part of the discussion. Establishing purposes for reading affects the way a reader comprehends.

Efficient Readers Focus on Metacognitive Knowledge That Contributes to Comprehension

Efficient readers know about their own reading and thinking processes and measure how much of the material they understand. Effective readers are cognizant of the demands imposed by different goals and by different types of reading material.

If, while you are reading this text, you realize that you have never considered the concept of metacognition before, you may discern that you still do not understand the concept and certainly are not ready to respond to an essay question about metacognition. You decide that you need to hear your instructor discuss the concept before you fully understand it. You may think you comprehend metacognition, but do not grasp how it relates to first graders learning how to read. You note questions that you want to raise during class discussion in order to develop a complete understanding. While waiting for class, you ask classmates about their interpretations of metacognition, and they share their ideas. After your instructor presents a lecture about the concept, you are able to reread the text with greater understanding. Your ability to recognize your level of understanding ultimately contributes to your comprehension of metacognition. As an efficient reader you were able to control your metacognitive processes to provide opportunities to increase your understanding.

The Reader Strategically Plans the Regulation and Monitoring of the Reading Act
The next part of the reader's strategic plan is to select the metacognitive skills and strategies necessary to understand the text. Babbs and Moe (1983) point out the following metacognitive tactics available to aid in comprehension: rereading, skimming and summarizing, paraphrasing, predicting, looking for important ideas, testing one's understanding, identifying the pattern of text, sequencing events, looking for relationships, reading ahead for clarification, mentally executing the directions, and relating new knowledge to prior knowledge. Each of these tactics is used strategically by efficient readers.

One of the things you may do while attempting to understand the concept of metacognition is reread the text. After rereading, you may summarize or paraphrase the information in your own words, occasionally skimming the text to test your understanding. Not only do readers understand that these actions are to be used when needed, but they know when to use them effectively. An efficient reader knows which of the metacognitive strategies will be most effective and uses them to understand.

Metacognitive Strategies Include Evaluating the Effectiveness of the Strategies
As readers continue reading they are constantly judging whether their strategies are effective. They know if they understand and can evaluate their levels of understanding. An efficient reader will be able to say, "I didn't understand that information: I need to reread the material."

At this point you probably are making a decision about your level of understanding of metacognition. You may say to yourself, "I understand and can discuss the concept of metacognition so I will continue my reading." Or you may say, "I understand the concept well enough to contribute to a class discussion, but I certainly don't want to be evaluated on how much I know about the concept." Or, "I really do not understand this stuff. I sure hope we discuss it in class."

Metacognitive strategies are used by efficient readers to focus on important and relevant text. The ability to determine the focus of reading suggests that readers control their actions. Effective instruction includes opportunities to allow readers to become aware of what they need to do to increase their comprehension. In other words, comprehension instruction provides for the development of a more metacognitively aware reader.

Assumptions about Comprehension Instruction

A complex interpretation of comprehension can be based on what is understood about prior knowledge, schemata development, differences in responses, text variation, and metacognitive strategies. Comprehension guidance with classroom activities should consider the following assumptions:

The Most Effective Method for Developing Comprehension Strategies Is Reading

Reading contributes to the store of knowledge, the schema for reading, and the development of metacognition. It is by far the most effective activity for cultivating the flexible strategies needed to comprehend texts. No activity will improve a reader's ability to comprehend better than reading. "Children do not learn to read in order to make sense of print. They strive to make sense of print and as a consequence learn to read," Smith writes (1985, p. 132). Regardless of students' previous experience or levels of reading ability, teachers need to encourage interaction with a variety of materials and establish many purposes for reading.

Young Readers Should Know Something about a Topic and the Text's Structure before They Are Asked to Read and Comprehend

The more experiences children have with a topic, the easier it is for them to understand the reading material. Conversely, the less information young readers have about a topic, the more the teacher must do to prepare them for reading. Often, it will be the teachers' responsibility to provide background when it is lacking.

The same is true of text organization. The more experiences children have with different texts, the easier it is for them to read texts with various arrangements. Reading a great variety of texts can provide the experiences so necessary for developing understanding from written language.

Readers Comprehend and Respond to Texts Differently

Comprehension is affected by prior experiences, individual schema development, the possibility of a multitude of responses, the idiosyncrasies of the text, and what is understood about reading. It is possible for children to read the same text and come away with different understandings and responses. Comprehension is shaped by interaction of the text and the reader and can be realized in several different ways depending on the reader. "There is, therefore, no correct reading for a text, but merely readings that are more or less complete . . ." (Cullinan, 1989, p. 9).

There Is No Specific Set of Skills That Can Be Linked with Comprehension

Reading instruction would be much easier if there were a specific set of skills that assure comprehension. A more realistic method is to consider comprehension as the effective use of many adaptable and flexible strategies (Pearson, Dole, Duffy, & Roehler, in press) that promote understanding.

The Environment Most Conducive to Comprehension Development Is Comfortable and Risk-free and Encourages Experimentation and Engagement in Reading

A risk-free environment encourages prediction and experimentation with strategies necessary for understanding, negotiating, and responding in a variety of ways. Reading can be risky business, and children need freedom to try their ideas and receive feedback in a nonthreatening atmosphere.

Comprehension Occurs before, during, and after Reading

Comprehension begins before a reader opens a book. The reader brings a great deal to the text before the reading begins. The interaction with print contributes to understanding, but the process can continue after the book is closed. Comprehension is completed in activities, experiences, and discussions before, after, and during reading.

Guiding Comprehension Development

There is very little support for teaching specific comprehension skills (Pearson, Dole, Duffy, & Roehler, in press), but much of the comprehension instruction in basals involves specific skills. Many teachers use workbook exercises and reading group discussions to teach traditional comprehension skills such as main idea, summarization, critical reading, or reading for specific facts and details. As researchers discover more about comprehension, traditional views of instruction are being amended and expanded (or, if you like, negotiated). Reading comprehension is more than the efficient application of multiple and flexible strategies. Many levels of comprehension and response must be expected from the diverse readers in our classrooms.

Instructional support for comprehension depends on a teacher's view of the process. Instead of viewing comprehension as something that is taught, teachers should consider themselves negotiators, facilitators, and guides who are available to help children make sense of text. There are some classroom procedures that support children's development of comprehension. Most procedures associated with comprehension involve one or more of the following aspects: concept development, demonstrations by the teacher, discussion and questioning techniques, discussion and interaction with others, and critical reading. Basic classroom procedures can occur at any time during reading. They may be used before a book is opened, while the reader is reading, and after the book is closed. Several basic activities that contribute to comprehension development are described in the discussion that follows.

Concept Development

To comprehend, children must have some knowledge of the concepts they are reading about. When children do not possess basic concepts about a topic, reading must begin by building the concepts and establishing some knowledge. Discussion, nonprint material, reading other material, and related activities help build conceptual understanding before independent reading on unfamiliar topics. The more children understand about concepts before they read, the easier it is for them to comprehend while they read.

An important feature of guiding comprehension development is providing readers with opportunities to redefine their understandings (Duffy & Roehler, 1987). Discussing a topic with others or writing about the topic are two ways for readers to grapple with what they have read. Discussion can clarify and help the reader integrate text material.

Discussion contributes to basic understanding. Panel discussions, debates, prediction exercises, and whole class discussions develop understanding that can be expanded by reading. Talking about topics before, during, and after reading provides teachers with opportunities to gauge children's initial understandings of and build experiences with a topic. When reading material includes many new concepts (e.g., science and social studies textbooks), teachers may want to schedule discussions and clarification activities.

Writing assists concept development in several ways. Writing predictions, identifications, and definitions before reading a text organizes thoughts and assesses knowledge. Writing activates thinking and provides opportunities for relating experiences and using vocabulary. Think about what you would do if your instructor asked you to jot down ideas associated with the term *comprehension* before you read this chapter. The request would cause you to reflect on what you know. You would use information from psychology, education courses, and life experiences to express your ideas. Writing would require you to use vocabulary associated with comprehension, identify relationships, and organize your thoughts. Writing would contribute to your understanding of comprehension before you read the text. Writing also helps identify what needs to be learned and clarified by further reading. For example, the experience of exploring ideas about comprehension would provide insights to what you needed to learn while reading this chapter.

Technology can be used to develop concepts. Pictures, slides, filmstrips, video cassette recordings, television shows, and computer simulations can familiarize children with topics they will read about. Teachers who plan for children to take part in support activities before reading about unfamiliar topics can be assured of higher levels of comprehension. Comprehension will grow if technology also is used after reading.

If children do not understand concepts in a particular text, reading other material can help them understand. Material can be read to students, or they can read the material themselves. Books that discuss the concepts in simpler terms, provide more pictures, or present information related to new topics can contribute to comprehension at any point. One of the advantages of literature-based instruction is the underlying assumption that many materials will be used for instruction. With many books available on different topics, it is relatively easy to find related material written in different forms or simpler language.

When children are reading about a concept or topic for the first time, much time should be spent in preparation. Information or ideas presented in any form before children are required to read independently will contribute to the child's ability to predict what the material is about and thereby improve comprehension.

Demonstration

Demonstrating is an important part of guiding comprehension development. One of the simplest and most effective comprehension activities to demonstrate is the reading act. Children who observe their teachers reading, both orally and silently, are provided with a display of how reading is done (Smith, 1988).

Demonstrations can occur any time during the reading process. "Talking through" behaviors that efficient readers take for granted are ways of demonstrating comprehension processes. For example, teachers can explain what they do when they do not understand the reading material. While reading aloud to the children, the teacher might stop and say, "This didn't make sense; maybe I should read it again" or, "I don't completely understand the way this text discusses this concept, so I will read out of this other book to clarify the idea." The teacher might clarify by pointing out that this is a technique that all readers should try when they are unable to understand the text. When processes are explained and encouraged, children take the responsibility to try the same techniques during their own reading. Teachers suddenly may realize after they systematically explain prediction and questioning strategies that children make predictions and ask questions with less direction.

Questioning

Questioning is a very important part of reading comprehension. Effective questioning contributes to students' establishment of reading goals and negotiation of what is understood from the passages. Questioning can occur before the reading to establish goals and motivation, during the reading to clarify and monitor the understanding, or after the reading to negotiate, extend, and assess comprehension.

While most experts agree that questioning is important and contributes to comprehension, there is no clear-cut evidence of whether teachers' or students' questions are the most effective comprehension strategy (Pearson, Dole, Duffy, & Roehler, in press). The most reasonable way to deal with questioning is to include teacher and student questions in the reading process. When teachers ask the right questions, they are demonstrating what is important during reading. There are some strategies that allow teachers to ask more effective questions. Pearson (1982) outlines guidelines for questioning children during reading instruction:

1. Questions about reading should focus students' attention on appropriate background experiences. Teachers should be able to activate prior knowledge so a student is more able to predict. One effective strategy to help children remember and activate their own experiences in relation to the story they are reading is to describe the plot and ask the students what they would do if they were in that situation.

Sam, Bangs, and Moonshine (Ness, 1966) is one example. This is the story of a girl, Sam, who has a difficult time discriminating between events that really happened and events in her imagination (her dad calls her fabrications "moonshine"). Her fantasies place her cat, Bangs, and a friend in danger. Some questions to activate background knowledge might include: Have you ever said something that was not true and, as a result, placed someone in danger? Have you ever been in danger or known that someone was in danger and couldn't do anything about it? How did it feel? Have you ever lost a pet in a big storm? Any of these questions would prod children to think about their own experiences before reading and allow them to use their experiences to predict the development of the story.

2. Questions about reading should help students learn what is important.

One way to produce effective questions is to create a framework for questioning based on the structure of the story. The structure of the story or story map can be used to ask questions that elicit response to the story based on details of the story (Pearson,

1984) and those requiring personal reactions to the story. When teachers consistently use the outline of a story to guide children's reading, it provides their students with a predictable framework for understanding and recalling the story (Pearson, 1984) and contributes to the development of story schema.

The following outline of *Sam, Bangs, and Moonshine* could be used to develop effective questions to guide the reading and discussion.

Theme: Not understanding the difference between imagination and real events can cause dangerous misunderstandings.
Setting: Island near a large harbor.
Characters: Father, Sam, Bangs, Thomas
Plot (Important Events):

- *Thomas believes everything Sam says. Sam tells several stories to Thomas, including the tale that she has a kangaroo. Thomas comes to her house every day and begs to see the kangaroo. He follows her around hoping to see the animal.*
- *One day when Sam's father is out on his fishing boat, Thomas follows Sam and Bangs to Blue Rock Cave near the ocean to see the kangaroo. Sam leaves Thomas at the cave while she goes to the "moon" and returns home without Thomas.*
- *After Sam returns home alone, a storm develops. She can't find Thomas or Bangs.*
- *Sam's father returns home and sets out to find Bangs and Thomas. The father finds Thomas but not Bangs, and Sam realizes that her imagination contributed to losing her cat.*
- *Bangs finds his way home, and Thomas recovers from being lost in the storm.*
- *Sam's father buys her a gerbil that looks and hops like a kangaroo. When Sam begins telling her father that the gerbil is a kangaroo, he helps her realize that saying the gerbil is a kangaroo is "moonshine" and not real.*

This brief outline provides a "map" for questions and discussions. When the teacher does pose questions, the questions should be neither too specific nor too general, and they should allow children to respond in different ways. The responses should require that children go beyond literal interpretation of the text and use higher thinking to respond (Pearson, 1984). Some questions requiring children to take a variety of stances would be:

1. What do you know about the setting, and how did the author develop the setting?
2. What events contributed to your understanding of Sam and her feelings?
3. What events contributed to Sam realizing the danger of "moonshine"?

Other questions could focus on the aesthetic response to the literature.

1. Describe the most memorable part of this story.
2. Does this setting remind you of any place you've lived or visited? How is it different from where you live?

3. Did any of the characters remind you of someone you know? How?
4. Which of Sam's moonshines will you remember after you have read the story?

Some questions can combine analytical and personal responses.

1. What techniques did the author use to make you think of your own life as you read the story?
2. In what ways was the setting developed so that you could compare it to your own home?

Making Decisions about the Reading Material

Comprehension instruction should provide opportunities for children to make decisions about the material they are reading. When judgments and comparisons are made as a result of reading, the term used to describe these decisions is *critical reading*. Critical reading skills may involve establishing the author's purpose, inferences suggested in the text, or evaluating the content for truthfulness, bias, or fairness (Whitmer, 1986). Critical reading should be encouraged from the time children begin reacting to text. Even young children can be guided to discuss what they like and don't like about a story or how one story is different from another.

A type of critical reading involves comparing and contrasting stories and reading material. In addition to evaluating the text, most comparisons and contrasts involve some type of categorization to contribute to general understanding of the story. Children should be taught to note likenesses and differences while reading. Some questions that encourage an analytic response and contribute to critical reading strategies include:

1. In what way are the characters in two books alike/different?
2. How are the two settings different?
3. Which of the stories is more realistic?
4. Does this story represent life as we know it?

Questions that allow children to respond based on their own experiences would be phrased this way:

1. Do either of the books remind you of something that has happened to you?
2. Which of the settings is more like where you live?
3. Could this story have happened where you live?
4. Which of the stories would be more apt to happen where you live?

Instructional Strategies

Comprehension strategies are nurtured and developed in an atmosphere that encourages reading, sharing, writing, and discussing the literature that children read. There may be times when children read without being required to respond. Sustained silent reading

(SSR) (chap. 4) is one opportunity. But general comprehension is guided by requiring some type of response. There should be many opportunities for free responses to literature. Children can share with whole groups, small groups, teacher–student conferences, and student–student conferences. When guiding children to an understanding of the texts they are reading, teachers should facilitate and guide instead of directing a specific outcome. Much of how teachers help children gain understandings from texts has to do with facilitating or negotiating the literature in an appropriate manner. Facilitation can occur in discussions, student–teacher conferences, responding to journal reactions (Readers' Workshop, chap. 4), or even well-planned centers. But there may be times when teachers wish to plan to focus on comprehension. These comprehension activities help children prepare for the independent reading activities that are the core of literature-based instruction. Teacher-directed comprehension activities will not be used daily during reading, but occasionally for specific purposes. Some of the times when more teacher-directed comprehension activities are required are:

1. to introduce a format that will be used by groups of children discussing literature. Activities can be used by children to progress through literature without the aid of the teacher. Activities that allow children to focus on comprehension can provide time to discuss which reading strategies were or were not helpful (Harste, 1989).

2. when children seem to be having a difficult time coming away from texts with any meaningful responses. Direct focus on some of the strategies allows the children to understand what is involved in the comprehension process.

3. when a new text arrangement or genre is introduced. Children need assistance in realizing that comprehension is obtained by using different strategies for various texts.

4. when a particularly difficult concept is presented in the literature. Many will automatically think of difficult concepts in expository texts such as science and social studies, but there are times that narratives offer concepts that call for teacher guidance in understanding.

5. to observe and watch how children respond to literature in an organized session. Organized comprehension strategies allow the teacher to assess how children are going about understanding what they are reading. Discussions that occur while children are participating in the activities help them become more aware of their own reading process, too. In other words, they can become more metacognitively aware of their personal reading behaviors when they are involved in effective comprehension activities.

6. when children seem to have difficulty with specific comprehension strategies such as using prior knowledge to predict and confirm.

Structured comprehension activities can be planned to encourage gaining more meaning from print, but these activities must be meaningful. They should be used as an opportunity to understand meaningful texts. The discussion that follows describes some of the most common comprehension instructional patterns as well as some innovative structures evolving from recent research. These instructional strategies are effective with all types of children's reading material, including exposition and narrative.

Reciprocal Teaching Strategy

Reciprocal teaching strategy (RTS) involves a dialogue between teachers and students about segments of text (Palinscar & Brown, 1986). It was developed for use with children who have great difficulty comprehending texts. Palinscar and Brown, the researchers who have thoroughly investigated this technique, tested it with different ages, in small groups, and whole class settings and found it to be successful in many situations.

The RTS dialogue is guided by the use of four strategies: summarizing, question generating, clarifying, and predicting, which are used during all phases of reading. The teacher and students take turns assuming the role of the leader of the dialogue.

When introducing RTS to students, the teacher explains the strategy and why the students will learn the procedure. Children are told that it is important to have strategies that help them comprehend and remember what they read. Strategies are introduced one at a time, practiced, and learned before putting all the parts together as RTS.

Predicting

Students hypothesize what the author will discuss. Students use pictures, titles, headings, and subheadings to predict what will occur. Confirming or disproving the hypothesis becomes one of the purposes for reading the text.

When students are introduced to prediction, they should understand that a prediction is a guess based on something they have read or understood from the book. They begin their predictions with the title of the story or pictures from the book. For example, as children begin reading *Just A Dream* (Van Allsburg, 1990), they use the title to guess that the book is about a dream of a character. By viewing the picture on the front of the book, they are able to predict the story could not really happen because the boy is in a bed that somehow has landed in a tree. A further prediction might involve the cat sitting on the bed. After making initial predictions, children are encouraged to revise their predictions as they read and understand more about the text.

Questioning

''Real-life'' situations help to illustrate question formation. Children ask each other questions about themselves and in the process brainstorm a list of question words (*who, what, when,* and *where*). In addition, the teacher demonstrates questioning as the class reads a variety of texts. When the children learn how to formulate good questions, they begin generating their own queries.

Summarizing

Summarizing allows readers to integrate the information in the text, but children often have a difficult time condensing material. A great deal of explanation will help children with this part of RTS. Depending on the readers' abilities, summarization can be explained with sentences, paragraphs, parts, or whole texts. It is also easier to summarize short texts or texts with headings and subheadings. While students are learning RTS procedure, they are more successful summarizing short passages. As they gain experience, the amount of text they can process expands. Students need a great deal of practice with summarizing information. The teacher probably will need to assist children in this part of RTS longer than any of the other three parts of the dialogue.

Clarifying

Students monitor their comprehension when they attempt to clarify what they have read. One way to encourage monitoring is to constantly call students' attention to the fact that what they read should make sense. Students are encouraged to ask for clarification whenever there is a word or concept they don't understand. Children learn how to clarify through discussion. For example, when reading *Just A Dream* (Van Allsburg, 1990), the teacher might ask readers to clarify what it means to ''rev'' a bulldozer. As children understand what it means to clarify, they become responsible for making sure they understand the concepts and vocabulary. It becomes their responsibility to ask for clarification when they do not understand text material.

Before RTS is used as a dialogue, students must understand each part of the strategy. Palinscar and Brown (undated) suggest that television and movies are useful for teaching children how to question, monitor, summarize, and clarify. After the students understand the four strategies, initial instruction begins. At first the teacher is principally responsible for initiating and sustaining the dialogue. Over time, the teacher will give more responsibility for sustaining the dialogue to the students. Teachers take less and less responsibility for the dialogue as the children gain experience with the strategies (see Box 6.1).

ReQuest (Reciprocal Questioning)

ReQuest is a comprehension strategy that encourages students to question as they read (Manzo, 1985; Tierney, Readence, & Dishner, 1990). The questioning allows them to focus on the prediction skills so necessary for improving comprehension. Although ReQuest originally was designed to be used with exposition in various subjects, the technique can be used with small groups or whole class situations with many types of text. It is particularly effective when children do not have the prior knowledge necessary for understanding texts.

ReQuest (see Box 6.2) can be presented as a game and should be used with text that is challenging to the students. The students first read an assigned portion of the text and are told that they will exchange questions with the teacher afterward. After silent reading the students ask the teacher questions about the text. The questions can involve recalling parts of the story, responding to the information or plot sequence, or replying with specific facts.

After the students ask questions, it is the teacher's turn to ask the questions. Teachers should use the types of questions they wish the children would ask. After both the teacher and children have asked questions, another portion of the text is read. After all have read the next section, the questioning continues until the students have enough information to predict what might happen next. The predictions are made after each question exchange, and the teacher elicits validation from students by asking, ''Why do you think so? . . . Read the lines that prove it . . .'' After the predictions, the sequence continues with silent reading.

BOX 6-1

Reciprocal Teaching Strategy (RTS) Dialogue

After explaining RTS and talking about each of the processes involved, a discussion somewhat like the following could occur after reading a few pages of *Just a Dream* (Van Allsburg, 1990).

Predicting

T: I still agree with my original prediction that this story is about sleeping. But I predict that we will learn more about what Walter dreams.

S1: Yes, I first predicted that it would be about sleeping because of the title and now he is going to bed. I agree with your prediction.

S2: I predict something weird is going to happen. The book just feels weird.

S3: I predict that he will dream about robots and stuff.

S4: I predict he will dream about his birthday. . . . Maybe he will dream about presents.

S5: Well, I predict he will dream about the future because it gives us a clue. Right here, it says ". . . he traveled to the future . . ."

Questioning

T: The question I have is, why did the author have the boy throw away the trash?

S1: Yes, I want to know that answer, and another question I have is still, on the front of the book, why is his bed in the tree?

S2: What do you think he will get for his birthday?

S3: The question I have is, do you think his neighbor will be in the book again?

Clarifying

T: I'm having a hard time understanding about him throwing away the trash. Could someone help clarify why he would want to sort the trash into three trash cans?

S1: Oh, you know, it has to do with environment and everything.

S2: Clarify what you mean by that.

S1: Everybody says to recycle and put your cans in one sack, your glass in another, and paper in another.

S3: I'd like to clarify why the neighbor was getting a tree for her birthday.

S4: I think it would be about the environment, too. You know we should be planting trees to help replace those cut down and stuff.

BOX 6-1 *Continued*

Summarizing

T: I'll start the summarization: Walter doesn't seem to be very concerned about picking up trash.

S1: Yeah, he seems more interested in eating jelly doughnuts and watching television.

S2: He is also interested in robots and the future.

S3: Yeah, but something is about to happen to Walter.

An alternate ReQuest procedure is suggested by Fitzgerald (1983). Students are paired and read part of the text. The children may read the material orally or silently, depending on their reading ability. After reading the material the pair works together and generates questions from the reading material. The questions can be devised after reading short portions or the entire text. After establishing a set of questions, each pair of students exchanges with another pair who read the same information and completed the same procedure. Each pair then answers the questions for the other pair.

Another variation uses writing for response. After reading a small section of the text, a team of readers generates written questions. The collection of questions is given to another team to respond in writing. This variation would be appropriate for children only after they are familiar with the process and can complete the procedure without teacher guidance.

Story Structures

Story structures have been discussed as a guide for teachers for developing effective questions. But story structures also can be used to increase comprehension. An understanding of story organization provides the framework for classroom discussions, lessons, and writing. One of the most effective ways to promote children's reading and writing skills is to help them develop a "sense of story" (Lehr, 1987, p. 550) or story structure. Story structures are a way for teachers to organize questions and activities based on characterization, setting, theme, plot, and main events. Story structures provide the teacher with a method of developing an understanding of specific literary features.

Knowing about important features helps children better understand and remember the content of narratives (Spiegel & Fitzgerald, 1986). Children tend to use what they can remember of the story to discuss, understand and interpret. Children's comprehension is improved when they can label parts of the story and identify the framework or structure.

A focus on the elements of literature is appropriate as soon as children begin interacting with good literature. Even before children learn to read complicated texts,

―― **BOX 6-2** ―――――――――――――――――――

ReQuest Dialogue

The following script is a ReQuest dialogue between a teacher and a small group of children who are reading *Just a Dream* (Van Allsburg, 1990). The teacher and the children have their own copies of the book and have been instructed to read the first six pages, stop, and close the book. The teacher attempts to encourage questions that provoke high-level thinking.

T: We are going to play ReQuest so you can ask me any questions about what you have just read.

S1: What was Walter eating?

T: A jelly doughnut.

S2: What did he want for his birthday?

T: I don't know if it really said that. But I know he doesn't want a tree.

S3: Do you think there is any reason why the author told us that he threw away the trash? I mean, is there any reason why that's part of the story?

T: Wow! That's a good question. It really makes me think about the story. I'm not sure of the answer. Let's go back to the text and read that part and I'll answer the question.

After rereading the page, the teacher responds and moves to the next phase, which includes an opportunity for the teacher to ask useful questions.

T: Does this story remind you of anything that is happening in our world?

S4: I guess a lot of people throw things away and that reminds me of the environmental issues.

S3: It reminds me that I wouldn't want a tree for a birthday, either.

S5: The three trash cans make me think of that same thing. All the time we hear about recycling.

T: What kind of attitude does Walter have, and how does the author let us know what kind of person Walter is?

S5: Walter doesn't think about other people. He just wants his robots and planes. I know that because of what he says.

S4: Walter likes jelly doughnuts.

T: How do you know that?

S4: Well, he eats one in the story.

T: So the author lets us know about Walter by his actions or what he does.

The questions about this section continue for a while longer. After all questions are asked and discussed, the teacher asks for predictions about the next part of the story.

they can use pictures in picture books to develop their understanding of literary features. Whether in children's literature, in story books, tradebooks, or basals, the elements of literature can structure comprehension activities and encourage understanding. The following literary elements, which were discussed thoroughly in chapter 2, can be used to discuss the selections used during reading instruction:

Plot Development

Plot development focuses on the problems and solutions of the story and can be the basis for many discussions, writing, and listing activities. Plot most closely approximates the sequencing activities in the skills approach to reading.

Characterization

Understanding characters in a story has at least two advantages. By relating to the character and the actions of characters, children gain a better understanding of themselves and others. They increase their comprehension by understanding the characters in the story. Graves (1989) has shown that children's writing progress is affected positively by their understanding of characters.

Setting

A discussion of the setting of a story establishes the time and place of a story. The setting is important to the mood and credibility of the story.

Theme

A discussion of why the author wrote the story and the ideas that were communicated are especially beneficial. Theme is most closely associated with the traditional strategies of main idea.

Traditionally, junior high and high school literature studies have included a focus on story structure. Literature-based reading instruction at the elementary level suggests the importance of introducing literary concepts at the very beginning of children's introduction to good literature. Children do not seem to learn story structure easily on their own and are especially likely to profit from consistent and regular instruction in story structure (Spiegel & Fitzgerald, 1986).

When story structures are used to discuss classroom literary activities, writing can be affected. When reading activities are structured around story structures, teachers often see that knowledge reflected in the children's own narratives. Lynch (1986) suggests that young children can use and further develop their knowledge of story structures by writing original stories. Their writing reflects what they understand about the stories they read. Story structure instruction can provide a vehicle for integrating reading and writing.

Many instructional activities can emerge from a teacher focusing on the structure of a story. A simple procedure for introducing the elements can be implemented on the first day of first grade or kindergarten.

Introduce the Story Elements

Children are best introduced to story structures by developing their knowledge gradually. First graders might begin by understanding characterization or "who" in the story. Literature that presents strong characters could be selected to develop the concept of characterization. For example, *Hey Al* (Yorinks, 1986) presents a character with easily recognizable traits. The story begins, "Al, a nice man, a quiet man," and goes on to describe an unhappy janitor whose dissatisfaction sends him on a journey to a paradise. His dog, Eddie, is easily characterized as the "faithful dog Eddie, who lived in the east side apartment." Children's literature abounds with memorable characters, but books by Egielski and Yorinks such as *Hey, Al* (1986), *Oh, Brother* (1989), *Bravo, Minsky* (1988), and *Louis, the Fish* (1980), nearly always present strong and unusual characters that are easily described and fun to discuss.

Whatever literature is used, the teacher should focus on who is in the story for as long as it takes for children to understand the concept of characters and characterization. The development of literary concepts can be accomplished in a natural manner by identifying and discussing the character as the story is read. Use of the term *character* should be commonplace so that students become accustomed to the terminology. Children can participate in such activities as drawing pictures, writing, or role playing to reinforce concepts about characterization.

After the teacher is sure that most of the children have acquired an understanding of characterization, another element can be introduced. The same procedure can be used to develop the concept of setting. After reading books that focus on settings, children can draw pictures of a setting or produce a setting of their own in writing to reinforce their concepts about a story's setting. Yolen's *Owl Moon* (1987) is a good example of a high quality book that has a strong setting. The white, snowy countryside and the darker, quieter woods provide material for development of setting. *Hey, Al* (Yorinks, 1986) is another book that is particularly effective in developing setting since there are two contrasting settings and the artwork and descriptions make them particularly noticeable. *The Mysteries of Harris Burdick* (Van Allsburg, 1984) presents titles and captions for several wonderful pictures that suggest interesting situations. The title, caption, and picture can kick off a discussion of where the story takes place. After discussing a multitude of ideas, children can produce their own settings for the story.

After exposure to stories and literature, children begin developing an understanding of story structure. The children could add pictures of the characters to pictures of the setting. This process of drawing and discussion should help children distinguish story elements and understand how the elements are interrelated.

All five literary elements (characterization, setting, plot, theme, and main events) are introduced in the same manner, making sure that the class spends enough time on each element to develop it thoroughly. After children have developed the concepts of story structure, many comprehension activities can emerge.

Provide a Uniform Way for Children to Respond to Story Structures

Basing discussion and questions on story structures or maps is one way to familiarize children with story structure. But children can become explicitly aware of story structure if a consistent format is used to discuss it. One way to familiarize children with story structures is to produce an easily recognizable figure for children to use repeatedly. For example, a reproducible worksheet that is used with stories allows children to understand what they are supposed to recognize when reading a story. A story structure guide for first and third graders is illustrated in Figure 6.1.

Use the Story Structure to Guide Writing

The story structure also works well to guide brainstorming that leads to writing. After children have developed an understanding of the elements and structure of a story, the same framework can be used to produce original stories. One way to encourage the inclusion of all story elements is to use the story structure to brainstorm before writing. Some motivation should be provided, such as a wordless picture book, a picture, or event. Story structures guide brainstorming. The entire class is encouraged to brainstorm the type of character that could evolve in the story.

Children can use story structures to check whether their own stories provide all elements of good story structure. If all elements are not present in their own creations, editing should be encouraged. This activity helps guide children and expand their own writing to include all elements of a good story.

Use Story Structures to Develop Questions and Encourage Predictions during Instruction

Story structures can be used by the teacher to develop effective and comprehensive questions about the material. Effective questioning might include all story elements and provide a framework for discussion. Questions might include comparison and contrast with other stories or narratives or could serve as a basis for predictions before and during reading. Predictions based on the front cover could be encouraged. After seeing the first picture in the story or reading the first page, children could predict what type of character is in the story, a description of the setting, or make suggestions about the plot or events in the story.

Written *story frames* are one way to incorporate story structure or story elements in reading instruction (Cudd & Roberts, 1987). Story frames use some aspects of story structures and cloze. The process encourages summarizing and writing the missing sections where appropriate. Story frames often are used in basal stories, but can be easily adapted to any literature the children read. Different stories might use different story frames. A basic story frame would look like this:

Title
The problem in this story was
This was a problem because
The problem was finally solved when
In the end

Another type of story frame looks like this:

Title
In this story a   had a problem. His problem was

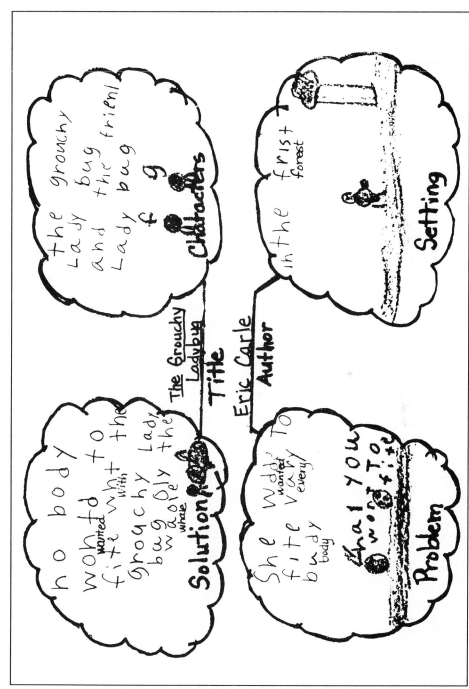

FIGURE 6-1 These examples illustrate the differences in first and third graders' productions based on story structure guides. *Continued*

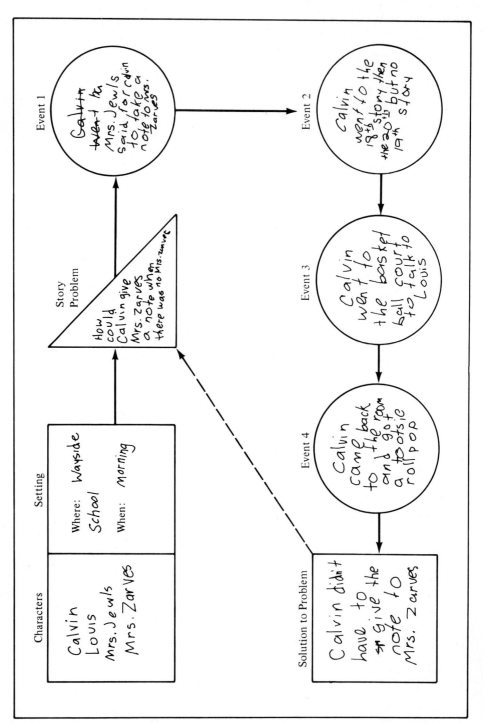

FIGURE 6-1 *Continued*

This was a problem for him because
Then one day a   had a good idea. She
This solved the mule's problem because
In the end,

Jennifer Dunham, a first grade teacher, uses the story structure format from the first day of school to guide discussions of the stories her students read. She believes her students learn to look for literary elements, and she has no doubt that story structure formats improve their comprehension strategies. The procedures she uses to introduce story structures are listed here and may be adapted for any age group.

1. Jennifer begins by identifying books that lend themselves to discussion of literary elements.
2. She first introduces the concept of character because her first graders easily identify the main character in the story.
3. The children discuss characterization for a day or two until they feel comfortable with the concept. The discussions occur naturally as the children read books together.
4. Usually, setting is the next literary element to be introduced gradually. Dunham begins by talking about where stories take place and uses a book such as *Clifford's Family* (Birdwell, 1966) to develop setting.
5. She continues introducing the elements through a natural discussion of the stories and showing how students might fill in the structure. Finally, her students are able to complete a story structure format that includes characters, settings, problems, and solutions.

At the beginning of the year, most students complete their story structures by drawing pictures. It is not long before they begin to use both pictures and writing to express their ideas, and by the end of the year many students complete their story structures in writing. Sometimes story structures are used to guide oral and written retellings. The children know and expect that classroom activities usually begin with some adaptions of story structures and evolve into other activities. They often complete a story structure to provide Dunham with information about their comprehension. One of Dunham's students children produced the first grade response in Figure 6.1. Older children may produce a graphic story structure as in the second example in Figure 6.1.
There is the danger that story structures always lead to analysis and factual recall and ignore how the literature affects the reader (McClure & Zitlow, 1991; Many & Wiseman, 1991). Even when using story structures, teachers should remember that the most mature responses to literature allow children to respond to what they are thinking, feeling, seeing, and hearing in addition to analyzing literary elements and recalling the facts.

Retelling

Verbal or written retelling contributes to comprehension of a text. Retelling requires the reader to organize the text in logical, cohesive thoughts and contributes to retention of the material. Retelling is a simple activity that also improves oral language development. This activity can be used with children's literature, language experience, or basal reader stories.

One way to implement retelling is to pair students during independent reading time. Each student is required to read silently and then tell his or her partner what he or she read (Koskinen, Kapinus, & Heathington, 1988). The following sequence suggests a plan for implementing retelling in the classroom:

1. The teacher should explain the purpose of retelling. What a child includes in a retelling is affected by the stated purpose. The teacher might ask children to read the story and share it with someone who has not heard the story or to read the story and talk about the action of the characters. Children must have a purpose for retelling the story, even if it is to share it with others.

2. The teacher should retell a story before requiring children to do it. This is especially important if the teacher is looking for a particular way of retelling a story. There should be many opportunities for observing retelling, and experimentation should be allowed.

3. Once the teacher retells a story, there should be opportunities for children to practice retelling it with the teacher's guidance. The teacher might work one-on-one or with small groups until each student is able to retell stories to the teacher.

4. Students should have time to practice retelling before sharing with their peers. After reading independently, students might talk to themselves aloud or even to a tape recorder. Short stories or passages ensure that everyone stays interested in the task at hand. Even stories that have been discussed all week in class could be retold. As students become more efficient at retelling, the teacher can select more complex stories for the activity.

Jennifer Dunham has her first grade students retell for many different purposes:

1. Sometimes they share with partners after their SSR reading. They enjoy having this time to converse with their neighbors, and there is no pressure since everyone is successful. Sometimes a few of the children volunteer to retell their stories to the entire class.

2. Another time her first graders retell a story after a literature selection is read. They often use story structures as their guides. In both of these situations, the rest of the class asks questions after the retelling to clarify and expand ideas.

3. Occasionally, Jennifer has her first graders introduce a book and "sell" their selections to the rest of the class.

Jennifer's techniques could be modified for use with older children. The choice of literature is the most obvious way to modify retelling for older children. As texts become more complex, retellings should be more sophisticated.

Written retellings contribute to comprehension. A written summary helps children focus on the story and translate what they understand into their own language. An identified purpose and audience are necessary to provide reasons for written retellings. Written retellings can be required for story reviews, sharing with others, or convincing others to read a story. Small groups of beginning readers can increase their understanding of a story by retelling it to be written during language experience. Not only do written retellings increase comprehension, they also provide concrete evidence of the readers' levels of understanding.

Cued Retelling

Cued retelling is a cooperative learning strategy that combines free retelling with cued response questions. Nancy Howard, a third grade teacher who uses many cooperative techniques (chap. 3) in her reading instruction, uses cued retelling as a way to assess children's comprehension. She likes this procedure because it gives the reader freedom to share personal recollections as well as to focus on recalling specific incidents in the material. This activity often results in children coming to conclusions about the differences in free recall and asking specific questions. After the children learn the format from Howard and role play, they can conduct the procedure on their own. The steps are as follows:

1. The teacher prepares cues. (See *Mirandy and Brother Wind* (McKissack, 1988) cues in Box 6.3.)

2. Students are paired and read the material to each other in unison or silently, depending on the abilities of the partners.

3. The first student writes or tells everything she or he remembers about the passage. This is a free retelling, and there are no requirements. This is a good time to encourage all types of responses from the children.

4. The student who is listening uses a cued retelling sheet to mark off what the first reader discusses. After retelling is completed, the items listed on the cued retelling sheet that were not mentioned are read as cues and the first student tells as much as he or she can. The second student asks, ''What do you remember about _____ ?''

5. The partners switch roles, and the process and cued retelling follow as before.

Nancy usually asks the reader with the most confidence to retell first so that the reader who may be having difficulty checks the items retold and is responsible for reminding the first story teller what he or she omitted. This allows the less confident reader more opportunity to be successful.

This activity allows a wide range of responses, but also provides a teacher with information about how a child is responding to texts. If the teacher sees that children are not discussing anything related to the text, the child may need to take part in more specific comprehension activities.

Interaction, Sharing, Discussion

Discussion already has been mentioned as a way to build concepts, but it is probably one of the most effective methods of assuring understanding of the reading material. Shanklin and Rhodes (1989) suggest that '' . . . reading comprehension is enhanced . . . through social interaction in the reading classroom'' (p. 496). Discussion is valuable when students read the same text or when they are sharing selections read independently. There should be opportunities for children to guide the discussion and ask questions. Reading can also be supplemented with media such as art or drama. Sharing can be formal or informal, occur in small or large groups, and can be teacher- or student-directed. There are several types of discussion and interactions that can be used to develop comprehension strategies. Books and literature can be shared in panel and roundtable discussions, book talks, choral reading, paired reading, assisted reading, persuasive

---

BOX 6-3

Mirandy and Brother Wind (McKissack, 1988)
Cued Retelling (Part I)

Ask your partner to tell everything he or she can remember about the story you have just read. Check off each idea as your partner mentions it. After your partner has told you everything he or she can remember, give the remaining cues one at a time. Allow your partner to tell as much as possible about each cue.

Free Retelling	Cued Retelling	Cues
_____	_____	It was spring
_____	_____	Partner at the junior cakewalk
_____	_____	Catching Brother Wind
_____	_____	Clumsy boy Ezel
_____	_____	Brother Wind strolling through the meadow
_____	_____	Mrs. Poinsettia, the conjure woman
_____	_____	Brother Wind jumped into the bottle
_____	_____	Ezel as Mirandy's partner
_____	_____	Making fun of Ezel
_____	_____	Dancing with the wind

Mirandy and Brother Wind (McKissack, 1988)
Cued Retelling (Part II)

Ask your partner to tell everything he or she can remember about the story you have just read. Check off each idea as your partner mentions it. After your partner has told you everything he or she can remember, give the remaining cues one at a time. Allow your partner to tell as much as possible about each cue.

Free Retelling	Cued Retelling	Cues
_____	_____	High stepping through Ridgetop
_____	_____	Mirandy's first cakewalk
_____	_____	Throwing pepper at Brother Wind
_____	_____	Orlinda as Ezel's partner
_____	_____	Conjures to catch Brother Wind
_____	_____	Colorful scarves
_____	_____	Brother Wind whooshed into the bottle
_____	_____	Asking Ezel to be Mirandy's partner
_____	_____	Mirandy and Ezel win the cakewalk
_____	_____	Colorful scarves around her wrist

speeches, and writing selections. Sharing also can be done in written responses to the literature. Sharing is limited only by the children's and teacher's creativity.

Directed Reading–Thinking Activity

The basal approach to developing comprehension strategies is usually a strategy known as a *directed reading–thinking activity* (DRTA) (Stauffer, 1975). Most basals use a consistent series of steps to present the stories and skills to the students. There are several identifiable procedures usually included in the overall presentation of basal lessons. The steps may have other labels, but can be defined as *prereading* activities, *during reading* activities, and *post-reading* activities or enrichment.

1. Prereading activities include establishing a purpose for reading, presenting unfamiliar concepts and vocabulary, and encouraging prediction.

2. During reading activities involve silent reading of several pages, the teacher asking questions afterward, and oral reading of the selection to support answers.

3. Post-reading activities include checking predictions, discussing the story, working on strategies and vocabulary, comprehension and decoding skills, and enrichment such as writing, drama, art, and discussion.

Overall, methods that basal readers use to encourage comprehension include questions to guide silent and oral reading, discussion of vocabulary, and opportunities to summarize what has been read. The questions asked during reading lessons require students to make predictions and offer support for them from the text. Children are encouraged to list their own predictions before reading the material. A text is divided into sections that teachers use to guide students to 1) predict, 2) read, and 3) provide evidence during reading. Questioning that requires prediction and support is similar to:

1. What do you think will happen?
2. Why do you think so?
3. What have you experienced or what has happened in the story to lead you to that prediction?

Most basal readers encourage teachers to use these strategies to develop comprehension. The DRTA is an easily recognized and familiar format used in many instructional situations. Discussions about texts in basals, children's literature, and even subjects such as social studies and science are developed around the DRTA format. The DRTA format offers a beginning teacher a structure for developing reading lessons and is a valuable tool if one is aware of a few pitfalls.

There are some concerns about using the prescribed format of the basal readers. The first is that basals tend to ignore the uniqueness of a reader's response to literature. When the DRTA is part of a basal reading lesson, it includes a structured, preconceived format that does not consider children's prior knowledge or schemata. Generally, the teacher's guide offers expected responses, and the variety of responses that might be produced by children is not considered. A teacher can overcome this concern by including questions that allow children to express their feelings and reactions as they read and relate their own experiences to what they are reading.

There are times when the stop-and-go nature of DRTA interferes with comprehension. Effective readers using well-organized texts do not need many interruptions to get some meaning from the texts. Fluent reading is usually a continuous, rapid activity that is hindered by stopping. While the constant prediction and confirming may be necessary for children who are experiencing a great deal of difficulty in understanding written texts, it is not necessary for readers who can respond to the material. Teachers who are aware of this potentially frustrating factor can plan to use the activity to meet individual readers' needs.

Finally, a classic study completed over ten years ago (Durkin, 1979) indicated that many teachers did not use DRTA appropriately. Teachers tended to skip the before and after reading components, which would be the most supportive of guiding comprehension. Instead, many teachers focused on the isolated skills and literal questioning suggested by the teacher's guide. This practice ignores prior knowledge and eliminates a valuable aspect of the procedure.

The use of DRTA is strengthened when it is viewed as a flexible procedure that allows for prediction, reading to see if predictions are appropriate, and providing evidence that the predictions were appropriate (Garrison & Hoskisson, 1989). A more liberal interpretation of traditional DRTA could provide help for students in negotiating texts. Students could be encouraged to make predictions with the idea that predictions not supported by the text will be changed. As the reading progresses, students could be encouraged to explain why predictions have been proved or disproved. Garrison and Hoskisson (1989) point out that as long as predictions are reasonable, there is no reason to establish new predictions, and the reading can continue. Their description of DRTA asserts, ''Many first rate stories at all levels support reasonable but mutually exclusive interpretations'' (p. 484). When DRTA allows for many interpretations, it supports comprehension development.

The vocabulary and concept building associated with DRTAs in texts and basals can be amended to focus on concepts and vocabulary that children identify as unknown or confusing. Children can be taught to recognize when they can benefit from clarification. Teachers can use the before, during and after structure of a DRTA, but instead of presenting basal suggestions, the concepts and vocabulary that children identify are the focus of before, during, and after discussions.

DRTA is similar to the other directed comprehension activities described in this chapter. DRTA is appropriate when children are reading difficult texts, need help with prediction and confirmation, and when the material is full of new concepts. DRTAs never should be the main focus of comprehension instruction nor should they be used exclusively. Time would be better spent in independent reading and free response to literature.

Comprehension and Listening

Listening and reading comprehension are both language processes that require the learner to construct meaning. Listening and reading require flexible use of many strategies and skills and may produce results that differ according to who is interpreting the information. Reading and listening have another important link. Research has shown that developing comprehension skills in listening directly affects reading skills (Pearson and

Fielding, 1982). Teachers can develop basic comprehension skills and strategies with listening or reading. Teachers do not need to wait until a child is capable of reading difficult and complex material to improve comprehension strategies. Listening to more complex material provides opportunities for learning. Instead of requiring children to read, the material is read to them. Many of the structures for gaining meaning from print can be used to develop meaning-gathering strategies while listening.

Writing

Reading comprehension and writing are related because of their common language (Kucer, 1987). They also share procedural aspects. Both reading and writing require previous experience with the topic. The reader or writer must know about a topic before beginning either process. Readers and writers must understand the language processes. They must understand vocabulary, sentence development, and mechanics. Readers and writers both revise understandings, negotiate texts, and refine meanings as they go along. Writers constantly revise their language and usage, and readers constantly revise their understanding.

When the two processes are used in instruction, they can contribute to understanding a topic. Writing about the subject is one way of sharing information and extending comprehension (Rhodes & Dudley-Marling, 1988). Writing is so closely associated with thinking that as children write, they develop their own thoughts and ideas about a story.

Encouraging written responses to reading material requires extended engagement with a text. The more time children spend with a text, the better the chance to develop greater understanding of the topic. The more time a reader writes and thinks about a story, the more comprehension is enhanced.

Writing contributes to comprehension when children see themselves as builders of comprehension. Their own writing is a way for them to understand topics while producing text. As they develop an understanding of how to produce a story, they understand more about how to read a story.

Comprehension is supported when children are asked to respond to what they read in various written formats. For example, free responses motivated by the request to write anything they want about a story encourages readers to think about the story and make a decision about what they read. Asking students to write about parts of the story that are like events in your life, or ''Does this story remind you of another story you have read?'' requires readers to link story events with their own lives. Many of the questions associated with reader response theory provide excellent probes for written responses to literature. As children write responses to literature, they become aware of additional insights and understandings, and their level of comprehension increases.

Learning Differences

Because comprehension is affected by prior knowledge and schema development, the different language and cultural backgrounds represented in the classroom have a great impact on how children understand text. Recognizing the differences is the first step in helping children of different languages and cultures become effective readers.

Language

Comprehending printed material in a second language can be a difficult and frustrating experience. Monolingual English speakers visiting another country gain a sense of what it is like to attempt to comprehend printed material without fluency in the language. That situation can lead to frustration and a feeling of helplessness. Children who are learning to speak English can be encouraged in a supportive classroom. Some techniques allow a teacher to understand ways to contribute to comprehension development for children who speak English as a second language.

There are great differences in how fast and well students learn English. Their comprehension of printed material is affected by the experiences they have had with oral and written language in their native tongues. These students never should be grouped together and considered homogeneous learners. They should be recognized as learners with differing abilities. Instruction should provide for the differences just as the differences among native speakers is considered.

Students may try to do exactly as they are told so that they can understand the language. If instruction focuses on sounds and parts of language, students will focus on sounds and parts of language. A heavy focus on sounds and parts of language may not be necessary because non-English-speaking students tend to focus on phonological aspects as they learn to read. Indeed, advanced learners of English do not tend to use semantic and syntactic cues well as they read. They seem to overuse decoding strategies at the expense of ways to gain meaning. For that reason, students learning English may need more explicit directions on how to comprehend written material.

It is important to recognize that the inability to talk about content in English does not indicate low achievement. Competence and instruction in two languages does not lead to lower levels of reading competence (Reyes, 1987). The ability to speak and read two or more languages in today's global economy is an asset and a measure of a well-educated person.

Teachers must be aware of and recognize differences in comprehension that result from speaking a second language. '' . . . [S]ensitivity to students, cultural congruence, and the informal social interaction . . . is believed to be critical in the development of the learning environment which are conducive to the academic success of bilingual students,'' Reyes writes (1987; p. 123).

Strategies that help children learning English as a second language to develop reading comprehension include all the suggestions that are good for native speakers. However, teachers may need to use a lot of predictable material, many supportive reading techniques, and much repetition to improve these students' comprehension strategies. Children who are learning English benefit from programs that rely on the integration of language processes. Just as the beginning reader of a native language needs a variety of activities for many purposes and in several media, students who are learning English as their second language need to see and hear language for meaningful purposes and for as many different reasons as possible. It is particularly important for children to spend much time listening in order to read and speak English. As the listening vocabulary accumulates, students can be asked to respond. Students' first reading activities can be an extension of listening activities that encourage all language processes (Guckes & Kandaras, 1988).

In addition to providing predictable activities, supportive reading techniques, and an accepting atmosphere, success for children who have limited proficiency in English can be enhanced by creating a language-rich environment and encouraging much interaction with other children (Holdzkom, Reed, Porter, & Rubin, 1984). Some of the activities for beginning readers, such as language experience and supportive reading techniques, can help children who are struggling to learn English as a second language.

Culture

One way to improve comprehension for children from different cultural backgrounds is to use instructional material that reflects their prior knowledge and experiences. Classrooms should provide texts that represent values, lifestyles, customs, and historical traditions for every child in the class. When contemporary material reflecting different cultural groups is not available, traditional literature can provide appropriate material for children to read. Folk tales, myths, and legends from many cultures are available and can support comprehension activities. A particularly effective comprehension activity is comparing the folktales of different countries. Comparing a European variant of *Little Red Riding Hood* and the Chinese *Lon Po Po* or *Cinderella* with the African variant, *Mufaro's Beautiful Daughters* (Steptoe, 1987) is an effective comprehension activity that also encourages multicultural awareness. If material reflecting some cultures simply cannot be found, language experience stories can be used to help children feel comfortable with their cultures.

There are times when lack of availability prevents a teacher from providing materials that match children's backgrounds. There are some activities that encourage and support comprehension development when children of different cultures are reading material that may not be familiar and comfortable. Discussion is very valuable for helping to close the gap between material and culture. Many of the concept-building activities already discussed are appropriate for dealing with cultural differences. Other activities based on nonprint and print materials help build the cultural background necessary for understanding reading material.

Comprehension activities can be more effective with differing cultural groups when teachers' attitudes reflect acceptance and understanding of all children. Teachers should understand that there may be differences in responses from children from different cultural groups. Children's previous experiences may produce ideas that differ from those of the teacher. Some children may respond better in a cooperative learning arrangement because their community encourages the completion of tasks in groups. Teachers should not lower their expectations because children comprehend and respond to reading activities in ways that owe to of their cultural experiences. Children still should be expected to learn the material, but teachers must understand that children will appreciate literature and reading material that reflects their beliefs. Responses to literature may differ, and different arrangements for learning may be necessary to meet the needs of children from different cultures.

One activity developed in a Honolulu school demonstrates how children learning English can improve their comprehension and language strategies (Au & Kawakami, 1985) as they respond in a culturally acceptable manner. As teachers ask questions, children respond to create a narrative. The teacher encourages all children to contribute, but always with the support of the group. The "talk story lesson" is not as quiet as when students speak in turn. Speaking out is not considered disruptive, but is accepted as contributing to growth in oral language and comprehension. Teachers do plan the questions to be asked, but expect varied responses and from more than one child at a time. The talk story lesson was developed for Hawaiian children and serves only as an example of culturally appropriate reading instruction. Teachers always should be aware of the importance of allowing children to respond in culturally comfortable ways.

DISCUSSION AND ACTIVITIES

1. Why is there no one method or material that is most effective for teaching comprehension? Brainstorm factors that might cause children to understand reading material in a different way. In addition to listing factors affecting comprehension, list an instructional method to reduce the effect of any one factor.

2. What material would be the easiest for children to read? Why is it easy, and why would you use that material for instruction?

3. Do you agree with the statement, "One activity that improves reading comprehension is reading aloud to children?" Why do you agree or disagree? List as many reasons as possible to support the way you feel about that statement.

4. Read a children's book and design a story structure of important elements to guide discussion and questions. Use the story structure to lead a small group discussion of the book. Include questions that require participants to respond to the text in various ways.

RELATED READING

Children's Literature

Reciprocal Teaching and ReQuest

Van Allsburg, C. (1990). *Just a dream.* Boston: Houghton Mifflin.

> *This recent Van Allsburg book is excellent for asking questions and making predictions about environmental issues. Each section of the story has a logical stopping place suggested by the picture arrangement, and it is not frustrating to stop and discuss during the reading.*

Expository Texts

Ballard, R. D. (1988). *Exploring the Titanic.* Illustrations by K. Marschall. New York: Scholastic.

> *This is the complete story of the Titanic and is full of facts and figures that allow children to understand the tragedy. The text is long and probably more suitable for upper grades, but there are concepts that need to be developed in readers of all ages.*

Retelling

Any of the beautiful examples of traditional literature would be good for developing retelling strategies because they evolved from the oral tradition. Children would have a particularly good time telling favorite traditional stories such as *Goldilocks and the Three Bears.* The wordless picture book *Deep in the Forest* (Turkle, 1976), which is a variation of Goldilocks, could stimulate retellings. Other favorites to retell are the nonsense stories that have their origins in traditional literature.

Story Structures

Van Allsburg, C. (1979). *The Garden of Abdul Gazazi.* Boston: Houghton Mifflin.

> *This fast-moving book would be good for presenting plot and conflict.*

Blume, J. (1971). *Freckle juice.* New York: Dell.

> Freckle Juice *has an obvious theme that is easily recognized.*

Paterson, K. (1978). *The great Gilly Hopkins.* New York: Crowell.

> *The first chapter of this book is one of the best examples of character development to be found in children's literature.*

Yorinks, A. (1986). *Hey, Al.* Illustrated by R. Egielski. New York: Farrar, Straus & Giroux.

> *Yorinks and Egielski use pictures and text to present two distinct settings.*

Yolen, J. (1987). *Owl Moon.* Illustrated by J. Schoenherr. New York: Philomel.

> *This is an excellent text that has a very distinct and integral setting.*

Books Cited in This Chapter

Birdwell, N. (1966). *Clifford's family.* New York: Scholastic.

McKissack, P.C. (1988). *Mirandy and Brother Wind.* Illustrated by J. Pinkney. New York: Alfred A. Knopf.

Ness, E. (1966). *Sam, Bangs and moonshine.* New York: Dutton.

Paterson, K. (1988). *Park's quest.* New York: Dutton.

Steptoe, J. (1987). *Mufaro's beautiful daughters: An African tale.* New York: Lothrop.

Turkle, B. (1976). *Deep in the Forest.* New York: Dutton.

Van Allsburg, C. (1984). *The mysteries of Harris Burdick.* Boston: Houghton Mifflin.

———. (1990). *Just a dream.* Boston: Houghton Mifflin.

Yolen, J. (1987). *Owl moon.* Illustrated by J. Schoenherr. New York: Philomel.

Yorinks, A. (1980). *Louis the fish.* Illustrated by R. Egielski. New York: Farrar, Straus and Giroux.

———. (1986). *Hey, Al.* Illustrated by R. Egielski. New York: Farrar, Straus and Giroux.

———. (1988). *Bravo, Minsky.* Illustrated by R. Egielski. New York: Farrar, Straus and Giroux.

———. (1989). *Oh Brother.* Illustrated by R. Egielski. New York: Farrar, Straus and Giroux.

Young, E. (1989). *Lon Po Po.* New York: Philomel.

REFERENCES

Au, K.H., & Kawakami, A.J. (1985). Research currents: Talk story and learning to read. *Language Arts, 62* (4), 406–411.

Babbs, P. J., & Moe, A. J. (1983). Metacognition: A key for independent learning from text. *The Reading Teacher, 36* (5), 422–426.

Baumann, J. F., & Schmitt, M. C. (1986). The what, why, how, and when of comprehension instruction. *The Reading Teacher, 39* (5), 422–426.

Brown, A.L. & Day, J.D. (1983). Macrorules for summarizing texts. The development of expertise. *Journal of Verbal Learning and Verbal Behavior, 22* (1), 1–14.

Cooper, C.R. (Ed.). (1985). *Researching response to literature and the teaching of literature.* Norwood, NJ: Ablex.

Cudd, E.T., & Roberts, L.L. (1987). Using story frames to develop reading comprehension in a 1st grade classroom. *The Reading Teacher, 41* (1), 74–79.

Cullinan, B. (1989). *Literature and the child* (2nd ed.). Orlando, FL: Harcourt Brace Jovanovich.

Duffy, G.G. & Roehler, L.R. (1987). Improving reading instruction through the use of responsive elaboration. *The Reading Teacher, 40* (6), 514–521.

Durkin, D. (1979). What classroom observations reveal about reading comprehension instruction. *Reading Research Quarterly, 14* (3), 481–533.

Fitzgerald, J. (1983). Helping children gain self control over reading comprehension. *Reading Teacher, 37* (2), 249–253.

———. (1989) Research on stories: Implications for teachers. In K.D. Murth (Ed.), *Children's Comprehension of Text.* Newark, DE: International Reading Association.

Garner, R. (1987). *Metacognition and reading comprehension.* Norwood, NJ: Ablex.

Garrison, J.W. & Hoskisson, K. (1989). Confirmation bias in predictive reading. *The Reading Teacher, 42* (7), 482–486.

Gentile, C. & Kane, S. (1989). A study of diverse responses to an allegorical text. In R.W. Blake (Ed.), *Reading, writing and interpreting literature.* Schenectady, NY: New York State English Council.

Graves, D. (1989). *Experiment with fiction.* Portsmouth, NH: Heinemann.

Guckes, L.R., & Kandaras, B. (1988). Speak it, read it: Simultaneous acquisition of language and reading skills. In K. Muller (Ed.), *Children and languages: Research, practice, and rationale for the early grades.* New York: National Council on Foreign Language and International Studies.

Harste, J. (1989). *New policy guidelines for reading: Connecting research and practice.* Urbana, IL: National Council of Teachers of English.

Holdzkom, D., Reed, L.J., Porter, E.J., & Rubin, D.L. (1984). *Research within reach: Oral and written communication.* Washington, DC: National Institute of Education.

Koskinen, P.S., Gambrell, L.B., Kapinus, B.A., & Heathington, B.S. (1988). Retelling: A strategy for enhancing students' reading comprehension. *Reading Teacher, 41* (9), 892–896.

Kucer, S. B. (1987). The cognitive base of reading and writing. In J. R. Squire (Ed.), *The dynamics of language learning.* Urbana, IL.: ERIC Clearinghouse on Reading and Communication Skills.

Lehr, F. (1987). Story grammar. *The Reading Teacher, 40* (6), 550–552.

Lynch, P. (1986). *Using big books and predictable books.* New York: Scholastic.

Mandler, J. M. (1984). *Stories, scripts, and scenes: Aspects of schema theory.* Hillsdale, NJ: Lawrence Erlbaum.

Mandler, J. M., & Johnson, N. S. (1977). Remembrance of things parsed: Story structure and recall. *Cognitive Psychology, 9* (1), 111–115.

Many, J.E. (1991). The effects of stance and age level on children's literary responses. *Journal of Reading Behavior, 23* (1) 61–85.

Many, J., & Wiseman, D. (1992). Analyzing versus experiencing: The effects of teaching approaches on students' responses. In C. Cox & J. Many (Eds.), *Reader stance and literary understanding.* Norwood, NJ: Ablex.

Manzo, A. (1969). The request procedure. *Journal of Reading, 412,* 123–126.

———.(1985). Expansion modules for the ReQuest, CAT, GRP and REAP reading/ study procedures. *Journal of Reading, 28* (5), 498–503.

McClure, A.A., & Zitlow, C.S. (1991). Not just the facts: Aesthetic response in elementary content area studies. *Language Arts, 68* (1), 27–33.

Murth, K.D. (Ed.). (1989). *Children's comprehension of text: Research into practice.* Newark, DE: International Reading Association.

Nessel, D. (1987) The new face of comprehension instruction: A close look at questions. *The Reading Teacher, 40* (7), 604–608.

Palinscar, A. S., & Brown, A. L. (1986). Interactive teaching to promote independent learning from text. *Reading Teacher, 39* (8), 771–777.

Palinscar, A.S., & Brown, A. L. (undated). *Reciprocal teaching.* Unpublished manuscript.

Paris, S.G., Oka, E.R., & DeBritto, A. M. (1983). Beyond decoding: Synthesis of research on reading comprehension. *Educational Leadership, 41* (2), 78–83.

Pearson, P.D. (1982). Asking questions about stories. *Ginn Occasional Papers.* Columbus, OH: Ginn.

———. (1984). A context for instructional research on reading comprehension. In J. Flood (Ed.), *Promoting reading comprehension.* Newark, DE: International Reading Association.

Pearson, P.D., Dole, J., Duffy, G., & Roehler, L. (in press). In S. J. Samuels & A. E. Farstrup (Eds.), *What research says to the teacher* (2nd ed.). Newark, DE: International Reading Association.

Pearson, P.D., & Fielding, L. (1982). Listening comprehension. *Language Arts, 59* (6), 617–629.

Probst, R.E. (1988). *Response and analysis: Teaching literature in junior and high school.* Portsmouth, NH: Heinemann.

Reyes, M. (1987). Comprehension of content area passages: A study of Spanish/English readers in third grade. In S.R. Goldman & H.T. Trueba (Eds.), *Becoming literate in English as a second language.* Norwood, NJ: Ablex.

Rhodes, L,K. & Dudley-Marling, C. (1988). *Readers and writers with a difference: A holistic approach to teaching learning disabled and remedial students.* Portsmouth, NH: Heinemann.

Rosenblatt, L. (1978). *The reader, the text, the poem: The transactional theory of the literary work.* Carbondale, IL: Southern Illinois University Press.

Shanklin, N.L., & Rhodes, L.K. (1989). Comprehension instruction as sharing and extending. *The Reading Teacher, 42* (7), 496–500.

Slater, W. H., & Graves, M. (1989). Research on expository text: Implications for teachers. In K.D. Muth (Ed.), *Children's comprehension of text.* Newark, DE: International Reading Association.

Smith, F. (1985). *Reading without nonsense.* New York: Teacher's College Press.

———. (1988). *Understanding reading.* Hillsdale, NJ: Lawrence Erlbaum.

Spiegel, D.L., and Fitzgerald, J. (1986). Improving comprehension through instruction about story parts. *Reading Teacher, 39* (7), 676–682.

Stauffer, R. (1975). *Directing the reading–thinking process.* New York: Harper & Row.

Tierney, R., Readence, J., & Dishner, E. (1990). *Reading strategies and practices: A compendium.* Needham Heights, MA: Allyn & Bacon.

Uttero, D. A. (1988). Activating comprehension through cooperative learning. *The Reading Teacher, 41* (1), 390–395.

Whitmer, J. E. (1986). Pickles will kill you: Use humorous literature to teach critical reading. *The Reading Teacher, 39* (6), 530–534.

Winograd, P. N., & Bridge, C. A. (1986). The comprehension of important information in written prose. In J. B. Baumann (Ed.), *Teaching main idea comprehension,* Newark, DE: International Reading Association.

7

DECODING, WORD IDENTIFICATION, AND VOCABULARY

MY FAVORITE WORD
There is one word—
My favorite—
The very, very best.
It isn't No or Maybe.
It's Yes, Yes, Yes, Yes, YES!

"Yes, yes, you may," and
"Yes, of course," and
"Yes, please help yourself."
And when I want a piece of cake,
"Why, yes. It's on the shelf."

Some candy? "Yes."
A cookie? "Yes."
A movie? "Yes, we'll go."

I love it when they say my word:
Yes, Yes, YES (NOT No.)

—Lucia and James L. Hymes, Jr., *Oodles of Noodles*

WORDS, words, words. They are such an important part of reading. Reading is much more than words, but there is no doubt that decoding to identify words and learn vocabulary contributes to reading. The instructional strategies for phonics, word identification, and vocabulary development are varied and numerous. The methods used to teach phonics spark a great deal of debate and confusion. Just how to teach and how much instruction is necessary and when that instruction should occur are questions that do not have easy answers. Educators, parents, and administrators all have opinions about the role of word identification strategies during reading instruction. These ideas and strategies are some of the most discussed and controversial issues associated with reading instruction.

Some of the questions that will be answered in this chapter are:

1. How do efficient readers use phonics, word identification strategies, and vocabulary?
2. What do children understand about phonics and word identification before formal reading instruction?
3. How do children learn the meanings of the words in their reading material?
4. What is the role of literature in the development of phonics, word identification, and vocabulary?

This chapter is divided into two sections. The first section discusses what is known about decoding and word identification and how that information is used to help children develop strategies for effective reading. Decoding is viewed as the process of learning in which sounds are associated with certain letters. Phonics is an approach to reading instruction that relies heavily on teaching decoding strategies. Decoding is one contributor to word identification or the ability to recognize words while reading. Decoding and word identification are discussed in the same section because they are interrelated and many instructional strategies are applicable to both. The second section of this chapter will deal with vocabulary development and how knowledge of meanings can be encouraged as children read.

Decoding and Word Identification

During the reading process the reader's main goal should be to construct meaning and not identify individual sounds or words (Goodman, 1986). However, efficient readers have well-developed decoding and word identification strategies that contribute to their understanding. Readers who gain meaning use what they know about decoding to sound out words and identify small parts of words to figure out words they have not seen before.

Often the term *cracking the code* is used to describe when readers automatically decode and use word identification strategies rapidly. This phrase suggests that inexperienced readers suddenly reach a point where they can decipher a mysterious word and read efficiently. Language-based, developmental views of reading do not recognize a certain point at which children become readers. Instead, reading is viewed as a developmental process in which language users accumulate knowledge about written language as they interact with texts (McGee & Richgels, 1990). This assumption also is used to explain the development of decoding and word identification abilities that children need.

Sound–Symbol Relationships

Effective readers are very familiar with the sound and symbol relationships of our language and understand how to use the sounds and symbols to help them determine the meaning of text. It is apparent that good readers are familiar with individual letters, have developed an understanding of the nature and organization of written symbols, and understand that language is composed of words and small parts of words (Adams, 1990). There is substantial evidence that what is known about sounds and symbols, or *phonological awareness,* contributes to the acquisition of reading as well as efficient reading behaviors (Lundberg, Frost, & Petersen, 1988). However, the relationship of phonological awareness, decoding, and efficient reading may be that of the chicken and the egg. The question becomes, ''Does phonological awareness (or decoding skill) facilitate the development of reading strategies, or do efficient reading behaviors facilitate the development of decoding strategies?''

Learning about sounds, symbols, and decoding evolves in the same way as other language strategies. Children begin to acquire knowledge about print through early interactions with written language. There is much evidence ''. . . that children experiment with letter sound correspondences long before they are accomplished readers or writers'' (McGee & Richgels, 1990, p. 329). As they begin to experiment, they acquire knowledge of the sounds and symbols of language. Much of the knowledge is demonstrated in their early reading and writing attempts.

Very young children begin by attending to the everyday print that surrounds them. Advertising logos may be the first symbols they interpret. During daily routines, parents and other adults demonstrate how language is used as they make lists, read signs, and write letters. When print surrounds them, children soon become interested in the forms of print and begin identifying names, sounds, and configurations of letters (Morrow, 1989).

Children also attend to print during story reading (Sulzby, 1985). When they first are read story books, they look at the pictures and pay little attention to the print. As they continue to gain experience with books, they begin to ask questions about the letters, individual words, or sounds of words (Yaden, 1985). Interest in print appears to follow the same developmental path that characterizes all language learning.

There are some decoding strategies that children must learn in order to be successful readers (Schickedanz, 1989). These include 1) a phonological awareness or understanding that language can be segmented in small units of sound; 2) the ability to use context and graphic clues in concert; 3) knowledge of letter names and sounds; and 4) an understanding of the conventions of English.

Decoding strategies are used by good and poor comprehenders while reading, but good comprehenders usually are more efficient at employing their knowledge (Beck & McKeown, 1984; McKeown & Beck, 1988). Poor comprehenders are often poor decoders. The logical assumption would be that direct instruction in decoding contributes to the effectiveness of a reader's strategies. However, some research suggests that even when poor readers are trained to decode so that their speed matches that of good readers, the poor readers still do not read text as well as the good readers (Beck & McKeown, 1984; McKeown & Beck, 1988). A conclusion is that decoding is necessary but not sufficient for effective comprehension (Beck & McKeown, 1984; McKeown & Beck, 1988). A focus on comprehension and understanding text is a necessity.

Even more vexing is the fact that there are times when decoding may interfere with comprehension. Many types of information contribute to comprehension. If a reader focuses exclusively on one type of information, reading will be interrupted. If the reader decodes very slowly, the reading process also will be interrupted. For decoding to be efficient, it must occur rapidly and smoothly in concert with knowledge of word meanings, syntax and language patterns, prior experience, and knowledge of what already has been read.

Phonological awareness, letter recognition, and familiarity with spelling patterns and spelling–word relationships should be developed in concert with real reading and writing (Adams, 1990). Many teachers like the idea of allowing children to learn decoding by reading and writing. It is obvious that it meets many of the requirements for meaningful and purposeful learning. But the lack of much direct instruction in the skills advocated by a language-based approach is the basis of an ongoing debate in reading education.

The Phonics Debate

Probably no other instructional strategy for reading produces as much debate as how much and when decoding skills should be taught in the classroom. *Phonics* is an approach to teaching reading based on explicit and direct instruction in decoding skills. In addition to the interest among teachers, parents have opinions about phonics instruction, and state or local standards often strongly suggest or even require that teachers present phonics instruction. Statewide testing systems often focus on phonics, so teachers feel obligated to teach it in their classrooms.

The debate about phonics began at least thirty years ago when Rudolph Flesch advocated that beginning readers be taught to read with a systematic introduction to decoding (Flesch, 1985). Another influential study (Chall, 1983) supported Flesch's views by concluding that phonics programs were more successful than other methods with beginning readers. As recently as 1986, Groff conducted research that supported beginning reading instruction based on phonics and specifically the presentation of phonics rules to beginning readers.

Recently, however, even phonics advocates advise against a continuous approach and suggest that the emphasis should decrease as students get older (Ryder, 1986). The authors of *Becoming a Nation of Readers* support teaching phonics to beginning readers, but advise, ''Do it early. Keep it simple. Except in cases of diagnosed individual need, phonics instruction should have been completed by end of second grade'' (Anderson, Hiebert, Scott, & Wilkinson, 1985; p. 43).

Other views of reading instruction rule out phonics altogether. Frank Smith (1985) builds a strong case for not relying on phonics instruction by saying ''. . . teaching a set of spelling-to-sound correspondence rules . . . just does not work'' (p. 49). He explains that the English language is unpredictable and that the lack of a one-to-one correspondence between the letters and sounds of language and the arbitrary nature of phonics rules make phonics instruction unreliable (Smith, 1988).

Kenneth Goodman believes that reading is made more difficult when language is broken up into "bite-size, but abstract little pieces" (1986, p. 5). His view comes from the belief that all reading instruction should be meaningful and "look like reading." This "whole language" view holds that children must focus on comprehension during all aspects of reading instruction. Whole language advocates believe that any experience that presents reading in isolation has no place in the classroom and that working with skills in isolation has little to do with reading (Altwerger, Edelsky, & Flores, 1987).

No view of reading instruction would deny the importance of decoding in the reading process. Decoding and sound–symbol relationships are important facets of reading. The debate centers on instruction and how much direct phonics instruction is needed to learn how to read. Teachers feel most compelled to teach structured phonics to beginning readers and when children are having difficulty learning to read. The question of the role of decoding in instruction has produced many studies, journal articles, and reading approaches of opposing views and opinions. If reading educators cannot agree on the right amount of phonics to teach, it is no wonder that teachers have a difficult time deciding how to approach decoding and word identification instruction.

The debate probably will continue because there are no easy answers or sure methods for teaching reading. Nearly all approaches to reading can be successful with some readers (Smith, 1985), and there are convincing arguments on both sides of the phonics question. Even as the controversy proceeds, teachers must make well-informed decisions about the role of decoding in their reading programs.

There is no specific answer to the question of how much phonics should be taught. Almost no one believes that systematic phonics alone is sufficient to teach reading (Fox, 1986). It seems that the current view is to teach only as much as children need and to teach it early. There is a rule of thumb to guide teachers' decisions about how to teach children the decoding necessary to become effective readers. Consider the language learning assumptions that provide a rational guide to all instructional decisions: Instruction should be meaningful, and children's decoding work should not be isolated from reading instruction. Isolating words to work on decoding skills teaches children decoding skills and does not teach children about reading. However, discussion and activities that provide opportunities for children to understand the relationship of decoding to reading are important.

Word Knowledge

Word knowledge implies the ability to identify, name, or label words while reading. Without word identification skills, a student cannot be successful at reading. However, when word identification skills are the only tools students have to work with, they will not be able to comprehend what they are reading. Word identification skills are one part of the delicate balance of strategies that promote efficient reading.

Word knowledge develops similarly to knowledge of letters and sounds. Children begin to recognize words in everyday print. They gradually begin to develop a sense of directionality of words and gain insights into the beginnings and endings of words.

Often the language of favorite story books is reflected in their word knowledge, and they may begin recognizing some words in their favorite books or in their names. When adults encourage and answer their questions and the children participate in other activities such as watching "Sesame Street" on television, it is easy to recognize how they begin to learn letters and words (Allen, Brown, & Yatvin, 1986).

If children have access to paper and pencils, their curiosity about words begins to be represented in their writing. Although they may begin by drawing and scribbling, their early attempts to convey words and concepts begin to produce letter-like forms and invented spellings. Children who have opportunities and experiences with print seem to be naturally curious about the words around them.

After readers begin interacting with a great deal of text and see words over and over, they begin to recognize some words automatically without thinking or considering the written symbols. These words usually are referred to as *sight words*. Usually the words that readers see most often are the words recognized immediately.

The text itself provides information about the words. A reader who possesses prior knowledge of a topic also will know and recognize the words used. Once readers determine the topics, they expect the words to relate to what they already know. As they begin processing the information, the text they have read contributes to their expectations about what words are likely be found in the text. Finally, what a reader understands about the text suggests the words that are found.

One important characteristic distinguishing good readers from poor readers is their ability to rapidly and efficiently identify words (Nagy, Anderson, Schommer, Scott, & Stallman, 1989). However, fluent, capable readers do not identify every single word and will use a variety of methods to identify words while reading. The techniques include the effective use of sound–symbol relationships, automatic word identification, contextual knowledge, and prior experience.

Structural Analysis

Structural analysis is a term often used in reading that relates to both sound–symbol relationships and word knowledge. Structural analysis involves the smaller parts of language sometimes necessary for understanding language as a whole. Small units usually referred to during structural analysis include roots, affixes, compound words, endings, contractions, and syllables. Words usually are not divided into small parts during real reading and writing, and instructional focus on these aspects of language should occur during meaningful language activities. For example, one of the times readers depend on their abilities to use structural analysis is when they need to use a dictionary.

Decoding and Word Identification Instruction

Although there is much debate over the manner and methods of presenting decoding and word identification in reading instruction, there are some assumptions that underlie the planning of literature-based reading instruction.

The Best Way to Teach Decoding and Word Identification
Is to Use Meaningful Reading Activities

The way to avoid isolating words and sounds is to base instruction on examples taken from stories children write and read (Harp, 1989). Children learn about words and decoding through repeated exposure to print. There is no better way to expose children to the way sounds, letters, and words work than to provide them with opportunities to read children's literature. Word identification can be taught as a part of actual reading and should contribute to the collection of strategies that allow a child to understand the text. There is no reason to introduce lessons about word identification unless the ultimate goal is to understand reading material.

The Ability to Decode and Identify Words Is Developmental

Just as in other language strategies, children with less experience are less effective with decoding and word identification strategies. Experiences and interactions with printed material increase children's understanding about all aspects of reading, including decoding and word identification. There will be times when children use decoding and word identification differently than adults. They should be given the time to hypothesize, experiment, and confirm their predictions about sounds, symbols, and words.

Writing Provides an Important Opportunity to Learn about Words and Decoding

Children's early print experiences involve an interest in print that can be demonstrated concretely in their writing. Invented spelling patterns (chap. 5) are a natural and acceptable way for children to demonstrate their knowledge of letters and sounds. This exhibition of natural language learning should be transferred to classroom learning. Children should be encouraged to try to write their ideas and attempt to spell and arrange words in their writing.

Reading Instruction Should Devote No More Time to Decoding and Word
Identification Than Is Necessary to Learn to Read

Decoding and word identification instruction should be a by-product of reading. It should never be the reading program or dominate the reading program. Decoding and word identification development should not take time away from reading and learning to love books.

Encouraging Decoding and Word Identification

The only reason for providing instruction in decoding and word identification is to help readers gain meaning when they read (Harp, 1989). There are times, however, when an emphasis on sounds and words is beneficial, and word identification and vocabulary development become the emphasis of discussion and activities. The key to effective reading instruction is to present it in such a way that children never lose sight of comprehension as the ultimate goal.

It is important that teachers understand words, word structure, and definitions of phonics terms and generalizations. Understanding decoding and phonics generalizations allows teachers to gain a more accurate perception of their role in furthering children's language growth and provides information necessary to discuss, describe, and explain an important component of the reading process. This does not mean that children must learn the phonics generalizations and rules. They may learn some, but only when necessary and beneficial to their overall reading competency.

Literature-based instruction encourages phonics and word identification development through participation in meaningful and functional literature experiences. By far the most effective method for promoting interest in the structure of words is to build awareness during daily reading and writing. Teachers should watch for opportunities during reading to focus children's attention on print in a natural way. For example, familiar beginning consonant sounds can be identified during language experience activities. Discussion of words and their sounds can occur naturally as children read, and children can be encouraged to use phonology as one way of clarifying and understanding the text.

Natural Opportunities

Children come to school with different levels of abilities and understandings about words. Children who have been exposed to books and had opportunities to write probably possess a great deal of knowledge about letters, sounds, and words. Other children come to school without that knowledge. Teachers need to plan experiences for children that will help them develop and use knowledge of words during reading. Children need several specific types of experience to develop word identification strategies that lead to efficient reading.

Children Should Be Able to Follow Print with Their Eyes as It Is Being Read to Them

This may develop naturally during the lap reading of the preschool years. Children who have grown up in homes where reading is done often gain some information about words by sitting with their parents and enjoying books. This experience needs to be repeated in some way during the early school years. Using big books, chart stories, and class sets of texts encourages children to follow print with their eyes and is extremely valuable. Shared and repeated oral readings during which children can see the text provide opportunities to become familiar with words.

Children Should Have the Opportunity to Manipulate Letters and Sounds by Writing

Writing implements and paper of all varieties should be easily accessible, and children should be encouraged to write. Children's first writing will contain invented spellings and are a means of exploring letter–sound relationships. Writing provides a concrete approach to letters and their sound relationships. Children develop knowledge of letters and sounds when they need to use language in meaningful ways. Very young children also can manipulate letters by playing with magnetic or sponge letters.

Children Should Have Opportunities to Manipulate the Print in Books

Book print can be manipulated to allow children opportunities to experiment with the nature of sounds and letters. The text can be reproduced on word cards, sentence strips, or other units so that children can rearrange the words and letters. Word cards and sentence strips allow children to interact and experiment with words and letters without having to produce the letters themselves. Teachers make word cards by reproducing words from the story on index cards. Children can manipulate the word cards in several ways. They can match individual word cards with words in the text to practice word identification. Children can use several word cards to produce their own sentences and focus on word order. Sentence strips are long strips of paper that reproduce a sentence from reading material, language experience stories, or children's original writing. Children cut the sentence strips in sections and rearrange words and ideas. Both word cards and sentence strips can be used with beginning readers to focus on smaller parts of text.

Another method that focuses children's attentions on words and letters within a text is some type of "window" that isolates parts of the text. A window can be made easily with two rectangular cards with notches cut on the edges (see Figure 7.1). When the cards are moved back and forth, they help the teacher isolate words and sounds in a text. Windows allow teachers to focus children's attention on words and letters in the context of actual reading.

Children Should See Teachers Writing

A natural opportunity to discuss words and their sounds occurs when children are watching the teacher write on the board or charts. Teachers who write and think aloud as they write demonstrate the importance of attending to certain sounds and letters. As teachers write, they can explain sounds and letters and even introduce phonics generalizations to demonstrate the importance of letter–sound strategies. The same opportunity exists when children dictate stories and texts to teachers during language experience. Words and sounds can become the topic of discussion during language experience, while the teacher is writing on the board or recording ideas on an overhead. Language experience and other demonstrations of writing allow children to see letters and sounds being reproduced in a meaningful context.

Children Should Be Encouraged to Talk about Letters and Sounds as They Read and Write

A teacher who demonstrates an excitement and interest in words and print will have children who also are interested in words. Each engagement with print offers opportunities for teachers to discuss and elaborate about aspects of letters, sounds, and words.

FIGURE 7-1 Windows made from notecards that can be moved to display different words or letters are a method for focusing children's attention to words or letters within a text.

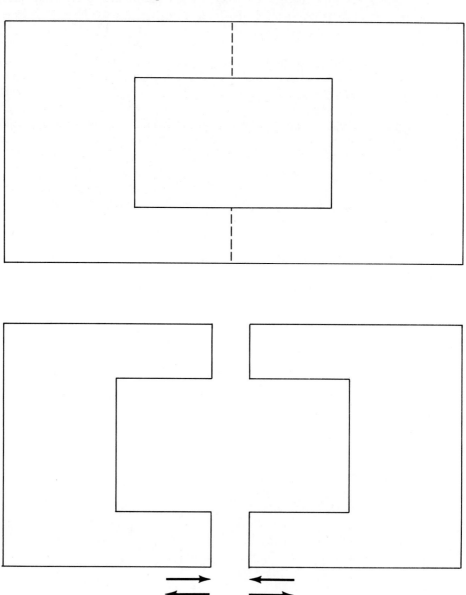

These experiences are effective with beginning readers and readers who are experiencing difficulties. In addition, there are some specific strategies that allow children and teachers to focus on the word identification techniques so necessary to reading.

Focused Opportunities

Basically, teachers want to focus discussions and activities on decoding in several instances: when a new concept is introduced, when children do not understand decoding and word identification after a great deal of experience with print, or when terms, labels, and concepts need to be understood in order to complete a reading and writing assignment.

When a teacher observes that one or more children do not seem to be understanding a certain aspect, opportunities should be provided for the children to use that aspect in their reading and writing. Letter–sound relationships can be discussed as part of a series of strategies that contribute to understanding and identifying new words in the text. Other strategies that can be encouraged are skipping the word, using context, predicting the word based on prior knowledge, and using decoding strategies if the other two strategies fail.

If children seem to be having a very difficult time grasping the basic and regular sound–symbol relationships, they should focus systematically on decoding and word identification skills. The emphasis on decoding never should occur exclusive of reading and teachers should not begin a systematic approach to decoding unless it is really needed. Children who are having a difficult time reading must continue to read and write, with decoding and word identification activities as part of the processes.

Children's writing may reflect a need for discussion of a particular element of decoding or word identification. This occurs when children have had enough exposure to print to recognize correct spellings; an example is when many children in the class are spelling *ed* endings as *t* or *d*. When children do not understand language parts and those misunderstandings show up in their writing regularly, teachers should provide opportunities for the children to discuss and use their knowledge.

The most meaningful time to focus on decoding, word identification, and structural analysis occurs when children have reasons for using the dictionary, thesaurus, and other references. Needing the dictionary to clarify or provide more information about a particular word can provide reasons for understanding the sounds and letter arrangements of words. Early readers must know how to use alphabetical order and beginning sounds to use the dictionary and reference material. When older children are encouraged to use the markings in the dictionary, decoding and syllabication become meaningful and important. Helping children understand diacritical marks and why readers and writers need them can develop a natural awareness of the importance of decoding.

Decoding and word identification may be part of developing a natural interest in word origins, derivations, and other linguistic principles. Some children are just naturally interested in the way words work and their pronunciation. One second grader announced to her teacher that she loved reading the first chapter of the Bible, Genesis. Curious about where the conversation was going and cognizant that Genesis contains a long list of biblical names, the teacher responded that it was nice to understand the ideas of the Bible during church discussions. ''Oh no,'' said the second grader, ''I can't understand a word that I read. I just love to listen to the words as I pronounce them.'' Some kids are like that. Others need a little encouragement. Teachers' enthusiasm about words goes a long way in encouraging children's enthusiasm.

Children who are involved in a great deal of reading and writing may become interested naturally in the structure and order of language. Teachers might consider designing a unit of study on the topic of words and word sounds. A study of phonology provides opportunities for teachers to introduce the origins and history of words and is particularly interesting when stories and poems that feature wonderful words and sounds are used to isolate interesting words, spellings, or patterns. Poems and other literature can be used to motivate decoding and word study.

Instructional Strategies

The instructional strategies that allow children a more structured focus on decoding and word identification should encourage children to become efficient readers and provide them with methods that provide independence in their reading and writing. Even though children can learn much about word identification strategies in the natural context of reading, there may be times when a teacher needs to focus on words and letters. The teacher should use activities that focus on sound–symbol relationships selectively and discriminatingly for children who need such instruction (Trachtenburg, 1990).

Word Pointing

Rhodes and Dudley-Marling (1988) suggest *word pointing* as a method for focusing beginning readers' attention on words and sounds. As books are read to children, teachers focus on specific aspects of the text by using their voices to point or vocally emphasize a particular aspect of the words. Reading words distinctly and emphasizing each word focuses children's attention on the words in the text. If teachers want to focus on specific types of words or letters, voice emphasis can highlight whatever aspects need to be considered. For example, if teachers want to emphasize the beginning consonant sound *c,* they should find material that includes the sound and allows their voices to focus on the *c* during reading. Big books or chart stories could be used in large groups. Although pointing slows the reading, the teacher should continue to demonstrate fluent reading.

Children can be asked to respond to the texts in the same manner to help them concentrate on certain aspects of print. For example, if a teacher wants to focus children's attention on the *bl* in *blend,* she or he could find a text that uses *blend* several times. The text could be read to the children, with the teacher emphasizing the *bl* sound. The children could reread the text in the same manner, and perhaps individual children could repeat the procedure. Discussion, writing, or the highlighting activity discussed later would reinforce the instruction.

Alphabet Books

Alphabet books offer a resource for teaching letters and letter sounds in the context of high quality reading material. Recent alphabet books provide interesting pictures and stories to support instructional strategies that highlight letter names, sounds, and language play. These books offer built-in motivation and a need for understanding and recognizing letter names and sounds while furnishing teachers with an opportunity to discuss individual letters.

Children can't help but focus on words and letter sounds when a text reads, "An amoured armadillo avoiding an angry alligator" in *Animalia* (Base, 1986) or, ". . . The F was firmly flattened" in *The Z Was Zapped* (Van Allsburg, 1989). Children read and reread the text and enjoy the pictures while learning about reading in general and beginning sounds specifically. Producing their own alphabet books modeled on those done by famous authors leads to more study of letters and letter sounds. For a discussion in greater depth on this topic, see chapters 2 and 5.

Jennifer Dunham explains that, as is common in all first grades, some of her students come to school without recognizing all their letters or knowing sounds. She feels these children must be provided with letter name–sound background information to be successful with many of the activities in her classroom. She uses alphabet books as follows:

1. At the beginning of the year, she reads many alphabet books with her first graders.
2. After reading and sharing the books, they discuss the books and recognize phrases and patterns in the texts.
3. The children brainstorm other words and phrases modeled after the alphabet book they are reading. They discuss letters and sounds as they brainstorm.
4. Each child makes a page that focuses on a particular letter and reflects the pattern in the alphabet book.
5. The activity continues as they illustrate their pages. The teacher helps the children match their drawings and texts.
6. The books are shared and placed in the library corner for independent reading times.

(By the way, Jennifer recommends this as an excellent "first of the year" activity for first graders.)

Predictable Books

Predictable books offer opportunities to increase a child's sight vocabulary. When children learn to read a predictable book from beginning to end, they establish an interest in the books and the words contained within. As children become involved in a book, they become more interested in learning about all aspects of the story, including the mechanics. This interest transfers to the words of a favorite story. The child soon recognizes words from a well-known story, which may be recognized in other contexts.

Repeated reading of predictable books is important for developing word identification techniques. Words confronted often are words that are easily recognized. The strong effect that frequency of usage has on word recognition can be a tool for reading instruction: the more often children see the words used, the greater likelihood that the words will become a part of their sight vocabulary.

Jennifer's first graders consult with each other while writing their alphabet book. Their conversations include many references to letters and sounds.

Teachers can facilitate a familiarity with words by providing opportunities for children to manipulate pieces of the text. Words from predictable books may be recorded on word cards and distributed to children to match the cards to the text.

Stories and Poems

Many children's stories and poems encourage play with words by presenting word families or by presenting words in an unusual way. Dr. Seuss and Bill Peet are good examples of writers who focus on word families. Several other children's poets provide opportunities for children to play with words and sounds. For example:

> Betty Botter bought some butter,
> "But," she said, "the butter's bitter.
> If I put it in my batter,
> It will make my batter bitter.
> But a bit of better butter,
> That would make my batter better."
> So she bought a bit of butter
> Better than her bitter butter,

And she put it in her batter
And the batter was not bitter.
So 'twas better Betty Botter
Bought a bit of better butter.

> —*Poems of A. Nonny Mouse* by Jack Prelutsky, 1989,
> New York: Knopf.

This poem could be used with voice pointing and word cards to develop an understanding of the *b* sound. A sample lesson using this poem might have this design:

1. Introduction: Write the poem on a chart or provide children with their own copies of the poem. Read the poem to the children. Repeat the readings and encourage them to follow along.

2. Ask the children to listen as you read the poem. This time as you read, point to the letter with your voice by emphasizing the beginning consonant sound. Ask the children what sound they hear most often.

3. After the children have identified the sound and have assisted the teacher in labeling the letter, let them identify names or other words that start with the same letter.

4. The teacher might say: "Let's write our own poem with *c*'s." Children brainstorm all the words they can think of with a *c* and write their own poem or story using as many words as possible.

These examples are ways to use a poem or book to focus on some aspect of word identification. Many texts suggest specific methods for introducing an element of word identification within the context of reading, while other selections offer opportunities to play with words and discuss how they are used in our language.

Reading Together

Many of the strategies for focusing children's attention on decoding and word identification involve the teacher and the students reading together. One strategy that allows children to work with complete texts, participate in repeated readings, and focus attention on specific elements of decoding and word identification is reading together. When one teacher recognizes that her third graders are not aware of a helpful decoding, word knowledge, or grammatical aspect, she plans an activity based on reading together by implementing the following procedures:

1. She identifies a text that contains the decoding or word identification the children need to practice. For example, she noticed that her children needed to discuss the *ly* suffix of adverbs and she found a text that used the adverbs and made a copy for the children. Another time she might use copies of familiar stories or exposition.

2. Each child has her or his own copy of the text to guide discussion. In addition, all children have access to different color markers.

3. The children begin by reading the text. After the children finish reading, they discuss the content and respond freely. The teacher and her students find time to enjoy the text together.

4. The teacher asks the children to reread the text and to notice the *ly* words. They discuss what the words do and how they are used.

5. The children reread the text and highlight the *ly* words. The highlighting provides a way to focus in context and also gives the teacher feedback about which children are understanding the concept.

Cloze

Cloze is a flexible instructional tool. Letters and letter sounds can be the focus while reading by using cloze to direct children's attention to the letters and letter names needed. Instructional cloze offers opportunities for children to develop phonics strategies while reading, and activities based on cloze can be oral or written.

To use oral cloze, the teacher simply reads a selection and stops at certain points to allow children to fill in the blanks. This is particularly effective for beginning readers when the teacher is guiding their attention to the print in a big book or large chart. Oral cloze can initiate discussion of the nature of the words and letters during reading or it can focus children's attention on specific sounds or letters.

Written cloze can be used to encourage children to use the beginning consonant or other letter patterns as clues to identify the missing word. One way of using written cloze to focus on word identification is as follows:

1. The text of a story or poem is copied, omitting any sounds, group of sounds, or words the teacher wishes to present to the class.

2. Children are encouraged to predict which sounds, letters, or words are missing. All predictions are recorded on a chart, overhead, or board.

3. After children have predicted the deleted letters or words, the teacher writes the missing element or part (e.g., the initial consonant if it is a word) in the blank.

4. The teacher writes each prediction on a word card, then holds each word under the blank to compare the supplied letter or word with the prediction. The comparison of the teacher's clue and the child's prediction forms the basis of a discussion to clarify word identification strategies.

Prelutsky's verse (1989) can provide text that focuses on the beginning consonant of *m*:

Mary had a little lamb,
A lobster, and some prunes,
A glass of m_____, a piece of pie, (milk)
And then some m_____. (macaroons)
It m_____ the busy waiters grin (made)
To see her order so,

And when they carried M_____ out, (Mary)
Her face was white as snow.

—*Poems of A. Nonny Mouse* by Jack Prelutsky, 1989,
New York: Knopf.

The teacher can introduce this selection by writing it with blanks on a chart large enough so that all children can see it. The poem could be read to encourage a variety of predictions, disregarding the *m* clue. The teacher keeps track of the predictions. After all predictions are made, the children eliminate those predictions that do not begin with an *m,* and finally they decide on the words that make the most sense in the poem. This procedure presents an opportunity to focus children's attention on one beginning consonant sound while reading and rereading. A decoding activity that uses cloze for initial consonants of missing words allows children to use all the strategies involved in reading and to learn about decoding cues.

Language Experience

Language experience was described as an approach to beginning reading instruction, but it can be used to develop knowledge of letters and sounds. The chapter on beginning reading instruction described language experience as children producing their own texts to read. The first graders in one class are presented with mini-lessons that focus on

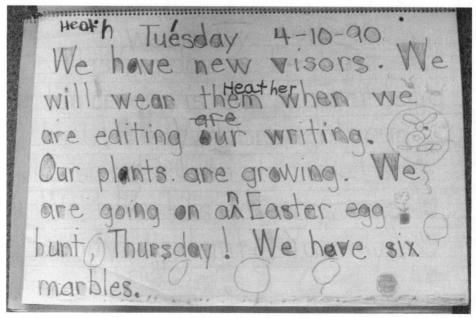

As Jennifer discusses specific word identification and grammar elements, she circles and writes on the language experience chart. Later, some of the children decorate and illustrate the pages.

phonics and word identification during their daily language experience activity. If the teacher notes that her children are not using some element in their writing or are having trouble using some basic phonics generalization in their reading, she focuses on the issue as they are writing together in their large chart-sized journal. For example, she noticed that many of her children were adding *d* or *t* instead of *ed* to make words past tense. The next time the use of an *ed* word came up in their language experience story, she discussed how to spell the ending and what it sounds like. She immediately saw evidence of applications in her children's writing.

Phonics and decoding activities are more meaningful if children can focus on word identification while they are reading. Instruction that provides opportunities to learn about decoding and word identification can reflect and support reading.

Basal Readers

Most phonics instruction is associated with basal reading series (Searfoss & Readance, 1989). Basal lessons begin with a presentation of decoding skills. Usually, phonics is emphasized on a workbook page or with isolated skill instruction that is completed before or after the children read the basal selection (Adams, 1990).

Basals usually identify specific decoding and phonetic skills for specific grade levels. The assumption is that the decoding and phonetic skills are introduced in increasing levels of difficulty as the grades progress. A basal series will teach and reteach phonetic skills over eight years of reading instruction. A list of skills from any basal series probably includes the following terms:

Match words	Short vowels
Capital and lowercase letters	Long vowels
Initial consonants	Diphthongs
Initial consonant clusters	R-controlled vowels
Initial consonant digraphs	Inflectional endings
Medial consonants	Plurals
Final consonants	Possessives
Final consonant clusters	Contractions
Final digraphs	Compound words
Syllabication	Base words and affixes
Prefixes	Suffixes

Basal series may differ in emphasis and approach to presenting individual phonics and the grade level at which each skill is presented, but most series present similar skills in some manner during reading instruction. Phonics terms often are used in curriculum, testing, and reading-related discussions. Just because you know these terms does not mean that children should be required to know them. But the terms can be used as you talk with children about reading. They will need to have the labels as they become more sophisticated in their language usage.

One criticism of the basal has been that it encourages an inordinate amount of time be spent on phonics instruction. Workbooks and skill instruction often focus on phonics and much independent desk work is spent completing tasks related to decoding. Many educators now agree that very little of this activity really benefits readers.

Any basal decoding and word recognition activity should be considered carefully and be based on the language learning assumptions presented in chapter 1. If the basal lesson does not support what is known about learning language, its usefulness should be doubted. Children can learn decoding and word identification without the isolated lessons of basal instruction, but that does not mean that teachers must not help children understand these very important elements of reading.

Foundations of Vocabulary Development

Children's development of vocabulary in their preschool years is nothing short of remarkable. Their first word is uttered around their first birthday, and by eighteen months they may use fifty words; at two years, they use 150 words; two-and-a-half years, four hundred words; three to four years, one thousand words, five to six years, two thousand to four thousand words (Allen, Brown, & Yatvin, 1986). It is estimated that by the time adults become fluent readers, they recognize fifty thousand words by sight (Smith, 1985).

The language learning assumptions that support other developmental language processes are applicable to vocabulary development. Children's vocabulary development is related closely to their cognition and understanding of the world around them. As they learn how to interpret their world, children learn the vocabulary they need to express their needs and ideas.

Children learn a great deal of vocabulary through use and exposure to language. They also predict, hypothesize, and confirm as they are learning. According to some researchers, vocabulary acquisition begins when children assign a probable meaning to a newly encountered word (Carey, 1978). As children continue to encounter the word, they complete their understanding of the concept represented by the word. Vocabulary development continues as children relate words and concepts to each other and expand their knowledge of the concept.

Think of how you become more acquainted with the vocabulary associated with literature-based instruction as you read this textbook. At first, because of your limited exposure to reading instruction, you may have associated what you knew about children's literature with the term "literature-based instruction." Now, after reading seven chapters and being exposed to related concepts in reading and class discussions, you may have not only increased your understanding of the term, but added new vocabulary to your knowledge. Words such as *schema* and *metacognition* have become part of your vocabulary as you understand more about the concept of literature-based instruction.

The amount of knowledge that children have about the words in their lives is remarkable. Children come to school with prior experiences that contribute to their vocabulary development. This acquired knowledge is used as they begin to read. As it turns out, children do not need to be taught every single word they recognize in texts. Frank Smith (1988) discusses vocabulary acquisition almost mystically as he writes:

> *There is something a little eerie even to think about how we might acquire and retain familiarity with relatively infrequent words. We meet them perhaps once a year, but it is not often we have to stop and wonder ''Haven't I seen you somewhere?''* (p. 130)

Assumptions of Vocabulary Development

Based on what is known about vocabulary development, there are several guidelines for planning vocabulary instruction:

Vocabulary Is Developed through Exposure to and Use of Language

Most vocabulary is acquired by talking, listening, reading, and writing. Many words encountered in reading are learned without the assistance of formal instruction. Explicit vocabulary instruction can cover only a fraction of the words students must understand (Nagy, 1988), and children add to their personal vocabularies by continuing to read and discuss their ideas.

Knowledge of Vocabulary Is Based on the Conceptual Understandings Children Possess

There is a strong relationship between vocabulary and what a reader knows. The development of vocabulary closely parallels the development of comprehension. If teachers ascertain that their students do not have much understanding of the concepts that support particular vocabulary, they must provide opportunities for concept and background development. Developing general concepts about a passage is much more important than having children memorize words and definitions.

Readers Learn Vocabulary That Is Meaningful and Useful

Newly introduced vocabulary must be used to be learned and understood. If a word is encountered and never seen again, it does not become part of the vocabulary. When students use new vocabulary frequently in their reading and writing, it is more likely to become permanent.

Guiding Vocabulary Development

Good comprehenders possess good vocabulary skills (Carpenter & Just, 1986). Readers' general knowledge of vocabulary indicates how well they comprehend texts (Nagy, 1988). However, teaching readers vocabulary does not necessarily contribute to a higher level of comprehension. Large vocabularies are related to, but not necessarily a cause of, good reading ability. Just as with decoding and word identification, it appears that vocabulary and comprehension are reciprocal.

Nagy (1988) makes the following observation about vocabulary instruction:

For children to learn large numbers of words, they need to be exposed to them. Teachers should include as rich a vocabulary as they can in their own speech without losing the students. There are numerous and varied ways to make the classroom a vocabulary-rich environment without making vocabulary a chore.'' (p. 23)

One traditional method of instruction has been to focus on definition and memorization of vocabulary. Children have been asked to find definitions for selected words and to memorize the definitions, usually in preparation for a test. A second method of vocabulary instruction has emphasized the importance of children's ability to use contextual clues to learn vocabulary. When children read texts that contain unfamiliar words, they are encouraged to deduce meaning by using information in the passage.

Nagy (1988) suggests that neither of the two traditional approaches can be effective when used as the only way to teach new meanings. He suggests two reasons why traditional vocabulary instruction is not always successful. One reason is that instruction does not always produce in-depth understanding of the concepts associated with the vocabulary. Mere memorization of dictionary definitions may not produce a reader who truly has integrated the basic meanings. Readers who parrot definitions and do not really understand the underlying concepts never acquire and use the words. Second, there are times when instruction may concentrate on developing vocabulary understandings not necessary for comprehending the text. It is not essential to understand all the vocabulary in a passage, and some words selected for study may not be needed to understand the text. If the words are not needed to comprehend the text, the chances of retaining and using the words are marginal.

Vocabulary instruction can be effective when several factors are considered. The amount of information the reader has about the vocabulary, the number of times the reader actually uses the vocabulary, and how necessary the vocabulary is for future understandings all affect how well the vocabulary is understood. Each of these factors must be included in effective instruction.

The existing conceptual base of the learner is one factor related to vocabulary instruction. When the reader possesses prior knowledge and experience about topics in the passage, the vocabulary is easier to understand. If the reader does not know much about the topic, teachers can enhance vocabulary development by providing appropriate background and concept development to support the words. The importance of developing the concepts associated with the vocabulary is based on research findings that suggest that concept development produces more gains in vocabulary than traditional instruction in definition and contextual identification (Pearson, 1984).

For example, new education vocabulary will be much easier for you to learn than vocabulary from engineering. If, as assumed, you have had a number of discussions, readings, and interactions about education and education-related topics, the associated vocabulary will be easier for you to grasp than the vocabulary associated with engineering. In order to understand the vocabulary in engineering you must have experience with the concepts and topics discussed. Otherwise, whoever is guiding you through the reading will need to spend a great deal of time helping you understand the basic concepts of engineering.

Also, the amount of interaction with vocabulary will affect how long you remember or how much you use the word. If you read only one chapter and discuss the term *literature-based* one time, you might not remember the term for very long. However, you probably will hear this term in one or more reading courses, a general methods course, a language arts course, and even during your student teaching, so you probably will be very familiar with the term and be able to use the vocabulary associated with the concept. The number of times you discussed, listened to others, or read about the term *literature-based* will determine whether you use the term in your own reading, writing, and speaking.

Yet another factor to be considered in vocabulary acquisition is the usability of the term. People tend to use words if they are popular and used often among peers, appear in reading material, and are recognized as important by other people (Blachowicz, 1985). If you and others around you use the vocabulary associated with a new concept, chances are good that you will begin to really understand the term.

When teachers plan vocabulary instruction, the selection of the words and concepts to be studied is important. There are three questions that help a teacher determine what is meaningful and usable:

1. Is the word important for the children to know in the future?
2. Will knowing this word help them figure out other important words?
3. Will understanding the word help the children understand the reading selection?

If the vocabulary word is important for one of these reasons, it should be a word that receives attention. It is impossible to spend time presenting lessons on all new vocabulary in reading material, so it is important to choose the vocabulary that will serve as the focus of instruction. The most obvious choices for vocabulary instruction are words that include concepts that are not a part of a student's everyday world. Instructional focus also is warranted when words are important for understanding the selection or because they are generally useful contributions to a child's vocabulary.

A subtle factor contributing to vocabulary development is the value that children place on understanding words and concepts (Nagy, 1988). There is a certain amount of pride in some people about the number of vocabulary words they can use. A certain amount of vocabulary learning depends on the motivation of the students.

The motivation for developing a personal vocabulary can be related to academic, social, and cultural factors. Teachers can best affect a child's attitude toward learning vocabulary by reflecting excitement and interest in new words.

Instructional Strategies

Instructional strategies that actively involve and help students become excited about words are the most effective (Jiganti & Tindall, 1986). Active involvement in vocabulary development usually means that the planned instructional activities are student-centered (Carr & Wixson, 1986). Student-centered activities focus on the children's interests and needs and contribute to their daily reading and writing.

Children's literature provides an excellent way to build vocabulary and encourage an interest in words. Literature provides a real reason for learning words. When children struggle to understand characters and their problems, they must understand and use the words that describe the characters. Expository texts offer many opportunities to enrich children's vocabulary. As children learn new concepts and expand existing ideas through reading, there is parallel vocabulary growth.

Many activities are student-centered, invite children to become active in vocabulary development, and use children's literature. Vocabulary activities should focus on structuring and relating ideas and using words repeatedly in reading, writing, talking, and listening (Nagy, 1988).

Listening

Reading to children is credited with contributing to oral language acquisition. There is much evidence to suggest that children learn vocabulary incidentally by hearing a story read aloud to them (Elley, 1989). When teachers stop reading to discuss new and unfamiliar words, vocabulary gains increase. This method of incidental focus on vocabulary allows readers of all abilities to learn vocabulary.

Sometimes, the combination of pictures and language in picture books produces conceptual information that is remembered for a lifetime. Many adult readers still remember such words as *rumpus* and *gnashing* from their exposure to Maurice Sendak's *Where the Wild Things Are* (1963). Pictures and text illustrate the concepts of ". . . the wild rumpus" and ". . . gnashing their terrible teeth" and develop understandings that last a lifetime.

The wide range of audio-visual versions of stories offers a method for children to hear stories and develop familiarity with vocabulary. Teachers can provide audio tapes of stories and encourage children to follow written texts as they listen. This allows for familiarity with the words as they sound and as they are written. Video cassette recordings also provide an opportunity for vocabulary development. The visual representation of the concepts supporting the vocabulary are concrete.

Brainstorming

Brainstorming what is known about a concept contributes to awareness and growth in vocabulary usage and allows children to relate words and ideas. Many vocabulary activities are based on a variety of brainstorming techniques. Brainstorming allows children to suggest words and make references that clarify new or relatively unfamiliar vocabulary. When children read the Caldecott Medal-winning book *Song and Dance Man* (Ackerman, 1988), they need to understand the vocabulary word *vaudeville*. Before reading the story, the teacher might ask the children to produce as many words as they know that are associated with the term. As the children begin suggesting related vocabulary, the teacher writes the words on a board or overhead. Words such as *jokes, dancing,* and *music* might be contributed by the class. The brainstorming serves as a basis for discussions that ultimately increase the conceptual experience related to the word and concept of vaudeville. In a way, brainstorming allows the teacher to use prior experiences of the entire class to help everyone understand the term.

Brainstorming is particularly effective when used to develop concepts about vocabulary that will appear in reading material, but brainstorming also can be used to interest and motivate children to explore and use other vocabulary in their speech and writing. Children can brainstorm overworked words such as *good* or *great* and find substitutions and related words to use in their writing and speaking. Brainstorming alone will not produce substantial vocabulary development, but will serve as a first step to many effective instructional strategies.

Mapping or Categorizing

When students have brainstormed words that are related in some way, the brainstorming can be made more effective by using categorization or mapping. After lists of words are brainstormed, students group the words and assign labels to the categories. After the words have been categorized, the teacher can add words that were not suggested that might increase understanding of the concepts. These categories and words can be assembled on a map that relates words and concepts.

Semantic maps can be used to develop relationships among words and concepts and to present the relationships in a visual way. Students begin by producing familiar words, phrases, and ideas associated with the targeted vocabulary. The mapping continues by extending their associations into multiple hierarchies based on words related to the main concepts. The maps are developed with definitions, words, or phrases based on related vocabulary. Children use their own backgrounds and vocabulary to develop semantic maps. A semantic map illustrating the development of the concept of meander is shown in Figure 7.2.

FIGURE 7-2 Mapping procedures can be used before and after reading to contribute to the development of concepts and vocabulary. Before reading, children brainstorm word associations to produce a visual "map" that develops understandings and associations connected with concepts. After reading, Nancy's third graders brainstormed what they had learned about a concept and arranged their knowledge into a semantic map.

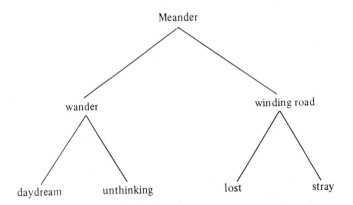

Maps also can be used to illustrate word families. The core word is identified and the map is developed to demonstrate the various forms of the word. A map of the words related to graph is shown in Figure 7.3.

Vocabulary Prediction

Vocabulary prediction is adaptable to many types of texts and provides children with opportunities to develop independence in identifying unfamiliar words as they read.

FIGURE 7-3   Mapping words helps children build concepts related to vocabulary.

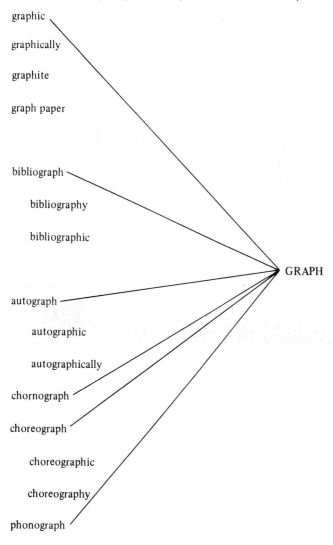

Vocabulary prediction can be some variation of the following (Rhodes & Dudley Marling, 1988):

1. The teacher prepares for vocabulary prediction by reading the material and selecting six to ten words that children may not know or are difficult for some reason. They may, for example, be used in unfamiliar ways or have multiple meanings.
2. The teacher introduces the words by writing them on the board, an overhead, or a large sheet of paper as shown in the photograph on this page.
3. The children predict what the words mean or suggest any ideas they associate with the vocabulary. All ideas are accepted, and discussion is encouraged. The photograph on this page shows some predictions made before third graders read *Two Bad Ants* (Van Allsburg, 1988).
4. The students are encouraged to read the material and see how closely the predictions match actual usage.
5. After reading, the students can add any ideas they associate with the vocabulary. Additional information will allow the class to clarify the terms.

Roberta records her third graders' responses to vocabulary predictions before they read. As she writes vocabulary predictions on the board, the children keep track of their responses in their journals.

Vocabulary can be predicted during reading, too. Identifying important vocabulary in the reading material and leaving blanks for the words also encourage prediction of meanings. Children can be encouraged to make predictions about words that would make sense in the blank. Cloze could be used instead of brainstorming to help children understand the word *vaudeville* in the example used earlier. The teacher could prepare a large section of text and omit the word when it appears. The students could be encouraged to use what they already have read to predict what word might occur in the text. Chances are they would not suggest the word vaudeville, but would predict words that they regularly use to discuss entertainment. After predictions are recorded, the class could discuss and compare the author's choice of *vaudeville* with the predictions of the class. Using cloze to predict the word that occurs in the text allows students to relate the new word to what they know.

Cloze can help students make judgments about the importance of the vocabulary. They may find that they do not need to identify the word in order to understand the text. An awareness that not every word must be identified to gain meaning from the text is an important lesson that must be learned by efficient readers. Cloze serves as a structure for discussion that allows the students to develop understanding of the vocabulary and strategies for learning vocabulary independently.

Reader-selected Vocabulary Procedures (RSVP)

Two activities illustrate child-centered instruction that encourages independence and vocabulary development. Watson (1987) suggests a vocabulary activity that allows students to select the vocabulary that is the focus of instruction. In addition, the technique provides the teacher with information about how well the children are reading. The procedure is as follows:

1. Children are given several strips of paper to use as bookmarks. The strips are cut from typing paper or notebook paper and are two to three inches wide and three to five inches long.

2. The children are instructed to read as usual, but when they encounter a word that they do not know and it interferes with their comprehension, they are to place the bookmark there and continue to read. Students are encouraged to continue reading until they reach the end or a logical stopping point. Every effort is made to not interfere with the fluency of reading.

3. At the end of the independent reading time or when they have reached a logical stopping point, the children are asked to return to where they placed markers. They select three or four of the words that most affected their comprehension.

4. The students record the words and the sentence in which they first encountered a word on the bookmark. The bookmarks are handed to the teacher.

5. The bookmarks can be used to organize instruction based on vocabulary problems the children identify. Children who are having difficulty with similar vocabulary problems can be grouped together for small group instruction planned by the teacher.

Another method is to provide a worksheet for students to complete, which allows for more independent vocabulary development. The worksheet is designed to guide students to select vocabulary words as they read. This procedure (Stansell, 1987) is known as the Reader-selected Vocabulary Procedure (RSVP) and begins by directing children to mark with a check any unfamiliar words they encounter during their reading. The reading is uninterrupted and continues until there is a logical stopping place. After they have read the material, they are asked to select several words they marked while reading. They then complete an activity sheet by filling in four columns headed, ''Words I Know After Reading,'' ''Important Words I'm Not Sure About,'' ''My Best Guess,'' and ''Resource'' (see Figure 7.4).

The students look back at the words they marked and write them in the appropriate columns. After the words are identified as words they know or words they are not sure about, students jot down meanings in the best guess column. The reference column can be used to write the definitions of words after class discussion, additional reading, or reference work that clarifies the concept.

Word Association Strategies

There are strategies encouraging an interest in vocabulary acquisition by encouraging children to associate familiar words with new concepts. One strategy described by Nagy (1988) encourages children to create their own vocabulary lists of words related to the theme of the selection, explore and categorize words on the vocabulary list, and share opinions about their ideas. The strategy is designed for high school and junior high, but a simplified version is effective with younger readers. Procedures for this word association strategy are as follows:

1. The teacher selects two words associated with the major theme or concept of the reading material. For example, to introduce the term *vaudeville,* the teacher selects two words, such as *joke* and *dance.*

2. The class is divided into small groups, and the children are asked to brainstorm as many words as they can that are associated with the word joke. The process is repeated for dance.

3. The students pair each of five words from their joke lists with five words from the dance lists. The students should be able to explain why each pair is matched. The discussions of why words are associated is valuable in building the concepts associated with vaudeville.

In this exercise the interaction between students is more important than the matching of word pairs. The discussions provide opportunities for the students to share their ideas and discuss the concepts that result in vocabulary growth.

A second example of a word association strategy is the versatile vocabulary strategy called ''We'd Rather'' (Wisler & Williams, 1990). This activity develops a rich conceptual understanding by providing associations with familiar concepts. During this activity, the children establish relationships by making decisions about the concepts associated with words. This activity would be guided in the following manner:

FIGURE 7-4 The RSVP worksheet encourages students to make predictions about word meanings.

Words I Know After Reading	Important Words I'm Not Sure About	My Best Guess	Resource
	Other Words I'm Not Sure About		

1. The teacher identifies words and concepts that are needed in order to understand a reading selection.
2. The teacher prepares key statements or questions that use the targeted vocabulary words. Phrases or sentences should be underlined or set apart in some manner. One third grade teacher selected vocabulary and concepts from *The Velveteen Rabbit* (Williams, 1983) and developed the example in Box 7.1.
3. Students work in small groups of four, and each group copies the phrases from the board or transparency onto strips of paper.
4. The students then use the strips to guide a small group discussion about what they would most like to what they would least like to have happen.
5. All the small groups share their rankings with the entire class. The sharing can produce a lively discussion based on the differences between the small group rankings.

As students discuss the rankings, they establish and use concepts and words related to the vocabulary. (Even kindergarten children can rank pictures according to the desired criteria. For example, What food do you like best? What is the fastest machine?)

Discussion and prediction are basic strategies for developing the concepts that allow children to learn the vocabulary necessary to comprehend reading material. Strategies that provide opportunities for children to predict, interact, and discuss the words help build the experiences needed for vocabulary development.

Encouraging Independence

One of the most valuable vocabulary development strategies that children can learn is how to figure out words by themselves. Much of this can be implied as children and teachers work through activities that encourage prediction and confirmation. Children also can be encouraged to determine the necessity of understanding some words and not

---

BOX 7-1

We'd Rather

We all have special times with special friends. Which of the following would you most like to have happen while you are with friends? Rank from what you would like most to what you would least like to have happen.

be *wedged* into a corner so you cannot move
line toys on the shelf in *succession*
wear a coat that is *shabby*
see the first buds of spring come through the *turf*
lose a special gold coin in the *bracken*
wear shoes until they are scuffed and *dingy*
feel *insignificant* while with friends
get a new dress made of pink *sateen*

---

others. Teachers can emphasize that words that do not contribute to comprehension do not always need to be understood.

Curiosity about words can be encouraged during all reading, writing, and language activities. Using dictionaries and other references is meaningful when children are attempting to understand a challenging text. They should learn that sometimes it's fun and interesting to note a new and unusual word. They also should understand and be encouraged to use in their writing vocabulary they find in their reading. Positive reactions from teachers when children use new and creative words in their speech and writing encourage more use of wonderful words.

Literature-based instruction encourages use of a wide vocabulary. Most teachers who use literature-based instruction can report concrete examples of children using new-found words. One teacher reports that the literature exposes her first graders to a rich vocabulary that is reflected in their language use. She tells of one student who had been struggling with reading and wrote a summary of Van Allsburg's *Jumanji* (1981). Words such as *appeared* and *approached* were featured throughout the child's summary. She doubts he would have used the words if he had not been exposed to them in the story. Another teacher relates how the word *cascaded* became a well-used word after her class read and discussed Yorinks and Egielski's *Hey, Al* (1983). The word appeared regularly in discussions and in writing long after the book was back on the shelf. What amazed her was that it was never a word that she selected for class focus. The children were enticed by the text to understand and use the word.

Basal Instruction

Basal readers and textbooks have had a great influence on the methods used to teach vocabulary. Generally, textbooks encourage a great deal of definition and context-related activities. The skills usually identified as vocabulary skills in a basal reader include the following:

- Rhyming words
- Instructional vocabulary
- Content-area vocabulary
- Context clues
- Multiple-meaning words
- Antonyms
- Synonyms
- Homophones/homographs

Basal reading lessons provide lists of vocabulary words to be taught. Usually, the vocabulary is selected because the words are difficult to pronounce, appear in the basal for the first time, or occur frequently in other material (Nagy, 1988). The basal series provides activities, worksheets, and workbook pages to focus on the vocabulary skills before, during, and after reading of the basal selection.

A teacher introduces "new" vocabulary before the story is read, or the new words and their meanings are found in the dictionary or glossary prior to reading. Often, decoding and vocabulary skill discussions are presented together. Vocabulary instruction continues during the reading. The teacher's directions may guide children's attention to specific vocabulary words during reading of the selection. For example, after reading a page of the selection, the teacher might ask, "What does the word *report* in the message mean? What is another meaning for the word *report?* After reading the selection, workbooks may focus children's attention on the vocabulary. They may be asked to write sentences, fill in blanks, or complete other exercises using the vocabulary.

The traditional methods of teaching vocabulary recently have been criticized for three major reasons:

1. Using only the strategy of providing definitions before reading the text does not usually improve comprehension (Nagy, 1988; Stahl, 1986). The presentation of definitions is only one small aspect of developing comprehension and certainly is not a complete approach.

2. A second criticism is the lack of opportunity to focus on students' needs. Structured language lessons based on a preselected word list cannot take into account the conceptual knowledge or experience of the children in a classroom.

3. Finally, traditional methods do not help children develop strategies for understanding words when reading on their own. In fact, by selecting which words are to be learned, designing methods for how they are to be learned, and directing where exposure to the words will take place, many traditional methods allow students to develop dependency.

Another concern related to vocabulary development and basals is that many of the texts produced for basals regulate the vocabulary in some way. For example, vocabulary may not be used until it is formally introduced or vocabulary with certain prefixes or suffixes may not be used until children have been taught the structure formally. This produces language that is unnatural and reduces the opportunity to introduce words and vocabulary incidentally as when the class picked up on *cascade.* One of the greatest problems with basal text materials is that controlled vocabulary creates texts that are not natural, do not sound like real stories, and therefore cannot generate the excitement of good literature.

Adapting Traditional Approaches

Basal and textbook approaches may not be as effective in developing vocabulary as many people would like to believe. There are a few modifications that could make the basal approaches more constructive when teaching children vocabulary necessary to understand text. Some basic factors that should be included in effective instruction are as follows (Blachowicz, 1986):

1. The teacher can activate students' conceptual knowledge and experiences by asking certain questions. Questions such as, "What do I know about these words?"

allow students to use what they know to begin building concepts about the reading material.

   2. Students should be encouraged to predict meanings based on the context in which words are found. Some prediction strategies encourage children to continue activating their experiences to understand concepts in the text. Questions such as, "What do I see in previewing the selection that can give me a clue as to what these words might mean?" allow predictions to help understand vocabulary.

   3. Students should be encouraged to read the text and discover how the author has used the vocabulary. Contextual clues can help students identify the author's interpretation of the concepts and how he or she intended to use the words.

   4. Students should be encouraged to change their original predictions and refine the meanings after reading the material. What is learned from the material can help build concepts that develop an understanding of the vocabulary.

   5. It is imperative that children continue to use the vocabulary. The words must be used in their daily conversation and writing before they can become a permanent part of the child's knowledge.

Writing

Writing allows students to experiment with both word identification and vocabulary usage. Not only does writing encourage the development of word identification and vocabulary, it also provides teachers with an opportunity to evaluate the growth and understanding of their students. When children write, there is concrete evidence of their language development.

   Children who are beginning to establish their knowledge of words and letters must be allowed and encouraged to write (Henderson, 1990). Writing encourages children to experiment with print and focuses their attention on the letters and sounds in a meaningful way. Writing provides reasons for learning about the letters, sounds, and spellings because that knowledge is necessary for the children to communicate their ideas effectively.

   As children begin to read and write, the interrelationship of the two processes begins to affect their vocabularies. Words they see in their reading begin to appear in their writing. Writing provides children with opportunities to use reading vocabulary in another context. Using reading vocabulary in writing increases the chances that new words will become a permanent part of children's language.

   Writing offers teachers concrete examples of phonetic and vocabulary growth. Children's spelling indicates how they perceive and understand the sound–symbols system and what rules they know about phonetics. The words that children use in their writing also suggest to a teacher what words they recognize in their reading. Also, using new vocabulary words or patterns of words from stories indicates that they are comprehending and learning from their reading.

   Children must have freedom to experiment with new vocabulary in their writing. Only when children know that their attempts at using vocabulary will be encouraged will they attempt to use new and interesting words in their writing. If they feel that misspelled words will be marked or interpreted as mistakes, they may use words that they are sure of spelling correctly and miss opportunities to practice new vocabulary. Children need to feel free to use new vocabulary and concepts in their own writing in order to learn.

Learning Differences

Most of the guidelines and instructional activities described in this chapter work with all children. In addition, there are some factors the teacher should consider when planning instruction for children who speak different languages and who are of different cultures.

Culture

Most children, regardless of their culture, are eager to be effective communicators. The identification of printed words can be affected by culture. Any cultural group comes to school with a rich experiential and verbal background, and the likelihood of reading success is as great for them as for other children. To assure all children's success, teachers should be aware of the way written and verbal language forms are viewed in children's cultures and how children are expected to interact with print. Increased awareness is the best way to interpret what children from other cultures are accomplishing. Responding to children of any culture with an awareness of and responsiveness to their backgrounds enhances learning about words and related concepts.

Language

Children who speak English with different dialects and accents have a particularly difficult time with traditional phonics instruction. They may not be pronouncing words as the teacher would or in the manner that diacritical marks would indicate "correct". Children who speak English with the strong accents of the south or New England, for example, may not always hear differences in phonology. The dialectal differences among children who speak English as a first language may be bothersome, but should not interfere with learning to read if a teacher is aware of the potential influence of dialect on phonetics.

The situation may be different when children come to school and do not speak English. When children speak other languages, several factors influence their understanding of phonics. The letters in English and other languages do not always represent the same sounds. In fact, there are some English sounds that do not exist in other languages. Spanish-speaking children, for example, may have a difficult time completing phonics activities based on the c or k sounds because those sounds do not exist in their language. Another difficulty that might arise is that the syntax of children's first language may vary from English syntax. The words may not even be in the same order as they might be in their native language. Both factors suggest that children who don't speak English as natives may have a difficult time understanding the phonetics or uses of English.

There is another reason why the emphasis on phonics should be moderated when teaching children who are learning English how to read. Children who are learning a second language tend to focus too much on phonics and decoding even when instruction does not encourage it. Because they may be lacking the ability to discuss some basic concepts in English, they depend on the concrete aspect of sounding out words at the expense of the comprehension. Instruction should not encourage them to focus on what may be too narrow an aspect of reading (Sutton, 1989).

Children who are learning English will gain meaning without sounding out every word, but instruction may be necessary to make this obvious to the students. One way to demonstrate to them that all words do not need to be identified is to allow them to read material that ensures success. Predictable books, repeated readings, and language experience activities provide them with opportunities to understand material and learn how the English language works. They will learn best about letters, sounds, and words by seeing them and hearing them in the context of real books (Franklin, 1986). Stories poems, and a wide range of other materials are an excellent way to teach children of all languages about the conventions of print.

Vocabulary and concept development is crucial to children who are learning English as their second language. They need many opportunities to discuss the meanings and to develop concretely the concepts they must understand. Concept development can be assisted with videos, charts, pictures, and concrete objects. Concept development should be repetitive and introduced in various ways. The child who is just beginning to speak English must have vocabulary that is useful, meaningful, and will be used often.

Krashen (1989) suggests that vocabulary is developed by reading as in the first language. He advises that pleasure reading is a most beneficial vocabulary (and spelling) approach for instructing second language learners. Unfortunately, chances for recreational reading generally are not provided to the child who is learning to speak English. Recreational reading is an inexpensive and practical suggestion for teachers who speak a language different than their reading students'. Reading some of the excellent concept books also allows children to improve their vocabularies.

Formal reading and writing should focus on the words students need in the classroom and in the world around them. For example, many words and concepts can be developed with a field trip to McDonald's (McGee & Richgels, 1990). Children can be exposed to everyday words such as *exit, stop, men,* and *ladies* during the visit. After returning to their classroom they can produce a language experience story explaining events and pictures taken during the trip. This activity encourages vocabulary development, contributes to sight vocabulary, and provides opportunities to discuss decoding in a meaningful context.

DISCUSSION AND ACTIVITIES

1. Select some reading material that you feel is appropriate for children and that contains some exciting vocabulary. Decide which words need to be the focus of vocabulary lessons.

2. Do you remember having to look up definitions of vocabulary words? How did that make you feel? Did it ever frustrate you, or did you feel you learned from the experience?

3. Do you remember completing worksheets that focused your attention on phonics and other word identification techniques? Did you enjoy working on these isolated skills? How will you change word identification instruction when you are teaching?

4. How will you explain to parents your approach to word identification instruction? Pair up with another member of your class and role play the explanation. Change roles and attempt to explain to another teacher how you teach phonics.

5. Find a term in the next chapter your instructor assigns and try one of the vocabulary development activities with a small group of your peers.

RELATED READING

Professional Reading

Binkley, J. R. (Ed.). (1986). Vocabulary [Special issue]. *Journal of Reading (1986), 29* (7).
Henderson, E. H. (1990). *Teaching spelling* (2nd ed.). Boston: Houghton Mifflin.

> *Henderson has been studying children's spelling development for many years and has many insights that can be applied to children's knowledge of words.*

Nagy, W. E. (1988). *Teaching vocabulary to improve reading comprehension.* Champaign, IL: Center for the Study of Reading.

> *This report presents a comprehension-based rationale and examples of effective vocabulary instruction. The article presents current ideas on vocabulary learning.*

Children's Literature

Ackerman, K. (1988). *Song and dance man.* Illustrated by S. Gammell. New York: Knopf.
Base, G. (1986). *Animalia.* New York: Harry N. Abrams.
de Regniers, B.S., Moore, E., White, M.M., & Carr, J. (Eds.). (1988). *Sing a song of popcorn: Every child's book of poems.* New York: Scholastic.
Prelutsky, J. (1989). *Poems of A. Nonny Mouse.* Illustrated by H. Drescher. New York: Knopf.
Sendak, M. (1963). *Where the wild things are.* New York: Harper & Row.
Van Allsburg, C. (1981). *Jumanji.* Boston: Houghton Mifflin.
———. (1987). *The Z was zapped.* Boston: Houghton Mifflin.
———. (1988). *Two bad ants.* Boston: Houghton Mifflin.
Williams, M. (1983). *The velveteen rabbit.* Illustrated by William Nicholson. New York: Doubleday.
Yorinks, A. (1986). *Hey, Al.* Illustrated by R. Egielski. New York: Farrar, Straus & Giroux.

REFERENCES

Adams, M.J. (1990). *Beginning to read: Thinking and learning about print.* Urbana-Champaign, IL: University of Illinois, Center for the Study of Reading.
Allen, R.R., Brown, K.L., & Yatvin, J. (1986). *Learning language through communication.* Belmont, CA: Wadsworth.
Altwerger, B., Edelsky, C., & Flores, B. (1987). Whole language: What's new? *The Reading Teacher, 41* (2), 144–155.

Anderson, R. C., Hiebert, E.H., Scott, J.A., & Wilkinson, I. A. G. (1985). *Becoming a nation of readers: The report of the commission on reading*. Washington, DC.: National Institute of Education.

Beck, I.L. & McKeown, M.G. (1984). Application of theories of reading to instruction. *American Journal of Education, 93*, 61–81.

Blachowicz, C.L.Z. (1985). Vocabulary development and reading: From research to instruction. *The Reading Teacher, 38* (9), 876–881.

———. (1986). Making connections: Alternatives to the vocabulary notebook. *Journal of Reading, 29* (7), 643–649.

Carey, S. (1978). The child as word learner. In M. Halle, J. Bresin, & G. A. Miller (Eds.). *Linguistics theory and psychological reality*. Cambridge, MA: MIT Press.

Carpenter, P.A., & Just, M.A. (1986). Cognitive process in reading. In Judith Orasanu (Ed.), *Reading comprehension: From research to practice*. Hillsdale, NJ: Lawrence Erlbaum.

Carr, E., & Wixson, K.K. (1986). Guidelines for evaluating vocabulary instruction. *The Reading Teacher, 29* (7), 588–595.

Chall, J. (1983). *Learning to read: The great debate* (2nd ed.). New York: McGraw Hill.

Cunningham, P. A., Moore, S. A., Cunningham, J. W., & Moore, D. W. (1983). *Reading in elementary classrooms: Strategies and observations*. New York: Longman.

Elley, W.B. (1989). Vocabulary acquisition from listening to stories. *Reading Research Quarterly, XXIV* (2), 175–187.

Finn, P.J. (1990). *Helping children learn to read*. New York: Longman.

Flesch, R. (1985, June 12). Why Johnny can't read: We taught him incorrectly. *Education Week,* 28.

Fox, D. (1986). The debate goes on: systematic phonics vs. whole language. *The Journal of Reading, 29* (7), 678–680.

Franklin, E.A. (1986). Literacy instruction for LES children. *Language Arts, 63* (1), 51–60.

Goodman, K. (1986). *What's whole in whole language?* Portsmouth, NH: Heinemann.

Groff, P. (1986). The maturing of phonics instruction. *The Reading Teacher, 39* (9), 919–923.

Harp, B. (1989, January). When the principal asks: ''Why aren't you using the phonics workbooks?''. *Reading Teacher, 326–327.*

Henderson, E. H. (1990). *Teaching spelling*. Boston: Houghton Mifflin.

Jiganti, M.A., & Tindall, M.A.(1986). An interactive approach to teaching vocabulary. *The Reading Teacher, 39* (9), 444–448.

Krashen, S. (1989). We acquire vocabulary and spelling by reading: Additional evidence for the input hypothesis. *The Modern Language Journal, 73* (4), 440–464.

Linfors, J. W. (1980). *Children's language and learning*. Englewood Cliffs, NJ: Prentice-Hall.

Lundberg, I., Frost, J., & Petersen, O.P. (1988). Effects of an extensive program for stimulating phonological awareness in preschool children. *Reading Research Quarterly, 23* (3), 263–284.

McGee, L.M., & Richgels, D.J. (1990). *Literacy beginnings: Supporting young readers and writers*. Boston, MA: Allyn & Bacon.

McKeown, M.G. & Beck, I.L. (1988). Learning vocabulary: Different ways for different goals. *Remedial and Special Education, 9* (1), 42–46.

Morrow, L. M. (1989). *Literacy development in the early years: Helping children read and write*. Englewood Cliffs, NJ: Prentice-Hall.

Nagy, W.E. (1988). *Teaching vocabulary to improve reading comprehension*. Unpublished manuscript, University of Illinois, Center for the Study of Reading, Urbana, IL.

Nagy, W., Anderson, R.C., Schommer, M., Scott, J.A., & Stallman, A.C. (1989). Morphological families and word recognition. *Reading Research Quarterly, 24* (3), 262–282.

Nelson-Herber, J. (1986). Expanding and refining vocabulary in content areas. *Journal of Reading, 29* (7), 626–633.

Pearson, P. D. (1984). Reading comprehension instruction: Six necessary changes. *Reading Education Report, No 54*. Urbana-Champaign, IL: University of Illinois, Center for the Study of Reading.

Rhodes, L.K., & Dudley-Marling, C.(1988). *Readers and writers with a difference: A holistic approach to teaching learning disabled and remedial students.* Portsmouth, NH: Heinemann.

Ruddell, R.B. (1986). Vocabulary learning: A process model and criteria for evaluating instructional strategies. *Journal of Reading, 29* (7), 581–587.

Ryder, R. (1986). Phonics in middle/secondary school subjects. In E.K. Dishner, T.W. Bean, J. E. Readence, & D.W. Moore (Eds.), *Reading in the content areas: Improving classroom instruction* (2nd ed.). Dubuque, IA: Kendall Hunt.

Schickedanz, J.A. (1989). The place of specific skills in preschool and kindergarten. In D.S. Strickland & L.M. Morrow (Eds.), *Emerging literacy: Young children learn to read and write.* Newark, DE: International Reading Association.

Searfoss, L.W., and Readance, J.H. (1989). *Helping children learn to read.* Englewood Cliffs, NJ: Prentice-Hall.

Smith, F. (1985). *Reading without nonsense* (2nd ed.). New York: Teachers' College.

Smith, F. (1988). *Understanding reading* (4th ed.). Hillsdale, NJ: Lawrence Erlbaum Associates.

Stahl, S.A. (1986). Three principles of effective vocabulary instruction. *Journal of Reading, 19* (7), 662–668.

Stansell, J. (1987). Reader-selected vocabulary procedure (R.S.V.P.): An invitation to natural vocabulary development. In Dorothy Watson (Ed.), *Ideas and insights: Language arts in the elementary school.* Urbana, IL: National Council of Teachers of English.

Sulzby, E. (1985). Children's emergent reading of favorite story books. *Reading Research Quarterly, 20,* 458–481.

Sutton, C. (1989). Helping the non-native English speaker with reading. *The Reading Teacher, 42* (9), 684–688.

Trachtenburg, P. (1990). Using children's literature to enhance phonics instruction. *The Reading Teacher, 43* (9), 648–654.

Watson, D. (1987). Reader-selected miscues. In Dorothy Watson (Ed.), *Ideas and insights: Language arts in the elementary school.* Urbana, IL: National Council of Teachers of English.

Wisler, N. & Williams, J. (1990). *Literature and cooperative learning: Pathway to literacy.* Sacramento, CA: Literature Co-op.

Yaden, D. (1985, December). *Preschoolers' spontaneous inquiries about print and books.* Paper presented at the annual meeting of the National Reading Conference, San Diego, CA.

8

READING TO LEARN
SPECIFIC INFORMATION

*The room they entered was big, square, well lit, and had a faint musty
smell. "It's reasonably comfortable, and if you like to read . . ." he gestured at
the walls. They were lined with shelves from floor to ceiling, and on the shelves
stood—Mrs. Frisby dredged in her memory. "Books," she said. "They're
books." "Yes," said Justin. "Do you read much?"*

*"Only a little," said Mrs. Frisby. "My husband taught me. And the chil-
dren . . ." She started to tell him how. Laboriously scratching letters in the earth
with a stick—it seemed so long ago. But Justin was leaving.*

*****

*Mrs. Frisby looked around her. The room—the library, Nicodemus had
called it—had, in addition to its shelves of books, several tables with benches be-
side them, and on these were stacked more books, some of them open.*

*Books. Her husband, Jonathan, had told her about them. He had taught
her and the children to read (the children had mastered it quickly, but she herself
could barely manage the simplest words; she had thought perhaps it was because
she was older). He had also told her about electricity. He had known these
things—and so, it emerged, did the rats. It had never occurred to her until now
to wonder how he knew them. He had always known so many things, and she had
accepted that as a matter of course. But who had taught him to read? Strangely,
it emerged that he had known the rats. Had they taught him? What had been his
connection with them? She remembered his long visits with Mr. Ages. And, Mr.
Ages knew the rats, too.*

*****

*She noticed at the far end of the room a section of wall where there were
no bookshelves. There was, instead, a blackboard covered with words and numbers written in white chalk. There were pieces of chalk and an eraser in a rack at
the bottom of it. The blackboard stood near the end of the longest of the tables.
Was the library also used as a classroom?*

—Robert C. O'Brien, *Mrs. Frisby and the Rats of NIMH*
(1972 Newbery Medal winner)

WHEN children begin their schooling, most experiences with reading and writing emphasize story telling or narration. Children in primary grades read narratives, including picture books, basals stories, and even social studies texts that tell stories. Repeated exposure to reading material and instruction ultimately requires them to become more flexible in their reading selections and strategies. When they begin the third or fourth grade, the materials they are required to read may include formats, contents, and arrangements that are different than narration. It is about this time that children are introduced to more in-depth exploration of subject areas through textbooks and nonfiction trade books. Magazines and newspapers play an important role in explaining daily events or special topics. Children need to comprehend directions and explanations in manuals, computer software, and other technical material to accomplish school work, hobbies, or other tasks. There are many opportunities for children to read expository texts that explain concepts, present ideas, and give directions.

Children are expected to learn by reading various forms of text. However, many young readers who are able to read narratives or short stories have a difficult time understanding exposition. School instruction should provide guidance in establishing strategies and abilities for reading to learn specific information. Some of the questions this chapter will answer include:

1. How is reading expository texts different than reading narrative material?
2. How should exposition be used in subject area instruction?
3. What can narratives contribute to learning about other subjects?
4. Is it possible to help children remember information they have read?

Reading to learn about subjects, concepts, and specific ideas requires the integration of many language skills and strategies. When children read to learn they are improving their overall reading abilities. Furthermore, the ability to learn about specific subjects and concepts through reading is easier if the proper reading strategies are employed.

Foundations of Reading to Learn

Reading can generate a wide range of emotional or factual results and reactions. Compare the reading of this textbook and a popular novel. When you read this text, you must understand certain ideas and concepts about reading instruction. You need to remember specific definitions, understandings, and ideas. However, during Christmas break, you may spend some time reading a novel that appears on the best seller list. The novel provides you with insights and understandings, but you will not be as concerned about remembering facts and details as you would be with a textbook. The purpose of reading, the context, and the text you are reading suggest differing strategies. Reading to learn involves different outcomes, different perspectives on the part of the reader, and different strategies when reading. As an efficient reader you have developed strategies to read and learn from both narratives and exposition.

Expository Texts

Reading expository texts is a basic activity through which learning occurs and is an important tool for building basic concepts, expanding personal knowledge, and understanding content. Exposition explains, informs, or directs (Slater & Graves, 1989) by presenting theories, generalizations, limitations, predictions, facts, specifications, and dates about persons, places, and things. The information presented in well-written exposition is more than a listing of facts and must be accompanied by explanations that allow the reader to relate to prior knowledge.

Most children do not come to school with the capability of understanding expository texts. Understanding exposition is developmental, is based on experiences, and a reader must read to learn efficient strategies for gaining information (Slater & Graves, 1987). Experience with exposition does improve abilities to comprehend, and as early as first grade children can begin developing reading strategies and abilities that allow them to learn.

Exposition looks different than text that tells stories. Often the information is arranged in several columns on each page, has boldface and italicized sections, and large printed headings within the text. Graphs, pictures, illustrations, and even questions are interjected throughout. Newspapers and history books may present similar types of information, but the arrangements are different. Even concepts may be presented in numerous ways. Two texts may present similar information arranged in different ways and explained in distinctive manners.

There are recognizable structures for expository texts. A particular structure often is recognizable because certain words signal a particular development (Richgels, McGee, & Slaton, 1989). The main structures are as follows:

1. Describing or collecting facts: presents lists or bits of information and uses cue words such as *first, second, third, next, then, finally, to begin, for example.*

2. Ordering or sequencing information: presents information in a chronological order and uses cue words such as *not long after, as before, after, when, since, during.*

3. Comparing and contrasting: presents similarities and differences between concepts discussed in the text and uses cue words such as *however, on the other hand, similarly, yet, different from, same.*

4. Presenting problems and solutions: describes a problem and one or more solutions and uses cue words such as *problem, difficulty,* and *solutions.*

5. Establishing causal links: demonstrates how events happen and why and uses cue words such as *therefore, consequently,* and *as a result.*

Understanding different text arrangements contributes to effective reading (Armbruster, Anderson & Ostertag, 1989). Since you have spent at least fifteen years reading exposition, you probably are familiar with textbook arrangements. Before you open a book, you can predict that each chapter will focus on an important topic, that there will be illustrations, charts, and boldface words to guide you through the reading. The prior knowledge you have of textbook arrangements contributes to your ability to understand the text. Readers who can explain how a text is arranged remember the content of what they read longer (Richgels, McGee, & Slaton, 1989) than those who cannot.

Direct instruction about expository text structure helps readers remember information. There are specific approaches that seem to help readers learn about text structures (Armbruster, Anderson & Ostertag, 1989). These approaches teach readers to be aware of headings, subheadings, and paragraphs or guide readers through graphic and visual representations of ideas in a text.

In addition to understanding text arrangements, the reader of exposition must understand basic concepts, ideas, and vocabulary about the topic presented. All the knowledge a reader possesses about a topic must somehow be organized in the reader's mind. The way all information about a topic is arranged mentally provides the basis for how concepts and ideas are understood and remembered. The elements of comprehension discussed in chapter 6 certainly pertain to the comprehension of exposition. The development and establishment of prior knowledge of the topic is extremely important when reading exposition to learn more.

When readers do not possess prior knowledge of a topic, the arrangement of the text greatly affects comprehension (Roller, 1990). Readers who are attempting to understand an unfamiliar topic are aided when they are reading a familiar and recognizable text structure. The text does not contribute information in the same ways to a well-versed reader. For instance, when children have not grown up reading and talking about dinosaurs, their science texts may be the first time they encounter the topic. The structure of the text presents relationships and definitions that children use to understand dinosaurs. A familiar text structure, such as one that compares and contrasts dinosaurs to modern reptiles, will be a great influence on the way children understand dinosaurs. The text builds and influences the child's schema. Children who already understand a great deal about dinosaurs will not depend on the text to establish relationships and they may be able to encounter unfamiliar text arrangements and structures and still come away with information.

Children come to school without much experience reading expository text. They can benefit from experience and from direct guidance in understanding elements and arrangements of the texts. Children are affected by the amount of experience they have with topics and the information they have about text structures. However, familiarity with text structure appears to be the most important element when children are learning about a topic for the first time.

Subject Area Reading

Exposition is used during instruction in subjects such as science, social studies, math, art, and music. At first glance it would appear that children who are efficient language users would be able to learn and comprehend factual reading material without assistance. The most effective readers of narratives probably will be able to use the textbooks effectively. However, because language is used differently and material is arranged uniquely, experience with the texts may not be consistent, background and concepts may not be developed effectively, and instructional arrangements may differ. All children can benefit from activities that guide them during subject area reading.

A great deal of subject area instruction is guided by textbooks prepared especially for classroom use. Since students seem to have a difficult time comprehending topics by reading textbooks, many teachers avoid requiring students to interact with and study the information in the book. Several studies indicate that students seldom are required to use textbook materials to read, think, or solve problems. Instead, teachers rely on reading aloud, lecturing, or discussing instead of requiring children to read. Flood and Lapp (1986) believe that students' limited contacts with subject area texts becomes particularly apparent as they progress through elementary and junior high and are less able to read textbooks. As a result of lack of experience, students often have a negative or passive approach to textbook reading and come away with little comprehension of the material (Davey, 1986). It would not be hard to understand how children never develop efficient exposition and subject reading strategies if they are not required to practice the skill.

The relationship between reading and understanding factual material is nearly synonymous. Subjects are learned through reading and writing. Success in subject areas is highly dependent on children's abilities to read and learn specific information. At the same time, while reading and writing are critical, the main focus of instruction is learning the content.

Children's Literature

While most subject instruction focuses on textbooks, children can learn by reading both expository and narrative children's literature. The wide variety of topics, structures, and formats available in children's literature provides readers with a wealth of print that will assist them in learning about specific topics. Fiction and nonfiction, magazines, and newspapers can be read out of school or in school to augment subject area reading. It is difficult to imagine how children could learn science, social studies, art, humanities, and even math without children's literature.

Assumptions for Reading to Learn

Reading to learn requires that children develop strategies for learning specific facts, understanding concepts, and remembering important information. Much learning occurs in the subject areas of the school curriculum and with the support of textbooks and children's literature. There are several assumptions that guide instruction in reading to learn:

Different Texts Require Flexible Comprehension Strategies
Both teachers and children need to understand that there are differences in reading text about specific subjects and text that tells a story. Expository text differs from narrative text in structure, arrangement, vocabulary, concept presentations, and so on. Different arrangements, presentations, and vocabulary should be identified, and specific strategies should be employed to understand various texts.

Children Need Successful Experiences in Reading about Specific Content
As with all other reading growth, the ability to read about specific content appears to improve as children mature and gain experience. Once the developmental aspect of

reading is accepted, it is easy to welcome children's first attempts. Children's responses may not always be mature, but will reflect their intent to begin understanding the world around them. Responses from children are necessary for learning and require a risk-free environment.

Children Will Need Prior Information to Understand Various Text Structures

Before children are asked to read specific content, there must be time to develop knowledge and understanding about the topic. Related concepts and vocabulary must be understood. In addition, students who possess the proper background about the reading material will be more successful in understanding what they are reading.

Subject Area Textbooks Are Only One Tool for Learning Information at School

Each subject has its own special instructional activities. Science has labs, social studies has problem-solving discussions and role playing, and art includes demonstration. Each of these activities can be supported by textbooks and children's literature. The textbooks should provide a supplement for instruction and should never be the sole activity required for learning and understanding a particular subject.

Encouraging Reading to Learn

Children's literature (both fiction and nonfiction) and textbooks can contribute to children's effective reading of specific content. Each of these resources has a somewhat different role in reading to learn.

Role of Children's Literature

Children can learn concepts, facts, and ideas from both expository and narrative children's literature. Literature can be incorporated into almost any subject in elementary school and can contribute to subject area reading in general. The range of topics presented in children's literature can be used to build knowledge, motivation, and interest to learn about any subject taught in elementary classrooms. Supplementing textbooks with children's literature increases opportunities to read and write about many different subjects.

Children's literature can be used in many ways during subject area instruction, but certain genres seem to be more appropriate for particular subjects. The suggestions in the following section are presented only as examples and should not limit the choices available for teaching subjects.

Social Studies

Literature can be used to develop a multitude of social studies concepts. Inclusion of children's literature in the teaching of social studies can enhance and support the study of history, geography, economics, and society. In addition, literature can be used to ensure a cultural representation of history, values, and customs. Books can be used to develop entire social studies units or can elaborate on and augment the subject matter of a textbook. Although all children's literature selections have the potential to contribute to learning social studies concepts, there are five specific types of children's literature that seem particularly adaptable.

1. Books that present facts and information in several different forms are an obvious supplement to social studies. Most obvious are the map books and atlases that are produced for children and could serve as a valuable resource in the classroom. In addition, there are children's books written about a wide variety of concepts, including cultural studies, habits, traveling, animals of different countries, and so on that can be used as a teacher prepares to introduce different topics.

The books describing specific historical events can motivate study and encourage historical understanding. One such book is Halliburton's account of *The Tragedy of Little Bighorn* (1989). The paintings, tinted photographs, and pictographs produced by the Sioux emphasize the human tragedy. The author begins with "Dead men do tell tales. Mostly little secrets . . . The tragedy of Little Bighorn is such a tale" (p. 9). The same event is chronicled in Freedman's *Indian Chiefs* (1987a). After children read these two accounts they can compare the presentations and discuss the differences in how the authors wrote about the event.

There are books about people who live in different regions of the world that allow children to see how life in other cultures may be different. One book that describes Americans with whom we may not always be familiar is *In Two Worlds: A Yup'ik Eskimo Family* (Jenness & Rivers, 1989). This book captures the similarities to and the differences from continental Americans and describes a group of native Americans often misrepresented in books and movies. Not only does this book capture a different American culture, it also details the changes that have come to the Eskimo way of life in the last fifty years. Pictures and text allow students to visit the homes of these citizens and be with them as they shop, go to school, visit the doctor, and hunt ptarmigans.

Some nonfiction books may present aspects of social studies not normally associated with children's literature. Economics and business successes are discussed in *The Fortunate Fortunes: Business Successes That Began with a Lucky Break* (Aaseng, 1989). This book recounts the successes of entrepreneurs who were responsible for such notable products as Baby Ruth candy and Wrigley's gum.

2. Biographies also increase the options for reading during social studies instruction. Any historical character or person that represents a certain era can be included easily in the study of history. Biographies provide insights into historical figures while presenting facts in an entertaining manner.

There are biographies of almost every American president and many of the famous Americans discussed in social studies curriculum. Abraham Lincoln probably has more biographies written about him than any other president. A recent book, *Lincoln, A Photobiography* (Freedman, 1987b), was a 1988 Newbery winner and contains prints and photographs to support the well-written account of Lincoln's life. This book could not help but add to the Civil War accounts in social studies textbooks.

3. Traditional literature is particularly important in classrooms that represent many cultures and ethnic backgrounds. Regional and ethnic folk literature is excellent for use in discussions of the similarities of all humans, as well as for forums on cultural differences. Comparing traditional literature from different countries encourages understanding of diverse cultures. When students read and compare literature variants such as *Cinderella* (Brown, 1954) and *Mufaro's Beautiful Daughters* (Steptoe, 1987) or *Little Red Riding Hood* (Hyman, 1983) and *Lon Po Po* (Young, 1989), they gain appreciation for different cultures and develop understanding.

4. Historical fiction is an extremely valuable source for social studies instruction. Historical fiction implies that history is people and not just events to be memorized. Good historical fiction such as *Johnny Tremain* (Forbes, 1946) is realistic and includes accurate facts with fictional characters. The fictional characters often interact with actual historical figures. Reading fictional accounts provides opportunities to compare what textbooks report about an event. The contrast between fact and fiction provides students with a chance to practice such skills as observing, questioning, predicting, hypothesizing, gathering data, comparing, interpreting data, and making inferences (Reed, 1985).

The themes of some historical novels are social problems. One method of exploring African-American history is to read such books as *Roll of Thunder, Hear My Cry* (Taylor, 1976) or *The Slave Dancer* (Fox, 1973). Historical facts are presented, but more important are the explanations of the motives and perspectives of the people who lived through the events.

Not only does historical fiction present facts, people, and places, it encourages the development of attitudes and general concepts about history through related reading, drama, artwork, and so on. For example, racial inequity is explained through Cassie's experiences in *Roll of Thunder, Hear My Cry* (Taylor, 1976). It is impossible not to feel the injustice that she and her family endure. Cassie and her brothers are humiliated daily as they walk to school and must endure the harassment of the school bus driver taking the white children to school.

> *Little Man turned around and watched saucer-eyed as a bus bore down on him spewing clouds of red dust like a huge yellow dragon breathing fire. Little Man headed toward the bank, but it was too steep. He ran frantically along the road looking for a foothold and, finding one, hopped onto the bank, but not before the bus had sped past enveloping him in a scarlet haze while laughing white faces pressed against the bus windows. (p. 8)*

Science

Children's science backgrounds are enhanced by well-researched, accurate books that focus their curiosity and provide information to supplement what is being studied in science. There are several types of children's literature that easily provide opportunities for reading and writing as well as information about certain science concepts.

1. Just as in social studies, information books provide a wide variety of printed material for teachers to use during science instruction. The number of concept books that support science instruction area are numerous. Almost any subject taught in the schools can be studied with concept and informational books.

Valuable science resources in children's literature are books about nature and life cycles. For example, *Wild Mouse* (Brady, 1976) discusses the life cycle and teaches the skills of observing and recording. The narrator discovers a wild mouse in the barn and observes and records the birth and growth of the babies. The diary format of this book can serve as an example for children in their science explorations and can suggest observation methods for the study of science.

Other books promote ecological awareness and respect for wildlife, and contain descriptions of scientific professions. *Two Orphan Cubs* (1989) by Brenner and Garelick tells the story of the adoption of two bear cubs after their mother is shot by a poacher. The job of a wildlife scientist is highlighted.

2. There are many project and experiment books that can augment certain types of science instruction. Project and experiment books can be simple, like Orii and Orii's *Straws* (1989), which presents experiments using straws, cards, and glasses to demonstrate the pushing force of air, or they can encompass more complicated experiments and projects. These books provide samples of instructional activities to support a unit of study or classroom discovery of an important concept.

3. High quality science fiction is based on scientific knowledge (Reed, 1985) and can become a teaching aid for science concepts. Science fiction explores the effect of technology on society and can provide opportunities to discuss the moral issues associated with scientific and technological advances.

Some science fiction is serious. *Z for Zachariah* (O'Brien, 1975) describes the aftermath of a nuclear war. It suggests the ethical and human issues that might accompany that event. *A Wrinkle in Time* (L'Engle, 1962) suggests the universal struggle with evil may continue in space. Such books can encourage high level thinking and in-depth discussions. Some science fiction is more lighthearted and can serve to motivate students to read the textbook to learn the underlying factual information.

4. Biographies can be used effectively in science to provide background or introduce a topic. Biographies of famous scientists provide background for concepts and underscore the effort behind scientific inquiry. An example is a commonly used biography of Louis Pasteur that illustrates scientific methodology while discussing the concept of pasteurization.

5. Even fiction can serve as a tool in science lessons. Some fiction encourages scientific observation. *Two Bad Ants* (Van Allsburg, 1988) is an example of fiction that could introduce the study of ants and their habits. While this book should never be the sole source of information on ants, it could be incorporated into scientific study of ants as an introduction, a motivator, or the basis of studying ants.

Math

Literature is not often considered a resource for teaching math, but there certainly are opportunities to include children's books in classroom activities.

Counting books can introduce math to young children. Counting books have many forms and can be used to encourage understanding of such concepts as one-to-one correspondence and counting with beautiful pictures, rhymes, or familiar narrative format. Most counting books are very simple, with the symbolic numbers and pictures of objects that represent the numbers. However, many of the books are quite lovely and may be clever and fun to read. *When Sheep Cannot Sleep: The Counting Book* (Kitamura, 1986) explains what sheep count on their sleepless nights.

Puzzle books for math can contribute to an understanding of problems and provide other opportunities for children to interact with numbers in written forms. Puzzle books are especially good for introducing math and math manipulation. Children may have difficulty understanding text that includes both words and numbers, and puzzle books can be used to provide experience in reading about numbers.

Art, Music, and Humanities

The uses of children's literature in the arts are unlimited. The variety of texts that make children aware of the beauty of the world around them is endless, and picture books themselves introduce beauty and art. Many children's illustrators are trained as classical artists and their work is recognized for its artistic merit. For example, Chris Van Allsburg and Maurice Sendak's illustrations are high quality artwork by trained artists.

There are several other ways that children's literature can be used to extend the study of art and music. Books such as *Gainsborough: A Biography* (Ripley, 1964) introduce us to the gay, witty Tom Gainsborough and his paintings. Children can learn that the English painter was a lovable and talented figure whose portraits and paintings have offered the world enjoyment for years. Children read about each of the subjects represented in his pictures and the stories behind the work. Ripley has produced biographies of several famous artists. A more recent book, *The Young Artist* (Locker, 1989), describes the life of a painter who must paint not as things are but how the king wishes. Locker, the illustrator and author, describes the creative process in his story and illustrates his text with beautiful paintings.

Musicians also become more tangible when historical fiction explains the events surrounding a famous composition. *The Boy Who Loved Music* (Lasker, 1979) presents the role of music in the eighteenth century and the importance of a famous composition. The pictures and the story help students picture the musical orientation of old Vienna. Yet another way to integrate children's literature in the study of music is illustrated by Isadora's *Ben's Trumpet* (1979), which describes the instruments associated with jazz. The shadows and shapes of this unusual book offer a format for instruction in art and music.

Teachers who use literature in their classrooms find that it encourages learning about a subject and increases reading ability. All kinds of literature teach children about the world around them.

Role of Textbooks

A basic resource for teaching subjects such as social studies, science, math, art, and humanities is the textbook. The organization of textbooks is similar to that of the basal reading series discussed in chapter 2. Generally, publishers provide graded series of textbooks in science, social studies, spelling, grammar, literature, and mathematics for grades one through eight.

Artwork and following directions can be integrated into a literature-based unit.

Organization

Although lessons may vary somewhat from subject to subject, most lesson structures include before reading, during reading, and after reading activities and discussions. This format is very similar to the arrangement of basal reading lessons. The before reading activities provide background information, develop vocabulary, and establish purpose. Skills instruction can be part of the introductory activities or part of the conclusion of a lesson. The skills that lessons emphasize are subject-related. For example, social studies might focus on globe and map skills and science might focus on inquiry skills. Teachers are given guidance in directing the reading and after reading activities through lesson plans suggesting discussions and activities that reinforce, reteach, or enrich the concepts and allow the teacher to establish what students have learned.

Textbook publishers provide teachers' editions that have many suggestions for instruction as well as specific lesson plans for particular units and concepts. Like the basal readers, they include supplemental materials. Social studies series might have maps, globes, and atlases, and science series might include lab manuals, microscopes, and charts.

Concerns and Considerations

Subject area texts have many of the strengths and weaknesses of the basal reading series. They may not always be well written for the students who are using them, they often are overused at the expense of concept development, and students often view these textbooks as boring and uninteresting.

It is not unusual to see a single textbook adopted and used in classrooms as the sole source of information on a subject. There are several reasons why using one textbook to present information to twenty to thirty children is doomed to failure. One of the first problems that arises is that children come to classes with differences in prior knowledge and interest about the topic. The difficulty level is determined as much by the background of the children in the classroom as the words in the text. The result is that the text will be too difficult for some students and too boring for others. Consider the third grader who has maintained an interest in dinosaurs since preschool years. That child may have been exposed to many books, a great deal of vocabulary, and understand many of the concepts associated with the topic. The third grade science text may be written to introduce students to the topic. The textbook material will be very easy for the dinosaur enthusiast and much more difficult for the student who has maintained other interests.

Sometimes children need different levels of motivation to encourage their interest in a topic, and textbooks do not always present the material in an interesting way. Perhaps you may be very interested in young children and see yourself working in a preschool setting. Chapter 5 may have been very interesting because you read about the reading and writing attempts of very young children. This chapter may not be nearly as interesting to you since you do not view yourself as a subject area teacher or as someone who hopes to teach older elementary students. Interest certainly affects the motivation for reading a textbook.

Instructional Contributions

Textbooks do have a role in subject instruction. Intelligent use of textbooks is flexible and involves several different instructional approaches:

1. Textbooks introduce and augment initial discussions of topics. They can be used as surveys to begin the study of a concept. Students can read sections, skim material, and become familiar with the vocabulary by using the texts. The textbook could provide the initial encounter with the topic and bring up questions students would like to answer. After surveying the texts and reading sections and viewing pictures, tables, and charts, students can predict outcomes and pose questions to guide further exploration. Textbooks can establish initial concepts about a topic, help students generate questions for research, and encourage prediction about vocabulary and concepts.

2. Textbooks can be used as an additional source with which children verify and compare findings from other reading material. Texts can guide the course of study or suggest a structure for developing activities, discussions, and learning experiences.

3. Textbooks can be used to summarize concepts after classroom activities and discussions. Textbooks usually are concise and would be an excellent way to review concepts. The questions and activities provided in texts and teachers' guides can be used to monitor children's learning.

Children learn important material if a large variety of printed material is available. Textbooks are not responsible for students' difficulties in understanding content, but total reliance on these texts may contribute to students' lack of motivation to learn. Effective use of texts suggests that teachers use their knowledge of the content, the students, and instructional methods to select the materials and approaches to subject area reading.

Instruction in Reading to Learn

There are many ways to contribute to children's abilities to read specific content, and teachers can provide opportunities for children to read effectively about subjects. Activities can be planned that allow students to learn more about the content and themselves as readers. Several components that should be included in teaching to read content effectively are concept development, text awareness activities, and vocabulary development.

Concept Development

Reading for content requires that students read material when they may not possess the background or basic concepts to facilitate their understanding. When students are expected to read material that is unfamiliar, attempts to understand what they read are frustrating and unproductive. Therefore, one of the most important instructional strategies associated with content reading is concept development. Specific tactics can be used to help students build basic concepts so that they are successful in reading factual and informative texts (Stansell and Deford, 1981).

Teachers Should Use Multiple Sources to Provide the Students with Background Information

Fiction and nonfiction books, magazines, newspapers, encyclopedias, guest speakers, video and audio recordings, and so on help students gain basic information about the topic. After students have developed some ideas about the reading material, they are more prepared to learn from texts.

Students Should Be Taught to Search for Additional Information in Various Parts of the Text

Students often read only what is assigned and do not realize that other parts of the material can offer information about the topic. Such strategies as using the table of contents and index to increase background knowledge and encourage prediction can ease comprehension when reading difficult material.

Reading Content Material Provides a Reason to Learn How to Skim

Students can be directed to skim the text in order to become familiar with the topic. Skimming provides an overview. Skimming also can provide the reader with a sense of how the text is arranged. Each of these opportunities provides students with a better chance of understanding the reading material.

The Teacher Can Help Students Coordinate Information in the Text with Other Reading, Class Notes, and Discussion

Readers should be shown how to use other information to help them understand assigned texts. When the class begins discussing an aspect presented in the text, the teacher can refer to other sources and even read aloud to the class. Using the textbook as a reference demonstrates an effective strategy to children.

Text Awareness

When students have not had much experience with subject area or expository texts or if they seem to be having difficulty using various texts, they should be given opportunities to develop awareness of the arrangement of textbooks. One method is to take class time to discuss such aspects of the books as table of contents, preface, glossary, and index. The teacher can explain appropriate uses of different aspects of the text. Text awareness skills can be demonstrated easily during class discussion. For example, as teachers prepare children for reading social studies, they can point out that the important words in the text are written in italics. The words be discussed to predict the focus of the reading material.

Students can benefit from planned instruction about text organization. A review of a specific instructional activity illustrates how teachers might guide children to a better understanding of text structures (Richgels, McGee, & Slaton, 1989).

1. To prepare for guiding students in effective reading of exposition, select a well-organized text. Well-organized texts present information logically and use illustrations, comparisons, compilations, and other means of elaboration. They use such words and phrases as *first, second, next, therefore, as a result, so that, in order to, because, similar to, different from, in contrast, however, but, on the other hand, problem, solution,* and *solve* to signal a particular text structure or elaboration (Richgels, McGee, & Slaton, 1989).

2. Once a well-organized text is identified, prepare a graphic organization. Graphic organizers are outlines of the text that show the presentation of the material. Tables of contents are simple graphic organizers, but more elaborate organizers should be used to illustrate text structure for readers. They might include key ideas from a passage and demonstrate relationships among important ideas. A simple graphic organizer for the beginning of this chapter, shown in Box 8.1, allows you to develop a schema or understanding of how ideas are presented.

3. Lead the children through a discussion that introduces the idea of different text structures. Richgels, McGee and Slaton (1989) suggest using blocks to establish the idea of different text structures with children. They write:

> *One way to demonstrate text structure is to have students build several towers out of toy blocks. Each tower should have the same structural pattern but use differently colored blocks. Make the point that even though each tower was made of differently colored blocks, all the towers have the same structure. In the same*

___ **BOX 8-1** _____

Graphic Organizer of the Introductory Section of Chapter 8

Foundations of Reading to Learn

Expository Texts	*Subject Area Reading*	*Literature*
Definition	Definition	Role
Description	Description	
Structure	Comparison of Reading	
Reading Approaches	Approaches	

way, tell the students that passages may be about different ideas, but each may be organized following the same structure. (p. 174)

4. After children understand the differences in text structures, introduce the graphic organizer and explain that it represents the structure of the passage.

5. Encourage children to write their own passages based on the structure you provided.

6. Students compare their passages with the textbook passage. Comparisons of their own writing and that of classmates can demonstrate how different ideas are accommodated by a common structure.

Vocabulary Development

The ability to recognize a vast number of words and use them correctly is a valuable skill for reading content. Without an adequate vocabulary, students learn far less than they are capable of and they cannot discuss or analyze what they read. Chapter 7 established that vocabulary is much more than memorizing lists of words and looking up their definitions. Teachers best help students learn the vocabulary by integrating vocabulary study and content study and encouraging students to use the vocabulary in speaking, reading, and writing.

Vocabulary instruction should focus on providing students with the strategies they need for dealing with vocabulary independently, rather than teaching individual words (Rhodes & Dudley-Marling, 1988). There are some guidelines for vocabulary development in reading content.

Students Need to Learn a Variety of Methods for Recognizing and Understanding Unfamiliar Words as They Read about Various Subjects
The methods include using reference material, writing, discussion, and reading additional sources to learn more.

Students Do Not Need to Understand Every Word to Comprehend the Text

One difficulty students may have is determining which words are important to the overall meaning of the text. Instruction should include opportunities to make decisions about the importance of the words students meet in reading for content.

Reading Should Provide Insights about How Words Are Used in the Text

Context is one important vocabulary strategy for content reading. Often, concepts and understanding of specialized vocabulary can be developed by reading the text. Students need guidance to understand that text provides some clues about vocabulary and word meaning. Students also must be aware that vocabulary can be clarified using other texts covering the same topic.

Vocabulary Development Can Be Encouraged by Discussion and Writing

Discussion can develop concepts necessary for vocabulary acquisition. In addition, discussion and writing provide opportunities for children to use newly acquired vocabulary. Vocabulary that is used is more likely to be retained, and a teacher who allows time for talking and writing ultimately contributes to students' vocabularies.

Prediction is used in many aspects of reading instruction and can contribute to vocabulary acquisition. Vocabulary prediction (Atwell & Rhodes, 1984) can be adapted for use with almost any text. A structured routine for predicting the meanings of a subject's vocabulary encourages discussion and interaction.

1. The teacher reads the text and selects six to ten words the students may not know. The words should be important for understanding the reading or should be words the students need to know in the future.

2. Students are encouraged to predict a definition for each word without referring to any source. Teachers can help students activate their own knowledge by encouraging them to use picture clues, root words, and subtitles to establish possible definitions.

3. After reading the text, the students discuss and amend their original definitions, provide insights into the meanings of the words, and discover how the text provided clues to the vocabulary. The teacher may have the children refer to the text and discuss why some predictions are eliminated and others are accepted. Prediction encourages children to use the text and vocabulary and to develop strategies that contribute to their independence in reading.

Instructional Strategies

Many of the comprehension and vocabulary strategies also are effective with content reading. Most activities that support reading for content can be planned for use before, during, and after reading. The following lists suggest structured activities. Most have been discussed and explained in previous chapters or are presented in this chapter.

Before

Discussion
Brainstorming
Visualization
Categorizing
Mapping or webbing
Free writing
Journal writing
Collaborative writing
Written conversations
K–W–L (discussed later in chapter)

During

Discussion
Choral reading
Echo reading
Shared reading
Directed reading activity (discussed later in chapter)
Reciprocal teaching strategy
SQ3R (discussed later in chapter)
Journal writing
K–W–L
ReQuest

After

Discussion
Categorization
Retelling
Mapping or webbing
Dramatization
SQ3R
Journal writing
Learning logs
K–W–L

Discussion is the most flexible instructional procedure teachers can employ. Children can share their ideas and learn from others, and teachers can establish what children are learning and provide additional guidance. Discussion provides the teacher with opportunities to demonstrate and encourage questioning procedures, reliance on support materials, interest in learning, and management of information. Discussion improves comprehension by building before reading concepts, guiding children during the reading, and clarifying ideas after reading the content. Discussion can occur between teacher and student, student and student, in small groups, or whole class settings. Discussion can be informal or part of a structured activity.

Directed Reading or Listening–Thinking Activity (DRTA or DLTA)

One of the most valuable instructional strategies for content reading is a standard format that provides for guidance throughout the entire reading process. Almost any comprehension-enhancing strategy can be designed for discussions and question formation, but the Directed Reading–Thinking Activity (DRTA) (Stauffer, 1969) is widely accepted for organizing discussions and questions. This strategy is also the basis of a basal reading lesson, but there are a few changes for content reading. Usually, DRTA or Directed Listening–Thinking Activity (DLTA) has three basic steps:

Prediction
Begin with prediction. The teacher asks such questions as, ''What do you think this text might be about? What do you think this text may be trying to explain?'' The teacher encourages predictions by showing pictures, reading from the first paragraph, and discussing the title. The students can skim the text to make predictions. Prediction before reading the material should increase motivation and set the purpose for reading.

Independent Reading
Guide the children to read for content. Discussion and prediction may continue throughout the reading. The amount of discussion and interaction depends on the difficulty of the text and the familiarity of the material. Children who are reading for content for the first time or are reading material with many concepts embedded in it may need to stop, discuss, and predict as they read. ReQuest, described in chapter 6, is an excellent way to support students while they are reading.

Conclusions
Encourage children to check their predictions and discuss the material. During this time the teacher can focus on vocabulary and concept development and begin expanding the children's ideas so they can contribute to discussions after they have read the material. Many conclusions can be developed with activities specific to the content (e.g., science labs, maps, etc.) These are flexible methods to provide children with opportunities to use their new information.

K–W–L

K–W–L is a technique to guide a class through specific activities before, during, and after reading (Carr & Ogle, 1987; Ogle, 1986). K–W–L allows children to establish what they already understand and what they want to learn about a topic. The *K, W,* and *L* each represent a specific activity. One teacher uses the following procedure with her third graders and combines cooperative learning techniques with K–W–L:

K = What I Know about the Topic

The *K* represents a before reading activity in which students discuss and brainstorm what they know about the topic. Brainstorming can begin by pairing students and allowing them to brainstorm all they know. One pair of students joins a second pair and the four combine their lists (see photograph below). Each group of four has a chance to share its ideas with the entire class, and the teacher records the ideas on the board or overhead. Students transfer the class responses to an individual worksheet. An individual worksheet, illustrated in Figure 8.1, is used to collect responses.

W = What I Want to Know

The *W* establishes the purpose for reading the material. Each group of four develops three questions to ask and shares the questions with the whole class. The teacher records all the questions on large sheets of butcher paper or a chart. As the entire class discusses the questions, other questions arise and are added to the list. Finally, all the questions are categorized, and predictions are made about how the text will answer the questions. The material then is read independently or in pairs.

L = What I Learned

Predictions confirmed by reading are circled and the other predictions are crossed off the list. Finally, the *L* portion of the worksheet is filled out by noting new information learned from the reading. Afterward, students discuss what they learned and answer the questions they asked before and during the reading. (One teacher has the entire class indicate which questions were answered by the texts by motioning thumbs up or thumbs

*The class establishes what they know and what they want to find out during their
"ant" unit. The K–W–L format guides the unit reading and research.*

K WHAT WE KNOW

W WHAT WE WANT TO FIND OUT

L WHAT WE LEARNED

CATEGORIES OF INFORMATION

A.
B.
C.
D.
E.
F.

FIGURE 8-1 K–W–L Strategy Sheets guide students as they read content area material. Source: D.M. Ogle, "K–W–L: A Teaching Model That Develops Active Reading of Expository Text," *The Reading Teacher* 39; 565.

down.) When questions are not answered, students can return to the text or research the answers elsewhere.

The K–W–L procedure is effective because it demonstrates strategic reading behaviors and encourages effective text use. The students are involved actively in establishing reading purpose and are responsible for finding out information. This procedure encourages independent reading behaviors while supporting content learning.

Mapping

Mapping texts can be an aid to comprehending all types of material, but works especially well when children are reading exposition. A map helps readers formulate their own graphic organizers. Mapping focuses attention on important aspects to be learned, creates a framework for understanding the structure and remembering text, and allows students to practice solving problems. Mapping can be done before, during, and after reading to support comprehension of the text. When mapping information from expository texts, several steps should be followed:

1. The teacher provides a basis for mapping by discussing the different structures of expository text. One of the easiest structures to use is the problem–solution format of many social studies textbooks (Armbruster, Anderson, & Ostertag, 1989).

2. Using a problem–solution example from a text, the students answer such questions as, ''Who has a problem?'' ''What actions were taken?'' ''Were there any results?''

3. Graphic organizers are used to record answers to the problem–solution questions as illustrated in Figure 8.2. Students can fill out the frames as they discuss.

Expert Groups

Sometimes students can teach each other what they have learned. One instructional strategy, JIGSAW, (Maring, Furman, & Blum-Anderson, 1985) is excellent for encouraging students to learn all they can about a topic and teach it to others. This activity requires involvement in two groups. First, students are a part of a research or EXPERT group in which they work together to answer individual questions. They are also members of a teaching–learning, or HOME group, in which they teach the information they have learned to other group members.

JIGSAW is a cooperative learning technique (chap. 3) that Nancy Howard and her third graders use frequently during social studies or science classes. To introduce this activity, she tells her students that each of them will belong to a HOME group and an EXPERT group. The procedure was used during a social studies unit that focused on certain Native American tribes.

1. The students started out in small home groups consisting of four students. The number of home groups depended on how many students were in the class. Nancy had five home groups with four students in each group. The first task of the home group was

FIGURE 8-2 Text structure frameworks help children understand and organize subject area information.

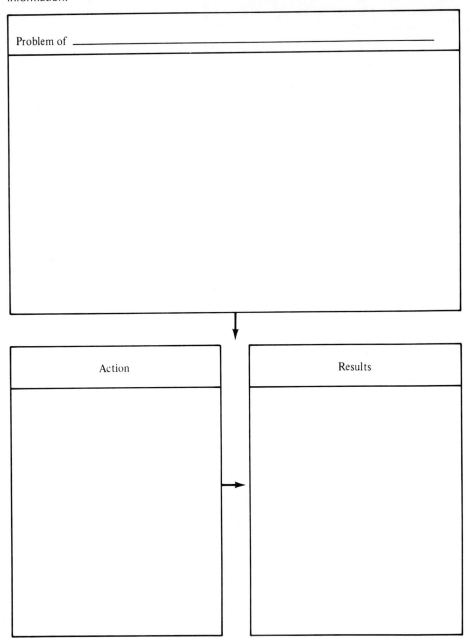

Problem of _____

| Action | Results |

Problem = something bad; a situation that people would like to change
Action   = what people do to try to solve the problem
Results = what happens as a result of the action; the effect or outcome
           of trying to solve the problem

Source: Anderson, T.H., Armbruster, B.B., and J. Ostertag, "Teaching Text Structure to Improve Reading and Writing," *The Reading Teacher* 43 (1989), 132.

to assign each member to a second group known as the expert groups. The assignments were made by the teacher but could be a home group decision.

2. Students left their home groups and reorganized in expert groups. There was one person from each home group in every expert group. When she organized her students for Jigsaw during her unit on Native Americans, Nancy had four expert groups, so there were five children working in each group. Each expert group focused on one area or main idea from the lesson. One expert group studied each of the four tribes included in her lessons: Pueblo, Woodlands, Northwest, and Plains Indians.

3. While in the expert groups, the children participated in reading, discussing, and completing tasks designed by the teacher to help them understand their topic. Nancy was very explicit about the activities that occurred in the expert group and provided guides for accomplishing tasks, questions to be discussed and researched, and books to be read. Figure 8.3 illustrates four study guides that provided the structure for the expert groups Nancy formed during during her study on Native Americans.

Nancy provided a great deal of guidance before she placed her students in small group work. She spent time with the whole class, showing them how to participate in small group work. The class practiced taking turns while reading and reading with a partner. They practiced discussing and summarizing information they had read so they could complete the processes during small group work.

4. After each expert group completed their tasks, discussions, and questions, and all members understood the topic, students returned to their home group. Now there was an expert on each topic in every home group.

5. Every expert shared information and taught their new understandings to others in their home groups. This procedure was also completely understood before students engaged in teaching. Nancy had demonstrated several appropriate ways to teach specific information before she expected her children to teach others in their home groups. She allowed the class to practice teaching with her direct guidance. When she felt the class was ready, she gave each member of the class the expert group task chart shown in Box 8.2, so they would understand exactly what procedure to follow. In the study of Native Americans, Nancy had the experts share the information with their home group by helping each group member to answer the same questions that guided the expert group activities.

Nancy is very enthusiastic about this activity and says it's one of the best strategies she has to guide her children as they read expository material. She also has used it when children read narratives to guide discussions about literary elements.

Readers' Response

Teachers need to help children look beyond the facts and view topics they are studying from different perspectives (McClure & Zitlow, 1991). As children read and learn about important topics and ideas, they should be aware of personal feelings and experiences. Expository texts provide readers with avenues for developing different perspectives of topics and reactions to the reading material.

A great deal of analysis is required when reading expository texts. However, children can consider the feelings, concerns, and desires associated with the content

FIGURE 8-3 PUEBLO INDIANS (Jigsaw Expert Questions)

PUEBLO INDIANS
(Jigsaw Expert Questions)

1   How did the Pueblo Indians feed their families?
_____
What did the raise?_____, _____, _____,
_____, _____, _____, and
_____ Circle the "three sisters."

2.   What did they make?_____
They were silversmiths and made_____,
_____, and _____ from_____
and_____.

3.   What did they believe would be received from the
dances?_____and_____

4.   What did the Pueblo's build homes with?_____
How were their homes built?_____
What were they called?_____

5.   How do the Indians get water for their gardens?
_____

6.   The Indian Children receive gifts to _____
Boys get_____
Girls get_____to teach
the_____

These four study guide worksheets guide Nancy's students during their independent and cooperative learning expert group exercises.

FIGURE 8-3 WOODLAND INDIANS (Jigsaw Expert Questions)

WOODLAND INDIANS
(Jigsaw Expert Questions)

1. How did the Woodland Indians get food for their families?_____

2. What did the women do?_____
    What did the men do?_____

3. What did the Woodland Indians live in?_____
    What was it made of?_____

4. What kind of shoes did they wear?_____

5. What was the Indian baby called?_____

6. What were the steps (in order) that were taken to cook dinner?
    1. _____
    2. _____
    3. _____
    4. _____

7. How were false faces made?_____
    _____

8. Why did the Indian wear false faces?_____
    _____

Continued

FIGURE 8-3   NORTHWEST INDIANS (Jigsaw Expert Questions)

NORTHWEST INDIANS
(Jigsaw Expert Questions)

1   Where did the Northwest Indians build their homes?

_____

What was the home made of? _____

2. What did these Indians carve on the trunks of the

trees? _____

What as this carved, painted pole called?

_____

What was it used for? _____

3. How did the Northwest Indians get food for their,

families? _____

_____

4. What did the women in the village do?

(1) _____

(2) _____

(3) _____

5. What did the women weave? _____,

_____, _____, _____, and

_____

6. What did they weave capes out of? _____

and _____

Continued

FIGURE 8-3   PLAINS INDIANS (Jigsaw Expert Questions)

PLAINS INDIANS
(Jigsaw Expert Questions)

1. What did the Plains Indians hunt?_____

2. What did the Plains Indians live in?_____
    What was the home made of?_____and
    _____

3. What was used to paint pictures on the homes?
    _____

4. Why did the Plains Indians live in teepees?_____
    _____

5. The Plains Indians used <u>all</u> of the buffalo. How did
    the Indians use the <u>meat</u>?_____
    <u>skins</u>?_____ _____ _____
    _____
    <u>bones</u>?_____
    <u>hoof</u>?_____
    <u>horns</u>?_____ _____ _____

6. What does the chief wear?_____
    What is it made of?_____
    What did these feathers bring? <u>great</u>_____

7. How did they talk to other tribes?_____

BOX 8-2

Expert Group Task Chart

- **READ THE INFORMATION**

  Decide how you will read the material.

  - **Take turns.**
  - **Read individually and silently.**
  - **Have someone read it aloud.**
  - **Read alternately with a partner.**

- **DISCUSS AND SUMMARIZE THE MOST IMPORTANT INFORMATION.**

  - **Use the study guide to help you identify the information you need to know.**
  - **Make notes of any additional information you want to share with your group.**

- **TALK ABOUT HOW YOU WILL TEACH THIS INFORMATION TO YOUR GROUP.**

  Decide how you will teach the information.

  - **Use your notes and study guide to explain.**
  - **Show illustrations from the book.**
  - **Draw a map or picture to demonstrate.**
  - **Ask questions to check for understanding.**

(Nelson-Herber & Johnston, 1989). Facts, figures, and events can be confronted in terms of the reader's own feelings about the subject. Encouraging a personal response to exposition is not only appropriate but desirable (McClure & Zitlow, 1991). Many events in social studies produce responses that reflect personal feelings, images, and thoughts. As children read about the 1989 changes in eastern Europe, they should be encouraged to think, "How would you feel if your state were divided by a wall and you could not visit relatives without governmental permission?" or, "How would you feel if you could not go in your car without being stopped by armed guards?" Sharing these responses increases comprehension and provides opportunities for children to reflect on the ideas.

Teachers who allow children to make connections between facts and feelings encourage a thoughtful and reflective environment in which children develop concepts and ideas. One of the easiest ways to encourage aesthetic response is to use poetry and prose on the topics being studied (McClure & Zitlow, 1991). When students study the Gulf War and read about the places, times, and events from expository text and the feelings in the prose of a short story such as "The Birds' Peace" (George, 1990), they understand the topic from a broad perspective.

> *On the day Kristy's father went off to war, she burst out the back door and ran down the path to the woods. Her eyes hurt. Her chest burned. She crossed the bridge over the purling stream and dashed into the lean-to she and her father had built near the edge of the flower-filled woodland meadow.*
>> *She dropped to her knees, then to her belly. Covering her face with both hands, she sobbed from the deepest well of her being. (p. 65)*

Students react to events, confirm their perceptions, and move beyond the facts when teachers require aesthetic responses to exposition. Personal responses to expository texts lead to reading and writing. The natural outlets for personal response are poetry, narrative, drama, and art. Varied responses to content must be viewed as valid, and sharing through reading, writing, and discussion allows all students to increase their comprehension of the information they read.

Theme Units

Ideally, information should be integrated by reading, writing, speaking, and listening. Additionally, content is taught best when topics are interwoven throughout the curriculum. This is more possible in some situations than others. It is most common for kindergarten through fourth grade teachers to teach all subjects to one group of students. About fifth grade, many school districts begin departmentalizing their subject areas and teachers may be responsible for English, science, math, art, or music. Because students often move from class to class in upper grades, the format for subject instruction may differ from grade to grade and school to school. First grade teachers may not teach social studies and science each day, and when they do teach subjects, they usually have opportunities to integrate reading and writing. Upper grade teachers may have their students for an hour a day, specifically for science or math instruction. Unless other teachers cooperate, it is difficult to integrate more than one subject. Whenever possible, subjects should be integrated throughout the curriculum. An effective way to manage this feat is through theme units.

Theme units suggest that teachers provide a variety of reading material and include a variety of academic areas in presenting a theme, a problem, an area of interest, or a topic to their students (Hittleman, 1983; Rhodes & Dudley-Marling, 1988). Planning units takes time, but usually results in a focused, in-depth study of a topic that is very rewarding.

1. Teachers begin planning by selecting a topic and considering students' needs and interests to determine what they will explore. Reading and writing are included in the basic plan. A unit may be based on a single topic, such as Vietnam or a book such as *Park's Quest* (Paterson, 1988) (see Figure 8.4). Many theme units have a variety of activities and last for varying amounts of time. Teachers integrate English, science, math, and social studies and plan multiple activities based on one theme.

2. Units require many materials and resources. Teachers have the major responsibility for locating resources, including children's literature, textbooks, reference material, audio-visual aids, and computer software related to the topic. Children can be encouraged to help the teacher collect material that supports the unit of study. They may search the library, find books at home, or provide items related to the topic. There should be materials to read at varying levels of difficulty and in various media that encourage the development of concepts relating to the topic.

3. The teacher needs to consider instructional activities, group arrangements, and evaluation for the unit. The activities should encourage the learning of basic objectives. Some of the activities suggested in the before, during, and after chart in this chapter can be part of a theme unit. Many theme units end with a project, such as a field trip, a presentation to other classes or parents, or a debate. Theme units include activities appropriate for individual, small group, and whole class learning.

Some teachers cooperate with colleagues to produce theme units, and there are commercially prepared units. Many science and social studies texts suggest ideas for theme units, while some literature suggests unit ideas. There are several unit plans in this textbook that illustrate different aspects of reading instruction. In addition to the unit plans in this chapter, chapter 4 presents a description of theme units as a way of organizing instruction and introduces a two-week unit based on *Two Bad Ants* (Van Allsburg, 1988).

Specialized Content Reading

There are some instances in which reading to learn subject matter requires very specific strategies and skills. Reading and understanding magazines and newspapers, mathematics-related material or reading to complete research projects are types of reading that may need careful attention.

Magazines and Newspapers

Magazines and other periodicals can be used to focus on math, social studies, science, and other subjects (Olson, Gee, & Forester, 1989). Contemporary problems such as pollution, war, peace, and economics are more current in periodicals (Cheyney, 1984) than in textbooks. Readers are exposed to vocabulary and comprehension strategies that will contribute to a lifetime of reading. Activities that focus on periodicals include:

1. Making periodicals available during independent reading times. Periodicals can be oriented to children or be the ones that adults regularly read such as *Time* and *Newsweek*.

2. Using periodicals as the texts for various activities. They may be used to build concepts, as a basis of discussion, and so on. Articles can be duplicated to give the entire class access. They can be used in research projects or to support theme units.

FIGURE 8-4   This teaching web demonstrates teaching ideas for reading/language arts, social science, science and art/music integrated by Katherine Paterson's *Park's Quest.*

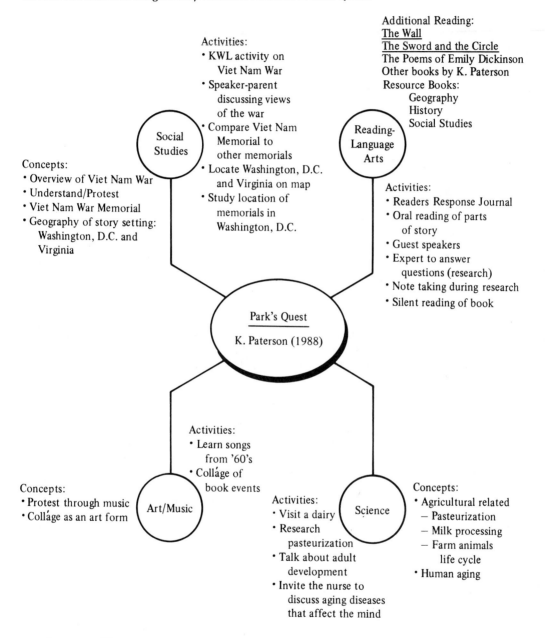

Summary of Story:

Park's mother will not discuss the death of his father who died in the Viet Nam War. Park is determined to find out about his father and travels to his grandfather's farm where he meets a ten year old Vietnamese girl. The strange girl, his grandfather, and farm activities bring answers and new understandings.

3. Using current periodicals to develop students' analytical and critical reading skills (Cheyney, 1984). Several periodicals presenting the same information can be read by individuals or small groups to compare information. Students can compare textbook information, television presentations, and other periodicals.

4. Using periodicals to teach successful reading strategies or differences in text structures. If students understand the arrangement of periodicals, they comprehend them better. Periodicals can be used to discuss editorializing, persuasion, comparing, and contrasting.

Math Reading Strategies

Mathematics is a language, but teachers rarely approach the subject as related to reading and writing. The textbooks associated with math are often the first barrier to viewing math as a language. Math texts often are thought of as exercise books instead of informational texts. In truth, math texts contain a great deal of reading material and information. Usually, math books include brief explanations, directions for solving problems, and many examples. As children reach upper grades, they are exposed to more and more story problems. Discussions and exploration can help children understand the arrangement and purposes of much of the text.

The vocabulary of math texts is especially bothersome. If the signs and symbols were not enough to warrant some confusion, the special usage of familiar words makes math a very demanding subject. Words such as *additive* or *property* may have completely different meanings in math books. A student's lack of background can lead to misconceptions in mathematics. The knowledge and concepts needed to read math text and understand the vocabulary and story problems should be developed in the way concepts of other subjects are.

Effective math teachers recognize the value of providing students with opportunities to talk about mathematics. Students rarely talk during math instruction, and the teacher's talk usually consists of asking direct questions, explaining, or discussing procedures (Small, 1990). Teachers should encourage children to verbalize their ideas and talk about numbers. They can discuss difficulties they have working problems and any confusion that results.

In addition, teachers should encourage children to write about mathematics. Although children cannot be expected to explain complicated mathematical procedures, some approaches encourage students to record their problem-solving process in a journal. Literature also can play an important role in helping children talk and write about numbers. Teachers can find stories that integrate the use of numbers in story telling.

Research

Content often establishes a need for students to research or find out more about a topic introduced in the textbook. Some specialized abilities help children read a variety of materials to provide in-depth information about a topic. Research requires the ability to state a problem, locate and read a variety of materials on one topic, take notes on the most important aspects, summarize information, and reach conclusions. Researching and reporting are difficult abilities to acquire, but are an exciting and motivating way to study all types of topics. A structured routine provides guidance for any age child:

Establish the Topic
The first step is to be sure that children know exactly what they want to find out. Establishing the research topic can be done by individuals or the entire class. The topic emerges from questions that arise from regular content reading and discussion, a special event that interests the children, or an object such as a bird's nest or bug.

Ask Questions
Research is most effective when children determine what they want to find out. Children can brainstorm what they think they know about a topic and list questions they would like to have answered. The K–W–L procedure provides an excellent format for establishing questions for research.

Design Methods for Inquiry
After the class has determined what it wants to find out, the children and the teacher design methods for answering the questions. This is the appropriate time to introduce different reference materials such as encyclopedias. Children also should know how the information is recorded and how it will be used. At the first opportunity for children to conduct research, the procedures should be established systematically, making sure children understand each step. Research can be structured and conducted similiarly to the EXPERT cooperative learning groups discussed earlier in the chapter. The worksheets and routines provide guidance for the children in completing their inquiries.

Share Findings
Children share what they have learned with one another, other classes, or visitors to the classroom. Students demonstrate their learning through discussions, written papers, models, drawings, or other creative products.

When the research process is established clearly and concisely, even first graders can find out more about a certain topic. Reading for research purposes is a skill that will benefit children throughout their lives.

Study Strategies

Studying is really a special form of reading (Tierney, Readence, & Dishner, 1985) and usually is associated with content reading. Developing study strategies requires explicit understanding of what must occur to retain information. Study strategies enable students to focus their attention, organize the text, practice, and use the material. Students need strategies that foster independence and comprehension monitoring. Teaching study strategies is not generally the main focus for elementary reading teachers, but spending a few class periods teaching the strategies enhances learning during instruction in upper grades and junior high school. By the time children reach the fifth and sixth grades, it is a particularly valuable skill.

Many of the strategies that promote effective studying contribute to overall reading improvement. Standal and Betza (1990) list several strategies essential for successful reading and studying:

- Scanning—Scanning involves sampling the text. The reader rapidly searches the material to answer a specific question.
- Skimming—Skimming is a quick survey of the text to get a feel for the contents.
- Outlining—Informal outlining helps students retain detail and understand cause and effect, sequence, and/or a complex point. Mapping can be used to teach outlining since the procedure is simply a graphic outline.
- Underlining and highlighting—As most college students can attest, underlining and highlighting are an important feature of studying. Since most elementary teachers cannot allow students to mark in their books, copies of passages can be used to demonstrate. Underlining or highlighting makes it easier to refer to important points.
- Note-taking—Around the fifth grade, students should begin developing the note-taking skills they will need later. Students need to be guided to listen and read for main ideas. The teacher can demonstrate note-taking during a presentation, such as a film or guest speaker, to which students and teacher listen.

There are many study skill systems, but Standal and Betza (1990) believe that most formalized study systems include five elements:

1. All forms of reading require that a purpose be established before reading. Students must be aware of the type of testing that will result or the responses expected.

2. Students can be taught to skim and scan first to gain an understanding of the direction of a passage or chapter. Predicting what the text will cover by reading the titles and headings, and looking at pictures and graphs is an effective strategy.

3. The reading that accompanies studying is flexible, silent reading. Students may be required to reread and remind themselves of the purpose.

4. After the initial reading, students skim the material to make sure they understand what they read.

5. Students can pretest themselves by closing the book and mentally recalling or writing all they remember. Students might attempt to write an outline of the material without the book, establish an informal journal about the material, or write a main idea to review the material.

An example of a study skill is the familiar SQ3R method. SQ3R stands for Survey, Question, Read, Recite, and Review. SQ3R provides a format that seems especially well-suited to students who are studying content. Students usually need guidance in the five steps of this study strategy.

1. Surveying before reading provides an overview of the passage. The question to be answered is, "What is this chapter about?" The student can use chapter titles, introductory paragraphs, headings and subheadings, concluding paragraphs, and end of chapter questions to develop an understanding of what the material will be about. The student uses subheadings and end of chapter paragraphs to develop a general outline (Vacca & Vacca, 1989).

2. The student asks questions that provide a purpose for reading the material in detail. The questions are developed from predictions of what the reader expects to find by reading the text.

3. The purpose of reading is to find the answers to the questions posed in step 2.

4. Students stop their reading and reflect on the answers to their questions. They attempt to answer the questions in their own words or in writing.

5. After the reading is completed, students attempt to recall the main ideas of the passage. Each heading can be read to verify answers given in the last step and to recall what was contained in particular sections.

Study skills are similar to comprehension strategies. Studying material is very efficient reading and is developed with extended practice and application. Elementary children who are introduced to methods that encourage good study habits and receive much guidance in the study strategies continue to use the skills throughout their schooling. Studying is intensive and effective concentration, and demonstrating the strategies during instruction provides a framework for students to be independent learners.

Writing

Students often are required to respond in writing to activities and assignments during subject instruction. More often than not, writing is used for testing, but is not considered an effective method for learning material. It is now becoming accepted that writing plays an important role in instruction in content. Writing has a dual role. Not only does it encourage content understanding, but also develops students' writing abilities. Often, the writing that is required is specialized. For example, a math teacher may have children write math problems, or a social studies teacher may expect children to demonstrate a knowledge of terminology. Students often are expected to write about what they read in subjects, but never taught how to write about what they read (Cunningham & Cunningham, 1987).

There are three identifiable benefits from encouraging writing in the subject areas (Frager, 1985). Writing may improve comprehension. Often, ideas are clarified and expanded as students write. Second, writing helps students organize their thoughts. Rearranging their words so that they make sense on paper requires students to organize their understanding of the topic. Finally, writing familiarizes students with writing skills necessary to communicate. Students must use the vocabulary and the language in a way that reinforces the concepts a teacher may be emphasizing during instruction.

Writing is not learned through osmosis (Gahn, 1989), and teachers need to help children learn to write in the subject areas. Instructional strategies that may be used across the curriculum include demonstration, guided practice, and feedback (Cunningham & Cunningham, 1987; Gahn, 1989). Before students are required to write in a class, the teacher should demonstrate what is expected several times. Examples of content writing could be provided by students, teachers, or professional writers who write about the subject. Students can compare their writing with others' to see how their presentations differ or resemble other products. Above all, students should practice a lot, allowing them to discover the process of writing about a subject. As students practice, feedback should be provided frequently. The feedback can include peer group reactions, teacher comments, and small group sharing.

Students who write about what they are learning are more able to recognize how and what they are learning. Learning logs rely on the reading–writing connection and work well in any subject. Students may use learning logs (Watson, 1987) to write about the subjects they are studying. After a concept development activity, experiment, or discussion has concluded, the students can be asked to write something they know now that they did not know at the beginning of the day. If students cannot think of anything they learned, they can describe what occurred during the activity. After a few minutes of writing, a sharing time provides opportunities for those who want to read what they wrote. The learning logs provide a forum for hearing new ideas or reinforcing newly formed ideas. Learning logs can be used and may be compiled into a class book, completed on chart paper in language experience style, or may include art and graphics.

Learning Differences

The learning and cultural differences that affect concept development, vocabulary, and comprehension are particularly important to consider when presenting content. There are special considerations that contribute to the education of all students.

Culture

Multicultural understandings can be developed during content readings and discussions using children's literature as a supplement (Stoodt, 1989). Music, art, and social studies are subjects that should include recognition of cultural differences. The textbooks and content should reflect and discuss differences, but children's literature provides additional glimpses of cultures in all aspects of the society and allows students to view the world through others' eyes.

Literature and expository text can recognize that various cultures in our society may have different reference points for similar events, concepts, and behaviors. A social studies concept as familiar as Thanksgiving can be viewed much differently depending on cultural experience. Native Americans often have been misrepresented in Thanksgiving discussions, and children of that culture certainly will have a perspective different from classmates'. Literature can be used to clarify and discuss the topic from a native American point of view. Yet another view of Thanksgiving is presented in Bunting's book, *How Many Days to America?* (1988), which will be familiar to recent refugees to our country. Understanding and acceptance of different cultures should be integrated throughout the curriculum, and children's literature provides opportunities for including different perspectives and consideration of different backgrounds.

Language

Children who are learning English as their second language may have great difficulty grasping the concepts and vocabulary of the subject material. Many of the instructional procedures emphasized in the chapters on comprehension and vocabulary are a necessity for these children. Many opportunities are needed to build initial concepts about the subject matter.

Children with limited English proficiency must have concrete examples of the concepts, such as experiences with actual objects, pictures, films, or other visual aids. Textbooks must be used with care to avoid imposing concepts and language that the children are not capable of understanding (Franklin, 1986). Discussion for the purpose of developing ideas is particularly important, and writing about the ideas through language experience or their own attempts is particularly valuable. Text generated by children can develop vocabulary and concepts and provide valuable and successful experiences with language. In addition, children's writing can provide additional reading material for the classroom.

Content reading is an excellent time to implement the narrow reading concepts suggested by Krashen and discussed in chapter 6. Children, regardless of their English abilities, will benefit from reading and rereading several different texts on the same topic. Each presentation can provide much needed concept and language development and will build the knowledge and experience so necessary for comprehension.

DISCUSSION AND ACTIVITIES

1. Divide the class into groups of four and brainstorm as many differences as you can think of in reading narrative and exposition. Establish a summary statement about your ideas. Share your summary with the class.

2. Review the teachers' manual from several different subject texts. How are the lessons different? List commonalities and differences.

3. When presenting a science or social studies lesson, how would you use the textbook to introduce the topic? How would you use the textbook to summarize the topic after classroom activities? Describe different uses of the text in each situation.

4. What must a teacher do to help children remember concepts and use vocabulary?

5. Review the different reading behaviors needed to be successful when reading for content. Review behaviors that are necessary for understanding and enjoying reading. How do the two purposes for reading differ? Compare your list with the lists of your classmates.

6. Select a concept or several vocabulary words from a social studies or science textbook. Find a children's literature selection that could be used to develop concepts necessary for understanding the words.

RELATED READING

The Journal of Reading includes many articles about content instruction. Many instructional activities and ideas in the *Journal* are effective and can be adapted to any classroom.

Muth, K.D. (1989). *Children's comprehension of text: Research into practice.* Newark, DE: International Reading Association.

> *This text explains the differences between reading exposition and narrative. If you feel you need to read more about this topic, this is an excellent combination of research and practical application.*

Standal, T. C., & Betza, R.E. (1990). *Content area reading: Teachers, texts, students.* New York: Prentice-Hall.

> *This book presents a complete discussion of content reading in concise, uncomplicated terms. The text includes a chapter on writing that presents strong justification and several activities for writing in the subjects.*

Tierney, R. J., Readence, J.E., & Dishner, E.K. (1990). *Reading strategies and practices: A compendium.* Newton, MA: Allyn & Bacon.

> *This collection of specific strategies for content reading is based on research and suggests specific procedures for implementing activities in the classroom.*

CHILDREN'S LITERATURE
MENTIONED IN THIS CHAPTER

Social Studies

Aaseng, N. (1989). *The fortunate fortunes: Business successes that began with a lucky break.* Minneapolis: Lerner.

Brown, M. (1954). *Cinderella.* New York: Macmillan.

Bunting, E. (1985). *How many days to America?* Illustrated by B. Park. New York: Clarion.

Durrel, A., & Sachs, M. (Eds.). (1990). *The Big Book of Peace.* Designed by J.B. Bierhorst. New York: Dutton.

Forbes, E. (1946). *Johnny Tremain.* Illustrated by L. Ward. Boston: Houghton Mifflin.

Fox, P. (1973). *The slave dancer.* Illustrated by E. Keith. New York: Bradbury.

Freedman, R. (1987a). *Indian chiefs.* New York: Holiday.

———. (1987). *Lincoln, A photobiography.* New York: Clarion.

George, J.C. (1990). The birds' peace. In A. Durell & J.M. Sachs, (Eds.). *The big book of peace.* New York: Dutton.

Halliburton, W. J. (1989). *The tragedy of Little Bighorn.* New York: Franklin Watts.

Hyman, T.S. (1983). *Little Red Riding Hood.* New York Holiday House.

Jenness, A., & Rivers, A. (1989). *In two worlds: A Yup'ik Eskimo family.* Photographs by Aylette Jenness. Boston: Houghton Mifflin.

Paterson, K. (1988). *Park's Quest.* New York: Dutton.

Steptoe, J. (1987). *Mufaro's beautiful daughters: An African tale.* New York: Lothrop.

Taylor, M. (1976). *Roll of thunder, hear my cry.* New York: Bantam.

Young, E. (1989). *Lon Po Po: A Red Riding Hood story from China.* New York: Philomel.

Science and Math

Brady, I. (1976). *Wild mouse*. New York: Scribner's.
Brenner, B., & Garelick, M. (1989). *Two orphan cubs*. Illustrated by Erika Kors. New York: Walker.
Kitamura, S. (1986). *When sheep cannot sleep: The counting book*. New York: Farrar, Straus and Giroux.
L'Engle, M. (1962). *A wrinkle in time*. New York: Garden City.
O'Brien, R.C. (1975). *Z for Zachariah*. New York: Atheneum.
Orri, E., & Orii, M. (1989). *Simple science experiments with straws*. Illustrated by Kimimaro Yoshida. Milwaukee: Gareth Stevens.
Van Allsburg, C. (1988). *Two bad ants*. Boston: Houghton Mifflin.

Art and Music

Isadora, R. (1979). *Ben's trumpet*. New York: Greenwillow.
Lasker, D. (1979). *The boy who loved music*. Illustrated by Joe Lasker. New York: Viking.
Locker, T. (1989). *The young artist*. New York: Dial.
Ripley, E. (1964). *Gainsborough: A biography*. London: Oxford.
Schroeder, A. (1989). *Ragtime Tumpie*. Illustrated by B. Fuchs. Boston: Little, Brown.

REFERENCES

Armbruster, B.B., Anderson, T.H., & Ostertag, J. (1989). Teaching text structure to improve reading and writing. *The Reading Teacher, 43* (2), 130–137.
Atwell, M.A., & Rhodes, L.K. (1984). Strategy lessons as alternatives to skills lessons in reading. *Journal of Reading, 27* (8), 700–705.
Carr, E., & Ogle, D. (1987). K–W–L plus: A strategy for comprehension and summarization. *Journal of Reading, 30* (7), 626–631.
Cheyney, A.B. (1984). *Teaching reading skills through the newspaper*. Newark, DE: International Reading Association.
Cunningham, R.M., & Cunningham, J. (1987). Content reading–writing lessons. *The Reading Teacher, 40* (6), 506–10.
Davey, B. (1986). Using textbook activity guides to help students learn from textbooks. *Journal of Reading, 29* (6), 489–494.
———. (1989). Active responding in content classrooms, *Journal of Reading, 33* (1), 44–46.
Flood, J. and Lapp, D. (1986). Forms of discourse in basal readers. *Elementary School Journal, 87* 299–326.
Frager, A.M. (1985). Content area writing: Are you teaching or testing? *Journal of Reading, 29* (1), 58–62.
Franklin, E.A. (1986). Literacy instruction for LES children. *Language Arts, 63* (1), 51–60.
Gahn, S.M. (1989). A practical guide for teaching writing in the content areas. *Journal of Reading, 32* (6), 525–531.
Hittleman, D. R. (1983). *Developmental reading, K-8*. Boston: Houghton Mifflin.
Maring, G., Furman, G.C., & Blum-Anderson, J. (1985). Five cooperative learning strategies for mainstreamed youngsters in content area classrooms. *The Reading Teacher, 38* (3), 310–313.
McClure, A.A., & Zitlow, C.Z. (1991). Not just the facts: Aesthetic response in elementary content area studies. *Language Arts, 68* (1), 27–33.
Nelson-Herber, J., & Johnston, C.S. (1989). Questions and concerns about teaching narrative and expository text. In K.D. Muth (Ed.), *Children's comprehension of text: Research into practice*. Newark, DE: International Reading Association.

Olson, M. W., Gee, T.C., & Forester, N. (1989). Magazines in the classroom: Beyond recreational reading. *The Journal of Reading, 32* (8), 708–713.

Rayner, K., & Pollatsek, A. (1989). *The psychology of reading.* New York: Prentice-Hall.

Reed, A. J. S. (1985). *Reaching adolescents: The young adult book and the school.* New York: Holt, Rinehart & Winston.

Rhodes, L., & Dudley-Marling, C. (1988). *Readers and writers with a difference: A holistic approach to teaching learning disabled and remedial students.* Portsmouth, NH: Heinemann.

Richgels, D.J., McGee, L. M., and Slaton, E.A. (1989). Teaching expository text structure in reading and writing. In K.D. Muth (Ed.), *Children's comprehension of text: Research into practice.* Newark, DE: International Reading Association.

Roller, C. M. (1990). The interaction between knowledge and structure variables in processing of expository prose. *Reading Research Quarterly, 25* (2), 79–89.

Schwartz, R. M. (1988). Learning to learn vocabulary in content area text books. *Journal of Reading, 32* (2), 108–117.

Slater, W.H., & Graves, M.F. (1989). Research on expository text: Implications for teachers. In K.D. Muth (Ed.), *Children's Comprehension of Text: Research Into Practice.* Newark, DE: International Reading Association.

Small, M. S. (1990). Do you speak math? *Arithmetic Teacher, 37* (5), 26–29.

Standal, T.C., & Betza, R. E. (1990). *Content area reading: Teachers, texts, students.* New York: Prentice-Hall.

Stansell, J.C., & Deford, D. (1981). When is a reading problem not a reading problem? *The Reading Teacher, 25* (1), 14–20.

Stauffer, R.G. (1969). *Directing reading maturity as a cognitive process.* New York: Harper & Row.

Stoodt, B. (1989). *Reading instruction.* New York: Harper & Row.

Taylor, B.M., & Samuels, S.J. (1983). Children's use of text structure in recall of expository material. *American Educational Research Journal, 20,* 517–528,

Tierney, R.J, Readence, J. E., and Dishner, E.K. (1985). *Reading strategies and practices: A compendium.* Boston: Allyn & Bacon.

Vacca, R., & Vacca, J.A. (1989). *Content area reading.* New York: HarperCollins.

Watson, D. (1987). *Ideas and insights: Language arts in the elementary school.* Urbana, IL: National Council of Teachers of English.

_9 EVALUATING READING BEHAVIORS

Every day Leo's father watched him
for signs of blooming.
And every night Leo's father watched him
for signs of blooming.
"Are you sure Leo's a bloomer?"
asked Leo's father.
"Patience," said Leo's mother.
"A watched bloomer doesn't bloom."
So Leo's father watched television instead of Leo.
The snows came.
Leo's father wasn't watching.
But Leo still wasn't blooming.
The trees budded.
Leo's father wasn't watching.
But Leo still wasn't blooming.
Then one day,
in his own good time,
Leo bloomed!
He could read!
He could write!
He could draw!
He ate neatly!
He also spoke.
And it wasn't just a word.
It was a whole sentence.
And that sentence was . . .
I made it!

—Robert Kraus, *Leo the Late Bloomer*

I T IS only natural for everyone involved with children to be both proud and concerned about reading and writing performance. Observing children's growth and evaluating their progress is a critical aspect of reading instruction. Effective instruction, interpretation of behaviors, and identification of areas needing guidance all depend on what teachers know about an individual child's reading and writing behaviors.

Evaluation is a mirror that reflects the learning and language processes occurring in a child's life. The mirror not only reflects what children are doing and how they are feeling about written language, it produces an image of what is occurring during instruction and allows teachers to learn more about their teaching and their professions. Some of the questions that will be answered in this chapter include:

1. What is the purpose of evaluation?
2. Who is interested in how your students read and write?
3. What feedback procedures are most important for the students? for parents? for administrators?
4. How can evaluation reflect instruction?
5. What evaluation procedures best reflect literature-based instruction?
6. How can a teacher keep track of a child's progress in reading and writing?
7. What is the role of standardized testing in reading instruction?

Children's language and reading abilities grow and change before our very eyes. Their growth can be documented. Evaluation is the process of keeping track of the changes that occur as children acquire knowledge of and experience with written language (Y. Goodman, 1989). Often, although not always, evaluation requires some type of judgment of children's reading behaviors. Children may be compared to others the same age, identified at a particular level of development, or contrasted with their own behaviors from an earlier time. At other times, effective evaluation may simply describe or document how children are reading.

Foundations of Evaluation

Teachers must evaluate what children know in order to plan for instruction. Evaluation allows the teacher to discover what concepts children understand and what experiences they need in order to continue developing as readers. When teachers know children, they are able to plan activities and interactions that motivate them to learn. Continuous and long range evaluation identifies growth patterns that result from experiences with print.

Good evaluation is grounded in observation. Teachers naturally watch their students daily and can tell you a great deal about the reading and writing behaviors in the classroom. They remember stories, incidents, conversations, endearing moments, and trying times. Teachers are "kid watchers" (Y. Goodman, 1977) and constantly are evaluating what is occurring in the classroom. Teachers are very good at observing children, and research has found that they are extremely reliable in describing reading behaviors and predicting reading success (Jewell & Zintz, 1986). But teachers must do more than Leo the Late Bloomer's father, who watched through the bushes and from behind furniture to see if Leo would bloom. They somehow must document the growth of their students in a way that contributes to planning classroom activities that encourage their students' reading development. In addition, the evaluation must be responsive to parents, colleagues, and others in the community.

Nature of Evaluation

The process of evaluation should support and parallel those events that occur in a literate class. One way to provide this support is to consider the language learning assumptions and the reading process just as in planning for any other component of reading instruction. Evaluation of the reading process should weigh reading that is done in real life contexts, consider the total language and learning processes, and recognize reading as developmental.

Understanding what children do as they read and write requires more than a forty-five minute test in which children pencil in bubbles to respond. It is also more than a single numerical score. Instead of one event and one number, evaluation is a continuous summary of the reading process over a long period of time. Evaluation concerns texts read, written, told, and discussed and collects information from children in several contexts as they read.

The reading process also is considered during evaluation. What children do before, during, and after reading are important activities that teachers must consider when making decisions about children and reading. If reading is considered a hypothesis-testing process in which children actively incorporate what they know with what is presented in the text, evaluation should reflect and explain how children go about the entire process of reading.

Reading is just one of the language processes. Evaluation in a literature-based curriculum documents all the language arts. All speaking, listening, and writing responses contribute information about how the child is approaching reading. It also works in reverse because the teacher learns what children know about language when their reading behaviors are evaluated. Evaluation simply cannot focus on reading without considering the other language processes.

Documentation of reading and writing behaviors must reflect that reading is developmental. The behaviors children display during reading are accepted as not only appropriate, but necessary at certain stages of learning (Y. Goodman, 1989). Teachers must view some of the responses as evidence that children are learning and establishing rules and predictions about reading. The unexpected responses that children produce are among the most valuable bits of information. Analysis of unexpected results provides information about a child's development and thinking about reading.

The nature of evaluation for literature-based instruction is more elaborate than the traditional method. Evaluation in a literature based curriculum includes examination of the entire transaction between teachers and students during the reading teaching/learning experience (Y. Goodman, 1989). This information can be collected from test scores, observations, checklists, work samples, and anecdotal records. It is compiled to explain the entire process of an individual child's reading behavior in several different settings.

Unfortunately, much of the evaluation required in today's schools focuses on the accuracy of skills and may not encourage documentation of the natural interactions with written language that occur in a classroom full of literature (Ammon, 1983). There are, however, very promising trends that affect reading evaluation and reflect changing attitudes.

Trends in Evaluation

The earliest concern about learning to read can be traced to Socrates, who described learning to read as knowing the letters of the alphabet (Stallman & Pearson, 1990). The major concern was whether children who were being taught to read knew the alphabet. Evaluating reading in this context was relatively simple. That view lasted until the early 1900s when the great educator John Dewey (Stallman & Pearson, 1990) suggested that reading instruction should begin at the age of eight, when the child possessed all the skills. This established the belief that some skills and abilities were necessary before children began reading.

Monitoring reading behavior began in earnest in the 1920s with the advent of scientific measurement and testing. The tests evolved after many became concerned that some children were not learning to read. Early tests were based on diagnosing strengths and weaknesses so instruction could be provided in deficient areas. The "deficient" view of evaluation prevailed until researchers in the 1960s began to consider that instruction was responsible for providing what children were lacking (Stallman & Pearson, 1990). Identifying skills, abilities, and teaching skills that were prerequisites to other skills became an integral part of reading programs, reflected in the basal approach.

Currently, research and philosophy about reading and writing reflect a developmental approach to reading. Reading and writing are viewed as the accumulation of written language knowledge that evolves from the environment and prior experiences. Many current evaluation procedures support earlier philosophies and do not reflect the current and developing views of reading and language learning. There are certain methods available that evaluate reading as developmental. Observation, checklists, and portfolios or collections of children's work are considered legitimate ways to chronicle children's growth. However, at the same time, many schools and states continue to require tests that look much like they did in the 1920s (Stallman & Pearson, 1990).

Although tests have been an evaluation tool for more than sixty years, they are viewed as too narrow or confined to explain many of the complexities of written language development. In particular, it would be erroneous to believe that formal tests can provide a total picture of literature-based instruction. Since evaluation should be ongoing, there are many opportunities to find out about children's reading performance during instruction and daily routines.

Feedback

Evaluation is not complete unless appropriate feedback is provided to those involved with children's reading and writing. Feedback is the way observation, portfolios, test scores, checklists, and other testing associated with reading are translated to students, parents, administrators, and other teachers. Each interested party may require a different method of evaluation and different methods of reporting.

Administrators—principals, superintendents, and curriculum directors—are interested in how the students in their school are doing as a group. That's not to say that they are not interested in individual students, but due to the demands of their positions, they often evaluate and monitor reading behavior from test results for large groups of children. Generally, they are very concerned about state-mandated and required test scores for the entire school district. Numbers and results of standardized tests are often required by state agencies, school boards, and other groups.

Parents also may be interested in the scores of the entire school, but their main concern is the information that describes their own child's progress. Test scores are not always meaningful to them, and they may need help interpreting the results. While parents do gain some information about their children's reading behavior from tests, the basic reports to parents are in the form of grades. Periodic grade reports are part of school culture and may involve many different interpretations. In view of the complexities of language and reading development, it would seem obvious that parents deserve more information about their child's reading than what test scores and grades explain. Any parent would be gratified to see the collections of reading and writing that describe a child's reading progress in a literature-based program.

Teachers who have the children in classes other than reading and those who will teach them in the future need a combination of reports so they can plan effective instruction. They are interested in the child's record of progress in previous years, in order to plan appropriate instruction. In addition, they benefit from such information as reading interests, behaviors, habits, and the child's responses to different instructional approaches.

Teachers who are primarily responsible for the child's reading instruction need to gather any information that will help the child during the year. They will use grades, test scores, and achievement. But they also need to know children's interests, behaviors, and habits. Teachers collect and organize enough information to satisfy the inquiries of any other interested groups and to plan effective instruction.

Teachers are responsible for the effectiveness of reading instruction and may feel a great deal of pressure about evaluation. Teaching abilities may be evaluated by the achievement of their students on some tests. The many requirements and demands of evaluation are difficult and time-consuming. The evaluation of children's schoolwork is part of the overabundance of paperwork often associated with teaching.

By far the most important feedback is that provided to students regarding their reading achievement. Methods of feedback can affect children for many years or even a lifetime and establish their opinions of themselves as readers. Often, the evaluation associated with reading is more for adults' benefit. Children seldom understand or need to know about standardized test results or their work in relation to others in their classroom, but they do need feedback about how they are doing in relation to where they started. The information they need is different from any other group that requires feedback. Portfolios and other methods of reviewing their work contribute to their views of themselves as language users. Evaluation of their interpretations of the process of reading is also an important aspect.

Evaluation is necessary to guide instruction and help the teacher and the child learn more about the reading and writing processes. The best approach to evaluating literature-based instruction is to be aware of the reading process and the developmental nature of language and learning. This is different from the traditional approach of the last sixty years, and current trends are toward a broader definition of evaluation.

Assumptions of Evaluation

Evaluating children's reading behaviors is a very involved task with a great deal of responsibility. Teachers who do this well have established several guidelines.

Evaluation Reflects the Developmental Nature of Language Learning

Evaluation must be sensitive to the changing behaviors of children as they learn to be effective language learners. When the developmental nature of reading is understood, behaviors are viewed as clues to how the child is interpreting the reading and writing processes. Certain types of behavior are to be expected. Developmentally appropriate behaviors should be recognized as important to reading instruction.

Evaluation Should Occur during Daily Reading Instruction

As much as possible, reading evaluation should be part of daily reading activities in the classroom. When evaluation reflects instruction and real reading involvement, the teacher can gain valuable and useful information from children's attempts. This technique allows teachers to evaluate ongoing instruction without using too much instructional time.

Evaluation Is Long-term and Continuous

Evaluation does not occur on one day or in one place, but considers different settings and situations. Results produced in 10 or 15 minutes are a reflection of that short time and not an overall reflection of children's reading abilities. A collection of writing and reading products explains much about reading and writing abilities. Most good teachers constantly evaluate during daily instruction. They judge when a child needs additional encouragement or support. Daily evaluation may be stored in teachers' heads, but this type of information can be documented with checklists, anecdotal records, or other informal methods.

Feedback Should Support Growth and Not Discourage Efforts and the Desire to Read

Because evaluation reflects the reading process, an environment in which children can predict and experiment with reading is important for their development. Evaluation should not discourage children from taking the risks necessary for learning how to read. They should have some opportunities to try things and fail without suffering any consequences from evaluation procedures.

Evaluation Procedures

There are many ways to evaluate children's reading behaviors based on the assumptions established for evaluation. On the other hand, there are several traditional methods of reading evaluation that may be required by school districts or state education agencies that are contrary to the assumptions of evaluation based on language learning. Changes in evaluation are occurring, but it will take reasonable dialogue and some compromise before all evaluation procedures are congruent with views of language learning and the reading process (Gaesser, 1990). In the meantime, teachers must understand and appreciate many of the common procedures prevalent in the schools.

Evaluating Emerging Reading Behaviors

As we begin to understand more about how children go about learning to read and write, the tools monitoring the growth should reflect what is commonly believed about their development. Most agree that standardized texts do not reflect the strategies that children demonstrate in beginning reading and writing. In addition, tests are only one type of measurement and do not reflect the full range of behaviors and what children are doing as they learn written language (Morrow, 1989).

Current research and beliefs about emerging readers demonstrate that children's initial efforts reflect a wide range of behaviors with books and print (Chittenden & Courtney, 1989). Furthermore, children may be acquiring and experiencing these events at different rates and in different ways. One way to look at the progress of very young readers is to document the behaviors they display (Chittenden & Courteny, 1989). Young children interacting with print constantly are inventing spellings, attempting to read aloud, and talking about what they are doing. Documentation can consist of the teacher's observations, forms and checklists designed to note information, collections of children's work, and samples of their performance as they read and write.

There are several categories of beginning reading behaviors that should be evaluated (Jalongo, 1988; Jewell & Zintz, 1986; Morrow, 1989). The categories and suggested evaluation procedures are listed here:

1. Emerging readers should develop an interest in and a positive attitude toward reading and books. Answers to the following questions help evaluate interest and attitudes:

    a. Do children spend free time looking at books?

    b. Do they flip rapidly through pages without attempting to look at pictures or print, or do children attempt to tell a story or act like they are reading when looking at books?

    c. Do children ask to have favorite stories read to them?

    d. Are they able to sit still and listen when a story is being read?

Observing children's behaviors during read aloud times is the most effective method of evaluating their interest in and attitude toward books. Occasionally, interviews or discussions with children can determine whether they are interested in and enjoy reading. Parents also can describe children's interest in books and reading. Checklists and anecdotal records can systematize the observations of teachers.

2. Emerging readers should develop concepts about books and stories. The following questions are useful for evaluating children's knowledge of books and stories:

    a. Does the child know about the parts of a book: the front, back, top, and bottom?

    b. Can the child distinguish print from pictures?

    c. Does the child know how to turn pages and identify where the reading begins?

    d. Does the child know what titles, authors, and illustrators are?

    e. Does a child have a sense of story structure and can he or she remember aspects of stories that have been read aloud?

These questions can be answered through observations or reading one-on-one with a child to observe his or her reactions to the book. Children's understanding of story structure can be evaluated by having them tell stories, memory read favorite storybooks, picture sequence or use such props as puppets or felt boards to reenact stories.

3. Emerging readers should develop concepts about print. The following questions are useful in evaluating children's acquisition of print knowledge:

    a. Does the child recognize some words, such as his or her name, on sight?

    b. Does the child point out individual words in print?

    c. Does the child recognize individual letters?

    d. Can the child identify the beginnings of words and use context and syntax to figure out words omitted from texts?

    e. Does a child recognize certain words that occur often in the environment such as STOP and EXIT?

Many standardized readiness tests appear to measure the print knowledge a young child possesses. But many of the concerns listed in the section on standardized tests should be considered before depending on the results. Some test publishers are becoming aware of the nature of beginning reading acquisition, and there are some tests that reflect the research on language learning. Marie Clay's Concept About Print Test (1979) and the Early Reading Test (Mason, Stewart, & Dunning, 1986) are tests that examine children's awareness of print in the environment and other beginning reading attempts (Morrow, 1989). In addition, observation, checklists, collections and descriptions of children's reading and writing attempts should be used to determine print awareness.

4. Emerging readers should begin to understand and exhibit writing behaviors. To evaluate beginning attempts to produce written language, ask:

    a. Does the child use paper and pencils to make markings on paper?

    b. Does the child experiment with letters and letter forms?

    c. Does the child print from left to right?

     d. Does the child respond when asked to read her or his writing aloud?

     e. Does the child copy words and letters?

Observation is one of the best methods of evaluating children's writing development. Observations can be documented with checklists designed to recognize beginning writing behaviors. A collection of writing samples also provides information about writing development. Teachers can maintain samples of the children's work in folders to be shown to parents and children when discussing writing behaviors.

Observation and Children's Contributions

Observation is one of the most valid and reliable measurements for any age reader (Moore, 1986) since teachers understand and can consider the entire situation (Searfoss & Readence, 1989). Observations are dependable because they are made during classroom activities and are based on the teacher's goals and objectives. Observation can explain current behavior or predict future behaviors. However, effective observation is demanding because the teacher must be aware of behaviors and make judgments during daily instruction.

Teachers learn a great deal as they observe children during classroom activities and keep track of findings in an organized manner. Yetta Goodman (1977) coined the term *kid watching* to describe informal evaluation. Kid watching techniques produce information through direct and informal observations. Goodman explains that kid watching should answer two questions:

1. What evidence is there that language development is taking place?
2. When a child produces something unexpected, what does it tell the teacher?

She believes that the learning environment provides opportunities for observation and that records should be kept on children during their daily language arts activities. Teachers should observe children in one-to-one interactions, small group discussions, and large class settings. Records can be compiled by taping oral readings or retellings.

Teachers who engage in kid watching make an effort to find out how children view reading outside the school setting, too. Children provide much of this information through interviews, class discussion, and writing. One valuable source of informal evaluation and monitoring may be provided by parents. Rhodes & Dudley-Marling (1988) suggest that parents are particularly valuable observers of their children's interactions with print outside of school settings because children may respond differently to books and reading at home. Parental reports can provide teachers with information needed to motivate or encourage children during classroom activities.

A great deal of information about children's reading development is available from daily instructional activities. Informal methods of evaluating and monitoring reading behavior can be embedded in classroom instruction, and some procedures can be completed by children. But to tap the wealth of information available from daily interactions with children, teachers need to establish methods of collecting, structuring, managing, and interpreting the information effectively.

Children may be observed reading and writing in response to assigned or recreational reading activities. Checklists and anecdotal notes are the basic tools of teacher observations, but interviews, inventories, and peer and self-evaluation provide additional information.

Checklists

The class roster can provide the format for checklists to chart and monitor information about reading behaviors. Dalrymple (1989) suggests methods of developing checklists for any activity in the classroom and explains that within a unit of study, she might use several checklists. As the teacher moves about the classroom, watching and monitoring students' work, the checklists can be marked for future reference. The teacher and children interact and discuss certain aspects of their work as they go about it. Responses from the students can provide the teacher with information for checklists such as those illustrated in Figure 9.1.

Checklists can be developed to monitor almost any activity or behavior. Experimentation by the teacher results in effective and useful checklists that contribute to the information a teacher needs for instruction.

Anecdotal Records

Teachers can keep notations in journals or on note cards to document classroom activities, behaviors, and events. Anecdotal records can be compiled for each child (their behavior in small reading groups might be chronicled, for example) or for the entire class. A good time to keep anecdotal records is when the entire class (including the teacher) is writing in journals. The teacher's journal might consist of a narration of classroom events that could be used to plan future instruction or work with individual children. Teachers who jot notes in their lesson plan books have helpful reviews of successful techniques that could be used in other situations. If one child is having a particularly difficult time during reading, a teacher might focus attention on the child to determine if there are any patterns of behavior that contribute to reading problems. One teacher carries a note pad with adhesive on the back as she interacts with children. If some behavior or comment is worth noting, she simply writes in on the pad along with the name of the child and the date. Later, the notes are attached to notebook paper in a three-ring notebook in which each child has a designated section. Many teachers use this type of information naturally and store many observations in their memories, but written records concretely document events that are necessary to consider in making effective instructional decisions.

Interviews and Interest Inventories

Discussing reading behaviors with students provides the teacher with a great deal of information about feelings and attitudes toward reading. There are structures for obtaining this type of information. The Burke Reading Interview (Burke, 1988) and the Textbook Handling Interview (Bixby & Pyle, 1988) are examples of interviews for evaluating students' perspectives of reading at different levels.

The interviews can be conducted during one-on-one reading conferences or the entire class can respond in writing. Teachers can conduct the interviews at the beginning

FIGURE 9-1 This basic form can be adapted to organize teachers observations in many literature activities.

Time Study Sept. '86 Literature	Read-Aloud Log Entries 3 Assigned No.	Quality	The Green Futures Discussion of Text	Response to Poem J. Prufrock	Text Compared to "Back to the Future"	Film Response to Time Machine	Task: Respond to own Lit. Re: Time
Mark	3	✓-	+	+ oral	+	+	0 → +
Todd	3	✓	✓+				W ✓
Sue	3	✓	–				0
Marge	3	✓	✓-				0 ✓-
Carol	3	✓	✓				0 ✓-
Don	3	✓	✓+				0/W ✓/✓
Richard	3	+	+		✓		0 ✓-
Scott	3	✓-	✓-				0 +
Melissa	5	✓	✓+	+W			0 ✓
Darrell	2	–	–				0
Nancy	5	+	✓+	✓+W		✓	W/0 +/✓
Tye	3	✓	✓	✓0	+		W ✓+
Peter	3	✓	✓				W ✓-
Kevin	3	✓	✓-				W –
David	3	✓	✓				W ✓
Derek	3	✓+	✓+				W ✓
Dawn	3	✓-	✓-				0 ✓
Maggie	5	+	+	+ 0/W	+	+	W ✓+
Emily	3	✓	✓-				0 ✓
Darin	3	✓	✓				W ✓
Trish	3	✓	✓				W ✓
Ellen	3	+	✓+				W ✓+
Jean	3	+	✓+		✓		W ✓+
Jane	3	+	✓+		✓		W ✓+

0 = Oral   W = Written

Source: K.S. Dalyrymple, (1989). "Well, What about his Skills: Evaluation of Whole Language in the Middle School." In *The Whole Language Evaluation Book,* eds. K.S. Goodman, Y.M. Goodman, and W.J. Hood (Portsmouth, NH: Heinemann, 1989).

of the year, and at two or three intervals to provide information about children's changing attitudes toward reading. The results of the interviews can be kept in portfolios to track children's changes over the year.

Attitudes and interests in reading affect children's involvement with reading. Children must be motivated to read in order to develop the strategies needed to become good readers. Developing a positive attitude toward reading is a significant step in helping children become lifelong readers. Interest inventories, incomplete sentence surveys, attitudinal interviews, and parental interviews (Searfoss & Readence, 1989) provide information regarding the child's reading attitudes and interests. Teachers can use these inventories to discover their children's reading attitudes and behaviors to help them in their classroom planning. Because a child's interests and motivations change so rapidly during elementary school years, it is particularly important to monitor this aspect of reading continuously. An example of the questions that might be asked in an incomplete sentence format is shown in Figure 9.2.

Conferences

Student/teacher conferences provide an opportunity to evaluate a child's reading behaviors and provide feedback. During conferences teachers can ask a child to read aloud, retell a story, or discuss what she or he is reading. This is an excellent time for children and teachers to discuss what type of reading is being done and goals for additional reading. Teachers can keep track of conferences in anecdotal records or on checklists.

Conferences may be conducted one-to-one or in small groups. During conferences, children can discuss current reading material and describe what they are thinking of reading in the future. Conferences are also a time for teachers to provide feedback, focus, and support for what children are doing.

The teacher's role in conferences is to listen to what children are saying about their reading and use this information to guide them in the future. The questions that guide discussions can originate in almost any topic, but some initial questions that are helpful are:

1. What did you enjoy about this book?
2. Read me parts of the book that you particularly enjoyed.
3. Who should read this book?
4. What would you like to read next?

These are just samples to demonstrate the type of conversations that might occur during a conference. Reading conferences are guided by the children's interests and needs and can't be guided by any set questions or established structure. Each discussion between child and teacher should reflect the individual situation and reading material. There is no right way to conduct a reading conference. The main factor to remember is that the teacher must listen and probe.

Children's Evaluations

Children also can be encouraged to monitor their own reading behavior. They might write in journals or discuss their reading metacognitively with teachers or peers. Journals can be used as a way for children to reflect on their reading interests and behaviors.

FIGURE 9-2   Children's responses to open-ended sentences can provide insights about their reading interests.

1. The best book I have ever read is _____
2. The best movie I have ever seen is _____
3. My favorite sport _____
4. Reading _____
5. On Saturday mornings I _____
6. My favorite television show is _____
7. If I could meet anyone in the world, it would be _____
8. I read _____
9. My favorite author is _____
10. I like to read in _____
11. Good books make me feel _____
12. Good stories are about _____

Teachers who discuss reading openly and freely often find that children will mimic them. For example, when teachers discuss their personal reading interests with children, explaining books they enjoyed or books that challenged them, they will find that children display the same behavior in writing and discussion.

Conferences offer another opportunity for self-evaluation. The teacher can guide children to discover what they have accomplished and what they need to do. Records of what has been done and the writing that children do in response to reading are used to focus children on their reading behavior.

Peer evaluation can be structured or informal. Teachers must explain peer feedback and be sure that all students understand that peer discussions are always positive. Peer evaluation is built on the assumption that everyone in the classroom is a collaborator in learning (Goodman, Goodman, & Hood, 1989). Effective peer feedback results from sharing and working together during reading activities.

Reading Portfolios

One new trend in reading assessment and evaluation is the use of a portfolio system to evaluate children's reading (Valencia, Pearson, Peters, & Wixson, 1989). Portfolios traditionally are used by artists, actors, and models to demonstrate their work and potential, but children can demonstrate their work and potential by collecting samples of their reading and organizing materials to chronicle their growth and development. A portfolio is a collection of materials indicating an individual child's reading behaviors. These include evidence of a child's level of comprehension, uses of literacy, metacognitive strategies, reading in different genres, purposes for reading, and attitudes toward reading.

There are several reasons why portfolios are logical ways to measure children's reading and writing behaviors:

1. Portfolios provide a way to monitor reading and writing activities. Portfolio information provides insights to how a reader approaches diverse texts and the variety of purpose that encourages reading and writing. The information in a portfolio emphasizes the uniqueness of individual students' reading and writing activities.

2. Portfolios collect information continuously throughout the reading and writing process. The insights offered by portfolios are not based on a single test, assignment, or response but allow the student and the teacher to view the entire process. Portfolios are designed to assess reading and writing behaviors as they evolve, grow, and change over a period of time.

3. Portfolios are multidimensional and can provide insights about many components of the reading process. They can demonstrate interest, motivation, independent reading actions, writing behaviors, metacognitive knowledge, and strategies that children regularly use with language. Much of the information gathered in a portfolio cannot be obtained with traditional measures of reading.

4. Portfolios encourage student reflection and self-evaluation. The information provided in portfolios helps readers evaluate what they've learned, how they've learned, and what they need to learn next. It is natural to evaluate and reflect when viewing work gathered over time.

5. Teachers who guide their students to compile a portfolio receive feedback about instruction. Portfolios provide information for making instructional decisions. Teachers who use the information to learn about students will plan effective instruction. Portfolio information allows teachers to systematically evaluate class progress and individual performance.

Most products of children's reading and writing can be used in a portfolio. Some of the portfolio requirements should be repeated during the school year to measure increasing reading efficiency. For example, self-evaluations based on a structured format and completed three or four times a year indicate changes in children's attitudes and behaviors toward reading. Self-evaluations provide information that cannot be elicited by conventional or standardized tests. The contents of a portfolio may vary, but most commonly include the following:

- Questionnaires measuring attitudes toward reading and writing
- Responses to literature
- Writing samples
- Reading and writing logs
- Teacher's observations
- Student self-evaluations
- Writing, both completed and in progress
- Classroom tests
- Summary checklists
- Copies of reading texts read during independent reading

Teachers use reading logs to determine growth in voluntary reading behavior (Au et al., 1990). Logs from a period of time, perhaps two weeks, can be reviewed to see how many books students read on their own. The reading logs and reading conferences provide information about students' voluntary reading, and a summary checklist, shown in Table 9.1, reveals the following information:

TABLE 9-1 Voluntary Reading Checklist

Number of books attempted	20
Number of books completed	2
Variety of genre	Yes
Favorite book	*Number the Stars*
Favorite author	K. Paterson

Comments: Seems to have difficulty finishing books. Discuss selection.

Portfolio collections are more effective when children and teachers plan procedures (Au et al, 1990; Jongsma, 1989). Together they can decide what goes into the portfolio, the purpose for collecting information, and even interpret and evaluate material in the portfolio. When planning a portfolio, teachers and children are selective about including information and look for ways to illustrate that readers understand the author's message, learn new information, read fluently, and exhibit an interest and desire to read. The focus of portfolio collections should remain broad and not concentrate on isolated skills or individual lesson objectives.

It is important that both teachers and children understand the purposes of the portfolio, the organizational format, and how the information will be used. Children and teachers establish specific directions for what information should be placed in the portfolio and who should be responsible for collecting the information. Some procedures state that teachers are responsible for contributing to the portfolio and other times children contribute to the portfolio. Children help with as much of the record-keeping and logistics of the portfolios as possible. For example, they could be responsible for developing a one-page table of contents listing everything included in the collection.

Valencia (1990) describes portfolios as larger than report cards and smaller than steamer trunks. Such a description leaves a great deal of room for interpretation and individual preferences. Probably the most realistic portfolio is a large expanded file folder. Whatever type of portfolio is selected, it should be easy for teachers and children to manage.

Both teachers and children should have access to the portfolios. The effectiveness of portfolio assessment increases when students and teachers discuss what is in the portfolios and how the information can be interpreted. Jongsma (1989) suggests that at least four conferences a year be devoted to portfolio information. The discussions can provide opportunities for teacher–student sharing as well as monitoring.

Portfolios are more than collections of graded papers. ''Portfolios should be viewed as a growing, evolving description of students' reading and writing experiences,'' according to Jongsma (1989, p. 264). The unique aspect of reading portfolios is that it allows the teacher and student to understand more about reading and writing.

Evaluating the Reading of Literature

Many evaluation and feedback techniques can be applied to children's literature. It is extremely important, however, that a teacher not allow monitoring procedures to promote associations between evaluation and children's literature. There are many other ways to obtain standardized information besides using children's literature. At the same time teachers must evaluate and monitor children's experiences with literature. Much of the monitoring and assessment of the reading of children's literature can be completed without interfering with the pleasure of literature.

Teachers who use children's literature in the classroom probably want to keep records of reading interests, books that children are reading, written responses to stories, discussion participation, and other anecdotal observations from recreational reading. Most informal measures suggested in this chapter are suitable for teachers to use in assessing the reading of children's literature. Portfolios are excellent methods for keeping track of literature read.

One method of keeping track of recreational reading is to require children to maintain reading logs of the titles of books they read during the year (see Figure 9.3). The dates each book was selected and completed, along with comments, are recorded in the journal. The journals may include reactions. Children can note if they finished the selection and whether they recommend the book to others.

Surveys provide additional information regarding recreational reading. Occasionally an entire class can be asked what they are reading and enjoying. The more teachers know about interests, reading habits, and how children feel about reading, the more effective reading instruction becomes.

Conventional Measures

Observation and children's contributions to understanding the reading process are very effective, but there are times a teacher needs a greater understanding of what is occurring during the reading process. When a child displays behaviors that indicate the reading process is not proceeding effectively and a teacher cannot identify the problem through observation, a more structured view of the child's reading process may be required. There are several conventional evaluation procedures that provide insights into what a child does while reading. (The term *conventional* is used to describe two procedures that involve specific procedures and analysis during administration.) These three procedures, cloze, Informal Reading Inventory, and Reading Miscue Analysis can be developed by teachers or kits can be purchased from publishers.

Informal Reading Inventory (IRI)
One of the most commonly used evaluation tools is the Informal Reading Inventory (IRI). IRIs originally were designed to help establish which basal reader level was appropriate for a child. Some IRI formats include procedures that allow a teacher to see what occurs during the reading process, such as analysis of a child's deviations from the print, and may be valuable in providing information about how children are reading basals and textbooks. Some school districts require that teachers administer an IRI to children once or twice a year. There are several distinct aspects of IRIs:

Selections and Questions
The IRI consists of graded reading selections and questions representative of text from the middle of a basal or another textbook. Sometimes two selections from each grade

FIGURE 9-3   Children can keep track of the books they read if a reading log is provided.

My Reading Record
Dawn A, Drury

number of pages	book read or heard	author	date started	date finished
124 pg.	Sideways storys from Wayside School	Louis Suchar	Aug. 28, 19	Sep. 19.
19 pg	The ture story of the three little pigs.	I	don't	no
32 . pg.	Polar Expres	Chirs Van Allsburg	Oct. 7	Oct.21
30pg.	Koulas & kangros	I don't know.	Oct. 23	Oct 29
pg. 26	Arthurs teacher trouble.	I don't know'	I don't know	
pgs. 127				
pg.5				

level are included. One selection is used for silent reading and the other for oral reading evaluation. Five or more questions about each passage are included.

Word Lists

To establish the appropriate level at which to begin IRI administration, children attempt to identify as many words as possible from graded word lists. The level at which the child recognizes one hundred percent of the words on the list indicates the level of reading at which the IRI should begin. For example, if a child identifies all the words on a third grade list and only ninety percent of the words on a fourth grade list, the first reading selection would be the third grade selection.

Procedure

Both the teacher and the child are provided with copies of the reading selection. The child begins reading the selection. As the child reads, the teacher marks anything the child reads that is not written in the text. The oral reading deviations from the text are called *miscues*. If the text appeared as "The horse jumped over the fence" and the child read "The house jumped over the fence," the word *house* would be a miscue. Miscues are marked on the text with an established code (see Box 9.1). The coding system allows the teacher to evaluate the oral reading at a later date by reviewing the text exactly as the student orally read.

Some miscues indicate a loss of understanding and others do not. When a child substitutes house for horse and does not correct the miscue while reading, the teacher assumes that comprehension is affected or altered. However, if the child rereads the word correctly and corrects the miscue or if the child read, "The pony jumped over the fence" instead of "The horse jumped over the fence," the teacher might assume that the miscue did not affect the meaning.

After the child has read the passage, the teacher counts the number of miscues that negatively affect comprehension and computes a percentage, which indicates the effectiveness of the child's reading. When computing the scores of an IRI, self-corrected miscues, miscues that do not alter sentence meaning, and miscues that are a result of dialect differences are not counted. To compute the percentage of correct words identified in the passage the teacher:

1. counts the total number of words in the passage and subtracts the number of miscues that affected the meaning.
2. divides the total number of words in the selection by the number found in step one.
3. Uses the resulting percentage as the word recognition score.

In addition to a word recognition score, the IRI provides a comprehension measure. Comprehension is measured by the questions accompanying the selection. Usually five questions are included with each selection, and the percentage of correct answers indicates the level of comprehension. If all five questions are answered correctly, the comprehension is one hundred percent; if four questions are answered, comprehension is eighty percent, and so on. The combination of word recognition and comprehension provides a formal level of reading. The IRI identifies four levels of reading performance (see Box 9.2).

BOX 9-1

Coding System for Oral Reading Miscues

Miscue	*Code*
Omissions	Cross out omission.
	The ~~dog~~ ran after the cat.
Added word	Use a caret to insert the word
	above the sentence.
	saw
	The dog ran after the cat.
	^
Reversal	Use a ⁀ to note the reversal.
	The cat ran after the dog.
Repetition	Draw line under the word.
	The <u>dog</u> ran after the cat.
Self-correction	Write the miscue and a *c* in a circle.
	doll Ⓒ
	The dog/ran after the cat.
Substitution or mispronunciation	Write the word above the text.
	doll
	The dog ran after the cat.

IRIs frequently are used to place children in special reading programs or to match individual children with grade level basals. Many basal companies provide IRIs with their series, and teachers often use IRIs to determine children's progress in reading.

Reading Miscue Inventory (RMI)

Reading Miscue Inventory (K. Goodman, 1973; Goodman, Watson, & Burke, 1987) is another oral reading evaluation of children's reading processes and their reading strategies. When children read orally they do not read perfectly, but make miscues or deviations from the text. Readers may correct or ignore miscues. The manner in which they react to the miscues suggests much about how they view the reading process. An analysis of the miscues while reading a selection can provide teachers with an understanding of children's reading behavior. The RMI is particularly valuable for children who seem to be having a great deal of difficulty comprehending or even attempting to use reading material.

Miscue analysis resembles the IRI during administration, but differs greatly in interpretation and results. The two never should be confused. Miscue analysis focuses more on analyzing the miscues than on obtaining a measure of reading ability or level of performance. Other differences include the teacher's selection of material for an IRI. The lack of established levels of reading and scores resulting from a miscue analysis distinguish it from an IRI. In miscue analysis, comprehension is measured with retelling and probing questions instead of the set of questions with expected answers found in the IRI. What results from a miscue analysis is a suggestion of the reading strategies needed to improve comprehension and an understanding of the reader's strengths.

BOX 9-2

Levels of Reading

- The instructional level is achieved when the student reads with 75 percent comprehension and 95 percent word recognition.
- The independent level is the level at which the reader achieves 95 to 100 percent comprehension and 100 percent word recognition.
- The frustration level is the level of reading at which comprehension falls to 50 percent and word recognition is below 90 percent.
- Listening comprehension is determined by reading a selection to students and allowing them to respond orally to the comprehension questions.

Experience and training are needed before a teacher is able to complete an involved miscue analysis. The procedure is time-consuming and difficult to arrange in a busy classroom. The purpose of this description was not to prepare one to complete a miscue analysis, but to describe the differences between miscue analysis and the IRI. Teachers who wish to use it will need to acquire more information to understand miscue analysis. This procedure is particularly valuable when working with children who are having an extremely difficult time with reading and provides a teacher with much information regarding individual reading behaviors.

Standardized Tests

Standardized tests have been one of the most prevalent and influential methods of determining children's reading successes and achievement and have had more of an impact on reading instruction than any one procedure other than the basal. Teachers for many years have depended on standardized measures to help explain the complex behaviors of the reading process.

Description
Standardized tests have specific instructions for administration and result in scores that have been standardized with comparisons to other children. A specific method is used to develop standardized tests. Before a standardized test is published, it is given to large numbers of children who represent the type of children the test is designed to measure. This procedure is known as *norming*. The group is representative of cultural, socioeconomic, and geographic groups that eventually will take the test. Test result averages, typical responses, and other statistics are gathered to determine average, grade and age equivalencies, and percentiles.

The information is used to develop tables and graphs that allow teachers to compare the results of their children with the results of the children in the norming population. For example, if the results of a test indicate an age equivalency of 8.5, they suggest that the child's efforts compare with those of children in the norming group who were 8.5.

Percentiles also are established by norming. If a child is in the 89th percentile at a certain grade level, that percentile indicates that of all children in the grade level, 89 percent scored below and 11 percent scored above these children. Tests that result in this type of evaluation and interpretation are known as *norm-referenced tests.*

The most common standardized tests are achievement tests that measure progress in a particular area from year to year. Achievement tests have subtests in such areas as reading, math, and writing, and measure whether a child has mastered certain subject areas. The standardized tests usually are given yearly and results become part of the child's permanent record. The scores on achievement tests are used to monitor overall achievement and may be used to place children in special programs such as gifted, talented, or reading resource classrooms. If a child scores a year or more above or below the expected grade level of achievement, he or she may be asked to take part in special programs offered by the school.

Interpretation

After a test has been given, a teacher usually interprets the results for further use and for parents. But interpretation can be complicated and difficult. The results of children's responses on the tests may be expressed in several different ways. The test results come to the teacher with an amazing number of scores and interpretation requirements.

The results of the Comprehensive Tests of Basic Skills may be reported to a teacher as shown in Figure 9.4. The first set of numbers listed after the subtest is the number of items answered correctly in that subtest. The second number is the scaled score, sometimes referred to as the raw score. This score is the basis for determining other scores. The scaled and raw scores can only be compared to the same student's performance on repeat administrations of the same test.

The next column indicates the number of objectives mastered. For example, one of the objectives in the reading subtest may be to measure the child's ability to identify root word meanings. If the child correctly answers the questions designed to measure that objective, it is considered mastered. The second number indicates the number of objectives there were to master in that subtest. So if a child has a 4/5 result in the mastery column, it suggests the child mastered four of the five objectives as measured by the standardized test.

The next column explains the child's performance compared to all other children in the nation who have taken the test. If a child's performance results in a national percentile of 89, then 11 percent of the children who have taken the test received a higher score and 89 percent of the children who have taken the test received a lower score.

Still another interpretation of the results can be seen on the chart labeled *Stanine.* The stanine is a statistical score from one to nine that roughly estimates achievement. Average scores fall in the fourth, fifth, or sixth stanine, while the lower stanines indicate lower achievement and higher stanines indicate higher achievement.

This particular standardized test includes a written interpretation of the results. Most standardized test results are reported to the teacher and parents in similar formats. Teachers need to be familiar with the method of reporting so that they can explain a child's performance to parents and other interested parties.

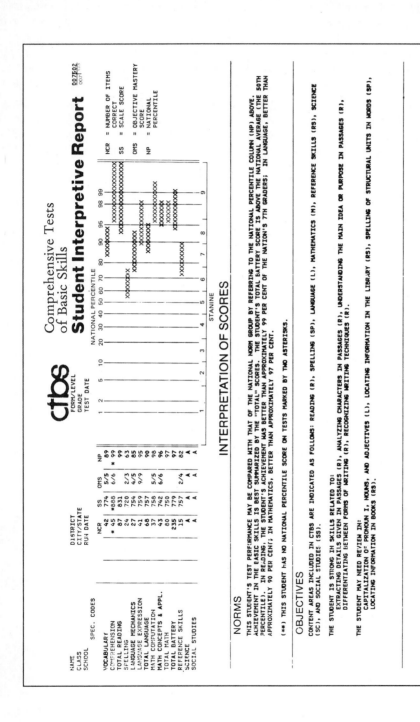

FIGURE 9-4 Students' reading behaviors as measured by standardized tests are often reported on a computer printout such as this one.

Concerns and Limitations

Every school system uses standardized achievement tests to document students' achievement and growth over time. Very few teachers accept the idea of measuring a child's total reading achievement with one score, but standardized tests are part of school and can provide a certain type of information. Tests can be used for statistical, administrative, and political reasons. But those who administer and interpret test scores should realize that, at best, standardized tests are a sampling of a child's reading ability in an artificial situation. The tests are administered in one class period and include short passages and multiple choice responses. As a result of many factors, tests may be biased against creative thinkers and students who are members of minority groups, and results can be skewed by anxiety and time constraints.

Standardized tests and basals are linked for several reasons. Traditional standardized tests focus on measurable written language behaviors like word recognition, sound blending, punctuation, and spelling (Rhodes & Dudley-Marling, 1988) that are presented in basal reading, language, and spelling series. Teachers may feel confident that basal series present the exact material that will appear on the tests and feel that if the material is not covered in detail, children will not be able to perform on the tests. This feeling often restricts reading instruction to basal series and prevents teachers from taking the time to use children's literature.

The tie between basals and standardized tests is a critical issue, but standardized tests are criticized for several other reasons. Many standardized measures evaluate reading comprehension with short passages written for the test. The passages often lack sufficient elaboration or context to help students comprehend and they do not match what students are reading in class (Valencia et al., 1989). In addition, traditional standardized tests fail to measure the students' background knowledge and how that important element affects comprehension.

There are more subtle dangers from the standardized testing used in our public schools when teachers "teach to the test." Some teachers seriously believe that test manufacturers can define what should be included in reading instruction and may look to tests to guide their curricular and instructional decisions. Unfortunately, the result is that teachers feel compelled to teach the information found on the test.

Another grave danger of the tests is the role that assessment may play in labeling a child. Children who do not perform well may be placed in special classes and, as a result of poor performance, teachers may expect less from a child. The dangers of labeling are many, but perhaps the most unacceptable is that once children are identified as below average, they rarely can remove that stigma throughout their schooling.

Standardized tests are not in themselves a detriment to reading development if teachers use them with caution. Teachers should be particularly aware of surprising differences between testing and classroom performance. Teachers know their students and should be able to predict how children will perform on a standardized test. If a child performs drastically differently than expected, the teacher should be alert to the causes. In addition, teachers should carefully interpret test results and make wise decisions about what the test results show.

Many people believe that there should be changes to improve the ways we assess children's reading achievement (Pikulski, 1989; Taylor, 1990; Valencia & Pearson,

1987). Pikulski's summary of the changes needed suggests that teachers and administrators should decrease significantly their reliance on standardized tests. He suggests that schools should review the number of tests given, the reading behaviors measured, and the interpretations and uses of the results. One of the main criticisms of reading assessment is that tests do not adequately reflect the goals of instruction or the process of reading.

Responding to Standardized Testing

Although teachers may see the fallacies of testing, they may not have a choice about administering tests to their students. Many states have laws that require the yearly administration of the tests. However, teachers can do a great deal to guide children through test-taking without jeopardizing their reading achievement. Teachers' attitudes toward the tests, providing a few opportunities to practice test skills, and explaining the nature of and reasons for testing can help children approach testing with attitudes that encourage solid scores and indicate achievement resulting from sensible instruction.

Teachers should maintain and display a positive attitude toward testing, reflecting confidence that good reading instruction will be demonstrated on standardized tests. If children can approach a standardized test with confidence that their reading abilities are strong, scores will reflect their capability and confidence.

Test-taking is a skill children should learn. It is necessary to learn the vocabularies, appropriate responses, and formats of standardized tests. Children will be faced with many types of tests, and teachers are doing them a disfavor by not discussing the procedures and roles of tests in our schools. However, as teachers familiarize children with test-taking formats, instructions, and directions, they should take care never to imply to the children that test-taking and reading are the same processes.

Children must learn how to transfer responses to an answer sheet, how to respond to short passages that may have multiple choice questions, and how to interpret directions. Children should participate in short drills that familiarize them with test-taking routines. Students need to learn how to manage their time when taking a test. They should understand how to continue the reading if they don't immediately recognize the answer and to keep moving through the responses even if they do not know the answers.

Children and teachers should discuss openly their fears, anxieties, and attitudes toward standardized testing. Explanations and discussions about how the results will be used and who will see them may put their minds at ease about their performances. They should understand that the test scores will be reviewed to see how much they have achieved in a year or to compare two years of school achievement. Tests should be viewed as another fact of life that is important, but not all-encompassing.

Mandated Tests

For the past twenty years, many states have been developing their own tests to measure public school children's reading achievement. At last count, forty-six states had mandated state-regulated testing (Valencia et al., 1989). Most state tests are simply forms of standardized tests that have been used for many years. Many state tests also include math and writing evaluations. These tests are used to determine how groups of children are reading, and the single score that is computed for each child provides precious little information about the child's written language development.

In response to concerns about the appropriateness of standardized tests, Illinois and Michigan have developed tests of reading comprehension that attempt to reflect current reading theory and emphasize instruction that focuses on meaning (Roeber & Dutcher, 1989). These tests measure the knowledge and skills that current research indicates are related to language. The assessments consist of a measurement of how children construct meaning and three supporting components: topic familiarity, metacognitive knowledge and strategies, and reading attitudes, habits, and self-perceptions. These tests have the potential to encourage strategic reading during the testing procedures and redefine the statewide assessment of reading (Valencia & Pearson, 1987). It is hoped that more states will look to these tests as models for their own tests.

Basal Assessment

Each basal reader includes its own procedures to identify children who do not master portions of units, themes, or skills. After a class or group completes a particular unit or level, basals provide a test that covers the information. The tests usually are available from the publishers, and the results of each child's performance are designed to help the teacher determine which children need additional instruction.

Usually, the tests are criterion-referenced to measure the students' mastery of objectives in each unit. The tests may be multiple choice and usually are administered to the entire class or group at one time. Often, two versions of the tests are provided to allow the teacher to test before and after the unit to see growth. The same concerns listed for standardized tests apply when these tests are required. Teachers who must administer the tests should focus on building the reading confidence and abilities of children through effective instruction and rely on good reading strategies to produce good results.

Grading

Some school districts require a teacher to provide a certain number of reading grades during each grading period. Atwell (1987) suggests that cumulative points are one way to provide grades. She explains that for each day that a student follows the guidelines established by the teacher, the student receives points. Over the grading period the points add up to one hundred. This becomes one third of the reading grade. She obtains the second third of the grade from the journals kept by students about the books they are reading. The journals are evaluated on frequency of response and depth of thoughts. The third part of the grade is derived from how nearly the student meets the goals of the reading program during that term.

There probably is no good way to grade in reading when a teacher is focusing on appreciation and lifelong learning as the main goal. It is difficult to establish a grade based on children's authentic responses to good literature. One way to approach this problem is to provide opportunities for two types of responses during the grading period. Some responses are completed with the expectation that they will be graded, and others only for feedback from the teacher or classmates. Children should understand or perhaps take part in decisions about which responses are considered for a grade. The students may select a series of examples from their portfolios to be graded or provide input into the grading procedure whenever possible.

It is unfortunate that grading may be the only feedback parents obtain about the performance and behavior of their children during reading instruction. Teachers constantly should attempt to find methods that allow parents and others to have realistic views of children's classroom reading behaviors.

Writing

Writing can provide information about a child's reading and language arts development. Children can write about what they are reading, and teachers can determine their comprehension and understanding from the children's written responses.

One of the earliest instructional procedures, language experience, can provide the first indications of a child's reading ability. As children dictate and read their own language, there is a concrete record for the teacher to collect. As children gain more reading skills and understand more about the structure of reading material, their dictated stories should reflect their increasing knowledge.

Journals can be used to keep track of reading and reactions to reading. As early as kindergarten, children can begin writing about the material they are reading. Pictures, one-word productions, short stories, and longer reactions provide information to the teacher about the reading growth of the children as they respond in journals.

There are many ways that writing offers concrete representation of the language behaviors, attitudes, and ideas that children develop about their reading. Writing has been suggested as a part of evaluation throughout the previous discussion. Writing also provides a way for the teacher to give feedback and respond to children's ideas. Activities that focus on writing can play many roles in the evaluation, monitoring, and provision of feedback necessary for reading development.

Learning Differences

Evaluation and monitoring are particularly sensitive when learning differences are considered. Formal testing is particularly nebulous when dealing with any type of learning differences. Not only are the children who may have differences in learning and language experiences more negatively affected by testing results, their attempts may be the most likely to be influenced by their differences.

Culture

Standardized tests traditionally have been biased against students who are members of minority groups. The difference in achievement reflected in the tests may be the result of any number of cultural differences. Students who have different learning styles may not produce high scores on tests. This does not mean that these students cannot think or learn. It simply means that these students might be more successful at learning in ways that differ from those measured by the tests.

The most obvious impediment to testing the culturally diverse is that test material and background of experience may not match. If the reading passages on the tests deal with events, activities, or ideas quite different from the child's experiences and background, the result will be lower scores. If the test refers to values different from those of the children, they may reject the information or consider it unimportant. Once a child experiences failure on the tests, the negative feelings may persist and extend to the succeeding years. Much can be done to overcome the effect of cultural differences if preparation encourages discussion and understanding of the tests and if feedback considers cultural differences.

Teachers must remember and be aware of the differences that culture might produce. The effect of culture on testing may be rooted in several causes. Teachers' perceptions, children's perceptions, school behavior, and the nature and importance of schooling (Bond, Tinker, Wasson & Wasson, 1990) can affect a child's performance on testing. The results of standardized tests must be considered with the possibility that cultural differences influenced the scores. There are better ways to measure a child's abilities than standardized tests, and the results of informal evaluation may produce a more accurate picture of reading behavior than a single score.

Language

Language differences pose additional problems in testing. Children who speak with a different dialect or who speak a different language may show lower achievement on standardized tests. The testing problems in measuring reading growth of children whose language is different than English resemble the problems associated with cultural differences. It is extremely difficult to obtain a measure of reading ability when children can neither understand nor speak English.

The causes of low reading achievement scores for these children are as numerous as those among English-speaking children. But many of the problems documented in evaluation may be a result of their inability to understand or speak English. The development of their language may be gradual and until they learn the language, traditional achievement measures of all types may indicate a deficit. When tests and measurements are interpreted, the fact that the child has language differences should be taken into account. It may not be possible to evaluate with tests what these children know. Teachers may need to use other methods of evaluation and monitoring to understand what these children are learning in school. The informal measures recommended for children of different cultures provide a more inclusive view of non-English-speaking children's development and achievements.

DISCUSSION AND ACTIVITIES

1. Brainstorm a list of agencies and individuals interested in children's performance on test scores. List many agencies and individuals that would be interested in actual classroom reading behaviors of children. Discuss a teacher's obligation to different groups of people.

2. What are some of the effects of the interest in children's test scores? Discuss how teachers react when there is an overemphasis on testing. What can happen to instruction when teachers are worried about test results?

3. Review the many methods of evaluation and monitoring. Evaluate which methods should be used to provide feedback to children. What are some of the ways that information can be presented to children to encourage their reading development?

4. Try to remember some of the feedback you received about your own reading development. How does it affect your view of yourself as a reader? Compare your and your classmates' negative and positive feedback situations. Discuss any instructional implications your memories may provoke.

RELATED READING

Professional

Goodman, K., Goodman, Y., & Hood, W. (Eds.). (1989). *The whole language evaluation book.* Portsmouth, NH: Heinemann.

This is an exploration of the many methods and procedures that allow a teacher to monitor classroom instruction and children's reading behavior in meaningful and productive ways.

Goodman, Y. M., Watson, D. J., & Burke, C. (1987). *Reading miscue analysis.* New York: Richard C. Owen.

Before attempting a miscue analysis, everyone should take the time to read this complete presentation of the procedure. The description allows one to see the difference between an IRI and a miscue analysis, but not necessarily to become efficient at conducting miscues analysis.

Valencia, S. (1990). A portfolio approach to classroom reading assessment: The whys, whats, and hows. *The Reading Teacher, 43* (4), 338–340.

Portfolios in reading are a new procedure that may require some exploration and development before implementation. This article is one in a series of recent Reading Teacher *articles that discuss the concept of portfolio assessment.*

Children's Literature

Some children's books allow teachers to use fictional events to discuss the testing and monitoring that children must experience. Each of these books has some relationship to the feelings that testing and monitoring can evoke in children.

For Younger Readers

Kraus, R. (1971). *Leo the late bloomer.* Illustrated by J. Aruego. New York: Simon & Schuster.

For Older Readers

Gilson, J. (1980). *Do bananas chew gum?* New York: Lothop, Lee & Shepard.
Magorian, M. (1981). *Good night, Mr. Tom.* New York: Harper & Row.
Voight, C. (1982). *Dicey's song.* New York: Atheneum.

REFERENCES

Allington, R.L. (1983). The reading instruction provided readers of differing reading abilities. *The Elementary School Journal, 83* (5), 548–59.
Ammon, R. (1983). Evaluation in the holistic reading/language arts curriculum. In U.H. Hardt (Ed.), *Teaching reading with the other language arts.* Newark, DE: International Reading Association.
Atwell, N. (1987). *In the middle: Writing, reading, and learning with adolescents.* Portsmouth, NH: Boynton/Cook-Heinemann.
Au, K.H., Scheu, J. A., Kawakame, A.J., & Herman, P.A. (1990). Assessment and accountability in a whole literacy curriculum. *The Reading Teacher, 43* (8), 574–578.
Bixby, M., & Pyle, D. (1988). Textbook handling interview. In C. Giles, M. Bixby, P. Crowley, S.R. Crenshaw, M. Henrichs, F.E. Reynolds, & D. Pyle (Eds.), *Whole language strategies for secondary students.* New York: Richard C. Owen.
Bond, G.L., Tinker, M.A., Wasson, B.B., & Wasson, J.B. (1990). *Reading difficulties: Their diagnosis and correction* (6th ed.) New York: Prentice-Hall.
Burke, C. (1988). Burke reading interview. In C. Giles, M. Bixby, P. Crowley, S.R. Crenshaw, M. Henrichs, F.E. Reynolds, and D. Pyle (Eds.), *Whole language strategies for secondary students.* New York: Richard C. Owen.
Chittenden, E., & Courtney, R. (1989). Assessment of young children's reading: Documentation as an alternative to testing. In D.S. Strickland & L.M. Morrow (Eds.), *Emerging literacy: Young children learn to read and write.* Newark, DE: International Reading Association.
Clay, M. (1979). *The early detection of reading difficulties: A diagnostic survey with recovery procedures.* Auckland, NZ: Heinemann.
Crowley, P. (1987). Teachers writing to learn in journals. In D. Watson (Ed.), *Ideas and insights: Language arts in the elementary school.* Urbana, IL: National Council of Teachers of English.
Dalyrymple, K.S. (1989). ''Well, what about his skills?'' Evaluation of whole language in the middle school. In K. Goodman, Y. Goodman, & W. Hood (Eds.). *The whole language evaluation book.* Portsmouth, NH: Heinemann.
Gaesser, V. (1990). Options for evaluation and assessment in an elementary school whole language program. In R.W. Blake (Ed.), *Whole language: Explorations and applications.* Brockport, NY: New York State English Council.
Goodman, K. (1973). Miscues: Windows on the reading process. In K. K. Goodman (Ed.), *The psycholinguistic nature of the reading process,* Urbana, IL: National Council of Teachers of English.
Goodman, K. (1986). *What's whole about whole language?* Portsmouth, NH: Heinemann.
Goodman, K.S., Goodman, Y.M., & Hood, W.J. (1989). *The whole language evaluation book.* Portsmouth, NH: Heinemann.
Goodman, Y. (1977). Kid watching: An alternative to testing. *Elementary Principal, 57,* 41–45.

Goodman, Y. (1989). Evaluation of students, Evaluation of Teachers. In K. Goodman, Y. Goodman, & W. Hood (Eds.), *The Whole Language Evaluation Book*. Portsmouth, NH: Heinemann.

Goodman, Y. M., Watson, D. J., & Burke, C. (1987). *Reading miscue analysis*. New York: Richard C. Owen.

Jalongo, M.R. (1988). *Young children and picture books*. Washington, DC: National Association for the Education of Young Children.

Jewell, M.B., & Zintz, M. (1986). *Learning to read naturally*. Dubuque, IA: Kendall/Hunt.

Jongsma, K. S. (1989). Portfolio assessment. *The Reading Teacher, 43* (3), 264–265.

Mason, J., Stewart, J., & Dunning, D. (1986). Testing kindergarten children's knowledge about reading. (Tech. Rep. 368). Urbana, IL: University of Illinois, Center for the Study of Reading.

Moore, D. W. (1986). A case for naturalistic assessment of reading comprehension. In E.K. Dishner, T.W. Bean, J. E. Readence, & D. W. Moore (Eds.), *Reading in the Content Areas: Improving Classroom Instruction* (2nd ed.). Dubuque, IA: Kendall/Hunt.

Morrow, L.M. (1989). *Literacy development in the early years: Helping children read and write*. Englewood Cliffs, NJ: Prentice-Hall.

Pikulski, J.J. (1989). The assessment of reading: A time for change? *The Reading Teacher, 43* (1), 80–81.

Rhodes, L.K., & Dudley-Marling, C. (1988). *Readers and writers with a difference: A holistic approach to teaching learning disabled and remedial students*. Portsmouth, NH: Heinemann.

Roeber, E., & Dutcher, P. (1989, April). Michigan's innovative assessment of reading. *Educational Leadership,* 64–69.

Searfoss, L.W., & Readence, J.E. (1989). *Helping children learn to read*. Englewood Cliffs, NJ: Prentice-Hall.

Stallman, A. C., & Pearson, P.D. (1990). Formal measures of early literacy. In L.M. Morrow & J.K. Smith (Eds.), *Assessment for instruction in early literacy*. Englewood Cliffs, NJ: Prentice-Hall.

Taylor, Denny. (1990). Teaching without testing: Assessing the complexity of children's literacy learning. *English Education, 22* (1), 4–75.

Teale, W.H. (1990). The promise and challenge of informal assessment in early literacy. In L.M. Morrow & J.K. Smith (Eds.), *Assessment for instruction in early literacy*. Englewood Cliffs, NJ: Prentice-Hall.

Valencia, S. (1990). A portfolio approach to classroom reading assessment: The whys, whats, and hows. *The Reading Teacher, 43* (4), 338–340.

Valencia, S., & Pearson, P.D. (1987). Reading assessment: Time for a change. *The Reading Teacher, 40* (8), 726–732.

Valencia, S.W., Pearson, P.D., Peters, C.W., & Wixson, K.K. (1989, April). Theory and practice in statewide reading assessment: Closing the gap. *Educational Leadership, 57–63*.

Watson, D. (1987). Valuing and evaluating the learners and their language. In D. Watson (Ed.), *Ideas and insights : Language arts in the elementary school*. Urbana, IL: National Council of Teachers of English.

10

GUIDING READERS WHO HAVE DIFFICULTY

It wasn't raining all that hard as I ran toward the corner office building. I could see the big letters on the silver canopy as clear as sunshine. But even after two months of glancing up at that sign, I still didn't know what it said. Not that it mattered much, so I didn't bother looking hard.

I knew my orthodontist was on the second floor. And that's where I was headed. But for all I knew the sign said Maniac Orthodontist Inside. *I couldn't read it or any other long words without a whole lot of wheels burning rubber in my head.*

See, I read like a second grader. And I'm not a second grader. I'm in sixth.

When I was in first and second grades they said I was a "slow starter." My mom and dad argued about that a lot. They didn't like the way it sounded. My teacher in Jersey, Mr. Spears, said that I was lazy and didn't try. That really bugged my folks and they tried teaching me themselves and that bombed. In the middle of fourth grade we moved west. Then last year in California the teachers started asking if they could give me these tests. Geez, that was some battle royal. Finally my folks said OK, but they didn't like the test results. See, they said I had this learning disability thing. And twice a week I got special lessons from this learning disability teacher. She was helping me some, I guess. But, I was still dumb. And then we moved again.

—Jamie Gilson, *Do Bananas Chew Gum?*

THERE are some children who do not do particularly well in reading and, what is more serious, the reading problems seem to increase with each passing school year. When students do not do well in reading instruction, there are ramifications for their school and personal lives. Failure in reading is implicated in several major societal problems. Profiles of high school dropouts, pregnant teens, delinquent and homeless youth (McGill-Franzen, 1989) all include high incidence of reading failure. Failure to read can affect economics: illiterate adults account for seventy-five percent of the unemployed (Adams, 1990). The increasing problem of illiteracy is affecting the quality of the work force and levels of productivity in industry.

Thousands of Americans suffer reading problems in silence, compensating in various ways for their inability to deal with written language. They develop excellent listening skills and avoid situations in which reading is required. Reading problems affect individuals from any socioeconomic or cultural group. Each year a teacher will have at least one child whose reading development is delayed or not progressing at expected rates. Despite much attention from educators, there are many unanswered questions about children who fail to become efficient readers. Some of the questions this chapter will address regarding children with reading problems are:

1. What causes reading problems?
2. How does a teacher know when a reading problem exists?
3. What does a teacher do to help children who are having difficulty?
4. Are there materials that are well suited to children who have different learning patterns?
5. How do children view their reading differences?

The factors related to failure to achieve in reading are varied and diverse. Similarly, teaching approaches and strategies for dealing with children who are experiencing reading difficulty are multifaceted. Many programs for dealing with troubled readers have been successful and just as many have failed. Programs that are successful with one child may be ineffective with another.

Children usually are identified as having reading problems from their scores on certain tests or their achievement and behavior during reading instruction. Even without formal or informal evaluation, ineffective readers are easy to recognize. They may read orally word by word, stumbling over the many words they do not recognize. Their oral reading is excruciatingly slow, and when they finish reading a passage they seldom have any comprehension of what they have read. Children who have reading problems seldom read books on their own and their products in reading and writing usually are inferior to other students' in the class. Because of the failure associated with reading and other school work, the child often suffers social and emotional problems that further interfere with academic progress.

Foundations of Reading Difficulties

Children who cannot read believe there are two types of readers: those who can read and those who cannot (Goodman, 1986). They usually place themselves in the "cannot" category. What struggling readers don't always know is that fluent readers do not always read effectively. Depending on the text, the situation, and the reader's attitude, it's possible for very successful readers to exhibit such behaviors such as slow, halting reading, lack of comprehension, and no motivation to complete a text.

Remember the engineering text discussed in the first chapter? There is the chance that if you pick up that text, you will not be able to comprehend it. Perhaps there is vocabulary that you do not recognize because you lack the proper background. Maybe you are not interested in the text and cannot motivate yourself to read it, or you may read every word, but when you complete the text, you do not remember what you have read. All readers can have problems in some situations.

Ineffective Reading Behaviors

There are several reasons why unproductive and ineffective reading behaviors develop. The most important reason for your lack of fluency when reading a engineering text probably relates to lack of prior knowledge and experience for understanding the concepts in the text. Since you did not possess the prior knowledge necessary for comprehension, you may have concentrated on word recognition to the exclusion of meaning. You may have read the text, but been unable to talk about it. When there is not much success built into the reading experience with a difficult text, you may experience a fear or concern that you will not be able to read the material. Because there was no reason, other than demonstration, for you to read an engineering text, you probably did not try very hard to finish reading it.

Most of children's difficulties in reading are not that different from what you experience when you are faced with the rare moment of ineffective reading. (Since you are an efficient reader, it doesn't happen too often.) When children are unable to use the three language cue systems (see chap. 1) in concert, they exhibit difficulty with reading. Usually, this breakdown is recognizable. They are unable to predict, their reading is slow, and they cannot identify words. They stumble over words, produce long pauses during their reading, and may even show physical discomfort. Another type of ineffective reading results when readers exhibit fluent oral reading behaviors but have no idea what they have read. Often, these readers have learned how to sound out words correctly and they are careful to get every word right. But they have a difficult time recalling or retelling what they have read. These *word callers* may have defined reading as identifying one word at a time (Smith, 1988) and this belief has focused their attention on one particular language system, such as graphophonics.

Another ineffective reading behavior associated with word calling is when readers attempt to read material for which they possess no prior knowledge or proper schema. They appear to be reading fluently, but there are several behaviors that indicate that comprehension is not occurring. For example, the word caller may produce miscues that are semantically unacceptable and when one is listening to their oral reading, it is clear that they have a difficult time following the text.

A third type of ineffective reading shows up in readers who may be fluent and can gain meaning from text, but simply are not motivated to read. This reader may resist reading during free time and rebel or act bored when a teacher encourages reading. They are nonreaders, not because of lack of ability, but because of choice. Motivating these children to read can be most challenging.

Often, these reading difficulties may overlap, making it difficult to know which problem to attack. For example, the child who cannot gain meaning from print may respond by acting unmotivated to read. Sometimes children may respond with one of these behaviors in one situation and show no evidence of a problem in another situation. If there are two or more children in one classroom experiencing a great deal of difficulty with reading, each may have a different combination of problems.

Reasons

Reading is much too complex a process to allow identification of one underlying cause that explains why some children struggle to learn how to read. It is probably more realistic to believe that reading problems are stimulated by a combination of factors, and in each case reading difficulties in school owe to slightly different reasons. Some traditionally cited causes for poor reading achievement usually include:

Physical Problems
While there may be some physical problems such as poor eyesight or hearing, or speech problems that pose difficulties in learning to read, these problems usually can be overcome. Allergies or childhood illness temporarily may affect children's abilities to progress in reading. Health problems that affect reading and other school learning situations are attended to by various health professionals in the schools. Some physical problems may not have easy solutions and may be serious threats to children's physical health. Often, poverty results in children not eating properly or receiving proper medical care. If children come to school hungry, sleepy, or scared of something in their home, they will have difficulty concentrating and learning at school.

Motivation
Children who are not motivated to read are called *reluctant readers*. Although not always the case, the reluctant or unmotivated reader may be a poorer reader than the rest of the children in the class. The unsuccessful reader gets caught in the cycle of not wanting to read because of lack of success and of being unsuccessful in reading because of the avoidance (Harris & Sipay, 1985). Motivation is one of the problems cited most often by teachers discussing reading instruction. Even children who learn to read may display lack of motivation in using books.

Emotional Problems
An overwhelming obstacle to instruction may occur when children have reading problems that have an emotional basis. In our very complicated world children sometimes must live in situations and deal with problems that are devastating. Many of these social and personal problems can cause students difficulty in their classwork, but reading achievement seems particularly susceptible to home and societal problems such as drugs, violence, divorce, poverty, and abuse. It is easy to understand why children would be distracted from reading if they were coping with any serious problems. It is important to remember that reading can provide children with an escape from some problems and with solutions to others.

Background and Language
The materials and instruction in the classroom should match the background and language of children. When there is a mismatch there is the potential for failing to teach a child to read. Children who have experiences different from what teachers expect sometimes have difficulty relating to reading material and classroom instruction. These

problems increase when children come to school speaking a language different from the language of instruction. Background and language should not cause reading problems, which often result from teachers' views of reading and instruction.

Instruction

Unfortunately, instruction itself may contribute to a child's reading problems. Because of the nature of classes and instruction, children who are succeeding at reading and the ones who are having difficulty may experience very different instructional patterns (Wuthrick, 1990). Children who are lagging behind in reading development usually receive less instruction in critical thinking skills and are more involved in working with isolated skills. Observation also reveals that children with reading problems have less time during instruction to be involved in actual reading, discussing, and responding to books, stories, and other reading material. When instruction focuses on isolated reading skills and avoids the development of critical reading strategies, children who are already behind may continue to lose ground.

Instruction also may contribute to reading difficulties when it does not appear meaningful or exciting to children. If reading instruction does not use materials or encourage activities that are meaningful to the child, motivation for involvement is less. Even college students who are efficient learners resist course work and reading that do not make sense, are not interesting, or have no direct relationship to their interests. A college student in this situation often justifies a lower grade in course by saying, "I just wasn't interested" or, "I saw no use for this course." If adults who have experienced some amount of academic success resist unmeaningful presentations, it is easy to understand that children would do the same.

Often, reading instruction does not reflect what children understand and accept about the world. Children may even be penalized for responding to school-related activities in ways that reflect their developing theories about language (Taylor, 1989). One reason that the Dick and Jane basals are not still used is because the life that they presented was so very far from what was understood about the world. This is very similar to the "Leave It to Beaver" phenomenon—the once-popular sitcom that presented a fairy tale version life. When materials and instruction do not reflect the lives or the language of children, it becomes very difficult to encourage learning.

Each child may have different reasons for not responding to reading instruction appropriately. Few problems have easy solutions, and most reading difficulties take a long time to overcome. Success with children who are experiencing reading problems depends greatly on how they view their successes and failures.

Historically, reading problems have been identified as originating with the children, and often children are viewed as having some deficit or block to learning how to read. Kenneth Goodman (1986) explains:

> *When pupils don't do well in a technologized reading and writing program, it's assumed there must be something wrong with them. . . . We blame their eyes, their brains, their central nervous systems, their diets, their noisy homes or their quiet ones, their neglectful parents or their over-anxious ones. (p. 55)*

Children are natural learners, and when provided with meaningful opportunities they will learn. This makes it difficult to continue to look at the problem of reading difficulty as originating with the child. Instruction needs to provide opportunities for learning to read. When so much is understood about how one learns to read, it is imperative that instruction begin reflecting what happens during the reading process.

Common Labels

School district requirements or state educational agencies often define methods of identification and provide labels for children with reading problems. Usually, children are identified as having reading problems if there is some difference between their ability and their performance or if they are assumed to be of average intelligence and they are performing one or two years below grade level in their work. Labeling and testing are used to place children in special programs and classes designed to help them overcome their reading problems. Some common labels associated with reading difficulty are listed in Box 10.1.

Helping children overcome their reading problems by placing them in special classes or programs results mainly from federal regulations (Allington & Broikou, 1988). Certain government funding is available only for children who meet certain requirements or have specific labels. Special classes and programs also are encouraged by teachers' views about reading instruction and how children learn to read. When it is assumed that poor readers are deficient or lack some skill or behavior, classes that offer compensatory instruction are justified. The belief that reading difficulty results from an absence of skills encourages intervention that is offered separately from regular reading instruction (Allington & Broikou, 1988) and requires children to leave the classroom. Often the special attention children receive is a result of how they are labeled. Instruction for learning disabled children may focus on different elements as compared to the instruction for children who are labeled remedial readers. For example, children who are labeled learning disabled may be taught reading strategies, time management techniques, and social skills, whereas those identified as remedial reading students may receive instruction only in reading strategies. The instruction will vary depending how children with reading problems are labeled. When programs are funded by the state or federal government they may require certain procedures or instructional activities to be implemented. Associating a child's reading problems with a particular label may suggest certain types of instructional procedures.

None of the labels associated with reading problems and failures has a universally agreed-upon definition (McGill-Franzen, 1989). When a parent, administrator, teacher, trainer, or any other individual uses a common term to refer to reading problems, it is wise to request a definition. Be sure to understand how an individual is defining the term before discussing classroom procedures for addressing the reading problem.

It is curious that none of the labels (see Box 10.1) refers to actual reading behaviors. After a child is labeled, a teacher needs to monitor behavior while reading a variety of materials and in many situations to determine how to help the child progress.

Sometimes the labels themselves are as detrimental as any difficulties the children face. It does not take long for children to realize that they are being treated differently.

─── **BOX 10-1** ──────────────────────────────────────

Common Labels Associated With Reading Difficulty

Learning Disabilities

Learning disabilities applies to students who have learning problems for many different reasons. The origin of a learning disability may include general language difficulties, lack of motivation, inappropriate instructional situations, or home environment. There is a history of establishing the etiology of learning disabilities from brain damage or other physiological disorders. But most agree that a very small percentage of reading problems result from brain damage or any other neurological dysfunction.

Dyslexia

Dyslexia has come to mean just about anything to do with reading difficulty and often is a confusing term that frightens parents and children and suggests some terrible scourge. If the term is used to discuss a child's reading behavior, it should be clear how the term is defined. Parents may use the term as defined in popular reading materials and principals may use the term as defined by a state agency or a local school district. The term may have different meanings with the two uses.

Remedial Reading and Poor Readers

Most regular classroom teachers are responsible for dealing with less skilled readers who are reading below most of the children in their grade level (Rayner & Pollatsek, 1989). Their IQ scores generally indicate that they should be reading better than they are, and it is difficult to separate these children from those who are identified as learning disabled. It may be that the only reason these readers have not been identified as learning disabled is the lack of referral to special agencies dealing with the learning disabled. Some schools may describe programs for children identified as remedial or poor readers as basic, developmental, or resource classes.

Disadvantaged

This term often is used to refer to children who are from low income homes and may have different language or cultural backgrounds than the schools expect. Often, it is the mismatch of backgrounds and not the fact the child is from a low income home or different cultural background that results in lower test scores and reading achievement. There is no doubt that conditions associated with low income may contribute to many educational and societal problems. Educators are now using the term *underclass* (Aaron et al., 1990) to describe children growing up in poverty without some basic necessities of life. Children who do not have the basic necessities of life may have some disadvantages, but this does not mean that they cannot learn to read.

Continued

BOX 10-1 *Continued*

At Risk

This is a generic term that has a connotation similar to disadvantaged and underclass. Children who are labeled *at risk* may be at risk of failing in reading. Often children are identified as at risk very early, perhaps as young as three or four, so that they can be provided with experiences designed to encourage reading achievement in school. There has been a great deal of federal and state funding to provide instruction for children who are at risk. One of the most successful federal programs, Head Start, is an example of a program designed to help the at risk child.

Mentally Retarded

Students who possess below average intellectual ability usually are placed in special classes for reading. Regular classroom teachers are not responsible for most of a mentally retarded child's instruction, although the child may be in a regular classroom during some part of the school day. If teachers do have mentally retarded children who are mainstreamed or spend some time in a regular classroom during their school day, they need to plan appropriate activities for the children.

Behaviorally or Emotionally Disordered

A student whose behavior results in socially unacceptable patterns may possess average or superior intelligence or could be learning disabled or mentally retarded. Some reading problems could result from emotional problems (Manzo, 1987) that are manifested in such behaviors as depression, unhappiness, and withdrawal. These problems might derive from home situations, school failure, or psychological or neurological disorders. Reading problems themselves might cause behavioral or emotional problems. Sometimes children who repeatedly fail in school develop emotional problems as a result.

They often think they are "dumb" because they receive special attention or must go to special classes. One of the most demanding tasks a teacher has is to deal with children's negative attitudes about their own performances.

Revaluing

Children who have reading difficulties usually believe they cannot possibly learn to read. Some of them carry several labels, have taken numerous tests, have worked with numerous teachers, realize their parents are upset, and still find that reading is an overwhelming task. It is not difficult to understand why they believe that something is wrong with them if they can't read. Every time they attempt a text and fail, it only reinforces the idea that they will never be readers.

The important thing to remember when dealing with children who have trouble reading is that they do have strengths and there are things they can accomplish with written language (Goodman, 1986). These children are often the last to recognize that they are successful at some aspects of language and may need to develop self-confidence about their skills. Goodman (1986) describes the process of building self-concept in troubled readers as *revaluing*. He emphasizes that the first thing a teacher must do when working with children who are having reading problems is to convince them that they *can* learn to read. Prior experiences may have convinced them otherwise since they usually have been told in various ways that they are failing. They often view themselves as unable to learn how to read. A teacher also must provide these children with meaningful activities that develop reading and writing strategies. It is extremely important for children who have reading problems to see the need for participating in reading and writing. Children who read without much trouble are able to establish their own reasons why reading is meaningful, but children who have problems may wonder why in the world they need to work so hard to accomplish such a difficult task.

Guiding Children with Difficulties

The development of instruction for students who may have different reading patterns is not different from good instruction for any reader. However, several assumptions can be made about children who are experiencing difficulties:

No Single Cause Can Be Identified as Contributing to Reading Difficulties
Many factors contribute to children's reading patterns, and different children have different combinations of patterns and approaches to reading. No generalizations can take care of all the difficulties associated with reading development. Each child deserves more than a generalization. Effective instruction for each child reflects the individuality of the child.

Children Experiencing Difficulty with Reading
May Need to Be Convinced They Can Read
Children are the first to know when they are not progressing satisfactorily in reading. They quickly learn to believe that they cannot read. One of the first jobs of the teacher may be to convince the child that reading is a learnable skill. Showing a child she or he can read may involve proving to them that their contributions and attempts are valuable. Revaluing (Goodman, 1986) is an important aspect of learning for a child who is experiencing difficulties.

A Plan for Guiding the Reader Who Is Experiencing Difficulty
Should Be Based on How the Student Uses Print
Although a teacher may be required by school policy to test a child, the best way to identify what the child can do is to watch the child reading. What children do suggests methods of improving reading behavior and becomes the foundation for helping a child who has reading difficulties.

Reading and Writing Breed Success for Children
Who Are Experiencing Reading Difficulties

It is most important that children who are experiencing difficulty with reading continue to read and write. More than any other children, they need to see real reading and writing. It is through this exposure that their knowledge of print increases and they become able to better use that knowledge to become efficient readers and writers.

Providing Instruction

Teachers who know their children well and observe classroom behavior systematically recognize ineffective reading behavior early. When teachers realize that a child's reading strategies are not developing as they should, they can use various strategies to identify what approaches and materials might encourage the child. The same tools that provide feedback for all readers also help teachers pinpoint potential roadblocks to reading development and identify effective instruction for children who may need special attention. Each of the monitoring techniques discussed in chapter 9 can provide insights to the child's reading difficulty (see Box 10.2).

Once a teacher can describe a child's reading behaviors, instruction and guidance must be provided to help the child become an efficient reader. Instruction must reflect meaningful and important reading opportunities. "Children who find it hard to make sense of reading need more meaningful reading, not less," Smith writes (1985, p. 148). Often, children who do not learn to read easily are required to participate in experiences that do not resemble reading. They may be required to work with computer programs, work sheets, or learn sight words without the help of context. Reading material that is very hard is another instructional impediment for children who are having difficulty. Readers with problems almost always are required to read texts that are very hard for them, while readers who are progressing satisfactorily read materials that are relatively easy. Children must observe and participate in demonstrations that show that reading is not an impossible task. "Children will fail to learn to read who do not want to read, who cannot make sense of it, or may even learn to approach reading in ways that will have the effect of always making it difficult or impossible," according to Smith (1985, p. 9).

What to do after describing reading behavior is still another part of the puzzle. Once children's reading behaviors are described, several alternatives and attempts should be available to provide successful reading opportunities for children. Effective reading opportunities must include integration of the language processes, and activities should include reading, writing, (Gaskins, 1988) and discussion (see Box 10.3). All children, particularly those who are experiencing difficulties, need to spend a great deal of time reading books and stories at levels at which they can succeed. It is important that teachers find material to use in reading instruction that allows each child to read. Children also should also spend a great deal of time writing. Writing supports the reading process and provides children with the opportunity to learn more about language. Finally, all children, regardless of their reading abilities, should have opportunities to discuss and interact with others about the material they are reading and the reading process itself.

BOX 10-2

Evaluation Methods and What They Identify

Methods	*Results*
Checklists	Identify and describe a specific strategy or summarize what children do when they read. Helps a teacher note developmental progress if checklists are completed several times each year.
Anecdotal records	Identify what children do as they read. print. Useful for observing behavior during independent reading. Good for gaining information about children who do not enjoy reading.
Interviews and Interest Inventories	Allow children to express feelings about reading and what they might enjoy reading. Used to identify situations in which children feel successful. Good for gaining information about children who are not motivated to read.
Conferences	Allow the teacher to find out what children are reading, check on comprehension abilities, encourage and motivate reading behaviors.
Self-evaluation	Allows children to express their feelings about reading. Provides information about children's self-concepts and what they feel that they can do. Describes behaviors of children who lack motivation to read.

Continued

BOX 10-2 *Continued*

Methods	*Results*
Reading Portfolios	Present a complete overview of children's reading behavior. Contain a variety of responses to literature and representation of behaviors.
Cloze	Provides information about children's ability to read a particular text, comprehension capabilities, and ability to use graphophonics and syntax. Instructional cloze can provide information about the child's understanding of the reading process. Helps identify children who are not using all language systems in concert.
Informal Reading Inventory	Provides a formal measure of reading levels usually associated with basal readers. Also produces a comprehension score and can provide awareness of the type of miscues produced during reading.
Miscue Analysis	Provides a measure of what percentage of miscues in children's reading interferes with comprehension. Demonstrates children's ability to retell a story. Helps a teacher identify whether children are focusing on one language system to the exclusion of another. Can help describe behaviors of word callers, children who have difficulty comprehending, and children who may use one language system to the exclusion of another.
Standardized Test	Provides a teacher with information on whether children focus on isolated parts of the reading process. Also provides information about how well a child can take a test.

—— **BOX 10-3** ——————————————————————————

Suggested Activities for Helping Children with Specific Reading Problems

Reading Behaviors	*Activities*
No Motivation	Reading aloud, buddy reading, sustained silent reading, discussion, drama, introducing new books, reading a variety of texts (including exposition), reading parts of books
Word Calling or Inability to Comprehend	Reading aloud, reciprocal teaching, retelling, interaction, instructional cloze, supportive reading, ReQuest, writing
Lack of Prior Experience	Discussion, reading other material, concept development, films, K–W–L, vocabulary story structures, mapping, reading aloud, language experience, caption writing, supportive reading
Not Using All Language Systems	
Semantics	Same as lack of comprehension
Syntax	Instructional cloze, reading aloud, language experience
Graphophonics	Instructional cloze, voice pointing, reading aloud, manipulating texts, writing

*All activities are discussed in this book.

——————————————————————————————————————

Planning Procedures

Instruction that motivates children, allows them to make sense of the reading, and helps them find out what effective readers do is important for all readers, but especially for those who are having difficulty with written language. There are several steps that must be completed in order to provide successful experiences:

1. Use observations, checklists, and other evaluation procedures (Rhodes & Dudley-Marling, 1988) to identify and describe what a reader does. Identify situations in which the reader is fluent and those in which the reader is unsuccessful. Many types of information contribute to a complete description of reading behaviors.

2. Plan instruction. Plans include those interactions with text that produce efficient reading. Reading and writing activities repeatedly demonstrate the process of efficient reading. Use materials that encourage success in reading and motivate the student to read.

3. Develop steps that can be taken to encourage the student's literacy development (Rhodes & Dudley-Marling, 1988). The plan considers the language assumptions for learning to read and includes authentic reading, writing, speaking, and listening to and about written language.

Instructional plans for readers experiencing difficulties consist of strategies outlined in the chapters on emerging reading, comprehension, decoding, vocabulary, and reading to learn specific content. When evaluations and descriptions of readers reveal that they are not able to use decoding strategies to predict, activities such as those suggested in the chapter on decoding become a focus for instruction. If children are word callers and do not comprehend what they are reading, instruction should focus on the type of activities suggested in the chapter on comprehension. If older children do not seem to have experience or interest in reading, activities such as those suggested in the chapter on emerging reading should be adapted so they are appropriate for older readers. (Some of those adaptions are suggested later in this chapter.)

Evaluating and providing guidance to help students who are having reading problems go hand-in-hand. Teachers continue to evaluate so that they can determine whether instructional plans are guiding the reader to success. Careful record-keeping and evaluation are a very important aspects.

Before, During, and After Reading

Some important factors must be considered when planning for readers who need extra guidance:

Before Reading
To provide reading experiences that are successful, it is most important to be sure that children with reading difficulties possess the background for reading the material. The more background a reader possesses, the more chance he or she will have to understand the text (Rhodes & Dudley-Marling, 1988). Often, a reader must learn how to activate the prior knowledge before reading the text. Students can be helped to develop background and activate what they know if they are shown how to preview the topic, understand the vocabulary, and determine the structure. Students with reading difficulties may need more concrete activities, such as seeing the material presented in films, or TV shows, or reading additional material on the topic first.

During Reading

Readers who are experiencing difficulties require a great deal of support while they read. The support is much more than telling them words or helping them through text. Discussions establish meanings, offer opportunities to share responses, and encourage questions so that the varied reading processes of all who read the text can be observed. Activities that focus on the reading process, the importance of prior experience, and an understanding of text structure are necessary parts of plans for those readers experiencing difficulties.

After Reading

Sharing and extending comprehension is a most important feature of guiding children with reading difficulties. Many activities appropriate for extending and sharing reading material resemble the enrichment activities traditionally presented in basal lessons. These opportunities are a necessity for children who are experiencing difficulties and are central for readers of all abilities (Rhodes & Dudley-Marling, 1988). These activities include oral and written sharing, answering questions, drama, art, and music.

The before, during, and after reading activities are imperative (see Box 10.4) for a child with reading problems. It is most important that instruction explicitly guide the child through each part of the process.

Materials

Literature offers a wealth of reading material appropriate for readers of all skills and abilities. Most of the material that will be successful with children who need to focus on efficient reading strategies are the same materials discussed extensively in previous chapters. Some materials are especially appropriate for providing meaningful and successful reading experiences for children who have problems in reading. Predictable and big books, picture books, poetry, short stories, nonfiction, and language experience provide built-in success for children.

Predictable Material

Books that have a good match between text and pictures, include rhythmical, repetitive, or cumulative patterns, use familiar sequences, and relate familiar concepts with familiar language (Rhodes & Dudley-Marling, 1988) provide a great deal of support for the reading process. Predictable books have been identified as effective in developing fluency and encouraging the development of word recognition strategies with troubled readers (Bridge, 1986). They are discussed in chapters 2 and 5.

Predictable picture books are widely accepted as appropriate reading material for children who are just beginning to read. While these books are charming and delightful for young children, the material for older readers should reflect different interests and language as well as provide them with a wide range of reading matter (Atwell, 1985). There are books that are predictable and appropriate for older readers. The advantage of

---

BOX 10-4

Before, During and After Activities Needed by Readers Experiencing Difficulties

Before Reading

Concept development, Vocabulary development, Text structure awareness, Concrete experiences, Alternate information sources, Related readings, Brainstorming, Visualization, Mapping, K–W–L, Learning logs, Journal writing, Written conversations

During Reading

Oral and silent reading, Discussion during reading, Teacher-directed strategies, Development of text knowledge, Feedback, Choral reading, Echo reading, Shared reading, Thinking aloud, DRTA, Cloze, RTS, K–W–L, SQ3R, Learning logs, Journal writing

After Reading

Sharing and extending text, Oral and written sharing, Art, Answering questions, Retelling, Drama, K–W–L, SQ3R, Journal writing, Learning logs, Readers' theater, Story maps and structures, Concept maps

---

using these books during instruction is that they are good for children of all reading abilities.

Books About Daily Life

Most realistic fiction for children mirrors their lives (Atwell, 1985). Judy Blume has been particularly successful at attracting young readers for many years. Her characters deal with such everyday problems as growing up, dealing with pesky siblings, and wishing for freckles. Many children can appreciate William Hatcher's consternation when his brother Fudge eats a pet turtle in *Tales of a Fourth Grade Nothing* (1972) or can identify with the boy who wanted freckles so badly that he buys a "freckle recipe" that makes him ill in *Freckle Juice* (Blume, 1971). The main characters are very predictable because readers can relate to the feelings and the situations that initiate the action. Other authors, such as Barte DeClements (*Nothing's Fair in Fifth Grade* (1981) and others) and Beverly Cleary (*Dear Mr. Henshaw,* 1983) provide worlds not very different from the worlds of children who read their books. Upper grade children will enjoy much of the young adult literature by such authors as S.E. Hinton, Richard Peck, and Paula Danzinger that discusses the pressures and concerns of becoming a teenager.

Books in Series

Stories in series are predictable and valuable materials for children to read (Atwell, 1985). Children who are having difficulty reading can be encouraged to become familiar with a series in which they are able to predict characters' actions, story format, and plot development. There is a multitude of series that deal with contemporary life. Though not always recognized as high quality but certainly popular with young readers are the Nancy Drew and Hardy Boys mysteries. A popular current series is Anne Martin's Baby Sitters Series. There are several books in each of these series. Children can be encouraged to predict because of their familiarity with these popular books. More sophisticated series, such as the science fiction trilogy of L'Engle, offer support with familiar characters and a topic that soon becomes familiar.

Encyclopedia Brown, Boy Detective (Sobol, 1963), *Choose Your Own Adventure,* and *Minute Mysteries* are guessing books with predictable formats. *Encyclopedia Brown* and *Minute Mysteries* explain an unlawful event or mystery, and the reader must predict "whodunit" or figure out how the crime was committed. After guessing outcomes or culprits, predictions can be checked at the ends of the books. The *Choose Your Own Adventure* books require children to make predictions about plot development by making decisions about the characters' subsequent actions. The story has different outcomes based on the decisions the reader makes. Prediction strategies are encouraged and demanded as children make their way through these books.

Picture Books

Picture books are used for enjoyment and instruction at the primary level, but middle school teachers and students rarely rely on them for reading material. Recent picture books are written for all ages, making them appropriate for use in middle school classrooms. Content, themes, and subjects of selected picture books provide legitimate sources of high quality reading material for adolescents. Describing the current perspective on picture books, Huck, Hepler & Hickman (1987) write:

> *Picture books, then, are for all children . . . The phenomenal growth of beautiful picture books for children of all ages is an outstanding accomplishment of the past fifty years of publishing . . . Picture books are also for adults, who find them potentially satisfying art and literature. (p. 240)*

Instructional activities that use picture books are suitable for middle school readers of all abilities, but are especially beneficial for those experiencing reading difficulties. The interaction of text and pictures and the role that pictures share in story development provide many opportunities for developing reading and language strategies. There are several reasons why picture books are especially suitable for reading instruction with middle school readers who have difficulty.

The motivation provided by the pictures is one positive feature they contribute to effective instruction of problem readers. The beauty and intricacy of the fine artwork lure unmotivated middle school readers. The diversity of media, perspectives, techniques, and technologies in recently published picture books is an enticement to read the text.

Well-written picture books present thought-provoking, entertaining ideas with concise text. Imaginative and literary language in a rapidly developing story is presented in a format that struggling readers are able to read and discuss in one session. Students who usually feel bewildered by long passages welcome the short narratives of the picture book format.

In addition, comprehension is enhanced when meaning is conveyed by pictures and texts. Pictures and text provide context and background that result in a more predictable text. Predictability increases when pictures provide clues to enable the reader to anticipate more easily what the author is trying to convey. When problem readers use highly predictable material, they can rely on their beginning reading strategies and focus their efforts on comprehension (Rhodes & Dudley-Marling, 1988).

Effective picture book instruction emphasizes the motivation of pictures, shorter length, and enhanced predictability. Exciting classroom opportunities emerge when the unique literary contributions of picture books are combined with instruction for middle school readers with problems.

Short Stories

Short stories for children present high quality literature in shorter format. Short stories may not seem as overwhelming to readers who are experiencing difficulties with other texts. Short stories are available from several different sources. Some short stories may appear in picture books. For example, most of Yorinks and Eigelski's picture book texts are short stories. In fact, Yorinks writes the text before Eigelski illustrates. Yorinks and Eigelski are among the picture book authors and illustrators who offer humor, well-developed vocabulary, and surprising turns. One of their more recent books, *Bravo, Minsky* (Yorinks, 1988), is an example of the drollery and absurdity that upper grade children enjoy.

Other "short" stories that would be successful with upper grade children include *Freckle Juice* (Blume, 1971) and *Dear Mr. Henshaw* (Cleary, 1983). Both involve high quality reading material that is representative of some of the longer texts written for older children. However, the chapters are one to two pages long and each book has fewer than one hundred pages and presents material that appeals to middle school readers. Other examples of shorter texts include *The Whipping Boy* (Fleischman, 1986), *Sarah, Plain and Tall* (MacLachlan, 1985), and *Number the Stars* (Lowry, 1989), all Newbery Medal winners. An additional advantage of using these books is that children who are successful at reading also enjoy and read the books, providing a great deal of opportunity for discussion among students of all abilities.

Another example of excellent reading material for middle school children who are experiencing difficulty are traditional short stories. Many well-known authors write short, concise stories that are excellent for children who read slowly or who dread reading. *Pricilla and the Wimps* by Richard Peck (1984) provides a young adult story in two-and-a-half pages. Adults and middle school children alike cannot escape the irony and shock of how the bad guy gets what he deserves in this well-written short story. This is just one good example of the plethora of excellent collections of short stories appropriate for upper grade readers.

Nonfiction

One problem experienced by problem readers when reading exposition is their lack of prior knowledge and experience. A way to provide students with the opportunities for developing background on topics is through the profusion of nonfiction available on almost any topic. All students benefit from being read to and reading from multiple texts on the same subject. Nonfiction can support subject area reading or the reading of novels. For example, if the class were reading *Park's Quest* (Paterson, 1988), a novel about a young boy who wanted to know more about his father who was killed in Vietnam, additional literature can be assembled on Vietnam. In this instance, the recent picture book by Eve Bunting, *The Wall* (1990), and other nonfiction accounts of the Vietnam war provide opportunities for discussion and additional reading that result in developing the reader's background. The additional knowledge makes it easier to comprehend the concepts in *Park's Quest*.

Poetry

Poetry offers brevity, depth of ideas, and predictability of language in one selection. The main advantage of poetry is that many great poems are short. The language and vocabulary are used creatively and imaginatively, but with text that may seem quite manageable to a child of any reading ability. The poems are easily reread several times in one sitting and allow children to become very familiar with the text. Poems offer much to think about in a very few words and can be the basis of involved discussions. The following poem (Rosetti, 1989) is simple and short, but poses discussion topics that run the gamut from environmental issues to kindness to humanity.

> HURT NO LIVING THING
> Hurt no living thing;
> Ladybird, nor butterfly,
> Nor moth with dusty wing,
> Not cricket chirping cheerily,
> Nor grasshopper so light of leap,
> Nor dancing gnat, nor beetle fat,
> Nor harmless worms that creep.

Most poetry uses language rhythmically or lyrically, which contributes to its predictability. Rhyme, repeated phrases, and expected rhythms provide clues to reading poetry.

Successful reading opportunities are provided by carefully selecting and using a variety of material. Some basal reading selections provide excellent resources for material. Effective basals can include well-written short stories, favorite poems, and other important literature. Teachers should survey available basals and find material that is representative of high quality literature and can provide successful reading experiences for all children.

Media and Technology

Media and technology contribute to children's reading in several ways. The videos of good books and stories motivate children to read the texts or provide a method for summarizing or clarifying ideas. Videos used before reading provide information that allow prediction during reading. If readers understand the story before attempting to read the text, it simplifies the process. The beginning of a video can tease children into reading the remainder of a book. Critical reading activities can be based on comparison of written text and visual interpretation. Videos used after reading encourage discussion and comparison of understandings and interpretations of two modes of story telling. The inevitable omissions and modifications of a video presentation can be described, compared, and evaluated with the written story.

A great deal of reading must occur to operate and respond to some computer programs, so computers should be considered a source of printed text that children are motivated to read. In addition, there are several computer programs based on literature. Sometimes children will work with computer text when they won't read the book.

Specific Strategies

Children with reading problems often are taught differently than children without problems. They may be moved to other classrooms or their reading instruction may be decidedly different than that of the more successful readers. As long as poor readers are taught differently, they will remain in special programs and not learn to read well (Allington, 1983; Allington & Broikou, 1988; Koenke, 1988). Allington (1983) believes that poor readers should not be pulled out of the classroom for instruction and encourages teachers to use the same methods to instruct good and poor readers. He suggests that poor readers should spend more time involved in reading instruction, focus on silent reading, read material that invites success, participate in a great deal of independent reading, and learn to self-correct their reading. One welcome trend of the 1990s is providing all children with high quality reading instruction, regardless of level of development or abilities.

Most of the strategies effective with children who need a great deal of support and success with reading are the same activities that benefit any children. The advantage to planning for the participation of all children in common activities is the increased potential for writing and reading with classmates and sharing common material for discussion. Common instructional activities decrease the potential for children to be labeled "dummies." There may be times when children experiencing difficulties may have to repeat a strategy more often, more slowly, or with different materials, but the strategies that involve children in authentic reading and writing contribute to all children's reading abilities.

Another guideline for helping children who are experiencing difficulties is to allow them to witness efficient reading and writing in many different situations and contexts. Not only must they have the processes demonstrated to them, they must be able to identify what efficient strategies look like and how they should go about reading. There are several activities that demonstrate real reading and writing:

Reading Aloud

No one argues the value of allowing time for the teacher or others to read aloud to children who are experiencing reading difficulty. While this activity is valuable for all students, it seems especially important for children who are experiencing problems. There several benefits from sharing good books through oral reading. The most obvious gain is relaxation and enjoyment for all involved. Other benefits include demonstration of fluent reading, identification of reading as an important activity, and introduction to different types of literature.

Children experiencing difficulty with reading need many opportunities to hear stories read aloud. Stories can be recorded or purchased on audio tapes and placed in listening centers so that children can listen to the stories unattended. Parent volunteers provide extra oral reading opportunities to small groups or individual children. Older or more capable readers can be used as an oral readers. Each occasion that children have to interact with exciting texts brings them that much closer to becoming efficient readers.

Supportive Reading

Poor readers often need opportunities to develop fluency or the ability to predict and process information quickly enough so that meaning is not lost. They may not understand how it feels to read without stumbling over words. One way to encourage fluency and ultimately comprehension is to plan supportive reading activities. Supportive reading techniques provide help for beginning or troubled readers in several ways (Buchanan, 1980):

1. Materials used for supportive reading are purposeful and meaningful, encourage predictions, and motivate children to read.

2. Materials used for supportive reading are predictable materials that improve chances for reading success. Rhyme, repetition, and familiar concepts offer much support to readers who are experiencing difficulties.

3. Repeated readings provide opportunities to become familiar with vocabulary, increase comprehension, and gain confidence in reading behavior.

4. Group reading techniques provide reading opportunity without the risk of failure. When two students or groups of children read together, there is support and help with words and meaning. No child ever feels under pressure to perform without support.

Supportive reading is most obviously exemplified by oral reading activities such as choral reading, but silent reading can be supportive when the first two conditions are met. Supportive reading activities should be part of instruction for troubled readers. The most supportive reading is accomplished when all four conditions are met during oral reading. The following activities demonstrate to children what is involved in fluent reading:

Shared Reading
Shared reading was described as a beginning reading instructional technique in chapter 5, but can be adapted for older children with reading problems. In shared reading, text is read aloud and children follow in their own copies of the text. In upper grades, class sets of short stories, shorter books (both fiction and nonfiction) or young adult novels

Reading aloud provides opportunities for all ability levels to be familiar with a common text.

can be passed out to all children in the class. They are asked to follow as the teacher reads the text aloud. The teacher might stop occasionally to discuss passages or stop randomly to ask a student to read the next sentence. Requiring students to keep track of the reading and follow the print meets the same objective as using a pointer to direct young children's attention to text in a big book. During discussion, parts of the text are reread to make a point or share specific information.

Oral Rereading
Teachers must plan opportunities for children with reading problems to reread texts they already have read. This provides practice and contributes to the development of fluency. Text can be reread in choral reading or readers' theater.

Paired Reading (Buddy Reading)
Students are supported in their reading efforts when two people are reading the same text aloud. The student may be teamed with the teacher or with another student; both read the text aloud. The pair should read the text smoothly and fluently without interruptions (Rhodes & Dudley-Marling, 1988). This technique also could be used by encouraging a student to read with a tape recorder.

Echo Reading

Echo reading is another instructional technique to increase the reading fluency of students who have difficulty. The material for this procedure should be predictable or material with which the student has some familiarity. Poetry would be acceptable. At least two readers participate. One reader reads a line or page of the material and the second immediately repeats it. This procedure is expressly for the student who is having difficulty with reading and should not be forced on students who do not need it.

Choral Reading

When more than one person reads aloud, a great deal of support is offered by all the readers involved. Choral reading is much like singing and children should be encouraged to use their voices in different ways to produce multiple effects. Poems usually are used for choral reading. The Newbery Medal winner *Joyful Noise: Poems for Two Voices* (P. Fleischmann, 1988) is an excellent example of the fine literature available for choral reading. Fleischman's collection encourages creative choral readings that mimic the drone of insects. He writes in the forward:

> *The following poems were written to be read aloud by two readers at once, one taking the left-hand part, the other taking the right-hand part. The poems should be read from top to bottom, the two parts meshing as in a musical duet. When both readers have lines at the same horizontal level, those lines are to be spoken simultaneously. (1988; p. iii)*

Choral reading does not have to be limited to poetry. Other narrative selections such as short stories, nonsense stories, or fables also may work well for unison readings. Short, simple, imaginative selections work the best.

Choral reading becomes much more effective if children discuss the selection and make decisions about how they should be presented. Preparation in choral reading can become a good lesson in comprehension (Buchanan, 1980) as children clarify interpretations and moods when discussing how many voices should read, effective volume, or sound effects.

Readers' Theater

Any story or portion of a story that has a lot of dialogue can be adapted to a readers' theater. A story becomes readers' theater when the oral reading is accompanied by dramatic actions or reading. Students are assigned to read the dialogue of specific characters, and a narrator is selected to read the descriptive parts of the story. The story is practiced to perfect the dramatic reading and interpretation of the story. There is always support from the text since the parts are not memorized and the dialogue is dramatized through reading. Although commercial scripts are available, teachers' and students' productions of scripts offer opportunities for writing, discussion, and rereading (see Box 10.5).

Language Experience

Language experience is another beginning reading instructional activity that adapts well to older children who might be experiencing difficulty. When children produce written text mirroring their own experiences and language, reading is as supportive as it can be. Any number of methods can be used to provide a scribe for the stories of older children. Children can take turns dictating to each other, the teacher can be a scribe, or a computer can be used.

Language experience can be used to focus on vocabulary and decoding. Text that children have dictated can be rewritten to leave out beginning sounds or certain vocabulary words as suggested in the emerging reader strategies. This instructional cloze procedure can be used to focus attention on certain aspects of the text with the support of contextual clues.

Language experience can be used in response to subject area or other expository texts for older children. After subject area discussions or reading, readers who are experiencing difficulty can dictate what they know about the topic to the teacher or another student. The dictated text can be collected for use as a reference for others in the class. The retelling contributes to comprehension, provides opportunities to use the vocabulary, and furnishes exposition for rereading at a later date.

Cross-Age Reading

Allowing older readers to read to young children is effective in helping older children become better readers (Labbo & Teale, 1990). This technique is used in upper grades by preparing for the storybook sharing. Books are selected, read repeatedly, and introductions can be planned by the teacher and the older children. The teacher can explain activities that would be successful with younger children such as prediction, discussion, and questioning. The older children can be encouraged to share their books in small groups to practice for reading to younger children. The older children visit the younger children's classrooms and read the book aloud. They may read to small groups of young children or older children. Labbo and Teale (1990) suggest a debriefing afterward to discuss what the older children learned.

Metacognition

Children who are successful readers know a lot about the reading process and what good readers should do. Children who are experiencing difficulties may not possess this knowledge. In other words, poor readers do not understand how to control their reading, or understand what strategies are needed for dealing with written language. Metacognitive insights, knowing what you know and when to use it, usually are develop as children read and write. Children who avoid reading and writing do not have opportunities to learn more about the reading process and themselves as readers. Metacognition can be learned. Teachers can help develop metacognitive awareness by providing students with opportunities to focus on strategies. Certain techniques increase metacognitive aware-

───── **BOX 10-5** ──────────────────────────────────

Steps for Readers' Theater

Select a poem, narrative, or expository text that can be adapted for a script. The following steps guide the class:

1. Read the selected text to the class.
2. Text is rewritten to identify readers as in the following selection from *Sarah, Plain and Tall* (MacLachlan, 1985, p. 24).

Narrator: Together we picked flowers, paintbrush and clover and prairie violets. There were buds on the wild roses that climbed up the paddock fence.

Anna: The roses will bloom in early summer.

Narrator: Anna looked at Sarah to see if she knew that I was thinking that summer was when the wedding would be. Might be. Sarah and Papa's wedding.

Sarah: I've never seen this before. What is it called?

Anna: Bride's bonnet.

Sarah: We don't have this by the sea. We have seaside goldenrod and wild asters and woolly ragwort!

Caleb: (Whooping) Woolly ragwort!
Wooly ragwort all around
Woolly ragwort all around.
Woolly ragwort grows and grows.
Woolly ragwort in your nose.

Papa and Sarah: (Laugh very loud.)

Text can be prepared by individual class members or language experience style.

3. After text is prepared, copies are made.
4. The scripts are distributed to the class, and the children reread what they have written.
5. Parts are assigned.
6. Students underline or highlight their speaking parts and read their parts again.
7. Students must practice expressive oral reading so feelings, emotions, moods, and tones are created.
8. The readers stand or sit before an audience. They read their parts with expression and minimal physical gestures.
9. (Optional) When a reader is not speaking, he or she turns and faces away from the audience.
10. The script is practiced and performed for another class or audience.

ness for readers who are having difficulty controlling the reading process and can be beneficial for all ability levels:

1. Brainstorming after reading a text with important information and asking students to explain their reasons for selecting their contributions can develop an awareness of the information they found important (Wade & Reynolds, 1989).

2. Categorization activities can be designed to help students identify main ideas, important details, and interesting but unimportant details and may develop into discussion that helps children decide what types of information they should pay more attention to.

3. Strategy lessons are designed specifically for individual reading difficulties and can be planned only after sufficient evaluation. Strategy lessons' main objective is to allow readers opportunities to discuss what they did while reading.

An example of an instructional approach that encourages the development of metacognitive strategies is reciprocal teaching. RTS, discussed in chapter 6, was developed specifically for use with readers who were not achieving up to grade level. Teachers who have used the technique have had a great deal of success in improving the comprehension strategies of readers.

Programs for Reading Problems

Many commercial programs are available to help children with reading difficulties. Programs come and go and may claim terrific results with specific reading problems. Teachers and administrators need to thoroughly research each new program before using it. Programs should be judged on their theoretical merits and their foundations for instruction. Some programs may possess excellent features while others may not have any substantive foundations to guide the activities. The programs may have set plans, employ workbooks or computers, and have specialized reading material. Only after thorough research and review should children be subjected to these programs. Parents are particularly susceptible to commercial programs, and teachers may need to provide guidance in response to parental interest. It is always best to review the programs carefully before recommending or using them.

Reading Recovery

A program that originated in New Zealand, Reading Recovery, was designed as an early intervention program for young at risk children (Clay, 1990). It is a highly successful program that offers extra instruction in addition to daily classroom lessons. It is an intensive, short-term program in which each child receives thirty minutes a day of one-on-one tutoring. Teachers who use Reading Recovery receive a year of special training in procedures. Teachers trained in this approach are extremely cognizant of children's responses and may vary instruction based on the child's interests and attitudes.

One important aspect of this program is the philosophy that children requiring help with reading need to be pushed along. Children who are already behind in reading must make fast progress to catch up with their classmates (Clay, 1990). One-to-one teaching and a personalized program designed to focus on a reader's strengths are the basis of the acceleration. In addition, children write and read daily. Sounds of letters and vocabulary are introduced through reading and writing instead of activities that isolate reading strategies. Children make good use of their one-to-one time and complete activities that support their reading development.

Teachers and children work closely during Reading Recovery lessons. They are placed side by side, and read, write, and talk collaboratively. Reading Recovery lessons (Pinnell, Fried, & Estice, 1990) include:

Reading Familiar Stories
Each day the child rereads familiar stories. Some stories are selected by the teacher to meet specific instructional objectives and other stories are selected and read by the student. Rereading is viewed as very beneficial, providing children with successful experiences in written language.

Recording Text Reading
The teacher observes the child's reading and records the reading with a type of miscue analysis. The information provided to the teacher during the child's response contributes to instructional decisions. Teachers must complete the training before recording and evaluating the text reading as suggested by the approach. Training is conducted at one of the few Reading Recovery centers in our country or by a district teacher who has attended the training sessions.

Working with Letters
Children may be asked to form words from reading material using magnetic letters or to manipulate letters for other reasons. If children do not need experience working with letters and letter recognition, lesson time is not devoted to this activity.

Writing a Message or Story
Every day the child composes a message. The messages may grow longer as the child gains experience in writing. Once the child produces a message, the teacher rewrites it on a strip of paper and cuts it into pieces to allow the child to manipulate the letters.

Reading a New Story
New stories are not read at first. The child and the teacher may discuss and build background for future reading. After discussion and questions, the child reads the story with support from the teacher

This program requires a great deal of training for teachers to be efficient, but it does produce good results (Clay, 1990). One of the difficulties is the intensive one-on-one involvement of the teacher and the children. Classroom teachers simply do not have the resources to focus attention on one child for extended and regular time periods. However, aspects of the basic program should be considered for working with younger or older at risk children in classrooms. Such elements as repeating readings of familiar text, building background before introducing new texts, and requiring daily reading and writing are important considerations for any program designed to help children learn how to read. The principle of acceleration can be translated to the classroom by making sure that children who experience difficulty in reading always are involved in meaningful reading and writing.

Special Reading Teachers

Many schools have teachers who specialize in teaching children who are having difficulties in reading. Programs to help children with reading may be referred to as *pull out* programs. Children may qualify for special reading classes by scoring low on tests or being unsuccessful with reading activities in the regular classroom. They leave their regular classrooms to receive instruction from the special reading teacher. This instruction should supplement classroom activities and is most effective when classroom teachers and special reading teachers work together.

The use of pull out programs is being questioned by educators, but schools still rely on this method for dealing with children who have reading problems. Teachers must be prepared to say what they think about the value of children leaving their classrooms to go to other programs. There are some times when children can benefit greatly from the attention received in a special reading class and other times when they would be better off staying in the regular classroom.

Children should be placed in special reading classes if they can be helped by small group instruction not available in the classroom, such as Reading Recovery. Special attention and more small group work is a positive attribute of special reading programs, particularly if the additional efforts increase the time spent in actual reading. One of the greatest potentials of special reading classes is the additional time for involvement with the reading process (Koenke, 1988).

Separate planning and instruction without cooperation between the special reading teacher and the classroom teacher can result in a more fragmented exposure to reading instruction. It is possible the child could receive very different instruction in each of the situations, compounding existing reading problems. When children are labeled and placed in special programs, there should be coordinated efforts to ensure that the programs are complementary and supportive (Allington & Broikou, 1988). Special reading teachers and regular classroom teachers should cooperate in programs to provide the child with the experiences that ultimately will improve reading. If cooperative planning and coordination is not occurring, it probably is not worth the child's time to leave the classroom.

Writing

Writing contributes to the development of reading strategies, and there is some evidence that writing does strengthen reading ability. Therefore, it is extremely important for children who are experiencing reading difficulties to write. Often, children who have troubles with reading do not like to write, and special reading programs provide few opportunities to write anything longer than a paragraph (Rhodes & Dudley-Marling, 1988). These children should be given every opportunity to write regularly and produce extended texts.

Students need to write about topics of interest and those about which they know a great deal. Writing experiences will be considerably more successful if young authors have many ideas to write about. It is particularly important for children who are developing self-confidence with written language to have freedom to write without a great deal of criticism. Students should focus on the ideas they have to contribute and not the correct forms, spelling, grammar, and punctuation.

Journal writing is an excellent method for encouraging children to respond to what they are reading. Atwell (1987) uses journals as the foundation of her Readers' Workshop responses. Each child is provided with a notebook and after reading any text, she asks them to write informal letters to her explaining their reactions to the books. She responds in a letter, reacting to comments, directing future reading, and making suggestions.

Journals are usually informal and provide opportunities for children to write frequently about their reading. They become a place for children to control topic selection and experiment with ideas and understandings. Occasionally, children can read entries to the class and the ideas can be used to start classroom discussion and sharing.

There may be students who produce unreadable entries because their written language abilities are not well developed. Gaskins (1982) suggests that these children be encouraged to write their ideas and read their journal entries to the teacher, who then records the ideas with standard spelling. They can reread the material using the assisted reading procedure if necessary.

Written conversations are another activity that encourages children to write. Children can carry on conversations by dividing in pairs and discussing a topic or book on paper. The pairs pass the paper when ready for the other person's response. If children produce ''talk'' that their peers cannot read, they need oral language support.

Rhodes and Dudley-Marling (1988) suggest several instructional modifications to written conversation. The teacher can respond to written conversation of small groups of children. Older children can be paired with younger children to participate in written conversations using the model described in cross age tutoring. Conversations can be written on a word processor. All these activities encourage informal, frequent, and motivational writing that builds children's knowledge and confidence about written language.

Learning Differences

During reading instruction children's differences often become the focus of attention. This is a very detrimental approach when working with children of different cultures and languages. It is especially important to recognize and respect the strengths of these children and to provide opportunities for their backgrounds to contribute to successful learning.

Culture

The main factor to consider is the contribution of cultural differences to the reading problems. Cultural differences may affect reading achievement in two ways. One link between culture and reading is the match or mismatch of background of the child, the reading material, and interpretation of text. The second way that reading is affected by culture is the effect of teachers' attitudes about the culture. If teachers do not understand the effect of cultural differences on reading behavior or if they expect children of different cultures to perform differently, reading achievement will be influenced.

Procedures and approaches that reflect cultural backgrounds and learning styles can be used. For example, African-American and Hispanic children's learning can be improved when they work in structured, but informal environments that include working together (Gilbert & Gay, 1985). In addition, teachers should attempt to identify materials that are relevant to different cultures rather than using materials that exclude cultural differences.

When cultural differences contribute to reading problems, every effort should be made to keep children in regular classroom situations. Cultural differences should be addressed in regular reading instruction. These children should never feel that their dignity and worth are measured by a test score.

If a teacher believes that a child's test score was affected by differing backgrounds or cultures, different modes of evaluation should be used to monitor and evaluate reading development. Children of different cultures never should be placed in reading programs unless the teacher is positive that there aspects other than culture affecting their performances.

Language

Non-English-speaking students depend on the school's help to ease them into the mainstream of society. The best teaching allows students who come to our schools speaking different languages to become independent learners. If only isolated, basic skills are offered to these students, they will not improve their language and thinking (Strickland & Morrow, 1989).

Teachers often estimate bilingual children's capabilities according to the facility demonstrated in English (Wallace & Goodman, 1989). As a result, children are identified as having reading problems and often are pulled out of their classrooms to participate in activities in reading, bilingual, or English-as-a-second-language classrooms. The danger is that children may receive significantly different instruction (Allington, 1986) than the instruction they are receiving in their own classrooms. The most effective programs are those that modify the instruction of the regular classroom.

There are several instructional procedures to help children with different language backgrounds. These are the same procedures that should be used with any child who is learning the language:

1. Children who speak another language should be placed in language-rich environments. There should be a great deal of discussion, reading, and writing. Books and writing materials should be available.

2. They should be encouraged to interact with others who speak English. It can be scary to try to talk to those who do not speak the language you know. The environment should make it less threatening so that children begin speaking to others and learn about oral language through usage.

3. Foreign-speaking students benefit from a great deal of shared, supportive reading and peer tutoring. Children should have many opportunities to read stories together.

4. Teachers must provide activities that recognize cultural and language differences. Using materials that reflect the culture and focus on contributions of the language allows the child to take pride in bilingualism.

A large part of being successful with children of different cultures and languages owes to the teacher possessing the appropriate attitude toward the students. The teacher must respect and accept cultural and language differences and realize that these differences may produce a variety of responses to activities.

DISCUSSION AND ACTIVITIES

1. List all the causes of reading differences that you can think of. Share your list with others in your class. Decide which factors a teacher can modify and which factors are most difficult for a teacher to overcome. Begin discussing what can be done in the classroom to alleviate some of the factors that lead to particular reading problems.

2. Interview a teacher and ask her or him to describe the behaviors that children who are experiencing difficulties often exhibit. Role play some of the negative behaviors the teacher describes and allow several of your classmates to react as a teacher might.

3. List different events that would contribute to successful reading experiences in school. Try to rank them in an order that indicates those that are most necessary for children with reading problems to experience.

4. Divide into four groups, each focusing on one of four grade levels: beginning (K–2), primary (1–3), middle grades (3–4), and upper grades (5–6). Have each group find five representative literature selections appropriate for children who may need more support than normal. Share your findings with the rest of the class.

5. Go back to the chapters on emerging literacy, comprehension, decoding, and vocabulary, and select one activity. How would that activity be presented differently to a child experiencing difficulty with reading? What would be the focus? Is there a section you might emphasize?

6. Try to think of a skill that you have had difficulty learning and remember how you felt when you didn't have immediate success (e.g., tennis, cooking, sewing, swimming, soccer, etc.). How long did it take you to be discouraged? How did you feel when you couldn't learn? Try to relate those feelings to the very young child who seems to fail over and over in school-related activities.

RELATED READING

Professional

Rhodes, L.K., & Dudley-Marling, C. (1988). *Readers and writers with a difference: A holistic approach to learning disabled and remedial students.* Portsmouth, NH: Heinemann.

> *You may have noticed that this book is often used as a reference to many topics discussed in this book. Rhodes and Dudley-Marling have done a superb job of discussing many aspects of working with learning disabled and remedial readers. The nice thing about this book is that the suggestions are good for any type of reader.*

Children's Literature

The annotated list that follows is of picture books that are especially useful with middle school children who have reading problems. It is by no means all-inclusive or complete, and teachers who use picture books quickly identify their favorites.

Ackerman, Karen. (1988). *Song and dance man.* Illustrated by Stephen Gammell. New York: Knopf.

> *Chalk drawings illustrate the story of a grandfather who once danced in vaudeville and now dances in the attic for his grandchildren. In addition to developing an understanding of vaudeville, this book could help students become aware of the talents and feelings of older people or to discover differences in music and entertainment.*

Bunting, Eve. (1988). *How many days to America? A Thanksgiving story.* Illustrated by Beth Peck. New York: Clarion.

> *This is a touching story that tells of modern refugees who face struggles and hardships to come to America. One can't read this book without thinking about what it must be like to leave home without any belongings and being thankful that America can provide a safe refuge. This is a very different Thanksgiving story.*

Cendrars, Blaise. (1982). *Shadows.* Illustrated by Marcia Brown. New York: Scribners.

> *A translation of a French poem, this text presents poetic language and suggests interpretive activities such as choral reading and drama. The artwork is spectacular and sets a dramatic tone for the poem.*

Hodges, Margaret. (1984). *Saint George and the dragon.* (Retold). Illustrated by Trina Schart Hyman. Boston: Little, Brown.

> *This beautifully retold traditional English tale is somewhat longer than most picture books. The beauty of the pictures is matched by the language as the tale of the dragon unfolds. The story is complete with knights and princesses and captures the imagination of middle school readers.*

Lioni, Leo. (1967). *Frederick.* New York: Pantheon.

> *Frederick is a mouse who daydreams instead of helping his peers collect food for the winter. But in the winter as they stay tucked away in their hole after the food is gone, Frederick shares his images of blue skies and green grass. This book is somewhat older than the other books mentioned, but it is an all-time favorite for teaching theme and allowing students to conclude that the world needs all kinds of people.*

Loebel, Arnold. (1980). *Fables.* New York: Harper.

Loebel has invented delightful fables accompanied by marvelous pictures and one-line morals. The vocabulary in the mini-fables is delightful and challenging. Loebel's book could be used to develop the concepts of main idea and theme or could be compared to traditional fables.

Sendak, M. (1988). *Dear Mili.* New York: Harper & Row.

Many middle school students are familiar with Sendak's classic, Where the Wild Things Are, *but* Dear Milli *is very different and appeals to children and adults on different levels. The story is a recently discovered Grimm's tale that took Sendak three years to illustrate. Critics suggest that it contains some of ''. . . the richest, most heart-rending illustrations Sendak has done to date'' (Mabe, 1989). Sendak has produced quality picture books for more than thirty years, and his impact on children's literature is impressive. His work would easily support a comparative study of artwork, content, and writing style.*

Steptoe, John. (1987). *Mufaro's beautiful daughters: An African tale.* New York: Lothrop.

A most beautiful version of Cinderella from Africa, this is another book that must be enjoyed before any instructional activities are pursued. It is a good book to compare with traditional fairy tales. It is an excellent representative of multicultural literature and all children, no matter what their ethnic backgrounds, can relate to this picture book.

Van Allsburg, Chris. (1979). *Jumanji.* Boston: Houghton Mifflin.

This is the story of a board game that leads to a jungle-land adventure. This is an excellent book for developing prediction strategies as well as motivating many writing activities. There are two strong, explicit themes.

———. (1984). *The mysteries of Harris Burdick.* Boston: Houghton Mifflin.

An almost wordless picture book that encourages discussion, imagination, and writing. It is an excellent source for brainstorming to develop understanding of such literary elements as characterization and setting. Even the forward suggests a written activity for middle school readers.

———. (1986). *Polar express.* Boston: Houghton Mifflin.

A beautiful Christmas story that focuses on one boy's experience with Santa Claus. Students can discuss the meaning of the silent bell while exploring their own beliefs about Christmas. This book quickly becomes a favorite of all ages and could be justified at any grade level simply for pure enjoyment.

Wiesner, David. (1988). *Free fall.* New York: Lothrop, Lee & Shepherd.

This unusual picture book proves that some picture books are published for older children and adults. The pictures in a large mural were divided and organized into a picture book format. The reader's understanding and imagination are guided by a poem on the jacket. There is no doubt that this surrealistic presentation will precipitate a great deal of discussion and could result in creative productions in various media.

Yorinks, Arthur. (1988). *Bravo, Minski.* Illustrated by Richard Egielski. New York: Farrar, Straus, & Giroux.

This is the story of one of the world's true geniuses, who is a composite of several talented people from all walks of life. One can't read this book without being drawn into history, geography, and scientific inventions. It is an excellent book for developing several subject area concepts. Yorinks uses humor to focus on important lessons in life such as, ''Never give up on something you want to achieve.''

Other Books and Stories Cited in This Chapter

Blume, J. (1971). *Freckle juice*. New York: Dell.

———. (1972). *Tales of a fourth grade nothing*. Illustrated by R. Doty. New York: Dutton.

Bunting, E. (1990). *The wall*. Illustrated by R. Himler. New York: Clarion.

Cleary, B. (1983). *Dear Mr. Henshaw*. New York: Morrow.

DeClements, B. (1981). *Nothing's fair in fifth grade*. New York: Scholastic.

Fleischman, P. (1988). *Joyful noise: Poems for two voices*. Illustrated by E. Beddows. New York: Harper & Row.

Fleischman, S. (1986). *The whipping boy*. New York: Greenwillow.

Lowry, L. (1989). *Number the stars*. Boston, MA: Houghton, Mifflin.

MacLachlan, P. (1985). *Sarah, plain and tall*. New York: Harper & Row.

Paterson, K. (1988). *Park's quest*. New York: Puffin.

Peck, R. (1984). Priscilla and the Wimps. in D. Gallo (Ed.). *Sixteen short stories by outstanding writers for young adults*. New York: Dell.

Rosetti, C. (1989). Hurt no living thing. In E. Carle (Ed.). *Animals, animals*. New York: Philomel.

Sobel, D. (1983). *Encyclopedia Brown, Boy detective*. Illustrated by L. Shorthall. New York: Bantam.

Yorinks, A. (1988). *Bravo Minski*. Illustrated by R. Egielski. New York: Farrar, Straus & Giroux.

REFERENCES

Aaron, I.E., Chall, J.S., Durkin, D., Goodman, K., & Strickland, D.S. (1990). The past, present, and future of literacy education: Comments from a panel of distinguished educators, Part II. *The Reading Teacher, 43* (6), 370–380.

Adams, M.J. (1990). *Beginning to read: A summary*. Urbana-Champaign, IL: Center for the Study of Reading, The Reading Research and Education Center.

Allington, R.L. (1983). The reading instruction provided readers of differing reading abilities. *The Elementary School Journal, 83* (5), 548–59.

———. (1986). Policy constraints and effective compensatory reading instruction: A review. In J.V. Hoffman (Ed.), *Effective teaching of reading: Research and practice*. Newark, DE: International Reading Association.

Allington, R. L., & Broikou, K. (1988). Development of shared knowledge: A new role for classroom and specialist teachers. *The Reading Teacher, 41* (8), 806–811.

Atwell, N.A. (1985). Predictable books for adolescent readers. *Journal of Reading, 29* (1), 18–22.

———. (1987). *In the middle: Reading and writing for adolescents*. Portsmouth, NH: Heinemann.

Bridge, C. (1986). Predictable books for beginning readers and writers. In M.R. Sampson (Ed.), *The pursuit of literacy: Early reading and writing*. Dubuque, IA: Kendal/Hunt.

Buchanan, E. (Ed.). (1980). *For the love of reading*. Winnipeg, Canada: CEL.

Clay, M. (1990). *The early detection of reading difficulties* (3rd ed.) Auckland, New Zealand: Heinemann.

Gaskins, R.W. (1982). A writing program for poor readers and writers and the rest of the class, too. *Language Arts, 59*, 854f–861.

———. (1988). The missing ingredients: Time on task, direct instruction, and writing. *The Reading Teacher, 41*, 8, 750–755.

Gilbert, S.E., & Gay, G. (1985). Improving the success in school of poor black children. *Phi Delta Kappan, 67*, (2) 133–135.

Goodman, K. (1986). *What's whole about whole language?* Portsmouth, NH: Heinemann.

Harris, A.J., & Sipay, E.R. (1985). *How to increase reading ability*. White Plains, NY: Longman.

Huck, C., Helper, S., & Hickman, J. (1987). *Children's literature in the elementary school.* New York: Holt, Rinehart & Winston.

Koenke, K. (1988). Remedial reading instruction: What is and what might be. *The Reading Teacher, 41* (7), 708–711.

Labbo, L.D., & Teale, W.H. (1990). Cross age reading: A strategy for helping poor readers. *The Reading Teacher, 43* (6), 362–369.

Mabe, C. (1989, June 1). Books point up Sendak's impact on children's literature. *The Houston Chronicle.* p. 3.

Manzo, A. (1987). Psychologically induced dyslexia and learning disabilities. *The Reading Teacher, 40* (4), 408–413.

McGill-Frazen, A. (1989). Failure to learn to read: Formulating a policy problem. *Reading Research Quarterly, XXII* (4), 475–490.

Pinnell, G.S., Fried, M.D., & Estice, R.M. (1990). Reading recovery: Learning how to make a difference. *The Reading Teacher, 43,* 282–295.

Rayner, K., & Pollatsek, A. (1989). *The psychology of reading.* Englewood Cliffs, NJ: Prentice-Hall.

Rhodes, L.K., & Dudley-Marling, C. (1988). *Readers and writers with a difference: A holistic approach to teaching learning disabled and remedial students.* Portsmouth, NH: Heinemann.

Rudman, M.K. (1984). *Children's literature: An issues approach.* New York: Longman.

Smith, F. (1985). *Reading without nonsense* (2nd ed.). New York: Teachers' College Press.

Smith, F. (1988). *Understanding reading* (4th ed.). Hillsdale, NJ: Lawrence Erlbaum.

Strickland, D.S., & Morrow, L.S. (1989). Developing skills: An emergent literacy perspective. *The Reading Teacher, 43* (1), 82–83.

Taylor, D. (1989). Toward a unified theory of literacy learning and instructional practices. *Phi Delta Kappan, 71* (3), 184–193.

Wallace, C., & Goodman, Y. (1989). Research currents: Language and literacy development of multilingual learners. *Language Arts, 66* (5), 542–551.

Wuthrick, M.A. (1990). Blue jays win! Crows go down in defeat! *Phi Delta Kappan, 71* (7), 553–556.

11

FAMILIES, COMMUNITIES, AND CHILDREN'S READING

THE ELEPHANT AND HIS SON

The Elephant and his son were spending an evening at home. Elephant Son was singing a song.

"You must be silent," said Father Elephant. "Your papa is trying to read his newspaper. Papa cannot listen to a song while he is reading his newspaper."

"Why not?" asked Elephant Son.

"Because Papa can think about only one thing at a time, that is why," said Father Elephant.

Elephant Son stopped singing. He sat quietly. Father Elephant lit a cigar and went on reading.

After a while, Elephant Son asked, "Papa, can you still think about only one thing at a time?"

"Yes, my boy," said Father Elephant, "that is correct."

"Well then," said Elephant Son, "you might stop thinking about your newspaper and begin to think about the slipper that is on your left foot."

"But my boy," said Father Elephant, "Papa's newspaper is far more important and interesting and informative than the slipper that is on his left foot."

"That may be true," said Elephant Son, "but while your newspaper is not on fire from the ashes of your cigar, the slipper that is on your left foot certainly is!"

Father Elephant ran to put his foot in a bucket of water. Softly, Elephant Son began to sing again.

Knowledge will not always take the place of simple observations.
          —Arnold Lobel, *Fables* (1981 Caldecott Medal winner)

PARENTS' involvement in their children's reading always has been influential, and over the years this parental role has been recognized and encouraged in different ways. More than ever, current practices in reading instruction are identifying the effect of the involved parent in children's acquisition of literacy. There are others who can make a positive impact on reading and literacy, too. Brothers, sisters, grandparents, caretakers, and community members can contribute to children's learning experiences. The acquisition of literacy more and more is viewed as a team effort of children, their home life, and the community in which they live.

A teacher who is aware of the importance of home and community involvement can plan and encourage reading activities that naturally involve others. This chapter will discuss the importance of collaboration in reading instruction and suggest methods and techniques that support parents' involvement in classroom activities. Specifically, the chapter will answer the following questions:

1. What is parental involvement?
2. How does parental involvement affect children's reading?
3. How can children's literacy development be encouraged outside the school setting?
4. What are the roles of family members and the community in the literacy development of children?

Teachers and parents must collaborate to provide effective opportunities for children who are learning to read and write. Parent, family, and community involvements can become an important support and resource for many aspects of reading and writing.

Family and Community Involvement

Extramural exposure to literacy has a great impact on how children feel about reading and writing. Literate homes and parents support and encourage their children's reading and writing development. If the community also is involved in children's literacy growth, children can't avoid understanding the importance of print.

Literate Homes

The influence and importance of parents' behaviors on reading was noted explicitly in the 1984 report on reading entitled *Becoming a Nation of Readers* (Anderson, Hiebert, Scott, & Wilkinson, 1985). That report stated that "parents play roles of inestimable importance in laying the foundation for learning to read . . . Parents have an obligation to support their children's continued growth as readers" (p. 57). In fact, parents are encouraged to become the "significant other" in children's learning experiences (Sandfort, 1987). No matter how old children are, a parent can affect their attitudes toward literacy development.

Many parents are interested in and actively involved with their children's educa-tion when they are in primary grades, but parental involvement usually declines as children reach the upper grades (Lucas & Lusthaus, 1986). By the time children enter middle school, parents may not realize they still play an important role in literacy development. A recent Carnegie report on middle school emphasizes the importance of parental involvement and calls for a reversal of the downward slide in involvement during the middle school years (Cohen, 1989). Parental involvement is an important factor in reading and literacy development throughout children's schooling.

The major contribution that parents make to children's literacy development is their initiation and demonstration of uses of written language in their homes and daily lives. The literacy behaviors that families encourage contribute to successful reading instruction. Barbara Bush recognizes that literacy is a shared goal of families and schools. As First Lady, she has chosen to focus on the family's impact on literacy while her husband is in the White House. She explains this interest (1989) by writing:

> *It's the home where a child should be first exposed to the joy of the written word.*
> *I go back to the memories of my mother reading to me; it's a moment all parents*
> *and children should share. Those first nursery books—even if the child cannot*
> *fully understand what's being read—can be an invaluable foundation for the*
> *school years ahead. (p. 10)*

The importance that family members place on reading is a crucial influence on children's acquisition of written language. The family's attitude toward literacy ulti-mately affects reading instruction. If literacy is valued at home, it is more likely that children will reflect that attention at school. When parents and families support reading activities, teachers' jobs are easier.

A literate home routinely reflects the value and importance of written language in several ways, and children who come from those homes usually have similar experiences and opportunities. The first ingredient usually held in common by children from literate homes is the availability of a variety and quantity of reading materials. Children in homes that support literacy usually own an average of eighty books (Morrow, 1983) and have access to libraries and other materials such as paper and pencils (Taylor, 1983; Teale, 1978).

Reading is usually a regular routine for children in a literate home. A wide variety of materials is read and for many different purposes. Bedtime reading is a regular practice, as is traveling with books, receiving books for gifts, and visiting the library. These homes also encourage experimentation with print by making paper and pencils available for writing.

Seeing other family members reading is also positive (O'Rourke, 1979). Children have the opportunity to observe family members reading books, newspapers, menus, recipes, signs, advertisements, letters, grocery lists, reminders, and checks. A literate home becomes a wide ranging demonstration of the uses and importance of reading and writing.

Parents who encourage literacy talk to their children about books and writing. They answer the many questions that curious young readers ask about print, seem to know the right questions to ask during reading, and how to encourage book discussions. It is not unusual to witness parents and children engaged in conversations about story content, letters, sounds, words, and pictures as they read. Parents become actively involved in reading by pointing, questioning, and playing with the language and they encourage their children to ask questions about what they are reading (Yaden & McGee, 1984). Not only do parents have an intuitive feel for stressing the importance of literacy, but they seem to be aware of their children's developmental needs. Book reading strategies modify and change over time to become more appropriate as children gain knowledge about written language (McGee & Richgels, 1989).

Some children, usually from literate homes, learn to read without formal instruction. In a classic study, Durkin (1966) found that preschool readers had a wide range of intelligence and represented several socioeconomic levels, but came from homes in which reading was observed and discussed and time for experimentation was allowed (Durkin, 1966). The activities that naturally occur in literate homes were present when children learned to read before school (Teale, 1981). Children who read early are read to, see people reading, have access to individuals who answer their questions, and experiment with paper and pencil. Literate homes contribute a great deal to children's natural development of reading abilities (Clark, 1976; Plessas & Oakes, 1964). Although these behaviors do not always produce a four- or five-year-old reader, there is no doubt that children who come to school with these experiences have a greater chance of becoming successful readers and writers.

It is never too soon to begin sharing books with young children.

Intergenerational Literacy

Recently there has been a great deal of focus on the literacy of the entire family. As a result a new term, *intergenerational literacy,* has emerged. This term refers to programs that develop positive attitudes toward reading and writing and improve literacy behaviors of both adults and children in a family. Intergenerational literacy programs are based on the assumption that improving the literacy levels of parents will affect positively children's written language development (Jongsma, 1990). A second focus of these programs is to teach parents how to read to their children and provide many of the experiences that are evident in homes that naturally support literacy. Children's literacy attainment correlates directly with the mother's educational level (Weinberg, 1988), and many studies have found that once parents increase their literacy skills, children's achievement also increases. Intergenerational literacy focuses not only on children's needs, but also on the needs of the adults who care for them.

Parents in the Schools

The effect of the home on children's literacy development is well documented, but there also is some evidence that parental involvement at school results in clear gains in the achievement of children (Henderson, 1988). Getting parents involved in school improves children's attitudes toward school and is viewed as a critical factor in overall school success (Rasinski & Fredericks, 1989).

There are several reasons why parental involvement results in gains in achievement and attitudes (Scott-Jones, 1988). Parents have worked with their children for five or six years before teachers become involved. Parents know their children and continue to have a powerful influence on their attitudes and learning. This influence results from the fact that, for the most part, parents of elementary age children control the environment and resources available to their children.

Each time a parent enters the school, more understanding and acceptance develop among all involved. When parents work and interact with teachers, the teacher is provided with another view of the child. At the same time, the parent understands what is occurring at school. Additional information about the child's situation at home or at school can only support learning activities. Understanding and acceptance expand to the community when several parents are present in the school. The presence of parents means that community values are represented in the schools. At the same time, parental involvement sends a signal that learning and schools are important aspects in the community. When children observe that learning is a concerted effort of important people in their lives, they are reminded of the importance of learning.

Parents can be a great help to teachers. They can offer extra ears to listen to children, extra hands to complete activities, and ideas and emotions to active class-rooms. A parent volunteer can fill a void where support is needed and provide aid to the teacher's instructional planning. When parents act interested and become involved in school, children will reflect that interest in their school work. School acceptance of parents' efforts recognizes that families and their values are important.

Parental involvement means different things to different people. Whatever the accepted definition, most agree that education cannot be provided by the school alone, but must be a collaborative effort between schools and families. Perhaps a satisfactory definition of parental involvement is that of an open invitation to parents and families to take part in their child's literacy development.

Community Involvement

Reading instruction can also be enhanced by others who are important to children. Community influences are linked to student success in schools (Mattox & Rich, 1977). All adults and peers who interact with children have the potential to contribute to perceptions of reading and writing. Role models from all aspects of life can demonstrate the importance of reading and the value of literacy. To develop a literate person, efforts must go far beyond the classroom.

Involving others in reading instruction may seem an overwhelming task at first. The results of involving parents and the community in children's learning are recognizable yet difficult to measure. No matter what level of family and community involvement a teacher manages to enjoy and encourage, there will be obvious and unexpected benefits.

Assumptions of Parental Involvement

Teachers can plan many types of activities to encourage parental and family involvement in children's literacy development. Planning and developing these activities should recognize some basic assumptions.

Literate Homes Provide Support for Reading and Writing Activities Required at School
The impact of the home on learning to read is being recognized as more and more important. Homes that provide a richly literate environment increase their children's chances of success at school. There is no doubt of the link between literate home experiences and literacy attainment.

Enlisting the Support of Families and Others in the Community Improves Attitudes toward and Achievement from Reading Instruction
No matter what level of involvement teachers encourage, parents and community efforts will affect children's reading and writing development. Involving others can provide teachers with allies and support while encouraging reading and writing activities.

Parents May Not Know What They Can Do to Encourage Reading Achievement
Many parents involve their children in activities naturally associated with child rearing and do not realize they are affecting their child's literacy development. Other parents do not understand exactly what they must do to support their children's literacy develop-

ment and need some guidance. Part of encouraging parents to participate is suggesting what they can do.

Levels of School Involvement

Involvement can come about in various ways, and parental interest ranges from passive to very active and will vary in quality depending on the social and personal situations of students and their families (Potter, 1989). The levels of parental involvement are identifiable. Epstein (1987) provides a description of how parents might become involved:

The First Level of Involvement in Schools Is That of Providing the Basics of Food, Clothing, Shelter, and School Supplies

Most teachers take the basic obligations for granted when, in reality, even the most basic requirements can be a struggle for some parents. Teachers should be alert for changing needs of children and understand that parents with different economic situations will respond to the basic needs in different ways.

A Second Level of Parental Commitment Is Becoming Involved in the Basic Communication Process between Home and School

Schools constantly should extend a line of communication to parents regarding their schools and children's activities. Communication should be positive and involve opportunities for parents to know about the daily routine. Too often the school contacts parents only when students have some difficulty. This may be one reason that parents do not always respond positively to contacts by the teachers. Teachers who become frustrated when parents do not respond to written or personal contacts should recognize that lack of attendance at school functions or failure to come to the school to discuss certain issues does not always mean disinterest in children's school work. Lack of response could reflect uneasiness of the parent in coming to the school or an inability to be released from work.

Many Parents Indicate Their Interest in Children by Becoming Involved in Ongoing Activities at the School

This includes visiting the classroom, attending programs, volunteering for specific jobs, and participating in actual instructional activities. Organized volunteer programs are established by schools and individual teachers to encourage parents and other community residents to take part in reading instruction.

Another Method of Involvement Is to Plan Activities That Allow Parents to Participate in Reading Instruction at Home

Home-based activities are especially valuable for working parents who want to become involved in their children's school work. Occasional homework assignments that ask the parents to read with the child, listen to the child read, respond to an interview, or react in a home–school journal are examples of ways to involve parents in literacy instruction.

Encouraging Involvement

Parental involvement in children's literacy makes sense, but isn't always as simple as it sounds. Parents may not know what to do, and schools may request a type of involvement that is not comfortable for individual parents. Teachers may not be aware of the range of activities that can involve parents and contribute to effective reading instruction. Parental involvement requires careful planning and organization for success. As a teacher plans to involve parents in classroom literacy activities, she or he should follow guidelines for successful involvement (Rasinski & Fredericks, 1988; Holbrook, 1985):

1. Parental participation is most effective when it is regular. The effect of children and parents routinely engaged in reading activities will be felt during classroom activities in ways that are not easily measured.

2. Reading activities for children and parents must be purposeful and should relate directly to the children's lives. Parental involvement will be much more successful if parents are responsible for motivating children to accomplish activities that have value and are interesting.

3. One way to assure purposeful activities is to be sure that the tasks look like reading and writing. Activities involving high quality literature and writing designed to accomplish a specific task encourage parents and children alike to become more involved in the activities.

4. Parents need to allow their children to move at their own pace. Activities should not force parents into cajoling or pushing their children. Planned activities provide opportunities for parents to support their children's endeavors in a relaxed and risk free manner. Spontaneity is a prime consideration for parents as they work with their children. The most effective involvement is that which occurs naturally out of interest in what the child is accomplishing. One of the simplest and most effective methods of parental involvement is discussion about reading.

5. Parents' values and abilities also should be considered as the teacher contemplates home–school involvement (Holbrook, 1985). Effective activities reflect parental values and varying parental competencies.

6. Finally, teachers can add to their support system by including caretakers as partners in reading activities. Babysitters, grandparents, and after-school day care personnel can and should become partners in reading development. Activities that easily include caretakers or others in the community include sharing books, ideas, and writing responses to interviews about reading and in journals.

Interferences

Even when the benefits of parental involvement are accepted and understood, certain attitudes and situations can interfere with interactions between parents and teachers. For example, parents may have experienced school failure and feel uneasy when asked to be involved with their children's classroom activities. If parents have not finished school, do not feel secure about their own reading and writing skills, or feel inferior to the teacher and other school personnel, it may be extremely difficult for them to believe that they have something to contribute. Parents' discomfort can increase if they do not understand what they are to do or feel they have nothing to offer. Once initial barriers are overcome, most parents will become involved in school activities if they feel welcome and understand what they must do.

Circumstances also can affect the amount of involvement a parent has in school activities. Personal or family problems can interfere with parental intentions to become involved in their children's reading and writing instruction. Divorce, supporting a family, caring for preschoolers, and lack of transportation can be factors in parents' levels of involvement.

Teachers also may contribute to the lack of parental involvement. Most teacher education programs do not discuss including parents as partners in their children's reading instruction. If the benefits are not explicitly emphasized, a teacher who has many tasks to complete may feel that parental involvement is an intrusion and represents another time-consuming element. It is easy not to include parents in ongoing classroom activities. But, since research demonstrates that children's reading achievement can be influenced when parents take an interest in school activities, it is worth the effort to find workable ways to involve parents.

Parents may continue to hesitate about becoming involved even after teachers make special efforts to include them in school activities. There are some ways to persuade and encourage even the most reluctant parents to become active in school activities (Fredericks & Rasinski, 1990):

1. Teachers should provide numerous opportunities for involvement and repeatedly invite parents to take part in classroom efforts. It will take parents time to get used to the idea of contributing to classroom instruction, and they may need to be invited more than once before they feel comfortable.

2. Parental and family involvement is much more successful if the entire school is working toward that goal. Schools that have very successful parental involvement programs actively recruit parents and involve them in many aspects of instructional programs. Reading instruction benefits from the whole school focus on parental involvement. If parents begin contributing when children are in the first grade, the third grade teacher will not need to work as hard to include them in classroom plans.

3. Parents respond to recognition just as children and teachers do. When parents make an effort to work with teachers, teachers should be quick to recognize and support them. Positive reinforcement can result in parents who view their part in reading instruction as a valued and recognized contribution to the child's academic career.

4. Students are effective recruiters and can do much to help convince their parents to take part in school activities. Many parents will participate in classroom activities at the request of their children much more quickly than if a teacher or principal asks them to help.

5. Involvement can include other family or community members. Older siblings, aunts, uncles, and grandparents should be invited to take part in literacy events. Community members who do not have children in school might be interested in participating and spending time at the school. There are many retired people who have much to offer and would enjoy helping young children get a good start in reading. University students often are eager to participate in school-related activities.

6. One of the factors most valuable in promoting parental involvement with reading is a classroom that welcomes them and makes them feel comfortable. Parents and others who wish to be involved always should feel welcome during times the teacher has set aside for classroom interactions.

7. Once parents are involved, they can help encourage other parents to work with children. When a teacher forms a team of parents who are regular classroom supporters, part of their task can be to recruit and organize other parents. Parents explain to other parents how to read aloud, listen to children read, or talk about books, or they can demonstrate activities that support classroom reading instruction.

9. Young mothers and fathers may have many other responsibilities that prevent them from contributing to school involvement. One way to help them is to provide babysitting and other special services that allow them the time to participate.

Specific Strategies

The strategies a teacher uses to communicate suggestions may range from personal letters and phone calls to school-wide contribution to curriculum decisions. There are activities appropriate for all levels of child, parent, and community involvement.

Providing Information

Informing parents about school-related activities is the simplest level of involvement. The traditional methods of providing parents with information about their children's achievement are term and end-of-term grade reports. Although systematic reports of school achievement have long been accepted, grades do not really provide parents with a full picture of school behavior and achievement of children nor do they encourage or suggest parental involvement. Some methods of reporting require that parents become involved and provide information to their children and teachers. Some of the methods informing parents about daily activities and their child's behavior include informal chats, personal letters, and class meetings. Open house dates and parent–teacher meetings should be planned regularly to inform parents about school activities. Many teachers use the first open house of the year to explain reading programs and talk with parents about their role in the process.

Written reports from the teacher inform parents about what is happening in school. The same information is conveyed during parent–teacher conferences. When a teacher does discuss a child's development with the parent, the report should be as positive as possible. Written and face-to-face discussions can be enhanced by displaying an accumulation of the child's work to illustrate the productivity of the child.

Many schools require teachers to contact the parents at certain times during the year. Teachers should continue to meet with parents as time allows. Parent contacts do not always need to be formal, and a few minutes of conversation as a parent picks up a child can be a positive encounter. Parents who are informed regularly about their child's development will be more comfortable providing support.

Children can be drafted into helping parents become informed about what is happening at school. The entire class can write a newsletter that is reproduced and sent home. This document can be read by parents or read aloud by children. Children can write letters to their parents periodically, telling what they have been doing in reading and writing and explaining what they have learned or what they have read.

Material written by children and shared with parents provides information about school activities and reading material for parents and children to enjoy. Any writing that is reproduced for the entire class to read can be sent home for parents to read. Some teachers establish a check-out system for books that have been published in the classroom. Children are encouraged to take home their class's published writing as reading material.

Organized parental involvement is based on providing information to parents in various ways. It lays the groundwork for allowing parents to learn about school activities and feel comfortable about taking part in certain events. Once parents feel comfortable, there are many ways to invite participation. The most successful activities are those in which parents are allowed to demonstrate and provide examples of certain reading behaviors. Such activities as reading aloud to children, listening to children read aloud, reading in unison with children, and actually demonstrating the reading process are excellent activities for parents to incorporate in their child care routines.

Reading Aloud

Usually when parents read to their children, they are completely unaware of the many values they are imparting. They approach reading aloud as a pleasurable and enjoyable event for all involved. That could be one of the most valuable lessons for children (Morrow, 1983). Nevertheless, children do learn many important ideas about reading and establish the groundwork for later development. Reading aloud provides children with demonstrations of the importance of reading and forms the basis of literacy development. Reading together provides a meaningful opportunity to discuss all elements of literacy. Talking about words and learning about the joys of literature evolve naturally. Even more important, reading aloud with children can bring families closer together. As they share stories, they learn more about each other.

There are a few simple suggestions to guide parental reading aloud:

Parents Should Read and Share Books with Their Children Often and Regularly

Parents from different cultural and economic backgrounds can understand the importance of reading aloud to their children. Even when parents do not possess excellent reading skills, they can look at books with their children and encourage children who can to read aloud and talk about the pictures in the books. Some parental involvement programs are ensuring that parents from all socioeconomic backgrounds are provided with books and basic reading aloud techniques so children can experience this valuable activity. There are some parental involvement programs in larger cities that send books home from the hospital with newborns to stress the importance of books in children's lives.

Parents Should Read a Variety of Material

Newspapers, letters, and recipe books can part of what parents share with their children. Teachers can contribute to the variety by sending material home from school when appropriate. If commercial books are not available for children to take home, parents can be provided with material written by their own children.

Parents Should Talk to Their Children about Books

Children and parents can discuss books they've read together, books read at school, and books they may have heard about. This activity is particularly valuable for parents who do not feel comfortable enough about their own reading skills to read aloud. Any parent can ask a child to talk about what she or he is reading at school and the books read independently at home.

Parents find it more difficult to become involved in the reading development of older children. When children become too old for bedtime stories, the opportunities for parents and children to read together decrease. Reading aloud may interfere with the independent reading of avid readers. Just because children become effective readers

Library visits are extremely effective when they are family affairs.

does not mean that parents no longer participate in and encourage reading. One thing that parents can do after children are reading fluently is to read the same books and discuss favorite passages. Parents also can become involved by asking the child to read a section aloud and a parent reads another section aloud. Even fifth and sixth graders will enjoy sharing parts of their favorite books. There are important reasons why parents and older children should continue to read and share ideas from literature. As parents and older children interact, it sends a message that reading is important. When parents share their ideas and books they have read, it suggests ways that reading is important out of school.

When children choose not to read on their own, parents can play an important role in motivating recreational reading by reading entire children's books themselves and sharing passages that they enjoyed. Library visits are a most effective way to encourage independent, recreational reading. Parents who provide opportunities for young readers to encounter good literature will do a lot to encourage independent reading.

Listening to Children Read

As children learn to read fluently, they like to read to their parents. Parents should listen to their children read aloud on a regular basis. Reading aloud together is spontaneous, direct, and effortless, and the contributions to reading development are numerous. This practice can vary from a passive listening role to a discussion of the content, story, and pictures (Wolfendale, 1985). No matter what beliefs teachers have about methods of reading instruction, parents listening to children read can be a support to classroom activities. Teachers can help by suggesting materials, specific activities such as paired reading, language experience, and methods of parental feedback and reinforcement.

Paired Reading

A program developed in the United Kingdom trains parents to engage in paired reading with their children (Topping, 1987). This technique is similar to the paired reading discussed in chapters 5 and 10. The paired reading designed for parents and children encourages the child to select reading material without regard for difficulty. If children select material that is too difficult for them to read aloud, the child is supported by reading in unison with a parent. The child signals to the parent when she or he feels capable of reading the text independently. An important aspect of this technique is that when parents read aloud, they demonstrate good reading. Other benefits are the increase in the amount of reading practice a child receives and the quiet time for parents to focus their attention on their children.

The paired reading procedure can be used by parents who do not read well. Parents who do not possess the reading skills or confidence can work with other family members who understand the technique. Parents supervise the activity and give praise and support. The process of pairing parents and children to read aloud does require some training either by teachers or parents who have used the technique successfully. Paired reading is a structured and positive method of parental involvement and when it was adopted in certain schools in the United Kingdom, it was successful with a variety of ethnic and socioeconomic backgrounds (Topping, 1987).

Models of Reading

Reading in front of children is another way parents can establish that reading is important (Smith, 1988). Parents who are reading in the home become models children want to imitate. Observations of parental reading may be one of the most powerful influences on children's reading success. It doesn't matter what parents are reading, but the frequency with which children see their parents reading seems to have a strong impact on attitudes toward reading. Parents can enhance the effect by sharing what they are reading and discussing their attitudes toward reading. Children learn a great deal from these encounters, and conversations often can encourage children to read on their own.

Providing Reading Material

Parents don't have to spend a lot of money to make print accessible to their children. The local library offers a great—and free—resource for reading material. Teachers can encourage use of the local library by organizing a field trip to acquaint children with the facility. Once children learn about the library, they encourage parents to visit.

Children's first library cards can be an important event in their lives. Using a library is a very grown-up thing to do. Parents and children can tour the library together to see how it is arranged and how to find the books. The library offers children and parents alike the richest source of reading material available, and frequent use encourages children to become lifelong readers.

Some parents provide collections of books for children to read at home; other parents cannot afford books. Teachers should identify opportunities to make books accessible to homes that cannot afford them. Parents should realize that giving books as gifts can make a lasting contribution to children's literacy development. There are programs such as one implemented by Reading Is Fundamental (RIF) that provides reading material to children who might not otherwise be able to afford books. RIF is a national nonprofit organization that has as its goal the encouragement of reading among young people. This organization makes it possible for children to own books without cost to them or their families (Graves, 1987). RIF can be contacted at the following address:

Reading Is Fundamental, Inc.
600 Maryland Avenue, S.W.
Suite 500
Washington, D.C. 20560

Parental Activity in the Classroom

Another way to involve parents in literacy development is to encourage them to visit the classroom. The classroom should be open to all parents, and each parent should feel comfortable visiting during reading instruction. Classroom visits could involve several levels of activity depending on the parent, the students, and the teachers' needs.

Classroom Visits

Observation is the minimum level of parental activity in the classroom. A teacher can simply have a set time when parents are encouraged to visit. They can observe reading and writing in action. Visits that have no obligation other than observing in a friendly, welcoming classroom encourage later involvement by the parent.

Parents' visits should familiarize them with the routines and procedures associated with reading and writing. Specific days can be identified for observing and taking part in the classroom routine. Parents can be involved in nothing but observing, but a regular classroom visitor cannot help but become involved in the give-and-take of an energetic and exciting classroom.

Once parents become familiar with classroom procedures and are comfortable, they can begin participating in classroom activities. One of the simplest things for parents to do is to share favorite reading material. Parents can be included in the daily read aloud sessions and share favorite children's books or read chapters from the novel being read by the entire class. Parents can be invited guests for silent reading activities. They can come ready to read with their books in hand and sit and read quietly with the class. Parents' presence during silent reading can provide powerful images of the importance of reading.

Parents as Volunteers

Once parents feel comfortable in the classroom, they may visit more often if they have a specific job or responsibility associated with the classroom routine. The jobs that parents can do in the classroom are endless. Parents can become scribes for language experience stories, or they can read to children who need more oral reading experience. They can help keep records of the books that are read and lead small groups of children who are ready to discuss the books they are reading.

Parents can begin assisting in the classroom by listening to children read aloud. The classroom emphasis can be reading for meaning and enjoyment. Butler and Turbill (1984) suggest that parents write the title of the book, the part read, and the date they listened to children read on a large bookmark. The bookmark becomes part of the regular record-keeping procedure.

Some jobs for parents might require some training. Workshops can be offered to train parents who want to help with such jobs as tutoring, producing language experience, or having conferences with children about their reading activities. Schools can actually increase involvement by initiating a workshop to explain cooperative school–home activities in all grades and subjects. When teachers want parents to get involved, clear guidelines and proper training assure successful parental participation. Parental training need not be complex and should include such steps as verbal instruction, demonstrating behavior, practice, feedback and reinforcement, and monitoring (Topping, 1985). Often parents who are seasoned volunteers can train recruits.

Parent–Teacher Conferences

The classic measure of parental involvement has been the parent–teacher conference often required by school districts. Unfortunately, these encounters are sometimes the result of children experiencing difficulty in school. Because of this, conferences often make parents feel insecure. Teachers need to communicate to parents about their children's progress, and conferences are a time to share what children are reading and writing as well as their behavior and responses in class. If teachers and parents have had other types of contacts, conferences will not be as difficult. Most parents really enjoy talking with others about their children, and conferences give them an opportunity to discuss progress, strengths, and potential problems. Conferences provide information to both parents and teachers, making their jobs somewhat easier.

The conference atmosphere should be comfortable and relaxed, allowing the parents to feel at ease. Descriptions of school behaviors can be provided to parents by sharing samples of work and anecdotes of classroom life. Children's progress in reading can be demonstrated with completed work from portfolios and teachers' explanations of accomplished objectives of instruction. Conferences are a good time to play a video of the child reading (Baskwill & Whitman, 1988), allowing the parents to see the child in action at school.

Conferences offer opportunities for teachers to interpret test results. Parents may not understand the purposes and results of a standardized test and may need reassurance that one test result does not serve as the total estimate of the child's reading ability. Teachers can alleviate many fears by discussing the entire gamut of children's classroom attempts. Portfolios, folders, work samples, and other records should support discussions during parent–teacher conferences.

Parents and Home Activities

One way to encourage parents to take part in their children's learning is to plan instructional activities requiring response from parents or family members. A parental or family discussion or response to a story can provide children with a great deal of encouragement to continue reading. A home–school link of this nature sends a message to children that family and teachers feel that reading is important.

Obtaining information about how parents respond to activities usually requires that students be the go-betweens for parents and teachers. Students can be given the directions for completion of the activity and convey the message to parents. Teachers clarify directions by demonstrating the expected results at school. The children's understanding can be augmented with a note explaining home-based involvement to parents.

Parental Response to Reading Material

Planning for parents to respond to reading material involves them in meaningful ways and ultimately encourages children's reading behaviors. There are many ways to provide a framework for parents to respond to books and other texts. Questionnaires, interviews, taped responses, and written conversations are examples of strategies that require parental response to what children are reading. Many techniques demonstrate creativity and embrace a wide range of responses.

One technique that involves parents was developed by a teacher who had many student-made books in the classroom. When students published a book, they left blank pages in the back. The books were checked out and taken home as independent reading material. Parents were asked to read the material with their children and to respond on the blank pages. The books also were available for parental reading during visits to the classroom. The parents were asked to respond to the text in writing during their visits. The readers' response page was introduced during an open house and continued throughout the year so all parents became familiar with the procedure.

Interviews

Another method of involving parents is to plan for activities in which interviews or stories told by parents are collected, organized, written, and reproduced as reading material. One common language arts activity that can be adapted for all ages is oral history. Basically, children establish a set of questions to ask parents or family members about a certain topic. The topic relates to some aspect of what is being studied in school. For example, if children are reading biographies in a theme unit, they could develop interview questions that everyone would ask a grandparent or neighbor about their lives. Each student could be responsible for writing up their own interview, or the interviews could be combined for a report on grandparents' biographies.

Another teacher designed a parental response activity based on family stories. During a unit that discussed the origins of traditional literature, each student was assigned to ask a family member to relate a favorite family story on tape. The students then wrote the stories in the words of the storytellers. The stories were typed, collected, bound, and added to classroom reading material.

Both are methods of allowing parents and family members to respond to classroom activities. The products of the oral interviews and the family stories help the children see that families can contribute to the reading process in many ways. The compilation of family ideas and stories provides concrete evidence of the personal value and importance of each family represented in the classroom.

Observation and Reporting

Parents can help teachers by observing and reporting behaviors of children as they read at home. During conferences or in personal letters, informal conversations, or questionnaires about children's home reading, parents can relate such information as what books children choose to read at home, attitudes toward reading expressed at home, and how children approach homework assignments. The feedback from parents provides insights into the best motivation and instruction for school reading. Reading aloud behaviors could be noted and compared with school reading aloud opportunities. A structured and organized report allows parents and teachers to work together to find what is best for the child. This type of involvement could provide the teacher with information that leads to more effective instruction.

Many levels of involvement can be expected from parents. But the ultimate goal is to commit parents to active home–school cooperation (Rasinski & Fredericks, 1989). This is the level at which parents and teachers plan together for home–school involvement and work together to implement the plans. Very few programs of parental involvement ever achieve this level of cooperation, and once achieved it is very difficult to maintain. Even so, this level of parental involvement should be the goal and desired outcome of each effort.

Writing

Writing is a good way to involve parents in the literacy activities of their children. Many of the methods described have involved writing by either the parent or the child. Writing activities provide a two-fold benefit for parent and child interaction. Writing supplies a format for responding to reading material, and the written responses produce additional reading material for classroom and home activities.

Language experience activities can be adapted for home–school collaboration. Parents serve as scribes for young children to keep journals, write captions, or tell stories. Children dictate to their parents at home and bring the results to school, or parents are scheduled to help the teacher who has planned these activities for individual children. When parents can be recruited to act as classroom scribes, teachers can hear twice as many stories during the school day as normal.

Written conversations between parents and children provide activities for travel, restaurants, and other quiet times. Once children learn how to do this at school, they can instruct parents in the logistics. This simple activity encourages reading and writing in a relaxed and fun atmosphere.

Interactive academic journals allow parents to be a part of their children's school work while becoming informed about specific classroom activities and content. A dialogue between teachers and students about content presented in the classroom becomes a unique and meaningful technique for parents when they are invited to write responses to the topics. The three-way journals familiarize parents with the content of instruction, and the interaction gives them an opportunity to assist their children and read and write in front of their children.

Journals are a flexible technique. One teacher begins each day with a journal entry on a large chart. The first grade students contribute to the journal by dictating the entry language experience style. Each Friday a different child takes the journal home. Over the weekend, parents listen to the child read entries and add comments to the pages if they wish.

Another teacher has a teddy bear for a class mascot. During the week the teddy bear participates in and observes classroom activity. The class helps the teddy bear keep a journal of ongoing classroom activities. Each weekend the teddy bear and its journal go home with a student. The student and parents provide a written account of how the teddy bear spent the weekend. The journal entry can be true or fanciful, depending on the child in charge of the weekend entry. The highlight of every Monday morning is reading what happened to the teddy bear over the weekend. The teddy bear spent one Christmas vacation in the hospital with a class member who was receiving treatment for an illness. When the class returned from vacation, the journal was full of entries from doctors, nurses, and the class member.

Parents often need to be educated about how a teacher reacts to spelling and grammar errors. Parents can become concerned if it appears that teachers are not checking the children's work for these errors. This issue can be addressed easily by making expectations about spelling and grammar clear and explicit to parents.

Learning Differences

Cultural and language differences have the potential to affect how parents respond to school-sponsored activity. Often, parents who have different cultural and language backgrounds feel uncomfortable with school involvement. A teacher who realizes that cultural and language differences provide additional resources for certain topics can encourage and motivate reluctant parents to become involved. If at all possible, parents representing all languages and cultures should be among the parents who visit classrooms. This provides a model of interest in school and sends a strong message about the importance of individual cultures and languages.

Culture

Parents with different cultural backgrounds may feel uncomfortable at school. These parents may realize that their backgrounds are different than that of the teacher and school personnel and may not feel at ease when involved in school-related activities. Teachers need to work extra hard to make these parents feel welcome in the schoolroom. Parents from different backgrounds may avoid visiting school because they do not know how to act or what to expect. Teachers often interpret this reluctance as not caring about their children. Parents from different cultures are no less concerned about their children than anyone else in our society. The level of involvement will vary with any group of parents, and teachers can safely assume that parents of different cultures are as concerned about the social and academic progress of their children as any other parents. As with all parents, these parents may need to understand what to do and learn how the teacher and family must work together to help the children become literate (Flores, Cousin, & Diaz, 1991).

Involving parents of different cultures in school activities and making them feel welcome in the classroom can provide a valuable resource for the classroom teacher. Not only can the students in the classroom benefit from the efforts of these parents, but the parents will contribute their knowledge and talents. Parents who represent various cultures can offer a great deal to social studies and world culture studies. They can demonstrate art, music, and language from their countries and may even be able to dress in traditional clothing to visit the classroom. Their backgrounds can be used to provide a rich and varied backdrop to regular school activities. Inviting parents of different cultures to speak to students about their backgrounds, demonstrate traditional aspects of their cultures, or to discuss events from differing perspectives can contribute to understandings in the classroom.

Language

Many of the same concerns and approaches suggested for multi-ethnic parental backgrounds can be applied to parents who speak different languages. Parents who are bilingual can become valuable resources for a classroom teacher. Parents who speak different languages can be used to take dictation during language experience, interpret stories as they are read aloud to the entire class, or otherwise serve as liaisons for children who are learning English. Parents who are bilingual might be used to help the teacher communicate with parents who are not bilingual. When new students come to class and do not speak English, bilingual parents can be used to help the children adjust to the new situation.

DISCUSSION AND ACTIVITIES

1. Try to recall how parents were involved with school when you were in elementary school. Do you remember if any parents helped with reading and writing instruction? Do you think it would have made an impression on you if parents were involved? Do you remember how you felt when your parent came to school?

2. Have one of your classmates take the role of a teacher and a second take the role of a parent who never graduated from high school. Let the teacher try to convince the parent that there is something she or he can offer to classroom reading instruction.

3. What are some of the special experiences that parents of different cultures and languages can offer to a class?

4. Suppose you had tried everything possible to involve the parents of your students and still got no response. What would be your attitude and what would you do to continue to invite the parents to be part of reading instruction?

5. Must every parent of every child visit your classroom to register interest in their children? What are some ways you can determine parental involvement if they don't visit the classroom?

RELATED READING

Professional

Parents will ask what they can do to encourage their children to read at home. Some books provide suggestions and ideas that parents can use to encourage reading at home. These books would be good for the parent organizations at school to own and circulate, or they could be offered as independent reading material when parents visit the classroom for silent reading.

Butler, D., & Clay, M. (1982). *Reading begins at home.* Portsmouth, NH: Heinemann.

> *This book describes how parents can instill a love of reading in children. The authors suggest an environment in which children read stories aloud, play word games, and draw pictures. It includes a short list of books for children.*

Clay, M. (1987). *Writing begins at home.* Auckland, NZ: Heinemann.

> *This book presents information about writing development and activities parents can use to encourage writing at home.*

Graves, R. (Ed.). (1987). Reading is fundamental. *The RIF Guide to Encouraging Young Readers.* New York: Doubleday.

> *This book is billed as a source of two hundred reading activities for parents and children. The activities are suitable for infants to children who are eleven years old. The book includes a recommended reading list compiled by RIF volunteers and a list of book clubs, books for parents, and organizations concerned with children's reading.*

Lee, B., & Rudman, M.K. (1982). *Mind over media.* New York: Seaview.

> *Lee and Rudman address those children who do read and write, but resist any suggestions to write during their time away from school. This book offers many ways for parents to help their children continue developing reading and writing skills at home.*

Taylor, D., & Strickland, D.S. (1986). *Family storybook reading.* Portsmouth, NH: Heinemann.

> *This book presents a step-by-step procedure for parents who want guidance in reading to their children. It includes pictures of parents and children sharing and reading storybooks. The descriptions and suggestions provide a wealth of information.*

Trelease, J. (1989). *The new read-aloud handbook.* New York: Viking/Penguin.

> *Trelease has motivated many parents to read aloud to their children. There have been four reprints of this book. Try to find the most recent so his treasury of great read aloud books will be current. This is probably the best known book about reading aloud to children.*

REFERENCES

Altwerger, B., Diehl-Faxon, J., & Dockstader-Anderson, K. (1985). Read aloud events as meaning construction. *Language Arts.* 62 (4), 476–484.

Anderson, R. C., Hiebert, E.H., Scott, J.A., & Wilkinson, I. A. G. (1985). *Becoming a nation of readers: The report of the commission on reading.* Washington, DC: National Institute of Education.

Baskwill, J., & Whitman, P. (1988). *Moving on: Whole language sourcebook for grades three and four.* Ontario, Canada: Scholastic.

Bush, B. (1989). Literacy: Our shared goal. *The Reading Teacher, 43* (1), 10–12.

Butler, A., & Turbill, J. (1984). *Towards a reading and writing classroom.* Portsmouth, NH: Heinemann.

Clark, M.M. (1976). *Young fluent readers.* London: Heinemann.

Cohen, D.L. (1989). Middle schools gain with 'focus' on child. *Education Week, VIII* (39), 1 and 11.

Durkin, D. (1966). *Children who read early.* New York: Teacher's College Press.

Epstein, J. L. (1987). Parent involvement: What research says to administrators. *Education and Urban Society, 19* (2), 119–136.

Flores, B., Cousin, P.T., Diaz, E. (1991). Transforming deficit myths about learning, language, and culture. *Language Arts,* 68 (5). 369–386.

Fredericks, A.D., & Rasinski, T.V. (1990). Involving the uninvolved: How to. *The Reading Teacher, 43* (6), 424–425.

Graves, R. (Ed.). Reading is fundamental. *The RIF guide to encouraging young readers.* New York: Doubleday.

Henderson, A.T. (1988). Parents are a school's best friends. *Phi Delta Kappan, 70* (2), 148–153.

Holbrook, H.T. (1985). ERIC/RCS report: Teachers working with parents. *Language Arts, 62* (8), 897–901.

Jongsma, K.S. (1990). Intergenerational literacy. *The Reading Teacher, 43* (6), 426–427.

Lee, B., & Rudman, M.K. (1982). *Mind over media.* New York: Seaview.

Lucas, B.J., & Lusthaus, C.S. (1986). The decisional participation of parents in elementary and secondary schools. *High School Journal, 69* (3), 211–220.

Mattox, B. & Rich, D. (1977). Community involvement activities: Research into action. *Theory Into Practice, 16* (1), 29–34.

McGee, L.M. & Richgels, D.J. (1989). K is Kristen's: Learning the alphabet from a child's perspective. *The Reading Teacher,* 43 (3). 216–225.

Morrow, L. M. (1983). Home and school correlates of early interest in literature. *Journal of Educational Research, 76* (4), 221–230.

Office of Educational Research and Improvement. (1988). *What works.* Washington, DC: Department of Education. (ERIC Document Reproduction Service No. ED 263 299).

O'Rourke, W.J. (1979). Are parents an influence on adolescent reading habits? *Journal of Reading, 22* (4), 340–343.

Plessas, G.P., & Oakes, C.R. (1964). Prereading experiences of selected early readers. *The Reading Teacher. 17,* 241–245.

Potter, G. (1989). Parent participation in the language arts program. *Language Arts, 66* (1), 21–28.

Rasinski, T.V., & Fredericks, A.D. (1988). Sharing literacy: Guiding principles and practices for parent involvement. *Reading Teacher, 41* (6), 508–513.

———. (1989). Dimensions of parent involvement. *The Reading Teacher, 42* (2), 180–182.

Sandfort, J. (1987). Putting parents in their place in public schools. *NASSP Bulletin,* 71, 99–103.

Scott-Jones, D. (1988). Families as educators: The transition from informal to formal school learning. *Educational Horizons, 66* (2), 66–69.

Smith, C. (1988). The expanding role of parents. *The Reading Teacher, 42* (1), 68–69.

Taylor, D. (1983). *Family literacy.* Exeter, NH: Heinemann.

Taylor, D. & Strickland, D.S. (1986). *Family storybook reading.* Portsmouth, NH: Heinemann.

Teale, W. (1981). Parents reading to their children: What we know and need to know. *Language Arts, 58* (8), 902–911.

Teale, W.H. (1978). Positive environments for learning to read: What studies of early readers tell us. *Language Arts, 55* (8), 922–932.

Topping, K. (1985). Parental involvement in reading: Theoretical and empirical background. In K. Topping & S. Wolfendale (Eds.), *Parental involvement in children's reading,* Beckenham, Kent, UK: Croom Helm Ltd.

———. (1987). Paired reading: A powerful technique for parent use. *The Reading Teacher, 40* (7), 608–615.

Trelease, J. (1989). *The new read-aloud handbook.* New York: Viking/Penguin.

Weinberg, H. (Writer and Producer). (1988). *First things first* (Television Film). Pittsburgh: Metropolitan Pittsburgh Public Broadcasting.

Wolfendale, S. (1985). An introduction to parent listening. In K. Topping & S. Wolfendale (Eds.), *Parental involvement in children's reading.* Beckenham, Kent, UK: Croom Helm Ltd.

Yaden, D., & McGee, L.M. (1984). Reading as a meaning seeking activity: What children's questions reveal. In J. Niles (Ed.), *Thirty-Third Yearbook of the National Reading Conference,* 101–109. Rochester, NY: National Reading Conference.

APPENDIX

Children's Book Awards

THE JOHN NEWBERY MEDAL is named in honor of John Newbery, the first English publisher of books for children. Begun in 1922, the award is presented each year to "the author of the most distinguished contribution to American literature for children." The author must be an American citizen. The selection of the winner is made by a fifteen-member committee of the Association for Library Service to Children and is published annually by the American Library Association. The following list includes the Newbery medal winners since 1922.

1922 *THE STORY OF MANKIND* by Hendrik Van Loon. Boni & Liveright (Liveright).
1923 *THE VOYAGES OF DOCTOR DOOLITTLE* by Hugh Lofting. Stokes (Lippincott).
1924 *THE DARK FRIGATE* by Charles Boardman Hawes. Little, Brown.
1925 *TALES FROM SILVER LANDS* by Charles J. Finger. Illustrated by Paul Honoré. Doubleday.
1926 *SHEN OF THE SEA* by Arthur Bowie Chrisman. Illustrated by Else Hasselriis. Dutton.
1927 *SMOKY, THE COWHORSE* by Will James. Scribner.
1928 *GAY NECK* by Dhan Gopal Mukerji. Illustrated by Boris Artzybasheff. Dutton. (McKay).
1929 *TRUMPETER OF KRAKOW* by Eric P. Kelly. Illustrated by Angela Pruszynska. Macmillan.
1930 *HITTY, HER FIRST HUNDRED YEARS* by Rachel Field. Illustrated by Dorothy P. Lathrop. Macmillan.
1931 *THE CAT WHO WENT TO HEAVEN* by Elizabeth Coatsworth. Illustrated by Lynd Ward. Macmillan.
1932 *WATERLESS MOUNTAIN* by Laura Adams Armer. Illustrated by Sidney Armer and the author. Longmans, Green (McKay).
1933 *YOUNG FU OF THE UPPER YANGTZE* by Elizabeth Foreman Lewis. Illustrated by Kurt Wiese. Winston (Holt, Rinehart & Winston).
1934 *INVINCIBLE LOUISA* by Cornelia Meigs. Little, Brown.
1935 *DOBRY* by Monica Shannon. Illustrated by Atanas Katchamakoff. Viking.
1936 *CADDIE WOODLAWN* by Carol Ryrie Brink. Illustrated by Kate Seredy. Macmillan.

1937 *ROLLER SKATES* by Ruth Sawyer. Illustrated by Valenti Angelo. Viking.

1938 *THE WHITE STAG* by Kate Seredy. Viking.

1939 *THIMBLE SUMMER* by Elizabeth Enright. Farrar & Rinehart (Holt, Rinehart & Winston).

1940 *DANIEL BOONE* by James H. Daugherty. Viking.

1941 *CALL IT COURAGE* by Armstrong Sperry. Macmillan.

1942 *THE MATCHLOCK GUN* by Walter D. Edmonds. Illustrated by Paul Lantz. Dodd, Mead.

1943 *ADAM OF THE ROAD* by Elizabeth Janet Gray. Illustrated by Robert Lawson. Viking.

1944 *JOHNNY TREMAIN* by Esther Forbes. Illustrated by Lynd Ward. Houghton Mifflin.

1945 *RABBIT HILL* by Robert Lawson. Viking.

1946 *STRAWBERRY GIRL* by Lois Lenski. Lippincott.

1947 *MISS HICKORY* by Carolyn Sherwin Bailey. Illustrated by Ruth Gannett. Viking.

1948 *THE TWENTY-ONE BALLOONS* by William Pène du Bois. Viking.

1949 *KING OF THE WIND* by Marguerite Henry. Illustrated by Wesley Dennis. Rand McNally.

1950 *THE DOOR IN THE WALL* by Marguerite de Angeli. Doubleday.

1951 *AMOS FORTUNE, FREE MAN* by Elizabeth Yates. Illustrated by Nora Unwin. Aladdin (Dutton).

1952 *GINGER PYE* by Eleanor Estes. Harcourt.

1953 *SECRET OF THE ANDES* by Ann Nolan Clark. Illustrated by Jean Charlot. Viking.

1954 *AND NOW MIGUEL* by Joseph Krumgold. Illustrated by Jean Charlot. Crowell.

1955 *THE WHEEL ON THE SCHOOL* by Meindert DeJong. Illustrated by Maurice Sendak. Harper (Harper & Row).

1956 *CARRY ON, MR. BOWDITCH* by Jean Lee Latham. Houghton Mifflin.

1957 *MIRACLES ON MAPLE HILL* by Virginia Sorensen. Illustrated by Beth Krush and Joe Krush. Harcourt.

1958 *RIFLES FOR WATIE* by Harold Keith. Illustrated by Peter Burchard. Crowell.

1959 *THE WITCH OF BLACKBIRD POND* by Elizabeth George Speare. Houghton Mifflin.

1960 *ONION JOHN* by Joseph Krumgold. Illustrated by Symeon Shimin. Crowell.

1961 *ISLAND OF THE BLUE DOLPHINS* by Scott O'Dell. Houghton Mifflin.

1962 *THE BRONZE BOW* by Elizabeth George Speare. Houghton Mifflin.

1963 *A WRINKLE IN TIME* by Madeleine L'Engle. Farrar (Farrar, Straus).

1964 *IT'S LIKE THIS, CAT* by Emily Neville. Illustrated by Emil Weiss. Harper & Row.

1965 *SHADOW OF A BULL* by Maia Wojciechowska. Illustrated by Alvin Smith. Atheneum.

1966 *I, JUAN DE PAREJA* by Elizabeth Borten de Treviño. Farrar, Straus.

1967 *UP A ROAD SLOWLY* by Irene Hunt. Follett.

1968 *FROM THE MIXED-UP FILES OF MRS. BASIL E. FRANKWEILER* by E. L. Konigsburg. Atheneum.

1969 *THE HIGH KING* by Lloyd Alexander. Holt, Rinehart & Winston.

1970 *SOUNDER* by William H. Armstrong. Harper & Row.

1971 *SUMMER OF THE SWANS* by Betsy Byars. Viking.

1972 *MRS. FRISBY AND THE RATS OF NIMH* by Robert C. O'Brien. Atheneum.

1973 *JULIE OF THE WOLVES* by Jean Craighead George. Harper & Row.

1974 *THE SLAVE DANCE* by Paula Fox. Bradbury.

1975 *M.C. HIGGINS, THE GREAT* by Virginia Hamilton. Macmillan.

1976 *THE GREY KING* by Susan Cooper. Atheneum.

1977 *ROLL OF THUNDER, HEAR MY CRY* by Mildred D. Taylor. Dial.

1978 *BRIDGE TO TERABITHIA* by Katherine Paterson. Crowell.

1979 *THE WESTING GAME* by Ellen Raskin. Dutton.

1980 *A GATHERING OF DAYS: A NEW ENGLAND GIRL'S JOURNAL* by Joan W. Blos. Scribner.

1981 *JACOB HAVE I LOVED* by Katherine Paterson. Crowell.

1982 *A VISIT TO WILLIAM BLAKE'S INN: POEMS FOR INNOCENT AND EXPERIENCED TRAVELERS* by Nancy Willard. Illustrated by Alice and Martin Provensen. Harcourt Brace Jovanovich.

1983 *DICEY'S SONG* by Cynthia Voight. Atheneum.

1984 *DEAR MR. HENSHAW* by Beverly Cleary. Morrow.

1985 *THE HERO AND THE CROWN* by Robin McKinley. Greenwillow.

1986 *SARAH, PLAIN AND TALL* by Patricia MacLachlan. Harper & Row.

1987 *THE WHIPPING BOY* by Sid Fleischman. Greenwillow.

1988 *LINCOLN: A PHOTOBIOGRAPHY* by Russell Freedman. Clarion.

1989 *JOYFUL NOISE: POEMS FOR TWO VOICES* by Sid Fleischman. Harper & Row.

1990 *NUMBER THE STARS* by Lowry Lors. Houghton Mifflin.

1991 *MANIAC MAGEE* by Jerry Spinneli. Little, Brown.

The Caldecott Medal is named in honor of Randolph Caldecott, a prominent English illustrator of children's books during the nineteenth century. This award is presented each year to ''the artist of the most distinguished American picture book for children.'' The following list includes the medal winners for each year since 1938.

1938 *ANIMALS OF THE BIBLE, A PICTURE BOOK*. Text selected from the King James Version of the Bible by Helen Dean Fish. Illustrated by Dorothy O. Lathrop. Stokes (Lippincott).

1939 *MEI LI* by Thomas Handforth. Doubleday.

1940 ABRAHAM LINCOLN by Ingri d'Aulaire and Edgar Parin d'Aulaire. Doubleday.

1941 *THEY WERE STRONG AND GOOD* by Robert Lawson. Viking.

1942 *MAKE WAY FOR DUCKLINGS* by Robert McCloskey. Viking.

1943 *THE LITTLE HOUSE* by Virginia Lee Burton. Houghton Mifflin.

1944 *MANY MOONS* by James Thurber. Illustrated by Louis Slobodkin. Harcourt.

1945 *PRAYER FOR A CHILD* by Rachel Field. Illustrated by Elizabeth Odon Jones. Macmillan.

1946 *THE ROOSTER CROWS* by Maud Petersham and Miska Petersham. Macmillan.

1947 *THE LITTLE ISLAND* by Golden MacDonald. Illustrated by Leonard Weisgard. Doubleday.

1948 *WHITE SNOW, BRIGHT SNOW* by Alvin Tresselt. Illustrated by Roger Duvoisin. Lothrop.

1949 *THE BIG SNOW* by Berta Hader and Elmer Hader. Macmillan.

1950 *SONG OF THE SWALLOWS* by Leo Politi. Scribner.

1951 *THE EGG TREE* by Katherine Milhous. Scribner.

1952 *FINDERS KEEPERS* by Will (William Lipkind). Illustrated by Nicolas (Mordvinoff). Harcourt.

1953 *THE BIGGEST BEAR* by Lynd Ward. Houghton Mifflin.

1954 *MADELINE'S RESCUE* by Ludwig Bemelmans. Viking.

1955 *CINDERELLA* by Charles Perrault. Illustrated by Marcia Brown. Harper (Harper & Row).

1956 *FROG WENT A-COURTIN'* by John Langstaff. Illustrated by Feodor Rojankovsky. Harcourt.

1957 *A TREE IS NICE* by Janice May Udry. Illustrated by Marc Simont. Harper (Harper & Row).

1958 *TIME OF WONDER* by Robert McCloskey. Viking.

1959 *CHANTICLEER AND THE FOX*, edited and illustrated by Barbara Cooney. Crowell.

1960 *NINE DAYS TO CHRISTMAS* by Marie Hall Ets and Aurora Labastida. Viking.

1961 *BABOUSHKA AND THE THREE KINGS* by Ruth Robbins. Illustrated by Nicolas Sidjakov. Parnassus.

1962 *ONCE A MOUSE* by Marcia Brown. Scribner.

1963 *THE SNOWY DAY* by Ezra Jack Keats. Viking.

1964 *WHERE THE WILD THINGS ARE* by Maurice Sendak. Harper & Row.

1965 *MAY I BRING A FRIEND?* by Beatrice Schenk de Regniers. Illustrated by Beni Montresor. Atheneum.

1966 *ALWAYS ROOM FOR ONE MORE* by Sorche Nic Leodhas. Illustrated by Nonny Hogrogian. Holt, Rinehart & Winston.

1967 *SAM, BANGS AND MOONSHINE* by Evaline Ness. Holt, Rinehart & Winston.

1968 *DRUMMER HOFF* by Barbara Emberley. Illustrated by Ed Emberley. Prentice-Hall.

1969 *THE FOOL OF THE WORLD AND THE FLYING SHIP* by Arthur Ransome. Illustrated by Uri Shulevitz. Farrar, Straus.

1970 *SYLVESTER AND THE MAGIC PEBBLE* by William Steig. Windmill/ Simon & Schuster.

1971 *A STORY, A STORY* by Gail E. Haley. Atheneum.

1972 *ONE FINE DAY* by Nonny Hogrogian. Macmillan.

1973 *THE FUNNY LITTLE WOMAN* by Arlene Mosel. Illustrated by Blair Lent. Dutton.

1974 *DUFFY AND THE DEVIL* by Harve Zemach. Illustrated by Margot Zemach. Farrar, Straus.

1975 *ARROW TO THE SUN.* Adapted and illustrated by Gerald McDermott. Viking.

1976 *MOSQUITOES BUZZ IN PEOPLE'S EARS* by Verna Aardema. Illustrated by Leo and Diane Dillon. Dial.

1977 *ASHANTI TO ZULU: AFRICAN TRADITIONS* by Margaret Musgrove. Illustrated by Leo and Diane Dillon. Dial.

1978 *NOAH'S ARK* by Peter Spier. Doubleday.

1979 *THE GIRL WHO LOVED WILD HORSES* by Paul Goble. Bradbury.

1980 *OX-CART MAN* by Donald Hall. Illustrated by Barbara Cooney. Viking.

1981 *FABLES* by Arnold Lobel. Harper & Row.

1982 *JUMANJI* by Chris Van Allsburg. Houghton Mifflin.

1983 *SHADOW* by Blaise Cendrars. Illustrated by Marcia Brown. Scribner's.

1984 *THE GLORIOUS FLIGHT: ACROSS THE CHANNEL WITH LOUIS BLERIOT, JULY 25, 1909* by Alice and Martin Provensen. Viking.

1985 *SAINT GEORGE AND THE DRAGON* adapted by Margaret Hodges. Illustrated by Trina Schart Hyman. Little, Brown.

1986 *POLAR EXPRESS* by Chris Van Allsburg. Houghton Mifflin.

1987 *HEY AL* by Arthur Yorinks. Illustrated by Richard Egielski. Farrar, Straus.

1988 *OWN MOON* by Jane Yolen. Illustrated by John Schoenherr. Philomel.

1989 *SONG AND DANCE MAN* by Karen Ackerman. Illustrated by Stephen Gammel. Knopf.

1990 *LON PO PO: A RED RIDING HOOD STORY FROM CHINA* by Ed Young. Putnam.

1991 *BLACK AND WHITE* by David Macaulay. Houghton Mifflin.

The Laura Ingalls Wilder Medal is given to an author or illustrator whose books (published in the United States) have made a substantial and lasting contribution to literature for children. Established in 1954, this medal was given every five years through 1980. As of 1983, it has been given every three years.

1954 Laura Ingalls Wilder
1960 Clara Ingram Judson
1965 Ruth Sawyer
1970 E.B. White
1975 Beverly Cleary
1980 Theodor S. Geisel (Dr. Seuss)
1983 Maurice Sendak
1986 Jean Fritz
1989 Elizabeth George Speare

Selected Regional and State Awards

ARIZONA YOUNG READERS AWARD
Department of Elementary Education, College of Education, University of Arizona, Tucson, AZ 85721. Awarded every two years from a master list of titles nominated by children, final vote by children.

BUCKEYE CHILDREN'S BOOKS AWARDS
State Library of Ohio, 65 S. Front St., Columbus, OH 43215. Titles selected in three divisions (K–2, 3–5, and 6–8) from children's nominations and children vote during Ohio Right to Read Week.

CALIFORNIA YOUNG READER MEDALS
California Reading Association, 3400 Irvine Ave., Suite 118, Newport Beach, CA 92660 and other sponsors. Preliminary nominations proposed by children become a master list from which a young reader medal committee determines final nominees. Children vote in four categories.

COLORADO CHILDREN'S BOOK AWARD
Colorado Council of the International Reading Association, 1100 S.E. Frontage Rd., Fort Collins, CO 80524. A list of twenty most frequently nominated books by children is the master list from which children select one title by a living author, published within the last five years.

COMMONWEALTH CLUB OF CALIFORNIA AWARDS
Commonwealth Club of California, Monadnock Arcade, 681 Market St., San Francisco, CA 94105. For finest juvenile book on any subject by a Californian.

GARDEN STATE CHILDREN'S BOOK AWARDS
New Jersey Library Association, Children's Services Section, 116 E. State St., Trenton, NJ 08608. Recognize literary merit and reader popularity and are awarded to authors and illustrators.

GEORGIA CHILDREN'S BOOK AWARDS
College of Education, University of Georgia, Athens, GA 30602. Children in grades four to seven select the Georgia Children's Book Award winner and those in kindergarten through grade three select the Georgia Children's Picture Book Award winner from a list of twenty books by living authors, published within last five years.

KENTUCKY BLUEGRASS AWARD
Northern Kentucky University, Learning Resources Center-BEP 268, NKU, Highland Heights, KY 41076. Children in grades three to eight select a title from a booklist of titles published within a three-year period, compiled by award committee.

MASSACHUSETTS CHILDREN'S BOOK AWARDS
Salem State College, Education Dept., Salem, MA 01970. Two awards, voted on by grades four through six and seven through nine, are selected from among recent and older titles.

MICHIGAN YOUNG READERS' AWARDS
Michigan Council of Teachers of English, P.O. Box 892, Rochester, MI 48063. A committee of teachers selects a list from children's nominees, and children vote in two divisions, preschool through three and grades four through eight.

OHIOANA BOOK AWARDS
Ohioana Library Association, Room 1105, 65 S. Front St., Columbus, OH 43215. Awarded to an Ohio author or for the body of work of an author living in the state for at least five years.

PACIFIC NORTHWEST YOUNG READER'S CHOICE AWARD (Alaska; Alberta, Canada, British Columbia; Idaho; Montana; Oregon; Washington).
Children's and Young Adult Services Division, Pacific Northwest Library Association, c/o Children's Department, W. Vancouver Memorial Library, 1950 Marine Dr., West Vancouver, V7V 1J8, Canada. The oldest children's choice award (1940), it is selected from a master list compiled by librarians from suggestions by children.

SEQUOYAH CHILDREN'S BOOK AWARD
Oklahoma State Department of Education, Library Resources, 2500 N. Lincoln Blvd., Oklahoma City, OK 73105. Children in grades three through six vote from a master list of twenty titles chosen by the committee.

CHARLIE MAY SIMON CHILDREN'S BOOK AWARD
Arkansas Elementary School Council, Dept. of Education, State Education Building, 4 Capitol Mall, Little Rock, AR 72201. Arkansas school children, grades four to six, vote from a master list of titles selected by representatives from sponsoring groups.

SOCIETY OF MIDLAND AUTHORS BOOK AWARDS
Society of Midland Authors, 333 N. Michigan, Chicago, IL 60611. Awarded to a Midland author (twelve-state region) residing in, who grew up in, or has set a novel in the Midlands.

SOUTHERN CALIFORNIA COUNCIL ON LITERATURE FOR CHILDREN AND YOUNG PEOPLE AWARDS
Given to authors, illustrators, and contributors to the field of children's literature living in Southern California.

THE TEXAS BLUEBONNET AWARD
Texas Bluebonnet Award Committee, School of Library Science, P.O. Box 2236, Sam Houston State University, Huntsville, TX 77341. Students in grades three through six who have read or heard read at least five books from a master list of titles selected by adults vote for their favorite title.

MARK TWAIN AWARD
Mark Twain Award, Box 343, Butler, MO 64730. Children in grades four through eight vote from a master list compiled by award committee.

WESTERN HERITAGE AWARDS
National Cowboy Hall of Fame and Western Heritage Center, 1700 N.E. 63rd St., Oklahoma City, OK 73111. Awarded to juvenile book that best portrays the authentic American West. Awards selected by children.

YOUNG HOOSIER AWARD
Association for Indiana Media Educators, YHA Committee, 1120 E. 49th St., Marion, IN 46953. Indiana children, grades four to eight, vote for a favorite book from a list of twenty books selected by a committee. Books must be published in the five-year period preceding award. A second award is selected by grades six to eight.

INDEX

This page constitutes an extension of the copyright page.

p. 29 reprinted with permission of Charles Scribner's Sons, an imprint of Macmillan Publishing Company from *Shadow* translated and illustrated by Marcia Brown. Copyright © 1982 Marcia Brown.

p. 29 from *Owl Moon,* text copyright © 1987 by Jane Yolen, illustrations copyright © 1987 by John Schoenherr. Reprinted by permission of Philomel Books.

pp. 29 and 123 excerpts from *Brown Bear, Brown Bear, What Do You See?* by Bill Martin, Jr., copyright © 1970 by Holt, Rinehart and Winston, Inc., reprinted by permission of the publisher.

p. 32 excerpt from *Hey Al* by Arthur Yorinks. Copyright © 1986 by Arthur Yorinks. Reprinted by permission of Farrar, Straus and Giroux, Inc.

p. 32–33 excerpt from *Louis the Fish* by Arthur Yorinks. Copyright © 1980 by Arthur Yorinks. Reprinted by permission of Farrar, Straus and Giroux, Inc.

pp. 33 and 34 from *Mirandy and Brother Wind* by Patricia C. McKissack, illustrated by Jerry Pinkney. Text copyright © 1988 by Patricia C. McKissack. Illustrations copyright © 1988 by Jerry Pinkney. Reprinted by permission of Alfred A. Knopf, Inc.

p. 35 from *The True Story of the Three Little Pigs* by Jon Scieszka. Copyright © 1989 by Jon Scieszka. Used by permission of Viking Penguin, a division of Penguin Books USA Inc.

p. 42 Statement on Censorship and Professional Guidelines, approved by the Board of Directors of the National Council of Teachers of English, 1982. Reproduced with permission.

p. 55 from *Miss Nelson Is Missing,* by Harry Allard and James Marshall. Copyright © 1977 by Harry Allard. Copyright © 1977 by James Marshall. Reprinted by permission of Houghton Mifflin Company.

p. 87 from *Maniac Magee* by Jerry Spinelli. Copyright © 1990 by Jerry Spinelli. By permission of Little, Brown and Company.

p. 101 "Rules for Reading Workshop" reproduced with permission from Nancie Atwell: *In the Middle: Writing, Reading, and Learning with Adolescents* (Boynton/Cook, Portsmouth NH, 1987).

p. 112 reprinted with permission of Margaret K. McElderry Books, an imprint of Macmillan Publishing Company from *Worlds I Know and Other Poems* by Myra Cohn Livingston. Copyright © 1985 by Myra Cohn Livingston.

p. 146 reprinted with permission of Atheneum Publishers, an imprint of Macmillan Publishing Company from *Dicey's Song* by Cynthia Voigt. Copyright © 1982 Cynthia Voigt.

p. 185 from Lucia and James L. Hymes, Jr., *Oodles of Noodles,* © 1964 by Lucia and James L. Hymes, Jr. Reprinted with permission of Addison-Wesley Publishing Company, Inc.

p. 223 reprinted with permission of Atheneum Publishers, an imprint of Macmillan Publishing Company from *Mrs. Frisby and the Rats of NIMH* by Robert C. O'Brien. Copyright © 1971 Robert C. O'Brien.

p. 230 from *Roll of Thunder, Hear My Cry* by Mildred D. Taylor. Copyright © 1976 by Mildred D. Taylor. Used by permission of Dial Books for Young Readers, a division of Penguin Books USA Inc.

p. 242 reprinted with permission of Donna M. Ogle and the International Reading Association.

p. 244 reprinted with permission of Bonnie B. Armbruster and the International Reading Association.

p. 251 reprinted by permission of Curtis Brown, Ltd. Copyright © 1970 by Jean Craighead George.

p. 263 from the book, *Leo the Late Bloomer* by Robert Kraus. © 1971. Used by permission of the publisher, Prentice Hall Books for Young Readers/A trademark of Simon & Schuster, Inc., New York, NY 10020.

p. 273 reprinted with permission from Karen Sabers Dalrymple. In *The Whole Language Evaluation Book,* ed. Kenneth S. Goodman, Yetta M. Goodman and Wendy J. Hood (Heinemann Educational Books, Portsmouth NH, 1989).

p. 293 from *Do Bananas Chew Gum?* by Jamie Gilson. Copyright © 1980 by Jamie Gilson. Reprinted by permission of William Morrow and Company, Inc./Publishers, New York, NY.

p. 311 from "Hurt No Living Thing" by Christina G. Rossetti in *Sing a Song of Popcorn,* published by Scholastic Inc., New York.

p. 328 "The Elephant and His Son" from *Fables* by Arnold Lobel. Copyright © 1980 by Arnold Lobel. Reprinted by permission of HarperCollins Publishers.